Acclaim for

THE CAPTAIN

by Ian O'Connor

"Ian O'Connor is an ideal biographer for Derek Jeter. Ian is the same kind of thorough pro."
— **Tom Callahan, bestselling author of** *Johnny U*

"Long after Derek Jeter is inducted into the Hall of Fame, Ian O'Connor's work will be viewed as the definitive biography of the captain. Jeter has always managed to keep it simple, but as O'Connor shows, the shortstop is a complicated superstar."
— **Buster Olney, author of** *How Lucky You Can Be* **and** *The Last Night of the Yankee Dynasty*

"For years we've been telling young ballplayers to play and behave like Derek Jeter. Now we can tell them to read Ian O'Connor's *The Captain*. Finally, we have an inside look at the worthy successor to Ruth, Gehrig, DiMaggio and Mantle."
— **Dan Shaughnessy, author of** *Fenway* **and** *Reversing the Curse*

"Readers will welcome this candid account." — *Star-Ledger*

THE CAPTAIN

Books by Ian O'Connor

THE JUMP

ARNIE & JACK

THE CAPTAIN

The
CAPTAIN

The Journey of
Derek Jeter

IAN O'CONNOR

Mariner Books
Houghton Mifflin Harcourt
BOSTON   NEW YORK

First Mariner Books edition 2012
Copyright © 2011 by Ian O'Connor

www.hmhco.com

Library of Congress Cataloging-in-Publication Data
O'Connor, Ian.
The captain: the journey of Derek Jeter / Ian O'Connor.
p. cm.
Includes bibliographical references and index.
ISBN 978-0-547-32793-8
ISBN 978-0-547-74760-6 (pbk.)
1. Jeter, Derek, date. 2. Baseball players — United States — Biography.
3. New York Yankees (Baseball team) I. Title.
GV865.J48037 2011
796.357092 — dc22
[B]
2010049772

Book design by Brian Moore

Printed in the United States of America
DOC 10
4500632067

CONTENTS

Introduction

On Monday afternoon, July 6, 2009, more than 46,000 sun-splashed baseball fans inside the new Yankee Stadium witnessed something they never imagined they would see.

Derek Jeter getting in an umpire's face.

The captain of the New York Yankees had just made a wretched baserunning choice — another shock to the extended holiday weekend crowd — when he tried and failed to steal third with no outs in the first inning. The throw from Toronto Blue Jays catcher Rod Barajas to Scott Rolen arrived early enough for Rolen to recite the Greek alphabet before applying the tag.

Only Jeter being Jeter, he delivered the Toronto third baseman a lesson in resourcefulness right there in the infield dirt. The shortstop went in headfirst and used a Michael Phelps butterfly stroke to reach his arms around Rolen's glove and touch the base untagged.

Marty Foster, veteran ump, did what everyone expected him to do. He saw the ball beat Jeter by a country mile, saw Rolen drop his glove in front of the bag, and sent the foolish runner back to his dugout and his stunned manager, Joe Girardi.

But for once, Jeter did not retreat to the dugout. He told Foster he had reached the base before he was tagged, and according to the shortstop, Foster responded, "The ball beat you. He doesn't have to tag you."

The captain was incredulous. *He doesn't have to tag you?*

"I was unaware of that change in the rule," Jeter would say.

As the ultimate guy who played the game the right way, Jeter felt a rare rush of anger rising from his toes. He marched toward Foster in search of a more acceptable answer, and the Yankees' third-base coach, Rob Thomson, had to get between them. Girardi raced out to ensure Jeter did not earn the first ejection of his life, dating back to Little League, and the manager ended up getting tossed himself.

John Hirschbeck, crew chief, watched this scene unfold and said to himself what every living, breathing witness was thinking: "Wow, that's unusual." Jeter would rather get swept by the Boston Red Sox than show up an ump.

But more unusual would be the postgame conversation inside the umpires' room, where Hirschbeck held court with reporters while acting as a human shield for Foster, who showered and dressed behind a closed door. Thirteen years earlier, Hirschbeck had gotten up close and personal with ballplayer misconduct when Roberto Alomar spat in his face.

Like cops, umpires often adhere to a blue wall of silence. They have little choice but to protect each other. With players and managers emboldened by lavish guaranteed contracts, and with instant replay making infallible judges and juries out of millions of viewers, umpires are under siege from all corners. They are imperfect men burdened by the high-def, high-stakes demand for perfection.

And yet despite these truths, Hirschbeck faced the reporters gathered around him like campers around a fire and suggested he believed Jeter's account.

"In my twenty-seven years in the big leagues," the crew chief said, "[Jeter] is probably the classiest person I've ever been around."

Never mind that a day later, Foster would assure Hirschbeck he never told Jeter he did not need to be tagged (a claim Jeter vehemently denied, maintaining, "He knows exactly what he said"). Never mind that Hirschbeck heard Foster's version of what was said to the shortstop ("The ball beat you, and I had him tagging you") and decided even the classiest of players might have misheard something in the heat of the moment.

The crew chief's first instinct was to believe Jeter's version of the truth. "It would make his actions seem appropriate if that's what he was told," Hirschbeck said.

Yes, that was Derek Jeter in a nutshell: even an umpire would deem his inappropriate actions appropriate.

Months later, at a banquet announcing his son as *Sports Illustrated*'s 2009 Sportsman of the Year, Charles Jeter spoke for his wife, Dot, when he told the crowd, "One of the things that's really special for us is the fact that sometimes when we're traveling, people might come up to us and they often say, 'You know, I'm not a Yankee fan. But you know something? Your son has class and plays hard and we really respect what he's all about.'"

In the end, this is why millions of young ballplayers around America ask their coaches to assign them jersey number 2. Jeter does not embarrass the umpires or his coaches or his teammates or himself. His common acts of decency have made him the most respected and beloved figure in the game.

Funny, but Jeter never hit 25 home runs in a season. He never won a batting title. Never won a Most Valuable Player award.

But Jeter did win championships and a place in any debate over the greatest all-around shortstop of all time. He also won the title of patron saint of clean players in an era defined by performance-enhancing drugs.

When I told him in the spring of 2009 that I would be writing a book about his career, Jeter immediately replied, "My career's not over." I explained my goal — to author a defining work on his time with the Yankees as he was about to become the first member of the world's most famous ball team to collect 3,000 hits.

Jeter decided against making major contributions to this book, in part because he did not want fans to think he was basking in his own glory while there were still grounders to run out and titles to win. He had other reasons, I'm sure, but Jeter did agree to take some questions from me at his locker during the 2009 season.

For the record, this is my book, not his. It is a book shaped by more than two hundred interviews I conducted with Jeter's teammates, friends, coaches, opponents, associates, employers, teachers, admirers, and detractors (his detractors were actually admirers willing to address what they perceived as Jeter's human flaws) over an eighteen-month period.

But in truth, this book was built on thousands of one-on-one and group interviews I participated in with Jeter and his Yankees as a newspaper and Internet columnist who has covered the shortstop since his rookie year.

What was I searching for? The tangible explanation for Jeter's intangible grace. The passion behind his pinstripes. The fire beneath his ice.

In many ways, this book was born in my son's closet, filled with frayed and faded jerseys graced by the number 2. I wanted to explore why Jeter became as popular and iconic in his time as Mantle, DiMaggio, Ruth, and Gehrig were in theirs.

Jeter sure did not hit Ruthian homers, and he did not glide to the batted ball with DiMaggio's elegant style. Joe D. could have played the game in a tuxedo and top hat, but not Jeter. The shortstop had to work at it.

Yet Jeter survived an age of steroid-fueled frauds who dominated with their artificial moon shots, and of sabermetric snipers who used their forensics to shoot holes through his standing in the game.

Somehow, some way, the New York Yankees' shortstop remained the enduring face of his sport.

So that is the point of my book, to provide a simple answer to this complicated question:

How did number 2 get to be number 1?

THE CAPTAIN

1

The Kalamazoo Kid

LIKE ALL GOOD stories about a prince, this one starts in a castle. Derek Sanderson Jeter spent his boyhood summers around the Tiedemann castle of Greenwood Lake, a home near the New York/New Jersey border maintained by the Tiedemann family of Jersey City and defined by its medieval-looking tower and rooftop battlements.

In the 1950s, the Tiedemanns started rebuilding the burned-out castle with the help of their adopted son, William "Sonny" Connors, who did his talking with a hammer the same way Charles "Sonny" Liston did his talking with his fists.

More than a quarter century later, Connors, a maintenance worker at a Catholic church, would preach the virtues of an honest day's work to his grandson, who was enlisted as Connors's unpaid assistant when he wasn't playing with the Tiedemann grandchildren around the lake.

Derek Jeter was forever carrying his baseball glove, forever looking for a game. His grandfather was not an enthusiastic sports fan, but as much as anyone Connors showed the boy the necessity of running out every single one of life's ground balls.

Connors was a shy and earnest handyman who had lost his parents to illness when he was young, and who had honed his workshop skills under John Tiedemann's careful watch. Tiedemann and his wife, Julia, raised Sonny along with twelve children of their own, sparing him a teenager's life as a ward of the state.

Tiedemann was a worthy role model for Sonny. He had left school in the sixth grade to work in a Jersey City foundry and help his widowed mother pay the bills. At thirteen, Tiedemann already was operating a small electrical business of his own.

In the wake of the Great Depression he landed a job inside St. Michael's Church, where Tiedemann did everything for Monsignor LeRoy McWilliams, even built him a parish gym. When Msgr. McWilliams did not have the money to cover the scaffolding needed to paint St. Michael's, Tiedemann invented a jeep-mounted boom that could elevate a man to the highest reaches of the ceiling. He ultimately got into the business of painting and decorating church walls.

Around the same time, in the mid-fifties, Tiedemann was overseeing work on a 2.7-acre Greenwood Lake, New York, lot he had purchased for $15,000. His main objective was the restoration of a German-style castle that had been gutted by fire more than a decade earlier.

Tiedemann's labor force amounted to his eleven sons, including his ace plumber, roofer, carpenter, and electrician from St. Michael's — Sonny Connors.

"Sonny was a Tiedemann," said one of the patriarch's own, George. "We all counted him as one of our brothers."

And every weekend, year after year after year, this band of Jersey City brothers gathered to breathe new life into the dark slate-tiled castle, an Old World hideaway originally built by a New York City dentist in 1903. The Tiedemann boys started by digging out the ashes and removing the trees that had grown inside the structure.

They did this for their father, the self-made man the old St. Michael's pastor liked to call "the Michelangelo of the tool chest." The castle was John Tiedemann's dream house, and the boys helped him build additional homes on the property so some of his thirteen children and fifty-four grandchildren could live there.

"We weren't a huggy, kissy type of family," George said. "We weren't the Waltons. But the love was there, and it didn't have to manifest itself more than it did."

John Tiedemann was a tough and simple man who liked to fish, watch boxing, and move the earth with his callused hands. Long before he poured himself into the Greenwood Lake project, Tiedemann was proud of being the first resident on his Jersey City block, 7th Street, to own a television set. He enjoyed having his friends over to take in the Friday night fights.

He finally made some real money with his church improvement business and later bought himself a couple of Rolls-Royces to park outside his renovated castle. But Tiedemann was a laborer at heart, and he had taught his eleven sons all the necessary trades.

As it turned out, none of the boys could match the father as a craftsman. None but Sonny, the one Tiedemann who did not share Tiedemann's blood.

For years Sonny was John's most reliable aide, at least when he was not working his full-time job as head of maintenance at Queen of Peace in North Arlington, New Jersey, an hour's commute from the castle. Sonny would drive through heavy snowstorms in the middle of the night to clean the Queen of Peace parking lots by 4:00 a.m. He would vacuum the rugs around the altar, paint the priests' living quarters, and repair the parishioners' sputtering cars for no charge.

Sonny never once called in sick and never once forgot the family that gave him a chance. Every Friday, payday, Sonny would stop at a bakery and buy a large strawberry shortcake so all the Tiedemanns could enjoy dessert.

"Sonny was the spark that kept us going," George said, "because he never took a break." Sonny idolized Julia Tiedemann, and he liked to make her husband proud. If John Tiedemann wanted a room painted, Sonny made sure that room got painted while John was away on business so he would be pleasantly surprised on his return.

Sonny married a Tiedemann; of course he did. Dorothy was a niece of John and Julia's, a devoted Yankees fan who loved hearing the crack of Joe D.'s bat on the radio, and who hated seeing Babe Ruth's lifeless body when she passed his open casket inside Yankee Stadium in 1948.

Sonny and Dorothy, or Dot, would raise fourteen children, including another Dorothy, or Dot. The Connors family spent some time in the castle before moving to nearby West Milford, New Jersey, where Sonny served as the same working-class hero for his kids that John Tiedemann was for him.

Sonny and his wife took in troubled or orphaned children and made them their own, and it never mattered that money was tight. "Sonny went back to his own experience as a boy," said Monsignor Thomas Madden, the pastor at Queen of Peace. "The Tiedemanns took care of Sonny, so it was in his nature to take care of others. . . . And Dorothy had just as big a heart as he did."

One of their flesh-and-blood daughters, Dot, ended up in the army and was stationed in Frankfurt, Germany, where in 1972 she met a black soldier named Sanderson Charles Jeter, raised by a single mother in Montgomery, Alabama. They married the following year, at a time in America when the notion of a biracial president was more absurd than that of a human colony on Mars.

Naturally, Sonny did not approve of the marriage. He worried over the way the children would be treated, worried they would be teased and taunted by black and white. "Sonny was very concerned about that," Msgr. Madden said. "He would ask, 'Will they be accepted? Will they have to fight battles?'"

His questions would start to be answered on June 26, 1974, when Derek Sanderson Jeter was born at Chilton Memorial Hospital in the Pompton Plains section of Pequannock, New Jersey.

If Sonny initially did not have a relationship with his daughter's husband, that did not stop him from pursuing one with his daughter's son.

Derek was four when his parents moved with him from Jersey to Kalamazoo, Michigan, where Charles enrolled in Western Michigan University to pursue a master's and doctorate in social work. But every summer, Derek stayed with the Connors clan in West Milford and made almost daily visits to the castle in Greenwood Lake.

The Tiedemanns put down sand near the water to give the boys and girls the feel of a beachfront, and Derek's grandmother brought him over to play with the Tiedemann grandchildren and escape the heat. Derek was not looking for a chance to swim as much as he was looking for a partner in a game of catch.

"He was always talking about baseball," said Michael Tiedemann, one of John's grandchildren. They played Wiffle ball games and threw footballs and tennis balls around the lake. "And no matter what we played," Michael said, "Derek was by leaps and bounds the best athlete. He kept his eye on the ball and moved a lot faster than the rest of us did."

Despite the fact he was reed thin, Derek surely claimed some of his physicality from Sonny, a roundish but powerfully built man who stood five foot eleven and projected the body language of a dockworker — in other words, someone to be avoided in a bar fight. But it was Derek's father, Charles, who passed down the genetic coding of a ballplayer.

Charles Jeter was a shortstop in the late sixties when he arrived at Fisk University, a small, historically black school in Nashville. He was a shortstop until the coach, James Smith, told him he was a second baseman.

Smith had a pro prospect with a throwing arm to die for, name of Victor Lesley. Lesley was the reason the tall and rangy Jeter was moved to a less taxing infield spot.

Jeter was hardly thrilled with the demotion and yet never mentioned it to his coach. Though he did not have a male figure in his household while growing up — Jeter never met his father — he knew how to conduct himself as a perfect gentleman, a credit to the mother and housecleaner named Lugenia who raised him.

"Cordial, nice, carried himself the right way," Smith said. "I never heard Jeter use a curse word. Ever."

On a strong team composed of African Americans from the South and a small circle of Caribbean recruits from St. Thomas, Jeter was an excellent fielder and base runner, a decent hitter who liked to punch the ball to right field, and a selfless teammate who knew how to advance a runner from one base to the next.

Jeter was as reliable a sacrifice bunter as Smith had ever seen. "You could ask him to bunt with three strikes on him if the rules had allowed it," Smith said.

The head coach was the son of one of Nashville's first black police officers. Smith was only a few years older than his players, but he was a strict disciplinarian all the same, a man unafraid of leaving behind a couple of important players if they were late for the bus.

The Fisk team, he said, "used to be the laughingstock of the league," the Southern Intercollegiate Athletic Conference. He recruited better talent from American high schools, stumbled upon a pipeline to the U.S. Virgin Islands, and made sure his players were dressed in shirts and ties on road trips.

"They needed to know that when you go to Fisk," Smith said, "you represent something besides yourself."

Though Fisk had its share of white professors and white exchange students, Jeter and his teammates forever understood they were members of a predominantly black institution surrounded by a culture often hostile to African-American aims. So Smith took no chances. His student athletes were expected to be ambassadors of the school, the sport, and the cause of racial equity.

Charles Jeter fit the serious-minded mold. Only once did Smith have to reprimand him, and that was after Jeter was thrown out trying to steal second. Smith had never given him the steal sign, and when a teammate committed the same mortal baserunning sin the next inning, Smith went ballistic. "Gentlemen," he shouted at his players, "this is a team sport. Let's not put individual statistics ahead of the team."

Jeter was known for his hustle, for his willingness to run out ground balls, so he was the perfect apostle of this all-for-one, one-for-all approach. (Smith only heard of his dismay over being moved to second base through a relative years later.) Jeter did not play to inflate his numbers on the bases or at the plate. He burned to be part of a winner, so the demoted shortstop focused on being the best second baseman in the league.

Smith shifted the incumbent to right field to clear room for Jeter, whose quickness and hand speed made him a natural at turning the double play. Jeter had a glove as flat as a pancake, "and we teased him about it all the time," said Ulric Smalls, one of his teammates from St. Thomas. "When Jeter put it on the ground it had no shape, but he was flawless in the field."

Jeter got his chance to return to shortstop after Lesley left Fisk, and Smalls remembered him outplaying a Vanderbilt star who had all the big league scouts abuzz. Smith had left his coaching position before Jeter finished his collegiate career, but he had scheduled the likes of Vanderbilt so the scouts fussing over the white boys in the SEC would be forced to watch his players, too.

Buck O'Neil, the Negro League star working for the Cubs, was the only scout who made regular trips to Fisk, leaving Jeter without the stage he needed to display his command of the game's fundamentals.

Smith believed Charles had all the tools and talent to make it to the big leagues. "If he was playing at a different time and a different school," the coach said, "he might've made it. But Jeter just didn't have the opportunity."

Charles Jeter made sure his son had the opportunity by providing the strong and nurturing paternal presence he had missed as a child, and by embracing the same code of honor, decency, and hard work that had shaped the Tiedemann and Connors homes.

Starting when Derek was in kindergarten, Charles competed against him in checkers and in card games and challenged him to guess the value of an appliance on the television show *The Price Is Right*. Charles tried to beat Derek at everything, and he told his wife their son "needs to learn how to lose and how to play the game the right way."

Charles coached Derek when the boy was a Kalamazoo Little Leaguer, when Derek loved nothing more than throwing on his uniform, standing proudly before a mirror, and marching in the opening-day parade with his chin high and his shoulders thrown back, so proud to be part of a team.

Only one day Derek decided he was too proud to finish on the wrong end of a Little League score. He refused to join the handshake line to congratulate the winning team, and Charles got in his son's face and made a tough-love stand.

"It's time to grab a tennis racket," he barked at Derek, "since you obviously don't know how to play a team sport."

In fact, Derek knew how to play a team sport, baseball, better than any other kid in Kalamazoo. He could hit, field, run, and throw the ball from shortstop with more power and accuracy than any pitcher could throw it from the mound.

Derek would play all day, any day, for as many weeks and months as the Kalamazoo climate would allow. Of course, those summer days in West Milford and Greenwood Lake were best spent throwing around the ball, too, at least when Derek was not busy swimming in the lake with his younger sister, Sharlee.

The alternative? No, Derek did not take to the alternative work with his grandfather at Queen of Peace, especially when the chores involved a lawn mower and a wide-open field of unruly grass.

Over time Sonny Connors had grown close to Charles Jeter; the church handyman had gotten past his concerns for his biracial grandkids. But Sonny had a special bond with Derek, who lived to please Sonny as much as he lived to please Charles.

Sonny got a kick out of bringing his grandson to work. One day he asked Derek to mow a Queen of Peace football field that had the overgrown look of a Brazilian rain forest. All elbows and knees and ankles, young Derek was no match for the job.

"The poor kid was going crazy with it," said Madden, the Queen of Peace pastor. Derek was pushing the mower, emptying the bag, and pushing it again, and it was so hot the nuns felt sorry for him. They brought him inside, gave him a cold soda, told him to relax.

As soon as Sonny found out his grandson was cooling off and catching his breath, he ordered Derek to get back to work.

Sonny did not believe in fifteen-minute breaks, weekends, vacations, or holidays. "We used to open presents on Christmas Eve," Sharlee would say, "because our grandfather worked every Christmas Day."

Sonny did not want his children using the word *can't* in his home, and his daughter imposed the same ordinance on Derek and Sharlee. So when children laughed at Derek's claim that he would be a Yankee, and when teachers advised Charles and Dot to steer their son toward a more realistic goal, the Jeters did not budge.

No, the black social worker from Alabama and the white accountant from New Jersey would not listen to people tell them Derek could not be a big league ballplayer any more than they would listen to those who told them they should not marry for the sake of their children-to-be.

Derek refused to acknowledge those who thought he was banking on a fairy tale. "People laughed at it, and I just shrugged it off," he would say. "It just made me work harder."

The Jeters built their social lives around the ball field, particularly the Kalamazoo Central High School field just beyond the perimeter of their backyard. When Dot was not throwing Wiffle balls for Derek to hit in that yard, mother, son, father, and daughter were scaling the fence to take infield and batting practice. Derek hit his baseballs, and Sharlee hit her softballs.

"Some people go to the movies for fun," said Sharlee, who was Derek's athletic equal. "We went to the field. It was all part of being very close."

They lived something of a Rockwellian existence in their modest home on 2415 Cumberland Street, where Charles and Dorothy enjoyed watching *The Cosby Show* with their son and daughter, and where they maintained order by signing their children to binding behavioral pacts. Derek signed his just before going off to high school, and the provisions covered phone calls, television hours, homework, grade-point averages, curfews, drugs and alcohol, and respect for others.

Even back then Derek was one to live up to the terms of his deals. His teachers described him as industrious, self-motivated, and willing to lend a hand to a student in need.

"He epitomized what every mom wants in a son," said Shirley Garzelloni, Derek's fourth-grade teacher at St. Augustine.

Discipline and accountability were the laws of the Jeters' land. Charles was a full-time student by day, a drug and alcohol abuse counselor by night, and even with Dot drawing her accounting paycheck, money had to be spent judiciously.

One day Derek announced he wanted a pair of $125 basketball shoes he thought would improve his modest (at the time) leaping ability. His mother agreed on one condition: Derek had better wear those shoes and work on his jumping 24/7.

Sure enough, Derek would run and hop all over the family's small living room. "He knew it was important for us," Dot would say, "that if we were going to sacrifice $125, then he was going to give us his all."

On the field and in the classroom. By the eighth grade Jeter was a straight-A student who maintained his popularity with students of both genders. The boys were in awe of his athleticism, "and the girls were in awe of his personality and looks," said Chris Oosterbaan, his creative writing and history teacher. "There were many crushes on Derek Jeter."

The attention did not swell Jeter's head beyond the margins of his signed conduct clauses. Truth was, Derek would have signed anything as long as he was allowed to play baseball for the teams that would have him. And there was not an amateur team within a fifty-mile radius of Kalamazoo that did not want Charles Jeter's boy as its shortstop.

Derek was not anyone's idea of a braggart, but he had been telling classmates and teachers he would grow into a big leaguer as far back as fourth grade, inside Garzelloni's class in the basement of St. Augustine. Garzelloni asked her twenty students to declare their future intentions, and she heard the typical answers from most — doctor, firefighter, teacher, professional athlete.

Only Derek was not planning on being just a professional athlete; he had something far more specific in mind, a vision he shared with his parents as a child. He told Garzelloni's class he was going to be a New York Yankee, and the teacher told the student her husband — a devoted Yankee fan — would be happy to hear it.

Derek did not make this some grand proclamation; he just said it as if he were announcing his plans for lunch. "And if he said he was going to do something," Garzelloni said, "Derek was the kind of kid who did it."

Derek told anyone who would listen that he would someday play shortstop for the Yankees, the team his father had hated in his youth. Before Charles started rooting for the local Tigers, he was a National League fan from the South who did not celebrate Yankee dominance; the Yanks were among baseball's last all-white teams before promoting Elston Howard eight years after Jackie Robinson's debut at Ebbets Field.

Grandma Dot converted Derek on those summer trips to the castle and lake. She took her grandson to his first Yankee Stadium game when he was six, and years later Derek could not remember the opponent or the final score. "All I can tell you," he would say, "is everything was so big."

As big as the boy's ambition. Derek would stir his grandmother at dawn, throw on his Yankee jersey, and beg her to play catch in the yard. She always agreed, even if she knew Derek's throws would nearly knock her to the ground.

Soon enough Derek entered Kalamazoo Central High on a mission — to honor his own prophecy, the one laid out for him by his St. Augustine classmates in a 1988 graduation booklet that included forecasts of what the students would be doing ten years later. "Derek Jeter, professional ball player for the Yankees is coming around," one entry read. "You've seen him in grocery stores — on the Wheaties boxes, of course."

As it turned out, Jeter made his ninth-grade mark with a basketball before he made one with a baseball. Around Halloween in '88, Derek was dribbling a ball up and down and around a Kalamazoo Central service road just when Clarence Gardner was starting a road trip with the Central girls basketball team (Michigan girls used to play their basketball season in the fall).

The players pressed their noses against the bus windows and expressed wonderment over the freshman's commitment in the face of a late October chill. "They were all saying, 'You know he's going to be great,'" Gardner recalled. "Of course, some of them were talking about how cute he was, too."

It was the first time Derek Sanderson Jeter was known to have impressed a busload of schoolgirls.

It would not be the last.

Derek Jeter played basketball to stay in shape for baseball, but that did not stop him from approaching every possession as if all of his big league dreams depended on it. In fact, when he tried out for the Kalamazoo Blues, a high-powered team on the AAU and summer ball circuits, Jeter won a roster spot simply by outrunning and out-hustling boys who had played on stronger junior high teams than his.

St. Augustine was not a feeder program for the Blues, whose coach, Walter Hall, had never before seen Jeter play. Derek caught his eye with his speed and pure perimeter stroke. Hall also was impressed by his parents, Charles and Dot. The Jeters did not try to talk up their son during tryouts the way so many other parents did; Hall did not meet them until after Derek made the team.

Jeter was a reliable reserve player for the Blues, a team stocked with talent that would attract major college recruiters. Derek was the designated shooter, instant offense off the bench, and yet his intensity and willingness to dive for a loose ball and race back on defense to slow a fast break distinguished him from his more gifted teammates.

"Derek probably got dunked on more than anybody in the state of Michigan," said the Blues' assistant, Greg Williams. Jeter never gave up on a possession, even on a breakaway for the other team. Derek always thought he could catch an opponent and strip him, leaving him vulnerable to the slam.

Jeter separated himself from teammates in a more conspicuous off-court way. On trips to regional and national tournaments, when the rest of the Blues were wearing Michael Jordan jerseys or Detroit Pistons T-shirts, Derek was dressed from head to toe in Yankees gear, including the omnipresent gold Yankee pendant dangling from his neck.

His teammates kept teasing him about his allegiances, and Jeter kept assuring them what he had assured everyone else — he was going to be the Yankee shortstop someday, whether or not they reached the NBA.

The Blues often slept four to a room, and many a night their cheap hotels were filled with laughter over Jeter's baseball jones. They traveled to Kingsport, Tennessee, for a national tournament, and the one truth about the trip that intrigued Jeter the most was this:

Darryl Strawberry started his minor league career there.

Jeter was so serious about baseball and his favorite team, said Monter Glasper, one of his roommates, "he even wore Yankee boxers to bed." The Blues joked with him about that. "But you could tell he was never joking when he said he'd end up playing for them," Glasper said.

Once on the court, Jeter was no longer a daydreaming shortstop, but a basketball player as serious as Glasper and Kenyon Murray, who would earn scholarships to Iowa. If Jeter was not a strong ball handler, at least not by top-shelf AAU standards, he was among the Blues' best shooters and defenders and perhaps their most fearless presence in the final minutes of a frantic game.

Jeter's favorite shot was the three-pointer from the corner. David Hart, a point guard who would earn a scholarship to Michigan State, would penetrate and kick it to the gunner many Blues likened to the Pistons' trigger-happy reserve, Vinnie Johnson.

"It didn't matter if Derek had missed twenty shots in a row," Hart said. "If the game was on the line and he got the ball again, he was putting it up."

Jeter's parents, Charles and Dot, took in every game from the stands, "and it was definitely unique," Hart said, "because I came from a two-parent home, too, but a lot of our guys didn't." Charles and Dot filmed the Blues' games, and with no operating budget to speak of, the Blues' coaches would borrow their film and show it to the team on the locker room or hotel walls, complete with Dot's running commentary on her son's play.

Dot knew the game. "Sometimes she was hollering, 'Go, baby, go,'" Williams said, "but she was very on point. She could be very critical of Derek's performance."

So could the Blues' coaches. During one film session, Williams drove Jeter to tears by repeatedly pointing out open big men in the paint while he was firing away from the perimeter. The assistant coach had to apologize to Derek a few times for shredding him in front of the team.

But all in all, Jeter was a basketball coach's best friend. The Blues played a powerhouse Oklahoma team in one prominent national event, "and on paper," said Hall, their head coach, "we didn't belong in the same gym with those guys. And Derek came off the bench and shot Oklahoma right out of the tournament."

Everyone agreed Jeter had major college ability, even if basketball rated as a distant second love. Derek had what his father called a quiet arrogance on the court. "He always wanted the last shot," Charles Jeter said. "He usually didn't make them, but he was never afraid to fail."

The Blues made their share of overseas trips to compete against the best available international competition, and one summer they planned to travel to South America. Charles and Dot wanted Derek to make the trip for the cultural experience.

Hall talked them out of it, told them Derek could not afford to miss that much time away from baseball. The coach knew what his players did not.

The Blues were so caught up in the city game, in reaching for faraway NBA careers, that they paid little attention to what Jeter was doing on the diamond for Kalamazoo Central or for his summer league teams.

They knew he wore Yankee caps and jerseys and interlocking "NY" pendants, and they knew all about his prediction that he would land at shortstop in the Bronx. But they were shocked when they found out Jeter was far more proficient on a baseball diamond than they were on a basketball court.

The Blues were all so focused on earning Division I basketball schol-arships, Hart said, "it just didn't dawn on us that Derek was better than all of us in another sport. I mean, as it turned out, what we were doing was nothing compared to him. We were just trying to get into college, and this guy was already making himself a pro."

Courtney Jasiak was the first baseball coach to tell Derek Jeter he was not ready to play shortstop. Just as James Smith had moved Charles Jeter to second at Fisk University, Jasiak moved Charles's son to third on his sixteen-and-under Kalamazoo team.

A right-handed batter and thrower, Jeter was fourteen when he started playing for the twenty-one-year-old Jasiak, whose over-the-top, treat-every-game-like-it's-the-World-Series temperament un-nerved Derek. Jasiak put his team of teenage warriors in a men's city league to compete against twenty-five-year-olds, and when he went winless in his first eight games, the coach decided to jump his third baseman hard.

Derek rarely said a word during practices or games. "I was kind of crazy back then," Jasiak would say, "but I just felt he had more to give from a leadership standpoint and I let him know it."

Jeter responded, and Jasiak's Brundage Roofing team scored a cou-ple of victories against the men. Meanwhile, Brundage destroyed local opponents in its own age bracket and did so with a tiny sixteen-year-old at shortstop, Bobby Marks, an accomplished diver who made his mark in baseball by gobbling up everything hit his way.

"Derek did not like being shuttled to third base at all," Jasiak said.

He got some time in at short all the same, and Jasiak used to roll balls to Derek's left and make him field them with two hands. The teacher marveled over his pupil's lateral movement, and Jasiak assured people Jeter would someday be a first-round pick in the big league draft.

Derek did nothing at Kalamazoo Central to temper that optimism. On a bitter February day during his freshman year, Jeter showed up for junior varsity tryouts in the large and drafty Central gym. Norm Copeland, the jayvee coach, hit the prospects a series of soft grounders on the hardwood to test the strength of their arms.

Jeter fielded one and fired a ball on a line no more than three feet off the court. The poor kid assigned to catch it never had a chance; the ball crashed into the boy's stomach.

Copeland absorbed Jeter's long and lean athleticism, the foot speed, and the turbocharged arm and told his son to find the varsity coach, Marv Signeski. "He's got to see this kid," Copeland said.

Signeski watched from the balcony above the floor. "Hey," he called out to Jeter, "varsity tryouts aren't for another two hours."

Derek was one freshman who could have played on any varsity team in America. He remained with the jayvee because Central had an all-state baseball and hockey player at short, Craig Humphrey, leaving Copeland to try to maximize his phenom's potential.

The coach pulled Jeter aside after the team's first full practice.

"Derek," Copeland said, "I want to make sure you always give me 110 percent."

"Oh," Jeter answered, "you don't like the way I play?"

"No, I like the way you play very much. You're head and shoulders above everyone else, but I'm worried you might play down to the level of the other kids."

"OK. I understand."

Jeter understood. He loved baseball too much to ever dumb down his game.

Despite the vast difference between his skill set and his teammates', Derek never criticized a fellow player, never rolled his eyes or kicked the dirt over an error committed by a lesser light. He maintained his father's demeanor on the ball field and ran faster, threw harder, and hit better than his old man ever did.

But when he was a teenager, Charles had been the one with the better glove. "Derek was not a good fielder in high school," said one summer teammate, Chad Casserly. "He'd field the ball and then always pack his glove, pack it and pack it and pack it, before finally releasing the throw. He butchered some ground balls."

Jeter was a dead pull hitter, too, and pitchers started nibbling away on the outside corner of the plate. The Kalamazoo Central coaches worked with Derek to take those outside pitches to right field, and before they knew it he was spraying balls all over creation and developing an inside-out swing that would put batters twice his age to shame.

If Copeland was thrilled with Derek's progress, he pushed for more. The coach wanted Jeter to make regular appearances on the mound, too.

Derek liked to play deep at short to buy himself time on line drives, and to take advantage of his Nolan Ryan arm. During summer ball, when asked by *Kalamazoo Gazette* sportswriter Paul Morgan why he did not pitch, Derek shot Morgan a frightful look and said, "You're too close to the hitter. Somebody could get killed." Jeter, Morgan said, "wanted to be as far away from the hitter as possible."

Derek told his jayvee coach of a different fear, told him he was afraid that pitching might damage his arm. Copeland did persuade him to take the mound in one game, and Jeter threw eight warm-up pitches for eight strikes, and then he threw nine strikes to three batters who never once saw the ball. "But he didn't want to be there," Copeland said. "That was the one thing he was pretty emphatic about — staying at shortstop."

Jeter had no problem unleashing his fastballs at short. Kalamazoo Central was playing its local rival, Portage Central, in one jayvee game that devolved into a theater of the absurd for the Portage third-base coach.

Three times Portage batters ripped liners with runners on base, and three times Kalamazoo outfielders hit Jeter with their cutoff throws, and three times Jeter threw from the outfield grass to nail runners at the plate. From his dugout, Copeland saw the Portage coach fling his cap in the air before saying the following:

"I surrender. The first time I sent the kid, I didn't even bother looking at home plate to see the play and I couldn't believe it when I heard the umpire call him out. The second time I sent him, I watched it and I couldn't believe it when the ball got there so quickly.

"The third time I sent him, you made a believer out of me."

Jeter was promoted to varsity two-thirds of the way through the season, after Humphrey told Signeski he would clear the way by moving to second base. When the Central varsity faced Portage in the district playoffs, Jeter came to bat in a critical situation, with first base open. Casserly and Ryan Topham, another Portage player who was a summer teammate of Derek's, turned toward their head coach in the hope he would walk the freshman.

Bob Royer did not know enough about Jeter, so he chose to pitch to him. "And Derek hit a seed," Casserly said.

Jeter kept planting those seeds all over Kalamazoo, growing into one of the finest amateur players in the state. He played for Signeski and then Don Zomer at Central and graduated out of Jasiak's boot camp and into Mike Hinga's Maroons summer team, which played as many as seventy games a season. It was nonstop baseball for a kid who could not get enough, a charmed existence for a boy holding fast to his grown-up goal.

As the shortstop next door, Derek Jeter was the antithesis of Eddie Haskell. "He was like Beaver Cleaver, except a Beaver who didn't get in trouble," Hinga said. "Derek's mom and dad would've crushed him if he got in trouble."

By all accounts, Derek earned his parents' wrath a single, solitary teenage time, committing a felony—at least in the court of Charles and Dot—that would not even have drawn a parking ticket in most American homes.

Derek borrowed the family Datsun 310, joined some buddies for a night out, and ended up outside a house that was hosting a girls' sleepover. A friend tossed rocks at the house windows, a man emerged from the house to chase the boys, and the cops were called to the scene, the whole event inspiring Charles and Dot to deny their son car privileges for two months.

That was that for Derek, one small brush with his parents' draconian law. The Jeters did not have to worry about far more serious teen behavior issues; as a seventeen-year-old Derek told a family friend and a Kalamazoo scout, Keith Roberts, "Life is tough enough without drugs and alcohol."

Tough enough? Even as he projected an altar boy's disposition, Derek's was not a trouble-free youth, not when he was subjected to the bile spilling out of small and ignorant minds.

Sonny Connors's fears for his biracial grandchildren were realized. Though most of his teachers and coaches said they never heard others direct racial slurs at Derek, Courtney Jasiak recalled an incident after a play at the plate in a heated tournament game against a suburban Detroit team.

"They had this huge catcher," Jasiak said, "and he didn't like the way Derek came in. He called Derek the *N*-word. . . . The catcher got ejected, but Derek was about to fight him. We got in between them."

Growing up, Derek and Sharlee were sometimes called hurtful names. When Sharlee was young, Derek nearly threw a punch at one kid who called his sister an Oreo but did not succumb to the urge. "Why give them the gratification to where people know something bothers you?" Derek would say.

Dot Jeter moved to assure her children that everything would be OK, that she would deal with the offender's parents. "I'm going to take care of this," Dot said, and place the phone call she did.

Halfway between Detroit and Chicago, Kalamazoo was not unlike other midsize midwestern towns, where the vast majority of the 1980s populace appeared progressive-minded when measured against the whites who lorded over Charles Jeter's segregated South.

But Charles and Dot were once denied a vacant Kalamazoo apartment by a Jurassic-thinking realtor, and they were pained to see their children followed by suspicious salespeople, and to know their complexion drew stares from rude strangers.

"Kalamazoo's not too big," Derek would say, "but if you go somewhere with just your mother, you're a little bit darker than your mom. You go somewhere with just your dad, you're a little lighter than he is. So you got some funny looks. . . . Sometimes you felt the stares."

Charles and Dot did what they could to wrap a protective cocoon around their children.

"You can't get away from the fact there are racist people in society," Charles would say. "Some things happened, but our kids never let that affect them. We told Derek and Sharlee to chase their dreams, to not let anyone stop them."

When Derek closed in on his big league dream, sharpening his swing by swatting an endless procession of baseballs into a net installed in his garage, Keith Roberts heard the sounds of intolerance around the Kalamazoo Central batting cage.

"I know with some scouts it was an issue, that the Jeters had a biracial marriage," Roberts said. "I mean a few scouts, not a lot. You overhear scouts talking."

Roberts's older brother, Duane, was influential in integrating local schools and establishments and ran the Kalamazoo chapter of the

NAACP. "Kalamazoo is an accepting place," Roberts said, "but there is still some ignorance."

David Hart, Derek's basketball teammate with the Blues, sometimes traveled into Kalamazoo from nearby Battle Creek, met up with a fellow black player, Kenyon Murray, and a couple of white girls, and immediately felt a community's glare.

"It's a small town, not a melting pot like New York City," Hart said. "So you do have those little rules where you stick to your side of the tracks and I stick to mine. We didn't grow up in the South with traditional bigotry, but there was an underlying feeling there, an invisible line, and growing up you were always conscious of it."

The Jeters were so conscious of the invisible line, they suspected Derek was left off the all-district baseball team in his junior year of high school because of his biracial roots.

"I thought that definitely had something to do with it," agreed Derek, who batted .557 and hit 7 homers as a junior.

Though Jeter was clearly the best player in his district, it was hard to believe a disjointed group of high school coaches secretly conspired against him, especially because the state's coaches association would name Derek its player of the year the following season.

Much more likely, said Paul Morgan, the *Kalamazoo Gazette* sportswriter close to the Jeter family, the snub was the byproduct of Central's poor record and the fact that many district coaches did not see Derek play in person.

But the Jeters had their reasons to see ghosts where there were none. If nothing else, they refused to allow other people's ignorance to define who they were or what they would do.

Derek kept a 3.82 grade-point average as a senior, when he was considered the best high school ballplayer in the land. Surrounded by his trophies and plaques in his home, Jeter was asked by Morgan to name the award that made him most proud.

Derek immediately pointed to his eighth-grade math certificate. "I worked my butt off for that one," he said.

He was a member of the National Honor Society, a reliable tutor for freshmen lagging behind in their computer lab, and an A student in Sally Padley's fast-tracking British lit class who would draw himself in a coat of arms (as a Yankee on one side, a Central basketball player on the other) that was among the best drawings Padley had ever received.

Jeter had everything going for him: An arm so strong he would break the webbing of his first baseman's glove on a critical (and accurate) throw, costing his Maroons a trip to the Connie Mack World Series after hitting two long home runs in that very game. A confidence so unwavering he would take the big jump shots for the Blues, and for Clarence Gardner and Don Jackson at Central.

A heart so compassionate he would start a collection for a Central basketball teammate who had been arrested and could not afford a lawyer. As captain of the team, Jeter persuaded Gardner's wife to contribute $350 to the fund on the promise he would personally reimburse her — a promise he kept.

Derek's Midas touch knew no bounds. The shortstop with the Dave Winfield poster on his wall had Division I college coaches and major league scouts attending his games. The Yankee fan born twenty-eight miles from the historic ball yard in the Bronx had piqued the Yankees' interest. The pragmatist with the honors certificates displayed as prominently as his athletic trophies had pre-med possibilities lined up in the event baseball did not work out.

The baseball star with the steady high school sweetheart, Marisa Novara, also had fallback marriage plans in place. He was not just telling everyone he would become the shortstop for the New York Yankees — why stop there?

Jeter made another prediction to his summer coach, Courtney Jasiak, while they were working out in an indoor hitting loft, and to his summer teammate, Chad Casserly, while they were having a warm-up catch in the outfield.

"I'm going to marry Mariah Carey one day," Derek told them.

This was Jeter's vision of love, and it would have to wait. His vision of professional baseball needed to unfold first.

2

The Draft

ON THE MORNING of June 1, 1992, Julian Mock stepped out of his Cincinnati hotel and went on a three-mile run that would dramatically alter the course of baseball history. Mock was the Reds official who would make the fifth overall pick in that day's major league amateur draft, and he had two prospects in mind when he started his jog: Chad Mottola, an outfielder for the University of Central Florida; and Derek Jeter, a shortstop for Kalamazoo Central High School.

Mock was not sure if either player would be available at number 5, as baseball executives often did all they could to cloak their true draft-day intentions. But Mock knew his scouts loved Jeter, and he knew the big club was, in his words, "screaming for a power outfielder" in Mottola's mold.

The Reds were only a season and a half removed from a World Series sweep over Oakland, but they had taken a 74-88 plunge in 1991. Mock was facing a stressful decision, and jogging allowed him to get away from everything and clear his mind.

The New York Yankees would make the sixth selection in the draft, and Mock did not much care how his pick would affect theirs, not on a professional level. On a personal level, Mock cared very much about the Yankees, the team he had rooted for in his Selma, Alabama youth.

Selma was not just divided by white and black—it was divided by Joe DiMaggio and Ted Williams. There were two types of fans in Selma, Yankees and Red Sox fans. "If you said something about DiMaggio or Williams, those were fighting words," Mock explained. "You'd better have a record book in your pocket to back up your facts."

The local paper, the *Selma Times-Journal*, devoted plenty of coverage to the mighty Yanks up north, and Mock lost himself in the daily accounts. Of course, Selma's big league allegiances were altered on April 15, 1947, when Jackie Robinson arrived at Brooklyn's Ebbets Field.

"When Robinson came in," Mock said, "all the blacks in Selma were Dodger fans."

The following year, Mock and a couple of high school buddies jumped into a Chevy and drove 1,138 miles to Yankee Stadium without making an overnight stop. They saw the home team play the Red Sox and watched in awe as the great DiMaggio filled the ballpark with his presence and grace.

From their upper-deck seats in left field, the country boys from Selma could not get over the size of Yankee Stadium and the depth of the roars that greeted DiMaggio at the plate. Mock had made his first trip to New York in 1946, when he was working at the Selma post office for 99 cents an hour and yet somehow scratched together the $150 needed to get to Atlanta, hop on a train with a friend, and take in the Rockettes at Radio City Music Hall and the Giants at the Polo Grounds.

"Went to two plays, too," Mock said, "which I couldn't get out of soon enough."

He did not ever want to leave Yankee Stadium in late September 1948, but he needed to get back for classes at Auburn University, where Mock would become an outfielder with hopes of playing professional ball.

He ended up in the air force instead, got married on exit, and started a career in coaching and teaching in Atlanta. Mock led Murphy High to a number of city and state titles and was introduced to the scouting business by a fellow coach, Lem Clark, who was working for the Pirates.

Mock ended up as a territorial scout for the Reds, and then as their scouting director. He never completely surrendered his childhood affection for the Yanks.

Mock was a Mantle fan, he said, "until I found out he had permission to be with his wife for the birth of their baby and he didn't go. I went through the Horace Clarke era, and I stayed a Yankee fan until they got Reggie Jackson. I couldn't pull for a team that had a self-promoter like Reggie, but after he left I became a Yankee fan again."

Only on June 1, 1992, Mock woke up as the biggest Cincinnati Reds fan in the world. Would he go for Jeter, the high school phenom coveted by his own scouts despite the fact that Cincinnati's Barry Larkin was a twenty-eight-year-old four-time All-Star at short? Or would he go for Mottola, the older, stronger, more experienced player at a position of need?

By the time he completed his three-mile jog, Mock had his answer. He showered, dressed, headed to the office, and refused to reveal the name he would announce on the speakerphone when he walked through the door.

"I didn't tell a single person," Mock said. The scouting director was tired of the Reds' intentions getting leaked to the press. "One of the guys called me Columbo," he said, "but that's the way I wanted it to be."

As draft time neared, many in the Reds organization were merely hoping Jeter would still be on the board at number 5. With the first overall pick, the Houston Astros were considering the Kalamazoo kid and college star Phil Nevin. Cleveland, Montreal, and Baltimore would pick after Houston, and early indications had those franchises passing on Jeter for college prospects the likes of pitchers Paul Shuey and B. J. Wallace and outfielder Jeffrey Hammonds.

Those in the Reds organization who wanted Jeter figured they only needed him to get past the Astros at number 1. And yes, those Reds officials believed Jeter was worthy of the first overall pick. They saw him as the best high school player in the land, better than the warm-weather hotshots from California, Florida, and Texas.

In his frostbitten corner of Michigan, stuck on a losing Kalamazoo Central team, the biracial golden child who did not make the all-district cut as a junior became everybody's all-American as a senior, and only one thing was out of place in Derek Jeter's otherwise picture-perfect life.

The New York Yankees did not have a prayer of getting him.

Dozens of scouts tracked nearly every swing Derek Jeter took during his senior season at Kalamazoo Central, but none matched the profile of Harold "Hal" Newhouser. A Hall of Fame pitcher for the Detroit Tigers in the 1940s and 1950s, Newhouser was hired by the Houston Astros to find professional baseball players in a climate more likely to produce Big Ten football and basketball stars.

The wet and raw Michigan baseball season created a painfully small window for talent evaluation, and Newhouser attacked that window the way he had attacked American League hitters during the mid-forties, when he won at least 25 games in three consecutive seasons.

He would slide into long johns and corduroy pants, throw on two sweaters beneath his jacket, pull his woolly hat over his ears, and then make the 290-mile roundtrip drive from his Bloomfield Hills home to the Kalamazoo tundra to watch Derek Jeter quarterback his team at short.

The drive was worth it. What Newhouser saw in Jeter, Tom Greenwade had seen in a teenage prodigy from Oklahoma, Mickey Mantle, whom he signed for $1,500 while they sat in the scout's Cadillac.

"I don't know if Derek will play shortstop or end up in center field," Newhouser told Jeter's summer league coach, Mike Hinga. "But either way he's going to play in the majors for twenty years."

The old scout understood the Astros would not get Jeter for Mantle's $1,500, or for the 500 bucks Newhouser's hometown Tigers gave him to sign as an eighteen-year-old in 1939. The boy lefty gave $400 of his bonus to his mom an hour before a Cleveland Indians scout pulled up to offer a brand-new car and a $15,000 deal.

Newhouser was a young man of his word, so he stuck with the Tigers, made his debut with them in September of '39, and beat the Cubs in Game 7 of the 1945 World Series after the military refused his attempts to enlist because of his leaky heart valve. If Newhouser was known as an incurable hothead on the mound and in the clubhouse, he was a meticulous and even-tempered scout.

Before his 1992 induction into the Hall of Fame, an honor granted by the Veterans Committee after an endless three-decades-plus wait (some voters thought his wartime record was inflated by the watered-down competition), Newhouser scoured high school and sandlot ball fields for future Cooperstown immortals. He worked for the Orioles, Indians, and Tigers before landing with the Astros, and the prominent signings on his resumé were Milt Pappas, who won 209 games, and Dean Chance, who won a Cy Young Award.

Jeter was going to be a more prominent signing than both.

"He's the best I've ever seen," Newhouser told Don Zomer, Jeter's coach at Kalamazoo Central.

The professional scout made a profound impression on the amateur coach. One day at practice, Zomer spotted a solitary figure in the stands he had taken for a father waiting to give his son a ride home. The man approached Zomer behind the batting cage and introduced himself, and the coach was struck by the stranger's tanned, leathery face.

When Newhouser offered his name, Zomer nearly fell over. Some scouts paraded around in their blazers, the coach said, "but Hal had on an old jacket and a stocking cap and looked like he was going hunting."

Newhouser was going hunting for sure — hunting for a player whose signature would ease the sting of the Astros' 97-loss season in 1991.

On assignment, Newhouser made as little fuss as possible. He carried himself without any swagger, and he often did not bother bringing a radar gun to his games.

"I don't need a gun to tell me somebody throws fast," he would say.

Newhouser did not need any box scores or stat sheets to tell him Derek Jeter would be a twenty-year big leaguer, either.

"Derek is so natural," the scout told his wife, Beryl. "Derek has the most wonderful pair of hands I've ever seen."

Newhouser was hardly the only big league scout left breathless by Jeter's exploits at Kalamazoo Central. In fact, when Central played a double-header against the local rival, Portage Central, and its own highly touted prospect, Ryan Topham, more than forty scouts braved the mid-April sleet and snow and turned the Portage field into an *American Idol* audition ten years before the show's debut.

Topham, Jeter's summer teammate with the Maroons, had already signed a National Letter of Intent to play at Notre Dame. The Fighting Irish chased a Jeter-Topham daily double and had booked Derek and his parents for a campus visit.

Jeter told Gary Tuck, a Notre Dame assistant and former Yankees coach, of his pinstriped aims. Tuck was hoping Dot Jeter's Irish-American roots would help convince Derek that the road from Kalamazoo to the Bronx ran through the emerald fields of South Bend.

"My mother wanted me to go to Notre Dame," Derek would say.

As academic-minded people, the Jeters insisted their son prepare for college despite the intensifying interest from the pros. Derek seriously considered offers from Notre Dame, Miami of Florida, and Michigan, and despite his mother's preference, he was leaning toward Miami.

His Michigan visit with the Wolverines' head coach, Bill Freehan, an eleven-time All-Star catcher with the Detroit Tigers, changed everything. The Jeters liked Freehan and his assistant, Ace Adams, who met the family in an Ann Arbor restaurant in the hours before Michigan hosted Notre Dame in the Big House. They had the restaurant all to themselves.

"Do you think Derek will ever play here?" Dot Jeter asked.

Adams about choked on his food.

"Mrs. Jeter," he replied, "Derek could have started for us in tenth grade."

Michigan was just coming off NCAA probation for violations committed under Bud Middaugh, and the Jeter signing represented a home run in every literal and figurative way.

The way Adams saw it, Jeter was the best player Freehan had ever recruited. The assistant thought Derek would be worth five runs to the Wolverines in every game — he would save two in the field and produce three at the plate. Beyond that, Charles Jeter delivered a scouting report Michigan had yet to hear from a recruit's father.

"My kid never disappointed me one day, ever," Charles told the Wolverines' staff.

The day Jeter called with word he was committing to Michigan, Freehan walked into the coaches' office and broke the great news. "He's coming with us," Freehan said.

"Goddamn," Adams replied. "All that hard work paid off."

But had it? Would Jeter hand back the scholarship and turn pro if he was drafted high in the first round?

Adams remained worried. The big league scouts were everywhere, he said, "and they were all lying to us, telling us they weren't going to take him."

All those lying eyes were on Jeter for that Saturday double-header against Portage early in Derek's senior season.

The teams were not the main attraction, as Portage was a suburban power and Kalamazoo the city long shot hoping to win half its games. Instead everyone wanted to see the duel between fast friends, Jeter versus Topham. They played together across three summers, traveled together to tryout camps, stayed over at each other's homes.

Jeter entered the double-header with three homers in his first two games, and with the clear understanding that, on this stage, he was the Jordan and Topham was the Pippen.

Only neither could run anything approaching a fast break in this snowy, dreary, rainy weather. "A typical Michigan baseball day," said Eric Johnson, a Portage pitcher.

The teams knew they had to play on a day like this, if only because full-fledged storms usually washed out a third of the area schedule.

Topham made the first impression. With Kalamazoo holding a 3–1 lead in the opening game, the Portage star ripped a first-inning fastball through the sleet and over the 345-foot sign in right.

Jeter was moved to answer, and quickly. In the third inning, he lashed at a 3-1, eye-high fastball from Portage's Chris Quinn and sent it screaming into the pine trees beyond the 385-foot sign in center.

The shot whistled straight over Topham's head; the outfielder did not even turn to watch it clear the fence. Johnson, playing shortstop at the time, could not get over the flight path of the ball.

"If I was on top of second base, I could've jumped and caught the thing," he said. "It was one of those jaw-hitting-the-ground moments, because nobody could believe how hard Derek hit that ball. It was exactly what the crowd had come to see."

In the sixth inning, the crowd of fans and scouts saw something it never expected to see — a Derek Jeter strikeout, his first and last of the year. Derek was facing a 2-2 count, two outs, bases loaded, when his summer league teammate, Chad Casserly, fired a slider that caught the outside corner of the plate.

The umpire gave Jeter the benefit of the doubt, and the Portage side let the man behind the mask hear it. Casserly came back with the same pitch in almost the same location, this time missing the plate by a hair, and Jeter started heading for first base.

Only Derek was halted by the sickening sound of an umpire calling him out. Jeter spun around with his head tilted, shot the masked man a crooked smile, and headed for the visiting dugout to retrieve his glove.

Zomer jumped all over the ump. "And I just ran off the field while everybody cheered," Casserly said.

Portage won, 12–8, and the scouts milled about before the start of the second game. Some were carrying stopwatches to time Jeter and Topham on their sprints from the batter's box to first base. Others were carrying radar guns to time Jeter's throws from shortstop to first, throws clocked at 90 miles per hour.

Derek was very much aware of the scouts, at least those who were not hiding in their cars or behind trees in order to conceal their interest. Jeter stole glances at them whenever he could, the way a shy teen steals glances at the prettiest girl in his third-period history class.

Derek was desperate to be noticed, and so when he hit a dribbler toward short in the first inning of the second game, he exploded out of the box and raced hard against all those stopwatches timing him to first.

Johnson, another friend, was Portage's starting pitcher, and one who had eagerly anticipated this matchup. He was happy he had gotten Jeter to hit this slow roller, at least until Derek beat out the throw on a bang-bang play.

But as soon as Jeter crossed the bag it was clear he was in distress. In his zeal to reach base safely and post a blazing time for the scouts, Jeter extended his final stride, caught his spikes on the outfield side of the soaked bag, rolled over his ankle, and began hopping on one leg.

A hush swept over the entire field, leaving Johnson to think, "Oh, no, what just happened?" Portage was going to defeat Central whether or not Jeter was in the lineup, only this moment was not about winning and losing on a high school scoreboard.

"You could tell everyone was thinking, 'I hope this doesn't hurt Derek's chances,'" Johnson said.

Jeter was helped off the field by his father, and Kalamazoo went down by a 10–0 count. Derek was terrified he might have suffered a broken ankle, and he was only slightly relieved when the doctor told him he had a high ankle sprain and could miss most of the year.

The injury could have cost him hundreds of thousands of dollars and a place in the first round of the draft. Only the six-foot-three Jeter had an inner toughness that cut against the grain of his praying mantis build.

He missed a handful of games, slid his swollen ankle into a brace, and returned to his losing Kalamazoo Central team in high-tops and higher spirits. Derek was not about to let his human frailty defeat him.

Jeter could not match his .557 batting average and 7 homers from his junior year, but he did hit .508 and finish with 23 RBI despite the fact that his injured ankle stripped him of all his home-run power.

The numbers were good enough to earn Jeter plenty more than the all-district honors that had escaped him in 1991. The American Baseball Coaches Association and *USA Today* would name Jeter their national High School Player of the Year, and Gatorade would name him its High School Athlete of the Year.

As it turned out, Derek's draft status did not begin deflating the moment he blew a tire on the first-base bag at Portage. Hal Newhouser still believed Jeter was the best amateur prospect in America, high school or college, and he was hell-bent on the Astros selecting him with the number-one overall pick.

With the Reds picking four slots behind Houston, Reds scouts Fred Hayes and Gene Bennett wanted their team to be ready to scoop up the Astros' potential fumble.

But Hayes and Bennett were not making the final call for Cincinnati any more than Newhouser was making the final call for Houston. Scouting directors, general managers, and team owners did not make a habit of watching high school games in the Michigan rain and snow, at least not the way their scouts did, and yet they were the ones responsible for deciding who was worth drafting and who was not.

Sometimes those decisions were not about speed and power, but dollars and cents. So veteran scouts who were not in prime position to sign Jeter knew enough to hang in there with the Kalamazoo kid.

Dick Groch was one of those scouts. He was hiding in plain sight at Jeter's games, avoiding eye contact with the shortstop, and declining to introduce himself to Jeter's coach.

Zomer took calls all day from scouts needing directions to Kalamazoo Central, from scouts asking for weather reports and places to eat. Sometimes the phone rang in the small hours of night, and Zomer never cared.

"When you're doing it for a kid like Derek," he said, "you don't mind at all."

But Dick Groch did not bother to set up a meeting or even to stop by the batting cage to say hello.

"Never met him," Zomer said. "I had no idea who he was."

Groch was employed by the New York Yankees, and as draft day approached, he was finally emerging from the bushes and preparing to pounce.

Dick Groch first saw Derek Jeter at a baseball camp in Mount Morris, Michigan, where the shortstop fielded ground balls, showed off his arm, and ran the sixty-yard dash. Groch was standing next to an assistant coach at Michigan State who was taken by the teen's talents and who wanted to get Jeter on his mailing list.

"You'd better save your postage," Groch told the coach. "That kid's not going to school."

The Yankees' scout had been watching Jeter for only half an hour when he ruined that Michigan State assistant's day. Groch had been a junior baseball coach for eighteen years, and he had seen dozens of prospects come and go as a scout.

He knew a star when he saw one.

"When you look in the window of a jewelry store," Groch said, "it doesn't take long to see that big ring. If you've been in it as long as I had, you know the difference between going to the Kentucky Derby and the county fair."

Groch could not help himself. The young shortstop inspired the veteran scout to empty his considerable bag of metaphors.

"You travel so many highway miles to see players who have this flaw, or that flaw," Groch said, "that you figure somebody's got to be able to play this game. And then you walk into a ballpark one day and see it all, and you know it right away.

"Seeing Derek Jeter was seeing the personification of athleticism, the dynamics of energy. The ease with which he did things, the acrobatic way he moved his feet, the hands as soft as melting butter. This was Fred Astaire at shortstop."

Groch thought Ken Griffey Jr. was the best high school player he had ever scouted, and he put Jeter right there with Junior, who was more physically developed when he was Derek's age. Durability had been a question with Jeter, who did not even weigh 160 pounds, and Groch decided to see for himself if that question had merit.

He watched Jeter play four weekend games for the Maroons in oppressive July heat. "And his body remained alive; it was catlike quick," Groch said. "There was no sluggishness in his movements."

Groch tracked his blue-chipper all over Michigan. Sometimes the scout would watch Jeter from down the right-field line — "halfway in the woods," Groch said — just to see if Derek played hard all the time, or only when he thought the big leagues were watching.

Groch believed Jeter knew his identity, and which team he represented, even if the scout stayed clear of Zomer and avoided contact with the kid. So sometimes Groch would watch Jeter have a bad at-bat in the first inning, leave the field, and secretly watch the rest of the game from his car.

After Jeter returned from his injured ankle, Groch was on the way to an assignment in Columbus, Ohio, when his boss, Yankees scouting director Bill Livesey, stopped him in his tracks.

"Don't you know Jeter's team is playing?" Livesey asked.

"Bill, it's supposed to snow in Kalamazoo this weekend and Jeter's not playing on that ankle."

"Well, that's our kid, so you'd better go over and sit on him."

And sit on him Dick Groch did. The scout ultimately filled out a detailed report on Jeter for the Yankees to review, a report that read like this:

Long lean sinewy body. Long arms, long legs narrow waist, thin ankles. Live "electric" movements.

Above avg. arm, quick rel., accurate throws with outstanding carry. Soft hands, good range, active feet. Very good runner, 4.33 (R); 4.41 (R); Flow on the bases. Shows pwr potential. Quick bat.

Anxious hitter, needs to learn to be more patient at the plate. Swing slightly long.

"A Yankee"! A Five-tool player. Will be a ML Star! +5!!

Groch classified Jeter as a pull hitter. He ranked Derek's dedication, agility, and emotional maturity as "excellent"; his aptitude, habits, and coachability as "good"; and his physical maturity as "fair."

A scouting report score of 80 would be considered perfect, Groch said, "but getting anyone into the 60s is almost unheard of on the amateur level." He gave Jeter a raw score of 59 and an overall future potential grade (OFP) of 64.

But Groch preferred to focus on the narrative of a scouting report rather than the overall grade. Three scouts filed reports on Jeter to the Major League Scouting Bureau: Jim Terrell, an area scout; Dick Colpaert, a regional cross-checker; and Carroll Sembera, a national cross-checker.

Terrell described Jeter as a "straight away" hitter. He gave Jeter an OFP score of 59.9, compared his physique to that of "a young Mark Belanger," and was more impressed with Derek's "tap dancer feet" than he was discouraged by an offensive game that was "lagging" behind Derek's defense.

"All Star status likely," read Terrell's summation. "Born to play SS. Quality defensive tools compare with Barry Larkin — Reds."

Colpaert gave Jeter an OFP score of 60 but said his bat "will have to come on." Sembera was the toughest grader — he was known as "Mr. Chainsaw Scout" — but he allowed Jeter an OFP grade of 56.3 and offered only mild criticism of Derek's bat ("Will come around with maturity and added strength") and defense ("Did not get good jump fielding, was hesitant due to tender ankle"). Sembera's summation?

"All the tools to be a SS at ML Level."

Groch and the Yankees wanted as many fresh eyes on Jeter as possible. Don Lindeberg, a cross-checker from the West Coast, was flown in to Michigan to make sure the Yanks were not getting too enthusiastic about a hobbling player in a lousy climate.

Lindeberg did not need to see more than a game or two. "Jeter's got a rifle for an arm," he announced, "and there's not a kid in California as good as he is."

Groch was ready to make his predraft case to Livesey, who was already a Derek Jeter fan. Livesey and the Yankees thought highly of Stanford's Jeffrey Hammonds, a center fielder out of New Jersey who wanted to play in the Northeast, but they had a glut of young center fielders in their system and they figured Baltimore would take Hammonds at number 4 anyway.

Livesey had varying degrees of interest in the other candidates mentioned prominently at the top of the draft. He had a good feeling about third baseman Phil Nevin, the College Player of the Year out of Cal State–Fullerton. He appreciated the arm strength and breaking ball of Paul Shuey, the right-hander out of North Carolina, but had questions about his delivery and did not see Shuey as a good fit.

B. J. Wallace, the lefty out of Mississippi State? Livesey thought he would develop into a strong pitcher but worried that his development would come later rather than sooner. Chad Mottola, the power hitter out of Central Florida? Livesey had one scout who liked him, "but overall Mottola wasn't quite that high for us."

The Yankees considered a couple of pitchers — Jim Pittsley of Du-Bois Area High School in Pennsylvania, and Ron Villone of the University of Massachusetts — as serious backup options, and they kept their eye on Longwood University shortstop Michael Tucker, Miami (Florida) catcher Charles Johnson, and Florida State outfielder Kenny Felder.

Jeter? Livesey personally watched him play twice at Kalamazoo Central. He went in on a Friday, another miserable early spring day in the southwest corner of Michigan, and the field was too wet and muddy to get a solid read.

Livesey decided to watch some college players from Michigan and Michigan State over the weekend and then double back to Kalamazoo for a second look at Jeter that Monday. After watching the shortstop take BP and play a game on a dry track, Livesey was a believer.

"Oh, boy, I see exactly what they see," Livesey told himself while leaving the field. He instructed his scouts and cross-checkers to play it with Jeter the way Groch was playing it — by remaining as inconspicuous as possible.

They were trying to disguise their real interest in Jeter, Livesey said, "because a lot of things had to fall into place for us to get him."

A year after the Yankees made a record $1.55 million bonus payout to a high school lefty who threw 99 miles per hour, Brien Taylor, they needed a ton of luck for a chance to spend another first-round bundle on another high school kid. Livesey did not believe Jeter would get past the Reds at number 5 anyway; in fact, he did not believe Jeter would get past Ann Arbor.

In a meeting held before the draft, Livesey expressed one overriding concern about the player his scouts considered the number-one prospect on the board.

"Isn't this kid going to Michigan?" Livesey asked.

"No, he's not," Dick Groch shot back.

"The only place this kid's going is Cooperstown."

The night before the draft, the Houston Astros' decision makers gathered in a hotel conference room and made their final call. Their list of six candidates for the number-one pick had been reduced to two — Phil Nevin and Derek Jeter — and the time had come to reduce that list to one.

Dan O'Brien, Houston's scouting director, had seen Jeter play twice at Kalamazoo Central and found him to be a purposeful kid who never took a play off, and who already had an innate feel for the game. O'Brien felt Hal Newhouser was 100 percent right on Jeter's ability and makeup.

Bob Watson, Houston's assistant GM, watched Jeter once in person and came away believing the shortstop "was a man playing with boys." But Watson had a strong connection to Nevin — Watson's high school teammate and good friend, Astros scout Ross Sapp, had coached Nevin years earlier.

"I'd trust Ross on anything," Watson said, "and he gave us a great report on Nevin."

The Astros actually thought Stanford's Jeffrey Hammonds might be a better prospect than Nevin or Jeter, but Hammonds's agent, Jeff Moorad, had warned Houston and other franchises not based in the

Northeast that his Jersey-born client yearned to play closer to home.

The Astros thought Jeter would be an easier player to sign than Hammonds. Watson had been having regular conversations with the shortstop's adviser, California-based agent Steve Caruso (high school prospects could not hire paid representatives without jeopardizing their amateur standing; they could only classify their agents-to-be as advisers).

Houston's assistant GM asked Caruso to submit the bonus figure he would be seeking if the Astros made his client the top pick. Caruso did not want to show these cards but relented and gave Watson a number that he said was "in the $750,000 to $800,000 range."

Caruso was asking for half of what the Yankees had given Brien Taylor the year before, so his was a reasonable request. But Houston had selected a number of high school players at the top of recent drafts, including two shortstops — Thomas Nevers of Edina, Minnesota, and Shawn Livsey of Chicago — in the first rounds of the 1990 and '91 drafts, respectively. This time around, team owner John McMullen favored a prospect who might bring a more immediate return.

McMullen was the former minority owner of the Yankees who famously said, "There is nothing quite so limited as being a limited partner of George Steinbrenner's." Holding the first pick, McMullen did not know that Steinbrenner's Yankees coveted Jeter with the sixth pick, and it would not have made a difference if he did.

McMullen set Houston's organizational tone on this one. So when Astros officials came to a decision on the eve of the draft, the result was not a surprise.

Houston thought Nevin would advance through its system faster than Jeter would. Back in Bloomfield Hills, Michigan, a veteran scout was about to receive the most disappointing phone call of his second career. Hal Newhouser had cherished those road trips to and from Kalamazoo, watching Jeter play baseball in the freezing rain before returning home for a hot dinner and a warm bath.

Newhouser had a healthy relationship with O'Brien, his boss, who understood his scout was working on a year-by-year basis. At seventy-one, on Cooperstown's doorstep at last, Newhouser was winding down his distinguished baseball life.

That phone call would abruptly end it. Newhouser took it in the upstairs office of his three-bedroom home and then walked downstairs to break the news to his wife.

"Well, I'm through with scouting," Hal told Beryl. "They picked Nevin and said it was an organizational decision. That means this is who we picked, and you don't count."

Beryl asked her husband if he was certain he wanted to quit, and the scout assured her his mind was made up. "Harold was very disappointed," she said. "He just thought it was such a big mistake, and he was the kind of person who, once he made a decision, he made it."

O'Brien maintained that Newhouser had never threatened to resign over Jeter, and that the scout did not tell him Nevin's selection was a significant factor in his retirement.

Beryl Newhouser saw it differently. Her man had been involved in the big leagues since he was a teenager, and more than half a century later he still loved a job that made him feel like a boy all over again.

"Harold was still looking forward to going into the Hall of Fame," Beryl said, "but after Houston didn't draft Derek Jeter, he didn't spend another day in baseball. Not one."

Cleveland had the number-two pick, and its young scouting director, Mickey White, saw Derek Jeter play on an injured ankle on a soaked field. White liked what he saw, but not as much as the Indians scouts who had watched Jeter run on two healthy feet.

Bill Livesey was there with White on that same ungodly afternoon, but the Yankee scouting director was experienced enough to catch Jeter again three days later. White was in his second year on the job, and he confessed that his time management skills left something to be desired. He did not return to Kalamazoo.

White had heard Houston would take Jeter at number 1, anyway, and later came to believe — despite Dan O'Brien's claims to the contrary — that the Astros picked Nevin because they thought he would be easier to sign than Jeter.

Either way, Cleveland had drafted Manny Ramirez the year before and Jim Thome in 1989 and was more interested in pitching. The Indians wanted the best arm in the country, and that arm belonged to Paul

Shuey, a right-hander out of the University of North Carolina. Shuey had his mechanical flaws, but he had a Juan Marichal leg kick that made his 95-mile-per-hour heater that much harder to see.

When you talk about the draft, White said, "it's like you're in a Fidelity Mutual discussion and you're trying to figure out what an investment is going to reap." The Indians thought a power closer out of the Atlantic Coast Conference was a better investment than a high school shortstop.

Montreal had the third pick, and its scouting director, Kevin Malone, was struck by Jeter's advanced professionalism and poise. The Expos had a history of drafting the best available athletes, and of absorbing the risk that goes with selecting the likes of high school stars Cliff Floyd, Rondell White, Marquis Grissom, and Larry Walker.

Only the Expos needed pitching — who didn't? — and in Mississippi State's B. J. Wallace they saw a dominant lefty who threw his fastball in the low to mid-90s and was projected to be a quality number-two big league starter.

Malone did not have a Yankee budget to play with, either. He worried about the possible impact Brien Taylor's $1.55 million bonus in '91 would have on Derek Jeter's asking price in '92.

Wallace was a safe and comfortable alternative. Montreal's scouts figured the lefty was only two years away from the majors, tops, so they gambled on the pitcher.

The Expos went against their norm. "Derek Jeter would've been our guy; he was our type of draft pick normally," Malone said. "Derek had all the tools and knew how to use them, and he was the best athlete there. But that was the one year we drafted for a need instead."

Baltimore was up next at number 4, and this was the one top spot in the draft where Jeter did not fit. The Orioles had their iconic Iron Man at short, Cal Ripken Jr., and they preferred college players to the teenage prom kings. They decided to go with Jeffrey Hammonds.

Baltimore had Jeter rated as the top high school player in the draft, "but I can't say he was on our radar screen," said Gary Nickels, an Orioles scout.

Nickels remembered his one trip to Michigan to see Jeter for two reasons: it was the last scouting trip he ever made with his father, who was dying of emphysema; and Derek's disposition suggested he would be a natural leader of a winning team.

"Jeter had an air of confidence about him," Nickels said. "A command of the situation."

That confidence and command had scouts for the Cincinnati Reds in a tizzy. They wanted to use the fifth pick to draft Derek Jeter in the worst way, and they did not know if their scouting director would let them do it.

Julian Mock was preparing to make or break the 1992 draft for his employer, the Reds, and for the team he once worshiped, the Yankees. His three-mile jog complete, his body fresh, and his mind clear, Mock would not open his heart for a single Riverfront Stadium soul.

As the first four picks came off the board that June 1 day, the tension in the Reds' conference room was thicker than the binders carrying the team's scouting reports.

Derek Jeter, the next Barry Larkin, was going to be available at number 5, and so was Chad Mottola, the next Dale Murphy.

At six-foot-three, 215 pounds, Mottola could have been featured on the "after" side of a muscle-building ad that pictured Jeter on the "before" side. The Central Florida outfielder was the only player other than Jeter and Phil Nevin whom the Astros seriously considered for the number-one pick.

The Yankees invited Mottola to work out for them as they considered their options for number 6, an invitation that was declined. Mottola told the Yankees he had played sixty games at Central Florida, and that he did not think a workout was necessary since he thought he would be chosen among the first five picks.

"I think the Yankees got offended," Mottola said.

He did not have an agent; he used his father as an adviser. Before the draft unfolded, a Reds scout negotiated a bonus figure with the Mottolas — $400,000 — and waited for Mock to make the final call.

Mock had two respected scouts who thought Jeter was the far better choice, even if he would cost Cincinnati double what Mottola would. A part-timer who lived outside Kalamazoo, Fred Hayes had watched Jeter play some three dozen times, and he loved the kid's talent as much as the Astros' Hal Newhouser and the Yanks' Dick Groch did.

Hayes told Gene Bennett, a full-time Cincinnati scout, that Jeter could play for the Reds as a high school sophomore, and he was only half kidding.

Hayes and Bennett first saw Derek in a Muskegon, Michigan, tryout camp. The camp had one hundred kids, Bennett said, "but Derek was the only one who made us say, 'Who is that guy?'"

Bennett and Hayes eventually sent the other ninety-nine boys home and kept Jeter around for some extra work. Over time they brought him to workouts at Riverfront Stadium, met his parents, and did everything they could to temper their enthusiasm for Jeter in the company of enemy scouts.

It did not matter that the Reds had selected a high school shortstop, Calvin "Pokey" Reese, in the first round of the '91 draft. "Jeter was a no-brainer for us at number 5," said Bennett, who had a remarkable track record for the Reds, signing everyone from Don Gullett to Paul O'Neill to Chris Sabo to Larkin.

Hayes had handed Jeter a Reds cap when he joined Bennett and Mock on a predraft visit to the Jeter home, and Hayes and Bennett left believing that Derek would be wearing that cap across his big league career.

"We were sure we were going to get him," Bennett said. "It was a done deal. He had blazing speed, he was smart, he hit rockets into the Riverfront seats when we had him in as a high school junior. Every single thing Jeter did was special."

With his team holding the first pick, a pick no team could sabotage, Newhouser did not mind sharing one little secret with Bennett. "No kid is worth a million dollars," the Houston scout told the Cincinnati scout. "But if one kid is, it's Derek Jeter."

Bennett did not need convincing, as he saw Jeter as Larkin's equal. To those who were concerned about drafting a shortstop when the Reds already had a young All-Star there, Bennett argued that Jeter could play center field and then move to short when Larkin broke down.

Mock wasn't so sure. Without Larkin, he told himself, Jeter would have been the guy hands down. But Larkin was there, and Mottola had already given a verbal to a price out of a small-market team's dream, $400,000, a steal at number 5.

Mock had seen Jeter once, and Bennett had pleaded with him to go back a second time and see the shortstop on a healthier ankle. The scouting director never returned to Kalamazoo, other than to meet with Jeter's parents.

So as Mock gathered with nine or ten other Reds officials in a conference room, gathered around a speakerphone that symbolized the outdated way baseball's elders conducted the draft (they practically used carrier pigeons to report the results), the guardians of his favorite boyhood team were holding their breath.

In Tampa, Yankees executives were huddled around their own speakerphone inside the Harbor View Room at George Steinbrenner's Radisson Bay Harbor Hotel. Those executives were feeling good after Bill Livesey, scouting director, made a morning phone call to his peer in Houston, Dan O'Brien, to ask what the Astros were planning to do at number 1.

O'Brien and Livesey shared a mutual respect, so the Houston scouting director told Livesey the truth: he was taking Phil Nevin. Livesey confessed he was hoping Jeter fell to number 6, and before their brief exchange ended, they both agreed the shortstop would develop into an outstanding pro.

Suddenly the outstanding pro-to-be was one pick away, and a wave of great anticipation roared through the Yankee room like a freight train in the night.

As soon as the Orioles made Hammonds official, a voice from the commissioner's office announced on the speakerphone that the Cincinnati Reds would select next. The Yankees had some twenty officials in their draft room, including regional scouting supervisors, a national cross-checker, Livesey, and Brian Sabean, the vice president for player development and scouting.

Days of mass coffee consumption and passionate debates had taken their toll. Nerves were frayed as the Yankees waited for the sound of Julian Mock's voice. Club officials were staring blankly at the boards in the front of the room that ranked the prospects by position, from top to bottom.

"We beat up those boards for three or four days," Livesey said. They kept changing the rankings, erasing names, restoring names, leaving at night, and then returning the next morning to do it all over again.

On draft day, Jeter's name was atop the list of shortstops, and everyone in the room agreed the Yankees should have and would have taken him had they owned the number-one pick. Livesey ran the strong preference for Jeter by Steinbrenner, which was an odd turn of events.

Commissioner Fay Vincent had banned Steinbrenner for life from the day-to-day operations of the club for paying a gambler, Howie Spira, $40,000 to dig up dirt on Dave Winfield, who happened to be Jeter's idol. Yet everyone knew the Boss was in full control of a shadow government.

"It's not like George disappeared by any means," said David Sussman, the Yankees' general counsel and chief operating officer. Steinbrenner readily offered his opinions on significant player transactions at quarterly partnership meetings (Vincent had allowed this). "George made it known in those meetings that he still owned the team," Sussman said.

Steinbrenner also made it known he was not especially fond of paying superstar wages to kids who had not proved a thing. The Boss came down hard on subordinates over the decision to pay Brien Taylor his record-shattering bonus.

But when Livesey ran Jeter up Steinbrenner's flagpole, assuring his employer the shortstop would be in the majors within four years, the Boss approved.

The Reds were about to make their move, and the Yankees' hour of reckoning had arrived. "It was a beehive of activity," Livesey said. "We had a lot of manpower in the room. People on our files, people working the boards, people erasing names, people making calls."

The Yankees had not been to the playoffs since 1981, and they were in dire need of a break neither Jeter nor his adviser thought they were going to get. Jeter was so sure he was going in the top five, so sure the Reds would take him if the Astros did not, so sure he had no chance of playing for his boyhood team, "I didn't even know the Yankees picked sixth," he said. "I thought I was going to Cincinnati and that I'd be stuck behind Larkin."

Wearing a University of Michigan shirt, Jeter paced about his home as he waited with his family for the call. Out in Sacramento, Caruso gathered with a few aides in his office and stared at the phone. "We were preparing to negotiate a contract with the Reds," he said.

Paul Morgan, the *Kalamazoo Gazette* sportswriter who had covered

Derek's high school career, was feverishly working his desktop at the newspaper's offices, hitting his refresh button over and over to get the latest Associated Press bulletins on a draft that was not televised.

Morgan called the Jeters after a couple of picks were made, and when the phone rang Derek jumped out of his chair. With four selections in the books and the Reds ready to go, the sportswriter called back and told the shortstop he would contact him the second the AP posted his name.

Jeter was overwhelmed by the very real possibility he would be selected at number 5. The franchises picking ahead of the Yankees knew of Jeter's pinstriped preferences, yet that did not shape their decisions. Like the teams that went before them, the Reds merely wanted the best available player at the best possible price.

Finally Julian Mock acted on his mid-jog epiphany. He leaned into the speakerphone and announced the Cincinnati Reds were using the fifth overall choice to take Chad Mottola of the University of Central Florida.

A cheer immediately went up in the Yankee draft room in Tampa, one loud enough to echo across the Bronx. Fists were pumped and backs were slapped. Somehow, some way, Derek Jeter had made it unscathed to the sixth pick.

Morgan called Derek with the news that the Reds had gone for Mottola, and that the Yankees were on deck. "Oh, God," the kid said. A series of fateful choices — gross miscalculations, some observers believed — left the teenage Jeter holding a winning lottery ticket.

Livesey wasted little time after the voice from the commissioner's office announced the Yankees were up next. The scouting director turned to Kevin Elfering, the assistant scouting coordinator and director of minor league operations, who was reviewing the large computer printout of prospects' names before him.

"Jeter," Livesey said.

Derek Sanderson Jeter.

Elfering found his name on the printout and noted his draft identification number — 19921292. Elfering did not have a single thing to do with the scouting of Jeter, but he had the honor of making it official. "All I did," Elfering said, "was say his name into the phone, Derek Jeter of Kalamazoo Central, and then he was ours."

Just as the commissioner's office was repeating what Elfering had said, Reds scout Gene Bennett walked into the room where Mock and other officials were gathered. Bennett could not believe his ears.

He heard a voice on the speakerphone say the Yankees had just taken Jeter, compelling the scout to blurt out, "Yeah, and the Cincinnati Reds take Babe Ruth." Bennett figured someone was pulling his leg, at least until a coworker told him, "Be quiet, we're on the hookup."

A sick feeling came over him. Suddenly Bennett realized Mock had actually taken Mottola instead of Jeter, "and I couldn't believe it," he said. "Without question it was the most disappointing thing that ever happened to me as a scout."

A prototypical five-tool guy with size, Mottola was thrilled to be a first-round pick, never mind a top-five pick. He took the $400,000 deal with the Reds because he wanted to play baseball, because it sure seemed like a lot of money, and because nobody had projected him as a high draft choice entering his final year of college ball.

But the fourth pick, Hammonds of the Orioles, would sign for $975,000. Even the twenty-fifth selection in that draft, Todd Steverson, scored a bigger bonus than Mottola did — $450,000 from Toronto.

"A big reason the Reds took me was my signability," Mottola would say. "When you're that young you think, 'Four hundred thousand to go in the first round? Great, where do I sign?' You don't realize people are trying to take advantage of you."

The Reds scout who saw Jeter the most, Fred Hayes, was just as devastated as Bennett. Jim Bowden, Cincinnati's thirty-one-year-old director of player development and a man on the verge of becoming the youngest general manager in baseball history, could not believe Mock had ignored Bennett's claim that Jeter could develop into a better player than the O'Neills, Sabos, and Larkins he had signed in the past.

Mock was not moved by anyone's counterarguments. He explained he did not know if Jeter would ever play shortstop for the Reds and figured Jeter might end up getting traded to another club.

"I thought of our needs," Mock said, "and of the fact I thought we had a superstar in Mottola."

Before he could do any of that explaining, Morgan was on the phone and speed-dialing the Jeters. The sportswriter knew if he did not get to Derek immediately after the Yankees selected him at number 6, he would never get through.

Morgan even beat the team and Dick Groch to the punch. This time Charles Jeter answered the phone.

"Charles, has he heard yet?" Morgan asked.

"No," the father answered.

"He's a Yankee."

Charles let out a cry of unmitigated joy and immediately handed the phone to his son.

"Derek, you're going to be a Yankee," Morgan told him.

"I can't believe it," Derek shouted. "I just can't believe it."

Morgan heard bedlam breaking out in the background, and the sportswriter let Derek go, knowing the Yankees would be trying to call. Morgan hopped into his car and headed to the Jeter home.

Meanwhile, Sharlee Jeter wrapped her big brother in a hug before her father shook Derek's hand.

"I'm so proud of you," Charles shrieked. "New York Yankees. That's your dream, man!"

It was as if Jeter had willed this to happen. All those years of wearing Yankee shirts and caps and pendants, all those promises to friends, teammates, and teachers that he would grow up to become the shortstop for the world's most famous ball team — they created some cosmic force too potent for an antiquated draft system to repel.

The dreamer was living the impossible dream, yet one that still required a signature and the rejection of a free education at Michigan.

The Yankees' Brian Sabean immediately began negotiations with Caruso, a labor relations consultant turned beginner agent who landed Jeter as a client after landing A. J. Hinch, the Oklahoma high school star.

Caruso would come to see Jeter as the second-best teenage prospect he had ever seen, right behind a Miami phenom named Alex Rodriguez. On a strong recommendation from Hinch's father, Charles Jeter had invited Caruso to Kalamazoo and, over a few slices of pizza, agreed to let him represent his son.

"Then [Scott] Boras showed up at the airport and he was bugging Charles a couple of weeks later," Caruso said. "Charles, to his credit, wouldn't let Boras come over because he'd already made a deal with me."

Caruso would go to bat for Jeter, a client he saw as "a skinny seventeen-year-old who barely said three words," a client who lived in a home modest enough to greet a visitor with a broken handle on the screen door. That modest existence was about to change in a big six-figure way.

Sabean faxed Caruso an opening offer of $550,000. The agent assured the Yankee executive these negotiations would not be nearly as acrimonious as the Brien Taylor talks but also told him that bid would not get it done.

Caruso wanted to beat the $725,000 bonus Toronto had given the California high school star Shawn Green and his agent, Moorad, the year before. As the faxes and phone calls went back and forth, Jeter phoned the Michigan head coach, Bill Freehan, to seek his counsel. Freehan was in a delicate spot — he wanted Jeter on scholarship in the worst way, but as a former All-Star catcher with the Tigers he understood the lure of the big leagues.

"The kid wanted to go to Michigan," said Freehan's assistant, Ace Adams. "No one knows this, but Jeter did not want to sign [with the Yankees]. He wanted to go to Michigan with his girlfriend, and he wanted to play there."

But the Yankees kept inflating their offer. Derek called the Michigan head coach and said, "Mr. Freehan, what should I do?"

"You've got to sign," Freehan finally told him. "You're crazy if you don't."

Adams was flabbergasted over his boss's show of integrity and good faith. "I don't think many college coaches would've ever said that," Adams said, "but Bill was such a classy guy."

Jeter listened to Freehan. On June 28, 1992, two days after his eighteenth birthday, Jeter signed an $800,000 deal with the Yankees that included a $700,000 bonus (Caruso's 5 percent cut amounted to $35,000) and enough to cover the full ride to Michigan that Jeter was giving up. His deal at number 6 doubled Mottola's at number 5 and beat those signed by the top three picks.

Freehan reached out to Adams, who was driving on the New York

Thruway and returning from the Cape Cod League when his boss broke the news.

"Derek just signed with the Yankees," Freehan said.

"Oh, shit," replied Adams, whose long journey home had just gotten three times longer.

Derek Jeter, who graduated twenty-first in a Kalamazoo Central class of 265, would not be continuing his education at Michigan. Instead, Charles Jeter would take his son to the airport for a flight to Tampa and a spot on the Yankees' rookie team in the Gulf Coast League.

When Charles took his last look at Derek before he boarded that plane, the father thought the son looked a lot younger than eighteen. After he returned to his car to begin the drive back to his Battle Creek office, Charles began to weep uncontrollably.

"As soon as the plane took off," Derek would say, "I realized there was no turning back."

His touchdown in Tampa marked the end of innocence. Derek was not an amateur prospect hobbling around in high-top cleats anymore. He was a corporate asset, a commodity, a highly compensated employee.

Charles did not know if his child was up to handling the transition. And in the first weeks of what was supposed to be a dreamy Yankee life, it became clear Derek Jeter was a boy ill prepared to become a man.

3

E-6

THE FIRST HIGH school player selected in the 1992 major league draft had a problem, and a big one:

He wanted to go home to his mother.

Derek Jeter could not hit a professional curve ball or fastball and could not get past the sinking feeling that all his fellow rookies and coaches in Tampa were asking themselves this one question:

How the hell did the New York Yankees make him their number-one pick?

"It was the lowest level of baseball," Jeter said, "and I was awful."

Alone in a faraway hotel room in the summer of '92, a child overwhelmed by grown-up stakes, Jeter could not get a grip on his runaway emotions. So he would call his parents, his sister, his girlfriend, and tell them that he had made a terrible mistake, that he should have taken the four-year scholarship to Michigan.

Sometimes the calls came at 2:00 a.m., long after Charles and Dot and Sharlee had gone to bed. The minute the phone rang they knew Derek had suffered through another dreadful day at the plate, and that he was busy trying to cry himself to sleep.

Night after night after night, Jeter sobbed for relief that would not come. "That was a nightmare," his father said.

Derek had been a sorry sight on arrival in Tampa, a scarecrow come to life. His ankles were so skinny, his high-tops flapped about even when they were laced as tight as could be.

Jeter would not be allowed to wear high-top cleats in games or practices (Yankee policy prohibited them), another reason he was not comfortable. Derek had never been away from home, outside of his summertime trips to his grandparents' place in New Jersey.

He was not in Tampa to play catch with Grandma Dot. He was not spending any long afternoons at the Tiedemann castle and splishsplashing around Greenwood Lake on the Yankees' dime.

The team was laying out $800,000, and the shortstop who was just days removed from his eighteenth birthday was supposed to honor the investment.

"We're expecting big things from you," George Steinbrenner told him the day they first met.

"And Derek was scared to death," said his agent, Steve Caruso.

Derek had his reasons. Finally done with his bonus negotiations, Jeter showed up late to the Class A rookie ball season and late to his first double-header.

"Everyone was looking at me," Derek would say. "I'm the number-one pick."

Jeter had felt the same stares bearing down on him while he ate in the dining room at Steinbrenner's Radisson Bay Harbor Hotel, and they unnerved him. No, he was not even remotely ready to play up to the numbers in his contract.

The same Jeter who struck out once in twenty-three games during his senior season at Kalamazoo Central struck out five times and went 0 for 7 in his first double-header as a pro in Sarasota. Derek faced a knuckleballer in the first game; he had never faced a knuckleballer. Derek faced a pitcher throwing 90 miles per hour in the second game; he had never faced a pitcher who threw so hard.

Barely 160 pounds, Jeter was hopelessly overmatched by the velocity of the pitching and the speed of the game. He made critical errors at shortstop, went hitless in his first fourteen at-bats, and started ringing up monthly phone bills that would approach 400 bucks.

"When you're in high school," Derek said, "you can't wait to get out of the house, be on your own and away from your parents telling you what to do. When you're down here, you realize you just can't go back."

Jeter would step into the batter's box and think about how many more hellish weeks he had to endure before he could go home. His games were played before a dozen fans, two dozen on a good day. Those games started under a blazing noontime sun so they would be over before the early-evening thunderstorms rolled in.

For once in his life, Jeter yearned for the sleet and snow of a Kalamazoo spring. Gulf Coast League scores and standings were not printed in the paper. Jeter was stuck in a forgotten time and place, and he wanted his parents to save him. He wanted his girlfriend, Marisa Novara, to visit him. He wanted Bill Freehan, the Michigan coach, to reassure him.

"Hang in there," Freehan told Jeter. "It's part of the process."

Derek could not help himself. The mind-numbing sameness of the routine — take early batting practice in the morning, grab something to eat, fail miserably in the game, stay for extra work in the evening, cry your eyes out at night — was wearing him to the nub.

Suddenly the very word banned by his grandfather and mother — can't — was the only word that rolled easily off his tongue. "The first few games," Jeter said, "I was just swinging at everything. I didn't have any idea where the ball was going."

Charles and Dot Jeter headed down to Tampa; Caruso had put a clause in Derek's contract calling for the Yankees to fly in the shortstop's parents at the team's expense. Novara also made a trip.

They told Derek the same things in person they had told him on the phone — everything would work out just fine. Charles reminded his son that an eighteen-year-old Chipper Jones hit .229 in rookie ball before hitting .326 the following season.

At that point in time, Derek would have made any Faustian deal to hit .229, never mind .326. He was melting in the oppressive heat, wasting away to nothing, wishing every solitary hour of every solitary day he was a college Wolverine instead of a professional Yankee.

Jeter's first official hit in the Yankees' employ was a bloop over the first baseman's head in the first game of a double-header. "Everyone was laughing with me," he said, "and that was a big load off my shoulders."

Derek went ahead and ripped off two singles in the second game, but his was a temporary refuge. When he showed up for work at the four-field minor league complex, Jeter never let on that he had been crying through the night in his room at Steinbrenner's hotel. His coaches and teammates did not realize it, and the banned Boss — forever lurking in the shadows — sure did not realize it.

"I had no idea he was that concerned about his ability to play professional baseball," said his manager, Gary Denbo.

How would he know? Every morning when Denbo arrived at the team's Hines Avenue complex, next door to the home of the Tampa Bay Buccaneers, Jeter and another eighteen-year-old prospect, Ricky Ledee, picked in the sixteenth round of the 1990 draft, were waiting for him in the picnic area, eager to be the first players in the batting cage.

They would also do extra conditioning after games, when most players had already fled the heat for the comfort of their air-conditioned cars and rooms. And through it all, Jeter wore a mask of clear-eyed determination.

He was hurting behind that mask. "It seemed nothing was bothering him, that he had a positive frame of mind," Denbo said. "I wish I knew. I would've helped him."

Denbo helped him more than he understood. When some in the organization were questioning whether Jeter would ever be a high-impact hitter at the big league level, Denbo tempered his leg kick and reminded him that the first part of his swing had to be an inside-the-ball move.

Derek quickly applied these lessons to the games, while most lower-level prospects needed two or three years before they could accomplish against live pitching what they were accomplishing in the cage.

Denbo also noticed Jeter was tilting the barrel of the bat toward the catcher when he moved his hands into the hitting position, or loaded. This was a fault common in hitters with long swings, but Denbo let the fault stand. The Yankees did not believe in breaking down prospects with too many tweaks too soon; they adhered to a thirty-day moratorium on suggested changes to a player's approach.

"They don't want to screw up the good things you did that got you here," Jeter said.

One last thing Denbo noticed about his shortstop: he was about the most polite and professional kid he had ever met.

Every single time Derek walked out of the cage, he thanked his coach or coaches for the help. "In professional baseball," Denbo said, "that just doesn't happen."

Overnight success does not happen, either. And even though Jeter responded to Denbo's teachings as few students did, he remained a prisoner of his own doubts and insecurities when holed up alone in his room.

Mark Newman, the Yankees' coordinator of instruction, did not know about the crying or the kid's wrenching struggle to find himself. Newman knew Jeter to be quick with a playful smile that could light up a clubhouse.

But one day he sat next to Jeter at his locker and asked how things were going. "You know, I don't think I can do this," Derek confessed. "I shouldn't have done this. I should've gone to Michigan."

Gone to Michigan? Newman was shocked by what he was hearing.

"Derek was about as distraught as it gets," he said.

The executive assured the shortstop that it was common to struggle, that nobody in the Yankees organization cared about his rookie ball batting average. Newman advised Jeter to carry himself the same way whether he was hitting .150 or .350, just so people knew his would be a consistent presence.

"You're not going to be a good player," Newman said, pausing for effect as Jeter shot him a look bordering on quizzical and pained, a look suggesting this was no way to comfort a beaten athlete.

"You're going to be a great player."

Derek's face widened into a smile. Newman had pushed the right human button, finding out what a legion of executives, coaches, teammates, and members of the news media would discover in the years to come.

Derek Jeter loathed criticism and thrived on positive reinforcement.

So nearly every time he saw Jeter, Newman would tell him, "Hey, you're going to be special. Stay with it. That's an outstanding swing." Denbo used the same lines, and Jeter responded just as the Yanks hoped.

By the end of his forty-fifth Gulf Coast League game, with a doubleheader left to play, Jeter had actually lifted his batting average near

.200. Derek had his first small triumph within reach, and privately all Yankee coaches and executives desperately wanted the .500 high school hitter to grab it.

"He had to get four hits the last day to get over .200," Newman said.

Derek Jeter got those four hits. And as soon as he did, Newman told Denbo to remove Jeter from the second game. "We wanted Derek to go home over .200," the executive said.

Only Derek and his final .202 batting average were not going home near the end of August 1992. The Yankees informed Jeter they were shipping him off to Greensboro, North Carolina, to finish out the South Atlantic League season, and it did not matter that the shortstop would finally escape the searing heat, play some night games, and perform before an actual crowd.

Jeter was crushed. Just when he had earned himself a chance to exhale, the Yankees threw him back into the Class A fire and ordered him to join a team that included a pitcher named Andy Pettitte and a second baseman turned catcher named Jorge Posada.

The Greensboro manager, Trey Hillman, picked up Jeter at the airport and was struck by the kid's composure. Hillman knew all about Derek's struggles in the Gulf Coast League, and he personally chauffeured the new recruit to the ballpark because, the manager said, "I didn't want him to be scared on his first day."

To Hillman, Jeter did not appear scared at all. The Yankees wanted Derek to play some baseball under the lights and to get acclimated to the team he was scheduled to join in 1993, and Derek projected an aura of confidence and calm.

But in Jeter's first game, Pettitte was slapping a punctuation mark on what would be a 10-4 season, and he was in no mood for some malnourished shortstop to come in and foul it all up.

On cue, Jeter started kicking around the ball on the left-hander's watch. "Look at this guy," Pettitte told himself. "Are you kidding me? This is our first-round draft pick?"

Jeter felt Pettitte was showing him up with his body language, and he did not forget it. The shortstop hit a home run to compensate for his defensive blunders, and Pettitte did not forget that, either.

Never mind that Jeter made 9 errors in 48 chances over eleven games. He hit a respectable .243 in Greensboro, and Posada said, "You saw what every Yankee saw, what every guy in the organization saw."

Poise. The same poise Jeter showed when he arrived at Yankee Stadium on September 11 as part of another trip Caruso had made a perk of the $800,000 deal. The agent wanted his client around the major league culture as much as possible, to make the ultimate goal feel only a few hard singles away.

When Derek walked into the home clubhouse, some Yankee veterans jokingly asked him for a loan. A year earlier, one clubhouse attendant, John Blundell, saw Brien Taylor pass through the same door, "and he looked like he was on Mars," Blundell said. "He was scared and didn't know what to say. Taylor was in awe of the pinstripes and the big league locker room, even though we were awful."

Jeter wore a different look. At eighteen, Blundell said, "Jeter walked in there and you knew in his mind and heart he felt he was with his peers, and Brien Taylor didn't have that presence at all."

Caruso, Jeter, and Jeter's family ended up in Steinbrenner's box near the dugout. The agent was sitting next to Derek, who had his legs and feet draped over a nearby seat, when a Stadium security guard asked Caruso in an annoyed tone, "Is he with you?" Derek straightened up, and soon enough a junior Yankee official came down to make sure everything was fine.

"If you need anything," Brian Cashman told Caruso and Jeter, "just let me know."

Derek did not need much that night or the following day, other than an update on the Michigan–Notre Dame game. He had enrolled for a semester in Ann Arbor and had attended his first classes the day before he arrived in the Bronx, where he spent part of Saturday, September 12, working out with the Yanks in full uniform.

"Everything was larger than life," Derek would say.

He did not get to meet his all-time favorite Yankee, Dave Winfield, who was playing in Toronto, but Jeter did share the field with the likes of Don Mattingly and Wade Boggs, and he did take a tour of Monument Park. Cashman was responsible for escorting Derek and his family around the Stadium, and the junior official who was a year away from becoming the Yankees' assistant general manager could not get over how much the supermodel-thin Jeter looked like the world's tallest batboy.

Derek had started a weight-training program at Michigan to supplement his summer workouts, and by year's end he would add 16 pounds to his frame and push his weight close to 180. "But he was still so gangly," Cashman said, "that you had to keep reminding yourself he was our first-round pick."

Cashman walked Derek and his family up the left-field side of the Stadium and escorted them into the Yankees' own Hall of Fame beyond the outfield wall. As they moved from plaque to plaque, monument to monument, Cashman figured this was the right time to make the Yankees' $800,000 bonus baby feel like a million bucks.

He turned to Jeter and said, "Maybe you'll have your number retired here one day."

Only Jeter was not worried about finding his way to Monument Park. He just wanted to get back to Michigan, back to the sanctuary of his dorm room, before the Yankees returned him to the school of hard knocks.

The following spring in Fort Lauderdale, Whitey Ford was walking past the batting cage at the Yankees' facility when a sight and a sound stopped him dead in his spring training tracks. Derek Jeter was taking his cuts on his first day of big league camp, and Ford decided to take in the show.

Jeter delivered smash after smash after smash. "When I found out he was a shortstop," Ford said, "I said, 'Jesus Christ, I can't believe it.'"

No, Phil Rizzuto never swung the bat like this.

Ford waited until Jeter was done, and then the Hall of Fame pitcher and the kid shortstop walked and talked until they reached the Yankee clubhouse. Ford complimented Jeter on his hitting, and he was taken by Derek's apparent modesty and easy smile.

"This kid's going to be around for a long time," Ford told himself.

The Chairman of the Board was struck by Jeter's arm and range at short, even if the infield instructor, Clete Boyer, would decree that Derek had "quite a ways to go."

Jeter was not going anywhere near the Bronx in 1993; he was in camp only to get a feel for how the Yanks went about their business. He hoped to make a strong second impression on team officials before heading back to Greensboro for a full season of Class A ball.

If nothing else, Jeter made an impression on Don Mattingly, just as he had made one on Whitey Ford. The shortstop and the veteran first baseman were finishing up a workout on a back field, all alone, the seats empty, not a player or team official in sight.

A spent Jeter had started walking off the field — no urgency or bounce to his step — when a jogging Mattingly came up behind him and in passing said, "Let's run it in. You never know who's watching."

Jeter caught up to Mattingly and the two raced to the clubhouse side by side. An elder's wisdom had hit home. From then on Jeter would do everything — even head to the showers — at full speed.

Team officials noticed. Jeter never expected to see the inside of a major league preseason game, never expected to hear the Yankees' manager, Buck Showalter, turn his way and say, "Get ready."

"Ready?" Jeter thought. "Ready for what?"

Ready to pinch-run for the New York Yankees, that's what.

Derek got his fifteen seconds of fame on the base paths, then was sent down to minor league camp with Brien Taylor on March 14, the same day the Yankees optioned a young pitcher named Mariano Rivera to the minors.

Before he knew it, Jeter was packing his bags and hopping into a car with a teammate and fellow shortstop he had befriended, R. D. Long, for the 645-mile drive from Tampa to Greensboro to rejoin the Class A Hornets. Long was not anyone's idea of a bonus baby; he was a college player at Arizona and Houston whom the Yankees picked in the thirty-eighth round of the '92 draft.

Five players were taken before Jeter in that draft, and 1,053 players were taken before Long. But as partners in middle infielder drills the eighteen-year-old phenom and the twenty-one-year-old long shot grew close and decided to be roommates.

They jumped into the car when camp broke and made the ten-hour drive to Greensboro. "We listened to Mariah Carey the whole way," Long said. "The kid had every single Mariah CD ever printed."

Mariah would be the background music for Jeter's long and painful journey from bungling apprentice to master of his trade. In Greensboro, where the Hornets competed in the South Atlantic League, a low-level Class A consortium known as the Sally League, Jeter would play for a team that included other prospects with big league potential, including Mariano Rivera, Shane Spencer, Mike Buddie, Mike DeJean, Nick Delvecchio, Matt Luke, and Ryan Karp.

The Yankee minor leaguers almost always knew how to carry themselves, and this group was no different. "We never had any problem with Yankee kids down here," said the Hornets' owner, John Horshok. "They were well behaved, and they had so much information and training, they were almost afraid to screw up and not end up being Yankees."

Coming off elbow surgery in 1992, Rivera was most determined to get his burgeoning career back on track. He had been a weeping mess himself as a rookie in the Gulf Coast League three years earlier, when the language barrier left him yearning to return to his native Panama.

But Rivera had adapted and grown up. One day in the Greensboro clubhouse he was barking at players, "Let's go to work, let's go to work," when Long threw his cup of water at Rivera just for the hell of it.

The water landed on a chart Rivera was holding, "and Mariano went ballistic and wanted to kill me," said Long, whom the pitcher chased around the locker room.

The Yankees were encouraged by Rivera's competitiveness and had high hopes for a few Hornets, but Jeter was the jewel of the system, the one draft choice outside of Brien Taylor the franchise needed to develop. He would play in a lost-in-time kind of place, World War Memorial Stadium, a crumbling concrete structure near the North Carolina A&T campus.

War Memorial opened in 1926 — "You mean there was a World War I?" one Hornet asked a Yankee official — and welcomed Charles Lindbergh a year later. Among the nation's oldest minor league parks, War Memorial was distinguished by the triple-arched main entrance, the perimeter resembling a backward J, the dim lights and choppy field, the wooden seats, the backed-up plumbing, the cramped clubhouses, and the pest-infested press box.

"When you walked in there," said Mitch Lukevics, the Yankees' farm director, "you felt like you were going to see Roy Hobbs."

Only Derek Jeter was supposed to be the natural on this Greensboro team, the teenage prodigy among more experienced and less touted Hornets in their early twenties. He would play for Bill Evers, a former catcher from Long Island who grew up wanting to be the next Mickey

Mantle, and for his trusted Gulf Coast League manager, Gary Denbo, who was Evers's hitting coach.

Jeter had returned to Denbo a little wiser, a little bigger, and a little less likely to cry himself to sleep. He matured some during his semester at Michigan and during his instructional league play that followed, and he gained confidence in February and March while working out with the Yanks.

Jeter had to negotiate one crisis of spring training faith — a veteran infielder, Dave Silvestri, was hitting him with a heavy dose of fraternity hazing, ordering Derek to perform menial batting practice tasks. But Gerald Williams, Yankee outfielder, assumed the role of Jeter's mentor and guided the shortstop through the turbulence, and Long took his own big-brother-Derek-never-had role on the road with them to Greensboro.

Meanwhile, as he surveyed the Fort Lauderdale camp prior to his departure, Jeter realized the gap between the big leaguers' talent and his was not quite as vast as he had thought.

So he did not arrive in Greensboro half as terrified as he had been when he arrived in Tampa the previous summer. Jeter hit the ball for the Hornets, sometimes with authority, and he fit in easily with the second baseman out of UCLA, Robert Hinds, and the other college boys on his team.

But in the field, Derek Jeter was booting balls left and right, Long said, "looking like a right fielder trying to play shortstop. He had gangly legs going in every which direction, gangly arms going in every which direction. If he picked it up, he threw it away. Every way you can make an error he made it."

Up in the tight and steamy War Memorial press box, where a rusty fan served as the air conditioner, Ogi Overman was reliving a bad dream. A few years earlier, the official scorer for the Greensboro Hornets had given a third baseman named Andy Fox most of his 45 errors. Overman nicknamed Fox "Glove of Stone."

"I'd give him the E-5," Overman said, "and he'd look into the press box and grab his nuts and give me the choke sign. He was a miserable third baseman."

Overman would point at Fox and shout obscenities at him, and no, it was not a pretty scene. But when he entered a Jeter error in the books, the official scorer knew to expect no such fireworks.

"Giving Jeter an error became a running joke," Overman said. "When in doubt, E-6." Only the scorer took no pleasure in the process. Jeter never complained about his rulings, he said, "and you could see him hang his head and pound his glove like, 'Goddarnit, how did I just do that?' I felt a little sorry for him."

Overman did not believe in home cooking or overzealous southern hospitality. An error was an error in his book, and the only time he ever cut a Hornet a break, Shane Spencer was the beneficiary.

Spencer was having a rough time at the plate when he lofted yet another benign-looking fly ball. The right fielder had to run a ways to reach it, but it was a catch he should have made. When the ball fell to the grass, Overman considered Spencer's struggles and his charity work in the community and awarded him a double.

Jeter caught no such break.

"So many of his errors were so cut-and-dried," Overman said. Jeter was on his way to setting the South Atlantic League record for errors, and every one of them was earned. "There was no flipping a coin to it," Overman said. "It would be a dribbler right through Jeter's legs, and I couldn't do anything about it."

Only somebody in the Yankees' front office could. That official did not want to hear about Jeter's dreadful footwork, his wildly inconsistent path to the ball, or his unreliable arm. He did not want to hear that the Harvard product at first base, Nick Delvecchio, was not making any plays to bail out the shortstop.

The official only wanted to hear that the Yankees' $800,000 first-round pick would stop getting humiliated by a Class A scorer. That official called the Hornets' general manager, John Frey, and screamed, "'Tell that motherfucking scorekeeper of yours to quit giving Jeter all of those motherfucking errors,'" Overman said.

The GM passed on the message to the official scorer. Overman was so enraged he almost quit on the spot.

Jeter was the one who kept his cool. He never blamed Overman, or Delvecchio, or the lousy field, or the lousy lights, or the lousy luck that landed him on this lousy field under those lousy lights.

Jeter blamed himself, and then tried to make it right. "He'd miss a

Sunday hop," Overman said, "and on the very next play he'd go eight steps into the hole, do a 360 in the air, and throw out the runner by a step. It was like he was redeeming himself, and the crowd would go crazy. Jeter was a very popular kid."

His redemptive plays were not enough to mute the growing chorus of front-office voices wondering if Jeter should be moved to center field. Gene Michael, Yankees general manager, decided to fly to Greensboro to see for himself.

Michael was uniquely qualified to evaluate Jeter. Like Derek, he was a skin-and-bones shortstop prospect (he would be nicknamed "Stick"), a talented basketball player on the side, and a fielder who had committed 56 errors in his first full minor league season.

"I didn't know they were counting mine when I did it," Michael said.

They were counting Jeter's for sure.

A Hornets executive, Tim Cullen, a former infielder for the Washington Senators and a member of the 1972 World Series champion Athletics, gave Michael this scouting report on Jeter:

"God Almighty, this is the worst shortstop I've ever seen. Where did you guys get him?"

Michael could not believe the Yankees' first-round pick could be so inept. Right away Michael noticed Jeter had advanced agility, a strong arm, and a spectacular talent for handling the slow chopper toward him. Michael noticed Jeter was playing with a first baseman who had trouble gathering his semi-wayward throws.

The GM also noticed Jeter fielded ground balls two or three different ways in the same game. He noticed Derek had no plan of attack, and he would tell him Cal Ripken Jr. compensated for his lack of range by applying the same robo-routine to every ball hit his way.

Another evaluator, Clete Boyer, told Jeter to stop catching the ball between his legs, to get it out in front. A lot of voices, a lot to change. Jeter was burdened by his fielding follies, but Michael and other Yankee officials were encouraged that Derek did not carry that baggage into the batter's box.

"The boy's making three errors a game and hitting .270," R. D. Long said, "and he tells me, 'I'm going to hit .400 this year.' I'm looking at the boy and saying, 'No way,' and sure enough he goes on a tear."

Only one year removed from his devastating debut as a pro, from his summer spent wanting to go home to his mother, Jeter was learning how to survive and occasionally thrive in a game built around failure.

Delvecchio, the Harvard grad, had spent the previous season in Oneonta, New York, watching high school boys fall apart at the plate and in the field.

Those boys never recovered. Jeter? He knew how to recover. One time he struck out with the bases loaded and came back to the dugout and declared, "That guy just showed me everything he's got. He'll never get me out again."

Jeter went 0 for 5 in another game and announced, "Tomorrow I'm going 5 for 5." He would go 4 for 4 before his last at-bat ended in a line drive to the second baseman.

Jeter's bat was not quite as powerful as his arm. Delvecchio was the second cutoff man once when the shortstop ran out to take a throw from deep left center. When Jeter turned and fired to the plate, Delvecchio found himself in the role of unnecessary middleman.

He had never seen a ball explode out of someone's hand like that; Delvecchio did not even think about catching it. He let the ball whiz by his ear and land in the catcher's mitt without a bounce, beating the runner by five feet.

"I know Derek's arm got injured," Delvecchio said. "I'm not sure how or why, but after that year his arm diminished just a little bit."

Either way, Jeter was staying in the moment. He was hitting and the Hornets were winning, creating a buzz among the locals and sometimes drawing sellout crowds of 7,500. The team's manager, Evers, had been promoted to the Class AA Albany-Colonie Yankees and replaced by Denbo, whom the shortstop adored.

Suddenly minor league life was agreeing with Jeter. He was taking to Greensboro, and Greensboro was taking to him. If it was not a perfect love affair, it had more to do with the thief who broke into his Mitsubishi 3000GT at the ballpark than it did the city's Old South roots.

In 1960, Greensboro had become ground zero for the civil rights movement when four African-American students from A&T sat at a whites-only Woolworth's lunch counter, starting a series of sit-in protests in cities around the South.

In 1979, five antiracism activists chanting "Death to the Klan" at a rally were gunned down by Klansmen and members of the American

Nazi Party in an incident known as the Greensboro Massacre. Fourteen years later, Horshok said, "you still had pockets down here in the South that . . . if you went into the wrong part of town and talked to someone's girlfriend, you could've gotten in a lot of trouble, if you know what I mean."

Jeter had friends of all colors and creeds, and he was sure to never marginalize his mother's heritage. Sometimes Derek told people he was black and white, and sometimes he told them he was black and Irish.

"Derek is biracial," said Long, "but he sees himself more as a black person. In high school he was a victim of prejudice a few times — even people he thought were his friends said things — and so that's his association."

Jeter had been cut by the jagged edges of racism in Kalamazoo the year before, when he parked his Mitsubishi outside a fast-food restaurant and heard kids in another car shout, "Take that car back to your daddy, you n-----," before speeding away.

"It's not Kalamazoo," Jeter would say of racism. "It's everywhere."

By all accounts, the overwhelming majority of Greensboro residents who came across Jeter did not care that he was black, or black and white. Delvecchio said his teammate did speak of facing prejudice on the road.

"People loved to get on him for who he was, the big publicity, the fact he was a first-round kid and biracial," Delvecchio said. "I know he had to put up with the nonsense of being biracial."

Delvecchio also said many minor leaguers were jealous of Jeter and would claim the Yankees "just got him because of his arm. He's going to be a pitcher. He can't play shortstop."

Jeter blocked out the negative noise, no matter how relentless or vile. Having just turned all of nineteen, Derek was strong enough to assume a leadership role. He would work the locker room to make certain everyone knew what restaurant and club the guys were hitting that night. In the pregame hours he would walk behind Denbo, smack him on the ass, and say, "You ready to go tonight?"

Greensboro had itself a playoff-bound team, and the community celebrated with the Hornets at the Grand Stand bar near the left-field seats. Jeter's older teammates were responsible social drinkers, but the kid shortstop was not one to sneak in a beer, not at the ballpark.

"Derek would sit out there all friggin' night drinking Coke," Horshok said.

Players, coaches, and townies would engage in karaoke contests at the Grand Stand, billed as the largest outdoor sports bar in North Carolina. Jeter, for one, saved his singing for road trips. "Derek had the worst singing voice on the bus," Delvecchio said. "He loved Mariah and Janet Jackson; he used to sing Mariah at the top of his lungs."

"I told him, 'You're horrible. You're worse than me.' And Derek would say, 'The first thing I do when I get to New York, I'm going to find Mariah Carey and go out with her.'"

Jeter was tooling around in his Mitsubishi and trying to persuade Delvecchio to appreciate Snoop Dogg and Dr. Dre. The teenager was mentoring the twenty-something college boys in more ways than one.

They would go to clubs together, "and Derek was underage in a lot of these places," Delvecchio said, "and nobody cared. . . . He occasionally had a beer here and there, but he never took it to excess."

The Hornets took turns approaching attractive women in these clubs. When it was his turn, Delvecchio rarely struck out. But when it was Jeter's turn, he said, the shortstop would get in the middle of the bar, "and he'd extend his index finger and point and motion for them to come over without making a sound. Without fail, they always came over. If Derek did that fifteen times with me, he was fifteen for fifteen. I never saw such confidence. The women absolutely loved him."

So did his teammates. Jeter did not walk about with an air of royalty. He carried himself like a thirty-fourth-round draft choice, like a player who had received Mariano Rivera's $3,000 bonus to sign.

Derek also was his baseball brother's keeper. After Rivera's surgery, Jeter counted his pitches in '93 and reminded Mariano he needed to be efficient to preserve his arm. The nineteen-year-old shortstop was looking out for the twenty-three-year-old starter.

Jeter built up his less talented teammates, never broke them down. A twenty-fifth-round pick, Delvecchio was a converted outfielder who had tremendous power (he was good for 21 homers and 80 RBI that year) but who struggled with his footwork at first base. He had a hard time picking up Jeter's throws from short under the poor War Memorial lighting, and he was likely responsible for a dozen of Derek's errors.

"And he never said a word to me about it," Delvecchio said. "That's how cool he was. He'd come over and say, 'Don't worry about it.' We all thought Derek was fantastic to play with."

Jeter would pass down lessons from his old man's playing days at Fisk University, too. Out of left field, Jeter approached Matt Luke, a big, strapping eighth-rounder out of the University of California, and handed him a page out of the Charles Jeter playbook.

"My dad always told me that you've got to get two or three hits against mediocre pitchers," Derek told Luke, "because when you face an ace you'll be fighting some nights just to get one."

Luke absorbed the thought and decided it made as much sense as anything a grizzled minor league or college coach had ever told him.

"And here's a high school kid telling me, a college kid," said Luke, who was on his way to a season of 21 homers, 91 RBI, and a .304 batting average.

No, Jeter did not let his mounting sum of errors ruin his Greensboro experience. The lost and homesick eighteen-year-old had slowly grown into this confident and independent nineteen-year-old.

Despite his age, Jeter was a credible leader. For 7:00 p.m. games he would arrive at War Memorial at 1:30 to do some soft toss and hone his inside-out swing as the Garth Brooks music blared on the stadium speakers. Jeter was almost always the first Hornet to arrive at work, even beating the team owner to the door.

Horshok was the owner of a local nightclub, the Rhino, and a carnival barker who knew how to create an electric small-time environment for his big-time prospect.

He booked concerts and Elvis impersonators and postgame fireworks shows and fired confetti cannons from the stadium roof. The team mascot, a giant red and blue wasp known as Bomber the Hornet, raced kids around the bases and always lost.

As executive director of the Major League Baseball Players Alumni Association, Horshok also kept a group of prominent friends that included Mickey Mantle, who showed up at War Memorial one day to shoot the breeze. The sixty-one-year-old Mick, who would soon seek treatment for his alcoholism, was en route to a golf tournament in Georgia, and he said his goal was to get there without having a drink.

"Hey, Mickey," Horshok said, "you know who Jeter is?"

"Yeah, yeah," Mantle responded.

"Well, you've got to meet him."

Mantle did not know the identity of any other Greensboro Hornets. Just Jeter. Denbo had Horshok ask Mantle if he would speak to the Hornets, and the Mick declined. He would only agree to talk to the teenager at short.

Horshok thought Jeter was destined to become a great player, he said, "so I wanted to make sure they met."

The team owner pulled Jeter out of the group and walked him into a handshake with a Yankee prodigy from a different time and place. They met along the outfield fence, and Horshok stepped away so they could talk one on one, $1,500 bonus baby to $800,000 bonus baby.

Horshok saw Mantle doing the talking and gesturing, and Jeter doing the listening and nodding. Long before he roamed center field and swatted 536 home runs and secured a place among baseball's all-time greats, Mantle had been a young shortstop who struggled with the burdens of great expectations.

They had a few things in common. Mantle might have been the most popular of Yankees, and Jeter clearly was the most popular of Hornets.

In fact, Jeter was just as comfortable with the townsfolk as he was with Mantle. He was a favorite of the team's booster club, and with the locals who wanted to make him feel at home.

"You'd see him go to potato salad, fried chicken, and hamburger cookouts with fans, when he didn't have to go," Horshok said. "Derek bought completely into what the people around here were all about."

Earl "Bubba" Clary was one of those people. A former placekicker at East Carolina and a sports nut newly divorced, Clary attended a businessman's special at War Memorial and ultimately opened up his large three-bedroom home to any Hornet who needed a hot meal or a place to stay.

Matt Luke and the third baseman, Scott Romano, moved in, and Shane Spencer and catcher Tom Wilson followed. Minor leaguers strapped for money and living three or four to a small apartment suddenly had bigger and better accommodations free of charge.

Jeter and his roommate, Long, crashed at Clary's for the final month of the season. At forty-five, Clary was a bachelor having the time of his life. He felt like the little boy he used to be, listening to Mantle play baseball on the radio. Jeter liked to call him Big Earl, and Clary would serve as the ballplayers' middleman when they were trying to score female companionship for the night.

When attractive women asked the Hornets for autographs, some players would include Clary's phone number with their signatures. "So after games we're over here watching *SportsCenter* at eleven o'clock," Clary said, "cooking some steaks on the grill, and the women would be ringing my phone. I was the players' agent, and I'd take the scraps. When we had enough women over here, I'd take the phone off the hook."

Only the 1993 Hornets were not exactly the 1986 Mets. They were a serious-minded lot hell-bent on winning the Sally League crown.

Ryan Karp, the lefty pitcher, was 13-1. Luke and Delvecchio provided the power, and despite his Gene Michael–tying 56 errors, Jeter was about to be named the most outstanding prospect by the league's managers.

Even though he remained skinny enough for Long to joke he might break his wrist on a check swing, Jeter would hit .295 with 5 homers, 71 RBI, and 18 steals. But Derek was not about numbers. He was about chasing the championships that were out of reach at Kalamazoo Central.

The 85-56 Greensboro Hornets had a chance to win the Sally League in a best-of-five series with the 94-48 Savannah Cardinals, an older team that did not have a fast tracker like Jeter on the roster. The series went to a winner-take-all game in Savannah, "and I built it up into the Super Bowl," Horshok said. "We had private planes down there, we rented banquet rooms, and the players got first-class treatment."

The Yankees even offered the Hornets $1,000 a man as a bonus if they won it all. "And when you're in low A baseball," pitcher Mike Buddie said, "that's a lot of money."

Greensboro needed its money player. With his team down late in that Game 5, Jeter shot a laser into the left-center gap with two runners on. It looked like a sure triple, maybe an inside-the-park homer, at least until a Cardinals outfielder named Joe McEwing reached the ball.

Jeter had already started his sprint from second to third when McEwing slid into the ball and intentionally kicked it under the fence. "A brilliant play," Buddie said.

Jeter was sent back to second base, a run was taken off the board, and Savannah would send the Hornets home with no trophy and no bonus to call their own. As much as the Yankees hated to lose any playoff series, even one in the bowels of Class A ball, they were excited about the fact that their prized shortstop rose to the postseason moment.

Jeter was Greensboro's best player. He was so good, in fact, that the beat writer who covered Derek, Charlie Atkinson of the *News & Record*, approached Ogi Overman, the official scorer who helped Jeter make Sally League history with his 56 errors.

"You do realize," Atkinson told Overman, "that Derek Jeter is going to hit .350 in the majors someday?"

Everyone was becoming a blind believer in Jeter's bat. His glove? That was an entirely different story.

Over in Cincinnati, the scouting director who had picked Chad Mottola instead of Jeter in the '92 draft, Julian Mock, kept throwing those 56 errors in the face of the Reds' new GM, Jim Bowden, who had backed the scouts in support of Jeter. (Meanwhile, Bowden hated Mottola's long swing from the first time he saw it, even if that long swing produced 21 homers and 91 RBI in Mottola's first full year of high Class A ball.)

Many executives around baseball — including more than a few in the Yankee organization — figured Jeter would not remain a shortstop. In the middle of the '93 season, Long sat down his teenage roommate in a diner and told him to prepare for a possible switch to the outfield. Long did not tell Jeter it would definitely happen; he told him to prepare for it to happen.

Jeter turned and shot him a blank look through those pale green eyes.

"I'm never moving from shortstop," he said. "It's never going to happen. Never."

Derek Jeter had been hit by a pitch on the left hand, and so his instructional league orders were to play defense, and only defense, until Brian Butterfield said otherwise.

The coach was the son of Jack Butterfield, a widely respected scout and development man with the Yankees who had died in a car accident in 1979. For Brian this was a dream assignment, a chance to have a former draft class valedictorian in his fielding lab for thirty-five consecutive days.

Butterfield's charge was clear: make sure the Yankees did not have to make their shortstop an outfielder. They started at 9:30 every morning at the minor league complex in Tampa, performed drills for sixty to ninety minutes, watched film of those workouts for thirty to forty-five minutes, and returned to the field to correct the mistakes found on the tape before Jeter played shortstop — without ever stepping to the plate — in afternoon games.

Butterfield thought Derek was too passive while receiving double-play throws at second and taught him to go get the ball. The coach changed Jeter's approach to grounders, showing him how to present an open and relaxed glove.

"Derek looked like a baby Doberman running around," Butterfield said. "Basically we had to break everything down."

The coach rolled balls to Jeter's left and right, hit fungoes at him, drilled him hard on slow choppers. Derek made the necessary adjustments so quickly and definitively, Butterfield said, "that toward the end of the instruction league he was taking a quantum leap."

By the start of spring training in 1994, Jeter was ready to validate everything the Dick Groches and Hal Newhousers and Gene Bennetts had said about him at Kalamazoo Central. He actually knew how to field a professional ground ball, and he was filling out with the help of the Yankees' strength and conditioning coach, Shawn Powell.

"The ugly duckling," said Bill Livesey, the executive who drafted Jeter, "had become a swan."

The Yankees needed to be right on Jeter, as they proved to be so wrong on Brien Taylor, the pitcher with the $1.55 million left arm. The previous December, while defending his brother's honor in a fistfight gone awry, Taylor had shredded his labrum and dislocated his shoulder, and the doctors were fairly certain he would never again touch 99 miles per hour on the gun.

Jeter had a maturity and a sense of purpose Taylor never had, and Yankee scouts, coaches, and executives loved to say the shortstop had a "good face" or a "sincere face."

Jeter had the right makeup, the loving two-parent home, and the clear commitment to be worth every penny of the Yankees' $800,000 investment. But Derek was only nineteen, and a lot can happen to a teenager to rearrange that sincere face.

He would make '94 the first special season of his professional baseball career. Jeter started the year with Tampa in the high Class A Florida State League, and before he shot through the minor league system like a comet in the night, a good friend helped show him how to perform off the field as well.

Out of upstate New York, the son of a former University of Maryland pitching coach, R. D. Long was a gregarious personality, a self-styled Charles Barkley inside Jeter's tight circle of less conspicuous friends. Long was an athletic six-foot-one utility man known for his speed, and he was hard to keep up with from one end of Tampa's anything-goes nightlife to the other.

Long went by the nickname "Hollywood." He visited Jeter's Kalamazoo home after the '93 season and was taken aback by the way Derek's bedroom was decorated. "It was wall-to-wall Mariah Carey posters," Long said. "Like a little kid."

R.D. assigned himself as the one to show the younger Jeter how to navigate the club scene. Up front, Long impressed upon Jeter the need to identify high-maintenance women.

"If that woman looks like a million dollars and puts it right in your face, that one you get away from," R.D. told him. "That one in the corner who is quiet? That's the one you go after."

After practicing all day in the hot sun, after torturing their bodies some more in Powell's weight room, Yankee prospects spent their nights indulging in the pleasures of the flesh. They were young and single, and the fact that they were recognized as potential millionaires did not hurt their batting averages in the clubs.

One prospect not named Jeter bragged about bedding nineteen different women over nineteen consecutive nights, a DiMaggio-like streak that few doubted. "We went out every night, going hard," Long said. "And 8:00 a.m. would come, my eyes can't even open, I'm telling myself there's no way in hell I'm going today, and I've got Derek Jeter knocking on my door saying, 'Let's go.'

"Athletes, we are hunters by nature. We can't help it. We are conquerors by nature. . . . And Derek and I hunted every night. But I saw him do his workouts on two hours' sleep, and it was the most incredible thing I ever saw. Derek was a maniac in those workouts. He was a monster, and that's why he was great. He was obsessive-compulsive regarding baseball preparation."

No matter how much boys-will-be-boys fun the minor leaguers had in Tampa, Jeter never let any of it negatively impact his work or his goals. But yes, the young Yankees were neck deep in fun, enjoying their red-blooded American fantasy.

"One thing me and Jeter used to do was have him play the shy brother," Long said. "I had to go in like a lion and push [a woman] back to Derek. We had good times, but Derek was always very respectful of every woman he'd meet."

His looks ensured he would meet a lot of them. While in Tampa, Jeter once pointed at a model pictured in a magazine and said he wanted to date her. One Yankees employee happened to know the model, placed the wingman's phone call, and weeks later Derek Jeter was dating her.

Jeter did not resemble that kid weeping in his hotel room anymore, wishing he had accepted the full ride to Michigan. He was tearing it up in the Florida State League, hitting .329 before leaving Long and other friends in his infield dust. Jeter was promoted to Class AA Albany-Colonie, where he batted an astounding .377 before playing his final thirty-five games in Class AAA Columbus, where he batted .349.

Jeter left a lasting mark on his old Greensboro and Tampa teammates when he flew back into town to support them in the Florida State League playoffs, but there was no turning back now.

He would finish the season with 50 steals, 68 RBI, 5 homers, and a .344 batting average, and he was named everyone's minor league player of the year. He would pull off the rare jump from Class A to Class AAA in a single summer, in part because of his defensive work with Butterfield. In 616 combined chances at the three levels in '94, Jeter committed 25 errors, or 31 fewer than he committed in 506 chances at Greensboro.

The word was out, and the Hall of Fame likes of Reggie Jackson were moved to watch Jeter in person. "But every time I went to see him," Jackson said, "he was already gone to the next level. I couldn't catch up to him."

Big league teams kept calling Yankees general manager Gene "Stick" Michael to see if Jeter was available. "Stick had to say no so many times it was ridiculous," said his assistant, Brian Cashman. "He was frustrated as hell. It was like, 'NO, I'M NOT TRADING DEREK JETER.'"

Jeter appeared ninety feet away from the majors, maybe less, when he arrived back in Greensboro with Long in December of '94, with baseball locked in the death grip of a strike that had killed off the World Series. The former Hornets were returning to attend Earl Clary's annual Christmas bash, and Clary picked them up at the airport.

"Hey, Jeet," Big Earl said, "you seen *SportsCenter* yet?"

"What do you mean?" Jeter responded.

"Well, the Yankees signed Tony Fernandez."

"Oh, yeah, Stick called me today and told me. That's OK. If I don't play for the Yankees soon, I'll call Steve Fisher. I'll go play college basketball and I'll quit baseball."

Clary laughed over the thought of Jeter replacing Jalen Rose in Fisher's Michigan backcourt and following up the Wolverines' Fab Five act.

"Jeet might've been joking," Clary said, "but he sure didn't sound like he was joking."

Baseball's labor war ended and Jeter started the 1995 season dead serious about landing in the Bronx for keeps. R. D. Long? He had stolen 37 bases for Tampa in '94 and was hoping to advance all the way to Class AAA Columbus the way his buddy had the year before.

Even as a thirty-eighth-round draft choice, Long was frustrated by his failed attempt to keep pace with Jeter. He had made tremendous strides in his game, earning a mention in *Baseball America* as a sleeper prospect to watch, but he was best known in Yankeedom as Jeter's good bud.

In 1995, Long was telling teammates that Jeter would become the highest-paid player in baseball, and that he would win more than one championship for George Steinbrenner. Not everyone was so convinced Jeter would end up as a multimillionaire or as a multichampion.

As late as 1995, some veteran baseball observers still were not sure he would even make a successful major league shortstop. "I wrote him up as being a third baseman, not no goddamn shortstop," said Ron Washington, the former big league shortstop who was a coach with the Mets' Class AAA affiliate in Norfolk, Virginia, when he evaluated Jeter.

"He used to go to his knees and catch balls. . . . But at the plate, Derek still had that winning aura about him."

That aura served Jeter well on the morning of May 28, 1995. With the Yankees' Fernandez down with a pulled rib cage muscle and with Kevin Elster hitting .118, Jeter got his first chance to make a fool out of Washington and a prophet out of Long.

His Columbus manager, Bill Evers, his first manager in Greensboro, called Jeter in his hotel room around 6:00 a.m.

"Put some water on your face and I'll be in your room in a minute," Evers said.

A terrible thought consumed Jeter's sleep-deprived brain. After reading all the trade rumors, after hearing the year before that he might get sent to the Marlins for Bryan Harvey, Jeter thought he had finally been dealt.

"I thought I was done," he said.

Evers knocked on his player's door, and Derek answered.

"Congratulations," the manager said. "You're going to the big leagues."

Jeter was stunned. He thought it might be a cruel practical joke, but Evers assured him Yankees manager Buck Showalter needed him to report to Seattle immediately.

Derek called home. "I'm out of here," he shouted to his father, Charles, the old middle infielder out of Fisk University who had been overlooked by the scouts.

"I'm going to the big leagues."

Derek packed his .354 Columbus batting average and headed for the Kingdome; Charles rose at 3:00 a.m. in Kalamazoo the next morning and headed west himself, while Dot stayed back to watch Sharlee's softball game.

Jeter found jersey number 2 waiting for him at his locker and was hit by the historical significance — the single-digit numbers were reserved for the Ruths and Gehrigs, the Mantles and DiMaggios.

Showalter threw him into the starting lineup, threw the twenty-year-old into the same infield as Don Mattingly and Wade Boggs. On May 29, 1995, Charles Jeter was among the 18,948 Kingdome fans watching as Derek went 0 for 5 and struck out in the eleventh inning with two outs and his friend Gerald Williams, representing the go-ahead run, on third. After the 8–7 loss, Derek and Charles could not find a restaurant that was still open and settled for McDonald's. Father and son were living the dream over Big Macs and fries.

The following night, with Seattle's Tim Belcher on the mound, Jeter struck out in his first at-bat before digging in for his second. This time Belcher threw a splitter that Jeter ripped through the left side of the infield.

Derek rounded first and felt an overwhelming sense of relief. An 0-for-6 start that felt like a biblical drought was finally over. When Jeter returned to the bag, Seattle first baseman Tino Martinez sized up the Yankee rookie and figured he looked about twelve years old.

Martinez was kind enough to add a gentle touch to the Little Leaguer's big league moment.

"Congratulations," he told Jeter.

"That's the first of many to come."

4

Rookie of the Year

JOE TORRE WAS sitting in what was supposed to be Buck Show-alter's chair, engaged in the most critical meeting of his new Yankee life. Torre had been fired by the Mets, Braves, and Cardinals, and his fourth time around was already being interrupted by a crisis of Defcon 1 angst.

George Steinbrenner worried that Derek Jeter was not ready to be a full-time Yankee at short.

The banned Boss had been reinstated by Commissioner Bud Selig in 1993, and he had long reinforced his own ideas on law and order. In the wake of his team's epic five-game playoff loss to Seattle in October of '95, the old shipbuilder had turned his ocean liner upside down, nudging the captain, Don Mattingly, into retirement, forcing out Showalter and his coaches, and replacing general manager Gene Michael with Bob Watson.

Steinbrenner fired his PR man, Rob Butcher, for having the nerve to go home for the Christmas holiday. Steinbrenner sacked Bill Livesey, the man who had drafted Jeter, and other minor league and development officials for allegedly failing to identify and develop enough winning prospects.

The Boss was no longer a diminished threat, sneaking around the edges of the commissioner's ban. The liberated Steinbrenner had been a tsunami of negative energy since Game 5 in the Kingdome, a game he spent trashing Showalter and praising his former player, manager, and GM, Seattle's Lou Piniella, in the visiting owner's suite.

It did not matter that the Yankees had not reached the postseason since 1981, or that they had rallied late in the year to earn the first American League wild card awarded under a newfangled playoff format. It did not matter that this Yankees-Mariners series was helping to win back baseball fans who had sworn off the sport after the players' strike wiped out the '94 World Series.

Once an assistant football coach at Northwestern and Purdue, Steinbrenner preferred an up-the-gut, cloud-of-dust managing style best suited to a Big Ten Saturday in the fall. He was never comfortable with Showalter's cerebral and detailed approach. At his core, Steinbrenner loved the passion and fire of the Billy Martins and Piniellas, no matter how often he fired them.

So during Game 5 in the Kingdome, Showalter was the easiest tackling dummy to hit.

"It was a combination of George second-guessing everything Buck was doing and elevating everything Lou was doing," said David Sussman, the Yankees' general counsel and COO who was seated next to Steinbrenner. "George's consistent theme was 'Our guy can't hold a candle to Lou. Lou is a much more experienced manager than our guy. This kid Buck doesn't know what he's doing.' It was very painful to listen to."

Steinbrenner actually showed a little humanity following the brutal eleven-inning loss, planting himself in a folding chair opposite a devastated Mattingly and whispering to the same first baseman who believed his owner had used the tabloids to run him out of town.

When reporters made their way toward Mattingly's locker, Steinbrenner got up, grabbed his captain around the neck with both hands, and squeezed. Mattingly was on the verge of tears — his one and only postseason appearance went down as a classic he could not win.

"It felt like a war out there," Mattingly said.

Showalter had been sobbing in his office, knowing he had likely managed his last game as a Yankee, when the man who wanted to fire him was consoling players in the clubhouse.

"We lost this series," Steinbrenner told the team, "but you guys played hard. We're ready to go. We're ready to start winning."

Some Yankee veterans who knew the Boss to be a terrible sport were shocked at what they were hearing. "For Mr. Steinbrenner to say that, as much as he hated to lose," Pat Kelly said, "that meant a lot to us."

The flight home felt like it was fifteen hours long, with the dead-silent coaches and front-office officials projecting a sense of doom and gloom in the front of the plane. David Cone, who valiantly threw 147 pitches in the Game 5 defeat, was feeling an intense pain in his right arm at thirty thousand feet. He could not even lift that arm, and he was thinking he would not have been able to make another postseason start had the Yankees advanced.

But in the back of the plane, some Yankees were playing cards, listening to music, and exchanging banter as if they had just finished losing some garden-variety series to the Mariners in the middle of May.

"It kind of surprised me," Sussman said. "I felt like it was inappropriate to be doing that."

Dramatic changes were on deck, highlighted by the stormy departure of Showalter, who refused to sacrifice the coaches Steinbrenner wanted him to dump. A Steinbrenner aide, Arthur Richman, gave the Boss a list of possible replacements that included Sparky Anderson, Tony La Russa, Davey Johnson, and Joe Torre.

Even before the Yankees were eliminated by Seattle, Showalter's coaches knew this list and this day were coming. Only minutes after the Yankees clinched the wild card at the end of their strike-shortened season in Toronto, Steinbrenner barreled into the coaches' office and declared, "If you don't go to the World Series, you're all fuckin' gone."

"Yeah, like we didn't already know that," a fading voice responded from the back of the room.

So Steinbrenner had his list of four, and it would be quickly whittled to one. Anderson chose retirement, La Russa chose the Cardinals, and Johnson chose the Orioles.

That left the Boss to choose Torre, an agreeable fifty-five-year-old Brooklynite who arrived in the Bronx with a career record of 894-1,003 and this unwanted distinction: he had played and managed in more games without reaching the World Series than any big leaguer dead or alive. A former catcher, first baseman, and third baseman, Torre had been a nine-time All-Star and, in 1971, the National League's MVP with the Cardinals.

But he had never reached the postseason as a player and had never won a single playoff game as a manager. It was such a tough sell to the public — Showalter had won 54 percent of his games; Torre, 47 percent — that Steinbrenner did not attend the November 2, 1995, news conference to introduce his man.

"Bob [Watson] and I are going to decide the baseball side of the situation," Torre said that day. "Until I see otherwise, I have no reason to think otherwise."

Steinbrenner thought otherwise the next morning, when he rose to a *New York Daily News* back page that read "CLUELESS JOE." The Boss called the aide who had recommended Torre, Arthur Richman, and screamed louder than that headline.

"What the hell have you gotten me into?" the Boss barked. Within days, Jack Curry of the *New York Times* reported, Steinbrenner showed up at Showalter's Pensacola, Florida, door and offered his not-so-dearly-departed manager a chance to replace Torre and bring back his entire coaching staff.

"I had two different contracts offered to me," Showalter would say, "one before they hired Torre and one after they hired Torre. They were going to make [Torre] president of the club."

Only Showalter would not be Steinbrenner's new-age Billy Martin. He had a handshake agreement with Jerry Colangelo to manage a concept known as the Arizona Diamondbacks, and he did not think an immediate return to the Bronx would be fair to Torre. So Showalter settled in the desert and announced to one reporter that his 1994 Yankees would have won the World Series if not for the strike.

Showalter had no such excuse for 1995. The experience of watching the Game 5 loss to the Mariners on videotape? "It's like watching *Brian's Song* with the lights off," Showalter said.

But now the burdens of managing George Steinbrenner's Yankees belonged to Torre, and with the start of the '96 season closing hard, the Boss and one of his most trusted advisers, Clyde King, were in Torre's office asking if Derek Jeter should be benched.

Actually, Steinbrenner was doing the asking, and King was doing the recommending. This was after the veteran Tony Fernandez had fractured his right elbow diving for a spring training ball in a game at the Yankees' shiny new facility in Tampa, Legends Field. A four-time All-Star at short, Fernandez was set to start at second base to make room for Jeter, and he was not happy about it. In fact, he had requested a trade.

That request had become moot. On the very day Fernandez got hurt, Jeter made two errors, including one on a throw to Fernandez two pitches before the second baseman got hurt. Jeter was struggling; he called his own spring training performance "terrible."

Sight unseen, acting on the organization's desire, Torre had reluctantly anointed Jeter his starter at short over the winter, at least until the rookie amended the statement to say the manager was merely giving him an opportunity to earn the starting job. "He said it better than I did," Torre conceded.

In '95, Jeter had hit .234 in thirteen starts for Showalter after Fernandez went down with the rib cage injury, and before Fernandez's recovery broke Jeter's heart — Derek was on the verge of playing his first hometown series in Detroit when he was sent back to Columbus.

Jeter was recalled in September, and after going nearly a month without facing live major league pitching, he became an emergency starter for a huge game in Milwaukee (Bernie Williams had missed his flight back from Puerto Rico after visiting with his wife and newborn child, angering Showalter and creating a hole in the lineup).

In the second inning, Jeter ripped Scott Karl's first pitch for an RBI double, impressing one veteran observer who was not around for the shortstop's first call-up in May.

"Buck took out Derek after Bernie showed up," said David Cone, who was traded from Toronto to the Yanks in July, "and I was thinking, 'Leave him in the game. That's OK, Bernie, you take the day off.' . . . When I saw Jeter run and watched how the ball jumped off his bat, I was like, 'Wow, this kid's got some talent. This kid's got it.' You could tell he wasn't intimidated and he wanted to play."

Showalter invited Jeter to sit in on the Seattle playoff series, an invitation that came with a warning. The manager told Derek he had better behave himself and take advantage of this chance to watch and learn how postseason baseball is played, or he would be sent home.

Jeter would later confess that Showalter's words practically left him afraid to leave his hotel room.

As it turned out, the manager and Cone appreciated the way the kid carried himself, and the respect he showed for the game. Jeter did not speak unless he was spoken to. He studied every move Mattingly made.

Jeter would have preferred to trade roles with Mariano Rivera, who was on the active roster and who could have potentially advanced the Yankees to the American League Championship Series had Showalter or anyone else fully grasped his ability.

But Jeter did learn something valuable in observing this franchise-altering defeat. "It let Derek see that beyond the money and the contracts there was still a passion for the pureness of winning," Showalter said. "He saw that it was OK for Don Mattingly to cry. He saw that losing that series made us all sick to our stomachs, and that pain helped Derek's development. It taught him to do everything he possibly could to avoid that feeling."

Jeter carried those lessons into spring training, 1996, with Showalter long gone. Only now Joe Torre's Yankees had a struggling novice at short, a utility man in Mariano Duncan at second, and the Greensboro Hornets' former Glove of Stone, Andy Fox, backing up both.

Jeter himself had been asking at least one team official, "Am I going to make the team? . . . Am I going to make the team?" So Steinbrenner and King joined Torre, his coaches, Watson, Watson's assistant GM, Brian Cashman, the GM turned scout, Gene "Stick" Michael, and other team officials in the manager's office to talk about a potential deal. The Boss gave the floor to King, a former Brooklyn Dodgers pitcher whose opinion had long carried a lot of weight — too much weight, many Yankee officials felt — with Steinbrenner.

King had served the Boss as a scout, pitching coach, manager, and general manager and as GM had been ordered by Steinbrenner to fire Yogi Berra sixteen games deep into the 1985 season, a decision that inspired Berra's vow to never again step foot in Yankee Stadium. Eleven years later, King had been watching Jeter in camp, and he did not like what he saw. "I think you guys have got a problem," King told the group.

He was not alone in this assessment. Tim Raines, a Steinbrenner acquisition, had seen a lot of shortstops in his sixteen years in the bigs, and he did not think Jeter was ready, either.

Raines was not in the room; King was, and he spoke his mind. He did not think the Yankees should open the '96 season with Jeter at short. The best available alternative on the board amounted to a trade with Seattle, of all teams. The Mariners were willing to deal Felix Fermin, a journeyman shortstop who had hit all of .195 in '95, for either Rivera or reliever Bob Wickman.

King was emboldened by the Boss's implicit backing, putting the Yankee coaches and officials on the defensive. "It was an intense meeting," Cashman said, and the intensity was written in the creases of the sun-damaged faces in the room.

Steinbrenner's outsize presence left everyone on edge, especially the new coaches on staff, and the waiting news media members lined up in the hallway did nothing to lighten the load. "It was almost like waiting for the puff of smoke when the papal decision has been made," Cashman said.

Some in the meeting reported that King pushed for Jeter to be demoted to Columbus. "I didn't say that," King would contend. "And anybody who says otherwise, that's an outright lie."

King swore he thought Jeter was ready physically, but that he just wanted to see the kid sit a couple or three games to get his legs underneath him. "I thought we were rushing him just a bit," King said, "but I never, ever said we should send him to Columbus."

Either way, King made it clear he wanted Jeter benched, and he had a captive audience in Steinbrenner. Torre had already discovered that no, Yankee baseball decisions were not the exclusive property of the manager and GM.

Torre and his coaches, especially Willie Randolph, the former Yankee captain and second baseman, spoke up for Jeter. When it was Cashman's turn to talk, the assistant GM was not afraid to tell it straight. Stick Michael had taught him to convey his feelings with conviction and to fight for what he thought was right.

In a meeting the previous fall, after the Yankees were eliminated, officials seated at a conference table were asked to identify their personal choice for the manager's job. "I'd go back and get Buck if we can," Cashman said. "I know Buck Showalter. I don't know Joe Torre, so I can't say yes, go get Joe Torre, and I can't say no, don't get Joe Torre."

This time around, Cashman voted for Jeter and against trading one of the pitchers for Fermin. He knew Michael had established a plan over the winter revolving around this article of faith: no matter what happened in the spring, Jeter would be the Yankees' shortstop for at least half a season.

Michael had even told Steinbrenner to avoid watching Jeter until the All-Star break, to stay away from games until the kid had a chance to make his mistakes and overcome them. So when he was called late into the summit in Torre's office, and then briefed on what had been discussed, Michael turned to King.

"You forget that I played the position," Stick told him, "and this kid is better than I ever was."

Michael then turned to Steinbrenner.

"We promised we wouldn't do this," he said. "Why are we even here? We were going to give Jeter a full shot, and we weren't going to utter anything until the middle of June."

"I know, I know," Steinbrenner responded. "I was supposed to stay home in Tampa and not say anything until July."

Everyone in the meeting laughed; for once in his life, the Boss had actually eased the tension in a room. Randolph said that Jeter would be fine, that the rookie had good hands and a better work ethic. Others chimed in with supporting thoughts.

"We went from 'We couldn't win with Jeter' to 'We couldn't win without him,'" Michael said.

So Clyde King was not going to win this meeting, and Derek Jeter was not going to lose his job. Watson called Seattle to say thanks, but no thanks.

The 1996 Yankees would try to win the franchise's first World Series title since 1978 by playing a kid at short.

"We'll be patient with him," Steinbrenner pledged. "Every year you look for Derek Jeter to stumble and he just doesn't. He dominated rookie ball so we moved him to [Class] A and he dominated there. We force-fed him to Double A and he dominated there. At Columbus, it was the same thing.

"I'm telling you, he could be one of those special ones."

The Yankees were snowed out on April Fools' Day in Cleveland, and so Derek Jeter, their first rookie to start an Opening Day at short since

Tom Tresh in 1962, had an extra twenty-four hours of anxious waiting to negotiate.

Jeter was nervous even before he saw the highlights of the Mets' own rookie, a Cuban defector named Rey Ordonez, putting on a defensive clinic in a 7–6 victory over the Cardinals, including an absurd throw to the plate from his knees that left the great Ozzie Smith offering the ultimate compliment.

"I'd have to say this guy is the second coming of me," the forty-one-year-old Wizard said.

So with the city wondering if the new kids on the block would build a Phil Rizzuto–Pee Wee Reese type of rivalry, Jeter had a tough New York, New York act to follow when he showed up at Jacobs Field. The Yankees were only hoping he would be another Bucky Dent and hit close to .250, make the plays he needed to make, and occasionally deliver a timely single up the middle.

Jeter had greater expectations for himself than that.

His mother, Dot, was in the crowd of 42,289 for this delayed opener; his father and sister had returned to Kalamazoo, Charles to work and Sharlee to play softball. Yankees owner George Steinbrenner was off in California filming an episode of *Seinfeld*, but he had left behind another laugh-a-minute production of the Bronx Zoo.

Kenny Rogers, his $20 million free agent acquisition, was told he would not even be in the rotation to open the season a day before Melido Perez lost his velocity and his temper and landed Rogers right back in the starting five, for the time being, anyway.

David Cone, the $19.5 million Opening Day ace, had nearly slipped through Steinbrenner's hands and signed with the Orioles, which would have been a disastrous twist of fate after the Yanks declined to offer salary arbitration to Jack McDowell.

Mattingly, the retired icon, had been replaced by Seattle's Tino Martinez. Mike Stanley, the popular catcher who was good for 18 homers and 83 RBI in '95, had been replaced by Joe Girardi, who was good for 8 homers and 55 RBI. And Buck Showalter, the manager who ended the playoff drought and whose fist-pumping introduction before the Seattle series made Yankee Stadium shake, had been replaced by Joe Torre, a three-time loser, a nice guy expected to finish last.

The pressure on Torre and his new Yankees was immense when

they faced the Indians, the defending American League champs. The turmoil and turnover colored this opener in ominous shades, a truth hardened by the presence of the rookie at short.

Jeter was wearing number 2, and for the second straight year the number almost came by accident. In '95, Jeter wanted his father's number at Fisk, 13, but it was already taken by Jim Leyritz.

The assignment of a single-digit jersey was no small matter in Yankeedom. Billy Martin was number 1, Babe Ruth number 3, Lou Gehrig number 4, Joe DiMaggio number 5, Mickey Mantle number 7, Yogi Berra and Bill Dickey number 8, and Roger Maris number 9. All those numbers had been retired.

"When you project a single digit at Yankee Stadium," Showalter said, "you'd better be right."

Showalter and Michael agreed Jeter was worth the shot. Nick Priore, the longtime equipment manager, was not so sure. When Priore assigned number 51 to the promising center fielder, Bernie Williams, Showalter asked him, "Don't you think Bernie will be a better player than that?"

"If it's fuckin' good enough for Willie McGee," Priore shot back, "it will be fuckin' good enough for Bernie Williams."

But Priore gave in on Jeter. So did George Steinbrenner, who told Showalter, "You'd better be right about this," words that did not shake the manager's faith.

"I knew by the time Derek proved he wasn't worthy," Showalter said, "I'd be long gone anyway."

In '95, Jeter batted .250 without a home run or stolen base in fifteen big league games, and he had homered only twice in 123 games in Columbus the same year. Maybe Priore did not think Jeter was single-digit material. With Showalter gone and Michael in a reduced role, maybe Priore thought he should act on his gut instinct.

Either way, the equipment manager decided to change Jeter's number to 19. His assistant, Rob Cucuzza, wrote down the number on a card and posted it above Jeter's locker.

"Robin Yount wore 19," Priore said, "and he started his career as a shortstop." If 19 was good enough for Robin Yount, the equipment manager reasoned, it would be good enough for Derek Jeter.

Only Derek saw it differently. "He came to me and said, 'You've got to get me number 2 back, you've got to get me number 2 back,'" Cucuzza said. "I think Derek was a little scared to go to Nick. I was caught by surprise that he was so locked in on number 2."

Was Jeter suddenly locked in because he realized the historical significance of number 2?

"Oh, I know Derek had that in mind," Cucuzza said.

Jeter was given number 2 and Torre number 6, and the odds were not good that both of these legacy gambles would pay off. The manager and shortstop were in this together, joined at the hip as they faced their greatest baseball challenge.

Jeter was batting ninth in Torre's order, and he represented the Yankees' sixth different Opening Day shortstop in six years. Jeter was facing a forty-year-old Cleveland pitcher, Dennis Martinez, who had been signed by the Baltimore Orioles before Derek was born. The rookie felt the butterflies in his stomach, butterflies with condor wings.

He struck out looking in his first at-bat when Martinez used a sidearm delivery that caught Jeter by surprise. Up again in the fifth inning, Jeter got ahead 2-0 in the count and waited to see if the ageless Cleveland starter would make a mistake. Sure enough, Martinez threw a high fastball, and Jeter turned on it as few thought he could.

He hit it 395 feet and into the left-field stands, giving the Yankees a 2-0 lead. "Wow!" Torre said. "I didn't see that all spring."

Joe Girardi had the same reaction, as did most of the Yanks. Clyde King, watching on TV, suddenly had an appraisal that sounded nothing like the one he had issued in Torre's Tampa office.

"When he hit that home run," King said, "I went, 'Wow, this could be some kind of player.'"

Of course, King and others were always more worried about Jeter's glove than his bat, and the rookie quieted those concerns, too. In the seventh inning, after he had already made a couple of fine plays in the field, including one in the hole in the second, Jeter used that glove of his to silence a gathering Indians threat.

Cone had kept Cleveland without a hit until Julio Franco's sixth-inning single, and he was still protecting a shutout in the seventh when Sandy Alomar Jr. laced a two-out double into the right-field corner.

With Cone tiring, Omar Vizquel lifted a bloop into short center that had the unmistakable look of a run-scoring single.

"It's 2–1," Cone thought to himself, "and I'm out of the game."

Only Jeter turned his shoulders and ran a mad dash against the ball. If he lost this race, Jacobs Field would have erupted, Cone would have been done, and the 1995 World Series runners-up would have seized enough momentum to finish first on Opening Day.

But as much as Rey Ordonez reminded Ozzie Smith of Ozzie Smith at Shea, Jeter would remind Omar Vizquel of Omar Vizquel in Cleveland. On the dead run, his back to the plate, Jeter beat the batted ball to its preferred landing spot.

His lunging catch made those 56 errors in Greensboro seem like two lifetimes in the past. "This kid's got some skills," Cone told himself.

"I had it all the way," Jeter said.

He had a highlight play to match Ordonez's, but the Yankees knew this catch meant so much more. The moment that ball landed in the webbing of Jeter's glove, the Yankees knew they would win the game.

Bernie Williams belted a three-run homer in the eighth, and Torre would celebrate a 7–1 victory by kicking up his feet on a desk and lighting a cigar in Red Auerbach form.

"He was everything you could ask for today," Torre said of Jeter.

Nobody cared about the kid's two strikeouts, not when Jeter gave the Yankees the two things he was not supposed to give them: power and world-class defense. On the home-run front, Jeter was telling those who asked that they should not expect too many more.

A clubhouse full of giddy Yanks did not want to hear it. When it counted, Jeter showed up as an entirely different player from the one who nearly lost his job in the preseason, and nobody on the visiting side rushed to throw cold water on that.

But one Yankee did not understand all the fuss. Matt Luke, Jeter's old friend and Greensboro teammate, had seen this movie dozens of times before. Luke replaced an injured Tim Raines on the Opening Day roster, and what he saw from the dugout was the same thing he had seen on so many minor league nights in so many backwater towns.

"Derek just walked into that Yankee locker room in '96 with the same laid-back swagger he always had," Luke said. "When you're a teammate of Derek Jeter's, he emboldens you, and that's a powerful thing. He gives you that confidence and ability to say, 'Hey, I can do this, too. I can get it done.'"

On the night Jeter got it done as the Yankees' full-time shortstop, he phoned another Greensboro teammate, Jeff Antolick, who had roomed with him in Tampa. Jeter was not calling to boast about his break-through moment in Cleveland.

He was calling to make sure Antolick did not have any problems closing the apartment they had rented from October through March. Jeter said he was happy the Yanks had won and did not mention a thing about himself, Antolick said, "and I had to finally say, 'Hey, you hit one out today.' He just said, 'Yeah, I got a good pitch to hit.' That's just how Jeet is."

Jeter had three hits and a walk and scored three runs in the Yankees' second game in Cleveland, a 5–1 victory for the pitcher who had "big-leagued" him in Greensboro in '92, Andy Pettitte. In that same game, Luke made his major league debut as a pinch runner for Ruben Sierra.

Derek was thrilled his friend from that special Sally League team of 1993 got in the game and scored on a headfirst slide past Alomar, if a bit disappointed that Torre pinch-hit for Luke in the seventh, denying him his first major league at-bat. The following day, when he reported to Jacobs Field, Luke forgot all about his near miss.

He was in the starting lineup in place of the hamstrung Sierra. He was finally going to get his cuts as a Yankee.

But in the cruelest twist of fate, the heavy rains and wind wiped out the game and — as it turned out — Matt Luke's career ambition. The Yanks re-signed Dion James and sent Luke back to the minors. Luke was waiting on deck to hit in the second game, and he was waiting for the skies to clear so he could serve as the designated hitter in the third game. So close, so far.

Luke never got an at-bat as a Yankee.

His friend at shortstop would get more than he ever imagined.

Surprise, surprise; Joe Torre had inherited a heck of a team. Don Mattingly's replacement, Tino Martinez, would overcome a hell-on-earth start to win over the jeering fans with the kind of power season (25 homers, 117 RBI) Mattingly had not even approached since 1989.

Martinez was able to weather the Bronx storm because a teammate kept talking him through it over their daily lunches. "Derek Jeter, a twenty-one-year-old kid," Tino said. "He kept telling me to relax, have fun, and play my game and the people will love me.

"Derek would be laughing at me, and it wasn't funny. But he'd say, 'Hey, we're playing baseball for the New York Yankees. Just enjoy it.' And I thought, 'You know what, this guy's right.' And I started relaxing and hitting the ball."

Joe Girardi overcame his own share of boos and the resentment over Mike Stanley's departure to hit .294 and establish himself as a coach behind the plate. Against the odds, Mariano Duncan, the journeyman who had batted .300 or better all of once in his ten-year career, hit .340 as the last-ditch starter at second base.

Bernie Williams arrived as a dynamic offensive force, batting .305 with 29 homers and 102 RBI and reminding everyone of the good work Stick Michael and Buck Showalter had done during George Steinbrenner's suspension, and after the Boss's return.

The Big Ten football coach in Steinbrenner had no use for those he deemed meek. Williams had the demeanor of a classical pianist, and he had allowed a taunting teammate named Mel Hall to reduce him to a quivering wreck — Hall had nicknamed Bernie "Zero" in Williams's rookie year of 1991 and reveled in his freedom to berate the young center fielder with impunity.

Williams never fought back, as he had been taught by his parents to maintain his dignity at all times. Instead of seeing Bernie as the stronger man for turning the other cheek, the Boss saw Williams as timid and soft. If Steinbrenner could have summoned the spirit of one of his heroes, George S. Patton, he would have slapped Williams's face with his batting gloves.

As it was, the old football coach wanted this blue-chip recruit from Puerto Rico stripped of his scholarship. Steinbrenner was not happy with the pace of Williams's development as a hitter. The Yankees had so much time and energy invested in the center fielder — they had stashed him in a Connecticut baseball camp before signing him for $16,000 on his seventeenth birthday — and yet Steinbrenner wanted to cut his losses.

He ordered Michael to call every single team until he found an executive who would take Williams off the Yanks' hands. Michael called his fellow general managers, left intentionally vague messages, exchanged fruitless banter about the weather and the cost of gas, and reported back to Steinbrenner that nobody, but nobody, wanted Williams.

And now Bernie was driving the ball all over the Bronx along with Martinez and Paul O'Neill, whom Michael acquired in a one-sided deal with Cincinnati in November of 1992, when Lou Piniella was sick of beating on O'Neill and saw something in Roberto Kelly that wasn't there.

In Mariano Rivera and John Wetteland, the Yankees had a devastating one-two punch in the bullpen and all the evidence needed to prove Michael and Bob Watson had been right to avoid trading Rivera for Felix Fermin, the would-be Jeter replacement who was released by Seattle before being signed and dumped by the Yanks for kicks.

Rivera's velocity had suddenly jumped 5 to 7 miles per hour and into the mid-90s in 1995, and the pitcher had transformed himself from a mediocre starter with no movement and no cutter into an indestructible setup man for Wetteland.

Andy Pettitte would go 21-8 in his second season in the bigs and would also make a sage out of Michael. When he was in trade talks with Seattle for Tino Martinez and reliever Jeff Nelson, Michael was told he needed to include one of the Yankees' two young lefties — Pettitte or Sterling Hitchcock — to make the deal work.

Michael liked Hitchcock and Pettitte. He elected to keep Pettitte.

Michael kept and acquired the right guys, Yankees who were tough enough to weather almost anything. David Cone, the heart of the rotation, was struck down in May by an aneurysm in his right shoulder that Watson would call potentially "life-threatening" before scrambling to retract those words.

In Columbia-Presbyterian, Cone was frustrated by his condition and by the fact that the hospital did not have cable TV. He had to listen to his Yankees on radio, and he wept when he heard his old Mets teammate, Dwight Gooden, throw a no-hitter against Seattle in his place.

Banned from baseball the previous year for his drug use, Gooden won the game for his father, who was facing heart surgery the following day. "I got a very good feeling about our season that night," Cone said. "I remember thinking, 'Wow, Doc's back. We're going to be OK.' I felt a responsibility to the team to be the number-one guy, and when

Doc covered for me, that made me feel we might have something special here."

The players were as resilient as their manager. In June, Torre was grinding hard for a come-from-behind victory in the first game of a critical double-header in Cleveland when Jeter stepped to the plate for the sixth time, the Yankees having turned a 6–1 deficit in the eighth into a 6–6 game in the tenth.

Jeter had already stunned the veterans around him with his unyielding belief in himself, and with his ability to focus under any circumstances. O'Neill was amazed that Jeter could be talking to front-row fans from the on-deck circle fifteen seconds before he would go up to hit, and that he could flip a switch once he arrived at the plate.

"Derek had so much confidence in himself," O'Neill said. "Tino and I thought that when you had a horrible day and you're 0 for 4, do you really want to get up in the bottom of the ninth and go 0 for 5, or are you just like, 'Hey, let's get 'em tomorrow'? Jeet was always sure he'd get up there to go 1 for 5."

This time Jeet only wanted to go 1 for 6. Sure enough, after he struck out with the bases loaded in the ninth, Jeter came up with the bases loaded in the tenth. He ripped a Jim Poole pitch to center for a two-run single.

Torre was feeling the rush of a dramatic victory over the defending American League champs in the first game when he took a phone call from his wife, Ali. Joe's older brother, Rocco, had dropped dead of a heart attack while watching the Yankees' victory from his home in Queens. Torre had been fearing this very bulletin about another brother, Frank, who had been in poor health and whose heart problems left him dependent on a pacemaker.

The logical choice for Torre was to hand over the second game and his injury-ravaged pitching staff to his bench coach, Don Zimmer, and catch the next flight home. Only Joe did not return to New York. He got three hits from Jeter and three innings from Rivera, managed the Yankees to a 9–3 victory, and completed a double-header sweep over the Indians with Brian Boehringer and Ramiro Mendoza as his starting pitchers.

Nothing stopped Torre's Yankees, not mounting injuries, not life-threatening aneurysms, not even death itself.

They held a twelve-game lead in the American League East near the end of July, and Jeter had added more than 40 points to a season-low batting average of .256. The rookie was thriving under Torre, who managed Derek with the Charles Jeter approach — almost always nurturing and understanding, but tough when tough was required.

Joe Torre was the father Derek Jeter always had.

"Derek was the kid Joe took under his wing," said Jim Leyritz, a second-string catcher with a first-string ego that annoyed Torre. "Joe loved the people who were somewhat perfect, who did the right things and said the right words. Derek was his kind of player."

As a rookie, Jeter needed less direction than most ten-year veterans. But when he needed it, Torre handled him with caution. "When Derek messed up, Joe would get on him, but he was always discreet about it," Andy Fox said. "Joe handled Derek the way he handled a lot of guys, but it was beneficial to Derek because he did it with a tone that said, 'Hey, I'm on your side. I'm with you.'

"Joe handled his stuff on the field. He would stand at shortstop during BP, and it would look like he was talking about the weather or the playing surface, but he was really getting on you about something from the night before. Derek responded to that. He never needed a lot of counseling, just a friendly pat on the ass, and Joe really connected with him."

Their temporary disconnects were kept to a minimum; Jeter made sure of that by constantly referring to his manager as Mr. Torre or Mr. T. But on August 12, while playing the White Sox in Chicago, Jeter hurt Mr. Torre through a rare lapse in judgment. With Cecil Fielder at the plate and Jeter on second in the eighth inning of a 2–2 game, Torre had one thought on his mind as he surveyed the scene:

This is exactly why we traded Ruben Sierra for Fielder, this two-out situation right here.

Of course, major leaguers are not supposed to make the third out at third base, not when dangerous hitters such as Fielder are planted in the box. But Jeter noticed that Chicago's middle infielders were ignoring him, and that third baseman Robin Ventura was playing back.

So on Alex Fernandez's first pitch, Jeter took off and lost his reckless gamble — Chicago's Ron Karkovice threw him out. Derek knew Torre had to rip into him the way the old Fisk University coach, James Smith, had ripped into Charles Jeter when he tried and failed to steal second — without Smith giving him the steal sign — on the first and last baserunning mistake of Charles's college career.

Rather than find a place to hide from his steamed manager, Derek Jeter sat right down next to Torre, temporarily disarming him. The manager rubbed the shortstop's head and, without malice, told him to get lost. But after the White Sox won on Harold Baines's tenth-inning homer off Wetteland, Torre was not cutting Jeter any breaks.

"You don't trade for Cecil Fielder to take the bat out of his hands," he said. "That's a play that stunned me. Coming from him, it really stunned me. He's a kid, and so you give him a certain amount of rope, but it's not a smart play."

Torre was normally reluctant to criticize his players in front of notebooks, microphones, and cameras, especially team-first achievers like Jeter. But on this one Derek had given him no choice.

Jeter got over it, and Torre was eager to move on. The manager knew he had something good going on in his clubhouse. Even after his best friend, Gerald Williams, was traded off to Milwaukee, Jeter was surrounded by Yankees who did not resent his teacher's-pet standing with Torre, or his boy-band popularity among the teenage girls in the stands.

The team's hardened veterans "rallied around Jeter, made him feel at home," said thirty-six-year-old Tim Raines. "It wasn't like back in the day when veteran players messed around with the rookie players and had them doing all kinds of crazy crap."

When healthy, Raines was a comforting presence to Jeter. Raines was twenty when his idol, Joe Morgan, was quick to offer him encouraging words, and now the aging Yankee wanted to give back to Jeter.

Derek did not have to endure what a young Bernie Williams endured in the form of Mel Hall, a bully's bully who tried to break Bernie down. A mid-season acquisition who had played thirty-two games for Showalter the year before, Darryl Strawberry joined the endless procession of big-brother types in Jeter's clubhouse. Strawberry re-signed with the Yanks on Steinbrenner's birthday, the Fourth of July, when the owner decided to buy a present for himself against Watson's wishes.

One more time the Yankees were borrowing from their neighbor's turbulent past, adding another prominent face from a period best defined by the titles the Mets did not win, rather than the one they did. Off his banishment for cocaine use, Strawberry had started working on Jeter's impressionable mind after the shortstop was called up in September of '95.

"He wasn't playing and I wasn't playing," Strawberry said, "and I'd be talking to him in the dugout or in the clubhouse, just telling him, 'Don't worry about it, your day is coming, bro. This town is going to eat you up. They're going to love you, trust me. You don't have star potential; you've got megastar potential.'

"Derek just looked at me wide-eyed like, 'Really?' You could tell he wasn't sure, but he was a great-looking kid who had it just like I had it. I told him, 'I had all this and screwed it up by making bad choices. Don't do what I did.'"

As Strawberry assumed the role of watchdog for Jeter (even if the son of a drug and alcohol abuse counselor did not need one), David Cone enjoyed a more playful relationship with the rookie. Cone and other veterans kept waiting to find something to ride Jeter about — his clothes, his shoes, his something, his anything — but the rookie never gave them an opening, not a single one.

Cone would tease Jeter about all those squealing voices in the Yankee Stadium crowd. "Be nice to those teenyboppers," he told Jeter, "because one of them will be your wife someday."

Derek laughed. Cone would watch Jeter peer into the stands and survey all the silly girls and women jockeying for his attention. "It's not bad to be you, huh?" the pitcher told the shortstop.

Cone would try his damnedest to pry information out of Derek about whom he was dating. "Just throw me some crumbs," Cone pleaded, but the rookie never would.

Jeter could spend hours listening to Strawberry, Gooden, and Cone tell him stories about the wild and crazy Mets of the eighties, a team that often treated a season as a six-month toga party.

Jeter wanted to know every last detail of every last anecdote. So Cone emptied his own considerable bag of salacious tales, starting with the time he was a single man in New Orleans trying to pick up a blond in a bar.

"I was cuddling up to her," Cone said, "and then I realized she had a big Adam's apple out to here. It took me an hour to figure it out . . . and

I started to question my own sexuality. At the end of the night, the joke was on me.

"Jeter loved that story."

Jeter loved this team, this clubhouse, this camaraderie, this boyhood dream come true. Before every game Jeter would walk up to Torre's sixty-five-year-old, Popeye-ish bench coach, Don Zimmer, and either rub his belly or the peach fuzz on his head. Or both.

The kid did not want his good luck to run out. He was the twenty-two-year-old starting shortstop of a New York Yankees team that had a good chance to return to the playoffs and, who knows, possibly win it all for the first time since 1978.

Jeter was not getting distracted by the media blitz, either. He was available and professional when approached by reporters at his locker, but he never threw open any windows on his soul. He spit out so many clichés, some wondered if he had learned them on a bus ride with the Crash Davis character in *Bull Durham*.

"Mattingly taught him that," Cone said. "Donnie told him, 'If you want to stay out of trouble with the media and you don't want them at your locker every day, just bore them to death.' Donnie was kind of joking, but Derek might've taken it literally."

Jeter found himself involved in one dustup he could not avoid. On September 12, with the Yankees' twelve-game divisional lead suddenly down to a frightening two and a half games, they found themselves facing a 95-loss Detroit team before all of 9,009 Tiger Stadium fans, half of them sounding like they came in from Kalamazoo.

Charlie Hayes and Andy Fox hit back-to-back homers off Jose Lima in the ninth inning to make it 8–3 in the Yankees' favor before Jeter came to bat. Lima proceeded to plant a fastball in the rookie's upper back, right below his neck, and Jeter responded by glaring at the pitcher.

Torre and a couple of players shouted at Lima; everyone inside the visiting dugout assumed the pitch was laced with bad intentions. Jeter took his base, and the next batter, Williams, got even in the purest possible way: he hit a grand slam that left him with eight RBI on the night.

Only the long ball that made it 12–3 was not enough. Under baseball's unwritten code of frontier justice, the Yanks would have been expected to avenge and protect Jeter, who had been hit by a pitch for the ninth time, and to send a message to future foes that they could not be intimidated.

Jeff Nelson was willing to settle the score in the bottom of the ninth. Twice he brushed back Detroit batters before Torre's pitching coach, Mel Stottlemyre, trotted out to the mound to remind the reliever he could not intentionally hit a Tiger, not when a suspension could have cost the reeling Yanks dearly in the playoff race.

Nelson backed off. The Yankees secured the victory without further incident, at least until they walked through the clubhouse doors and realized that Mariano Duncan, another of Jeter's many mentors, was in no mood to celebrate. Duncan confronted catcher Joe Girardi and profanely demanded an explanation for why no Detroit batter was hit. Girardi's biggest backer, Zimmer, stepped between them and had his own heated exchange with Duncan.

Asked if he thought about retaliating on his own — i.e., charging the mound and fighting Lima — Jeter said, "What can I do? I'm not a pitcher." If it sounded like the shortstop was upset that a Detroit hitter was not plunked, one teammate confirmed that suspicion.

"Derek felt kind of betrayed because we didn't protect him," Jim Leyritz said.

These were tense times for the Yankees, even if their most maddeningly self-absorbed member, Sierra, had been dealt to Detroit for Fielder, the powerful righty bat the team had lacked. Steinbrenner had already quit on the team, "because that's what George Steinbrenner always did when things got tough," one of his top officials said.

Steinbrenner assumed Peter Angelos, an owner he loathed, would steal the division. He assumed his Yankees would go down among the sport's all-time chokers, just like the 1978 Boston team managed by the Boss's current bench coach, Zimmer, and he was setting up Watson, baseball's first African-American general manager, to take the fall.

Watson had made a deal for a fifth starter, David Weathers, who was awful. He had traded Gerald Williams and Bob Wickman to Milwaukee for reliever Graeme Lloyd and outfielder Pat Listach, both of whom turned up in the Bronx with preexisting injuries.

Steinbrenner would call Watson four or five times a day, and there would be two or three shouting matches in those four or five calls. The GM put in a new door to Torre's Yankee Stadium office from the back hallway, he said, "to keep George out of the clubhouse. I kept him out of the clubhouse 95 percent of the time, because he brings an uneasiness with his presence."

That uneasiness swept over the Yankees like a thick and ominous fog. Doc Gooden was coming undone on the mound, the Yanks could not hit left-handed pitching, and their Cooperstown-bound third baseman, Wade Boggs, was furious that the team had traded for Hayes.

Andy Pettitte, the Yanks' best pitcher, had pain in his elbow, and Ruben Rivera, their most gifted outfield prospect, had been handed an important late-season role despite an alarming immaturity that embarrassed his cousin, Mariano.

Paul O'Neill started a brawl in Seattle after his old friend Lou Piniella had yet another one of his pitchers brush him back, and even then the Yankees were not inspired to play with the purpose and passion that had built their twelve-game lead. They were not even sufficiently roused by the remarkable return of Cone on Labor Day, when he made his first start in four months and threw seven no-hit innings at Oakland; the Yanks lost three of their next five.

But the Detroit series that saw Jeter get hit and his clubhouse nearly get flipped onto its ear by a heated argument over retaliation, or lack thereof, finally righted the Yanks. Torre used his greatest strength — his ability to meet chaos with calm — to turn around his team. He called a team meeting in that series, and in a tone one would use to speak to a small book club in a library, the manager told his players the following:

"We're not going to lose this division. We're going to the playoffs, and we're going to do well there. Just relax, go out and play, and don't try to put everything on your shoulders."

On cue, Jeter went 6 for 13 with 3 RBI and 7 runs scored in the three-game sweep, lifting his batting average to .313 and making for another significant homecoming.

It was in a Detroit hotel room where Jeter met his father and, over a box of pizza, told Charles he wanted to be a role model, wanted to give back, wanted to start a foundation like his idol Dave Winfield had.

Charles was surprised his son was ready to make the commitment. "It was his idea, he wanted to do it, and he was serious about it," Charles said. "I was very, very proud of that moment."

This was the first seed of what would grow into the Turn 2 Foundation, a program with a mission statement of keeping young students away from alcohol and drugs. Jeter was honoring his father's work, but he was not taking his eye off the ball.

He would rip through September with a 17-game hitting streak, the longest for a Yankee rookie since Joe DiMaggio's 18-gamer in 1936. The Yankees would win eight of nine, starting with that sweep of the Tigers and finishing with a stabilizing series victory over Baltimore.

Suddenly Steinbrenner was not berating Watson with the same intensity or frequency. Pettitte had been the rock of the rotation despite the elbow pain. Ruben Rivera had a huge hit against Baltimore, after a huge catch in Detroit, flashing some of the otherworldly talent that encouraged comparisons to a young Mickey Mantle and a hope — however thin — that he would someday grow up.

So on September 25, with the surgically repaired Cone on the Bronx mound for the first game of a double-header, the Yankees clinched their first division title in fifteen years by hammering Milwaukee, 19–2. Jeter contributed a two-run double to the ten-run second inning and joined his emotional teammates in a group hug near second base after Williams gathered the final out.

Torre cried in the dugout as cops surrounded the field and confetti and streamers fell from the sky. The Yankees waited until they won the second game of the double-header before they cut loose the champagne in their clubhouse.

"This could be the start of my greatest experience in baseball," Torre would say. The manager understood who was most responsible for the career-changing possibilities before him.

"Jeter and Mariano Rivera were our biggest X factors who came through," he said.

At that hour the kid shortstop had hit .375 over his previous sixty-four games, doing as much as any Yankee to hold off the Orioles. Jeter said he felt badly he reached the playoffs in his first full season after Mattingly made his first and last trip on the brink of retirement ("It seems kind of unfair, really," Jeter said), but he was not shy about his October objectives.

"We want to win it all," he said. "That's what we want to do, and that's what we play for."

Someone asked Jeter if he was prepared to deal with playoff pressure. "We'll find out Tuesday," he said, referencing the start of the Division Series with the Texas Rangers.

The previous Saturday, in a wild and crucial 12–11 victory over the Red Sox, Jeter had ended the game with his third hit and third RBI — a two-out single to center that scored Boggs in the tenth. "When the games mean more," the rookie said, "it's a lot easier to play."

Veteran Yankee observers realized none of this would have been possible with any of the Opening Day shortstops who had preceded Jeter in the past five years — Tony Fernandez, Mike Gallego, Spike Owen, Randy Velarde, and Alvaro Espinoza. Jeter would finish the year with a batting average of .314, with 10 homers and 78 RBI, showing more power than he showed as a minor leaguer and posting numbers that the Hall of Fame Yankee shortstop, Phil Rizzuto, never approached.

"Could he be the best Yankee shortstop ever? Absolutely," Rizzuto said of Jeter. "I don't think I've ever seen a young kid play with so much confidence. Mickey Mantle had the ability as a rookie, but not the poise. Jeter has both."

Jeter also had an unquenchable desire to compete every day. He played in 157 of the Yankees' 162 games and complained about the 5 in which he did not appear.

"When I rested him a few months ago," Torre said, "Derek told me, 'How am I going to catch Cal Ripken?'"

Catch Cal Ripken? Derek Jeter did not know it at the time, but during his first October as the New York Yankees' starting shortstop, he would not only have a chance to catch Ripken.

He would have a chance to pass him.

5

Champion

DEREK JETER WAS playing defense in his Yankee Stadium clubhouse, where inquiring minds wanted to know if the rookie had just choked. The Yankees had lost Game 1 of the Division Series to the Texas Rangers, and the shortstop was among the more conspicuous reasons why.

He had popped up with the bases loaded and had left six men on base in the 6–2 defeat. David Cone had been outpitched by John Burkett, but nobody questioned the accomplished veteran's stomach for the big-game fight.

Jeter was a different story. No matter how composed he appeared during the darkest hours of the divisional race, when the Yankees threatened to give away a twelve-game lead, this was October.

Nothing in August and September can simulate true October angst.

"All I can do is forget about it," Jeter said at his locker. "You can't sit here and dwell on it. . . . You've got to let it go."

Only Jeter wasn't one to let criticism go easily. "People have always doubted me," he said on the eve of the playoffs. "First, it was I couldn't stay at shortstop. Then I was from a small town. In the minor leagues, people said I couldn't hit, I couldn't field, then I couldn't hit at the major league level. There are probably still some who doubt me."

Jeter swore he approached his first playoff game just as he had approached the 157 regular-season games that preceded it, and reporters had a hard time believing it. Asked if he was concerned his shortstop would struggle to keep his cool in the heat of the postseason, Joe Torre had his answer before he left Yankee Stadium for the night.

On his way to the players' parking lot, done facing tough questions from the press, Jeter poked his head into Torre's office.

"Make sure you get your sleep tonight," he told his manager. "Tomorrow is the most important game of your life."

Torre shook his head and laughed. The kid was going to be all right.

Before Game 2, Torre acknowledged he preferred to lean on his veterans when his seasons were on the brink. "To me, Jeter is different," he would say. "I've been around a lot of young kids and a lot of rookies. He's done a lot of growing up this year. He doesn't see the postseason as something different."

So Jeter honored his manager's faith and delivered three hits in Game 2, including the decisive one in the twelfth inning. The Rangers held a 4–2 lead in the seventh and had the Yankees in a death grip — Torre's team could not possibly go to the Ballpark in Arlington, Texas, down 0-2, not after losing five of six regular-season games there while getting outscored by a 44–15 count.

But a Jeter single helped cut the deficit in half, and ultimately a Cecil Fielder RBI single sent the game into extra innings. After the Rangers failed to score with the bases loaded in the top of the twelfth, Jeter led off with another hit, moved to second on Tim Raines's walk, and then raced for third when Charlie Hayes put down a sacrifice bunt.

Dean Palmer, the Texas third baseman, fielded the ball and fired to first, but his rushed throw bounced in the dirt and skipped past the second baseman who was covering, Mark McLemore.

Jeter headed for home, scored the run that kept the Yankees in the series, and assured reporters once again he did not approach Game 2 any differently than he had Game 1, or Game 98 of the regular season in July.

"If I don't get a hit, you guys say I'm pressing," Jeter said. "And if I do get a hit, you guys say I'm not pressing. I felt the same way tonight as I did yesterday, but yesterday I didn't get any hits and today I did."

Jeter was back in his element, but that did not mean the Yankees were at ease as they traveled to a place a couple of headline writers described as Arlington Cemetery. The Ballpark threatened to be for the Yankees what Chicago Stadium and the United Center were for the Knicks — a place where New York seasons go to die.

Over a ten-year period, the Yankees were 13-42 in Arlington Stadium and the Ballpark. Billy Martin had one of his many bar fights in Arlington. Bobby Meacham once committed an error in Arlington that so enraged George Steinbrenner, the Boss sent him to Class AA because Class AAA did not represent enough of a demotion.

Years later, Torre decided to inject some confidence into his Texas-bound players by elevating the youngest among them. The manager had so much faith in Jeter entering Game 3, he moved him from the number-nine spot in the order to the leadoff position, where the shortstop had batted thirty-nine times during the regular season. A rookie whose tenth-inning error in a loss to the White Sox only seven weeks earlier had inspired the *New York Post* headline "SHORT-SLOP" was now charged to lead the Yanks into their not-so-little house of horrors.

Once again, Jeter responded to the manager he had come to see as a second father. He did make a rookie mistake in the field, failing to cover second base on a fifth-inning steal that led to the Rangers' go-ahead run. But with Texas holding a 2–1 lead in the ninth, Jeter led off with a single to left against Darren Oliver.

Following a single from Raines and a deep fly to right from Bernie Williams, Jeter was home with the tying run. Mariano Duncan drove in what would be the winning run, and the Yankees would play Game 4 with a shot to advance to the American League Championship Series.

Jeter managed a hit and an RBI groundout in that game, beating out a throw to first on what would have been a lethal inning-ending double play. But it was Williams's two home runs — one from each side of the plate — and spectacular performances from Mariano Rivera, John Wetteland, and the entire bullpen that allowed the Yankees to overcome a 4–0 Texas lead and claim their first postseason series victory since 1981.

Williams was mobbed in the visitors' clubhouse, sprayed with champagne and beer as his teammates chanted, "MVP . . . MVP." He had outlasted fellow Puerto Rican slugger Juan Gonzalez, who had five homers in the series but failed in his most critical Game 4 at-bat, allowing David Weathers, of all people, to strike him out with sliders on 3-1 and 3-2 counts, two on and nobody out in the fourth.

Without warning, the placid Bernie had the look of the devil in this series. Williams had come a long, long way from the day he was a clueless teenager in Buck Showalter's office threatening to return to Puerto Rico if the manager kept insisting he bat left-handed. Showalter responded by promising to call Williams's father — he knew Bernie was afraid of his father — and that was that.

"I'm like a volcano," Williams said after eliminating the Rangers. "You can't always see it, but I'm emotional."

The same held true for Jeter, the stoic fueled by the hidden flame within. He went from being a prime bum-of-the-month candidate after Game 1 to a budding Mr. October after Game 4.

Jeter batted .412 in the Division Series and now faced a best-of-seven showdown with the Orioles and their living legend at short. Right after the All-Star break, Jeter was the one who hit the shot heard 'round the American League East, breaking a 2–2 eighth-inning tie with a two-run homer off Mike Mussina that set up a four-game sweep at Camden Yards.

The Yankees left town with a ten-game divisional lead that so unnerved Baltimore's manager, Davey Johnson, he finally emasculated the Iron Man, Cal Ripken Jr., and inserted Manny Alexander at short. Ripken brooded at third base, Alexander went hitless in seventeen of his eighteen at-bats over six games, and the experiment died a quick and painful death.

The old man was moved back to short, and if he was a fading star in the field, he still had a presence at the plate. Ripken was still Ripken, and Jeter was still uncomfortable taking up space in the same paragraph.

"I haven't played a full year yet, so putting me there with Cal Ripken is ridiculous," Jeter said. "It's like he's the teacher and everyone else is the student."

Ripken remained a powerful force on a team that belted more home runs (257) than the '61 Yankees or any other club in the history of the game. At thirty-six, Ripken had managed 26 homers and 102 RBI. He had hit .345 against the Yanks in the regular season, and .444 against the Indians in the Division Series.

The standings said none of that mattered. New York had beaten the Orioles ten times in thirteen attempts and had gone 6-0 in Camden Yards, reducing them to an unwashed wild card.

"Secretly," Ripken said, "I've been hoping for another matchup against New York."

His double-play partner was hoping for something else. Roberto Alomar spat in the face of an umpire, John Hirschbeck, during a confrontation on September 27, and he knew Yankee fans would remind him at every turn. But outside of Alomar and Bobby Bonilla, a holdover villain from the other side of the Triborough Bridge, the Orioles were happy to be alive in the Bronx.

"I think it was fated," said Johnson, who had won it all with the '86 Mets. "I think this was meant to be."

Fate? Destiny? Playoff teams in all sports throw around those words as easily as they throw around used towels in a locker room. But in the first game of the last playoff series the great Ripken would play at shortstop, fate and destiny would collide near Yankee Stadium's right-field wall.

Derek Jeter put the ball in the air. Nobody knew it at the time, but one of Jeter's idols, Cal Ripken Jr. himself, helped put the twelve-year-old boy in the stands who would deflect that ball into history.

Eric Saland was a Yankee fan raised in Poughkeepsie, New York, a Mickey Mantle fan who went to eight or nine home games a year. So he was thrilled to be holding a ticket to Game 1 of the 1996 American League Championship Series between the Yankees and Orioles, scheduled to be played in the Bronx on October 8.

Saland and his son, Matthew, were all set to join another Bergen County, New Jersey family, the Altmans, in Yankee Stadium's right-field seats. Bob Altman did not buy the tickets for $175 a pop because he was a Yankee fan; he bought them because his son, Brian, had been a Cal Ripken Jr. fan since he was a second grader.

Brian was riveted by Ripken's Iron Man streak of consecutive games played, and he started collecting the shortstop's baseball card. But it was Ripken's simple act of kindness that made Brian a fan for life and set in motion a series of events that, three years later, turned the ALCS upside down and left Jeter the luckiest man on the face of the earth.

Brian was nine when his mother, Fern, had a sporting goods store make up an orange T-shirt with Ripken's name and number, 8, printed in white lettering. Her son would wear it as part of a Halloween costume made complete by eyeblack and an Orioles cap. The following year, with the Orioles in town and the Altmans holding tickets, Brian dug up the T-shirt and threw it on for the ride into the Bronx.

Bob Altman was working for Mike Bloomberg at the time, and one of the company's vendors had supplied him with seats near the Baltimore dugout. The Altmans arrived early enough to watch batting practice, along with dozens of fellow fans screaming in vain for Ripken's attention.

"Turn around for a minute," Bob ordered his son.

"Why?" Brian said.

"Just trust me."

Brian turned his back toward the batting cage, and in a fleeting moment of quiet that separated one thwack of the bat from the next, his father shouted, "Hey, Cal, check out the jersey."

Ripken actually looked over, smiled, and started heading straight for the Altmans. Brian's jaw dropped to his toes as the Iron Man locked his steel-blue eyes on him, this anonymous boy in his orange Halloween shirt.

Other kids buzzed about Brian as Ripken moved toward the railing, but the ballplayer barely noticed. "I was really nervous," Brian said. "This was my hero approaching."

Brian was speechless and shaking. He did not know what to do, other than hold out the ball he was carrying in his hand. "I'll sign your ball," Ripken told him, "but first let me shake your hand."

The boy and the ballplayer shook hands; Ripken signed the ball and jogged back to the batting cage while the other young fans begged in vain for him to return.

Right then and there, Brian Altman made a decision. He would not be embracing his family's allegiance to the Mets anytime soon. He would remain an Orioles fan, at least until the day Cal Ripken Jr. retired.

Three years later, despite his brief demotion to third base, Ripken had no intention of retiring. He had every intention of beating the Yankees in the ALCS and returning to the World Series for the first time since the Orioles won the title in 1983. Brian Altman had every intention of watching him try.

So his father scored the five Game 1 tickets, kept three for the family, and gave two to Brian's friend Matthew Saland and his father, Eric, who was looking forward to the night out as much as his son.

But just Eric Saland's luck, the rains came and turned an 8:00 p.m. Game 1 on October 8 into a 4:00 p.m. Game 1 on October 9. Eric worked in the trucking industry, and he had commitments in Hackensack, New Jersey that day. Eric pleaded with his supervisor to let him go to the game, but the man would not budge. They needed to make sure their outbound freight made it out, the boss explained, and Eric was some kind of pissed off.

The Salands had to return one ticket to the Altmans, who suddenly had a big decision to make that night in their Harrington Park, New Jersey home. Who should fill that fifth and final seat in the right-field stands?

The Altmans quickly agreed on the perfect candidate, a good friend of Brian's. Fern had met the boy's mother at the George Street playground and pond in Harrington Park, back when their children were two years old. They started talking, hit it off, and the families grew close. So ten years later, the Altmans decided Brian's twelve-year-old buddy deserved the first shot at the last Game 1 ticket. They placed the call to nearby Old Tappan.

They had Jeffrey Maier at hello.

The Altmans had already given Jeffrey his bar mitzvah gift the previous weekend, when the Maier party at the Pearl River Hilton was built around a World Series theme. They decided Jeffrey was a good enough kid, and a big enough Yankee fan, to deserve this second gift.

A center fielder and pitcher, Maier was the best twelve-year-old ballplayer in Old Tappan, a good baseball burb. Jeffrey was so hellbent on chasing and catching the ball, he once stopped a ten-year-old travel game cold by slamming into the outfield fence and cutting open his head in pursuit of a home-run shot.

Jeffrey felt the back of his skull and saw the blood trickling down his right hand. He was more upset he did not catch the homer than he was about a gash that would require seven stitches to close.

His parents were vacationing in Bermuda when they sent back word that their son was not to play in another travel game until they returned. On arrival in Old Tappan, Dick and Jane Maier were told by their housekeeper that Jeffrey was at his team's game, watching in the stands.

Dick and Jane headed to the field, only to find that their son was refusing to talk to them. You did not take baseball away from ten-year-old Jeffrey Maier without paying a heavy price.

Nothing had changed two years later, when Jane Maier wrote a note to the principal of Charles DeWolf Middle School asking that her son be excused from his final October 9 period, a gym class, because he had an appointment with his orthodontist.

She had no idea Jeffrey had a date with destiny instead.

"I should've known we were in trouble," Fern Altman said, "when Jeffrey got in our car with his mitt on."

His black Mizuno mitt. Jeffrey's parents had challenged him to bring home a ball. His grandmother, up from Florida for the bar mitzvah, had told him that morning, "If the Yankees don't know how to do it, you show them how."

Jeffrey was a Derek Jeter fan making it to Yankee Stadium for the second time. The year before, he had joined his father at a Yanks-Indians game played on August 13, hours after Mickey Mantle died inside Baylor University Medical Center. Jeffrey persuaded Cleveland's Dennis Martinez to sign his glove.

Dick Maier loved Mantle; he had his basement decorated with testaments to the Mick and Joe DiMaggio and other baseball icons. Growing up in Washington Heights, listening to every game he could find on the radio, Dick made his first trip to Yankee Stadium for a Red Sox game, hoping he would catch a foul ball from DiMaggio or Ted Williams.

He caught one from Jerry Coleman instead.

Some forty-five years later, Dick's son had failed to catch a David Justice foul ball during a Braves-Mets game at Shea. Jeffrey wanted desperately to get one. His black Mizuno had served him well on the Little League fields of Old Tappan, so he figured it might do the same around the great lawn of the Bronx.

Before Jeffrey jumped into the Altmans' car wearing his Emmitt Smith T-shirt ("E=TD2" read the vague tribute to the Dallas Cowboys' star) and his mitt, his father gave him a piece of homespun advice about sitting in right field. Jeter likes to go the opposite way, Dick told Jeff. Whenever there's a hard-throwing pitcher on the mound and Jeter at the plate, be ready.

The Altmans crossed the George Washington Bridge, drove down the Major Deegan, and pulled into a Stadium parking lot. Their five tickets were divided — three in the front row, and two five rows back. Bob and Fern decided the three boys — their son, Brian, Jeffrey, and Matthew Saland — should stay together, and that they should keep their eyes fixed on the kids from the rear.

Through seven and a half innings Ripken had a couple of hits, making Brian a happy — if isolated — face in the crowd, and the Yankees were down by only a 4–3 count, leaving Jeffrey and Matthew hopeful the home team could still pull this off.

But from their seats in the sixth row, Brian's parents were growing concerned over the hostile vibe being projected around them. The fans in right field, Fern Altman said, "were out for blood. As time went on, everybody was getting very drunk and the atmosphere was way too rowdy for us."

The Altmans were not about to leave; the boys would never have allowed it. So when Jeter came to bat against Armando Benitez with one out in the eighth, nobody on, Jeffrey Maier had one thought in his head as he sat in Section 31, Box 325, Row A, Seat 2:

This is the situation Dad talked about. Jeter in the box, power thrower on the mound, a talented boy with a glove in the right-field stands.

"I was on high alert," Jeffrey would say. "I was ready to go."

So was Jeter. He already had two infield singles and a stolen base to his Game 1 name, but he had stranded two runners on his most recent trip to the plate.

This time around, he lashed at the second pitch he saw from Benitez, a high 94-mile-per-hour fastball that drifted from left to right and over the heart of the plate. The ball sailed high into the black Bronx night, toward the right-field wall. Tony Tarasco, the Orioles' defensive replacement for the banged-up Bonilla, carefully worked his way back to the Nobody Beats the Wiz sign.

Behind Tarasco, behind the blue wall, a kid wearing a dark T-shirt and a black glove scrambled out of his seat and down a small flight of stairs as he tracked the majestic flight of Jeter's shot.

Jeffrey Maier was going after the ball as fearlessly as he had gone after it the day he gashed open his head on the jagged edges of a Little League fence.

The New York–born Tarasco settled under the ball right next to the Wiz sign, lifted his glove, and pressed the small of his back against the padding on the wall. Tarasco did not jump. He did not think he had to jump. The ball was heading right for the webbing of his mitt, until it wasn't.

A boy's glove had beaten a man's glove to the spot.

Maier had reached over the wall, following a twelve-year-old's instinct rather than the grown-up ordinances that prohibited spectators of all ages from interfering with the game, never mind a crucial play in the ALCS. Jeffrey felt the baseball smack into the heel of his glove and watched it bounce free as he tried to bring it into his body.

A dangerous scramble ensued on the Maier side of the wall, while a nasty argument broke out on the Tarasco side. Rich Garcia, the right-field umpire, was jabbing his index finger toward the sky to signal a home run as Jeter circled the bases. Tarasco immediately got up in the ump's face and berated him.

An enraged Benitez ran all the way from the mound to confront Garcia next, before Orioles manager Davey Johnson arrived to pull his reliever away. As Johnson jumped all over Garcia and earned his own ejection, Jeffrey Maier was receiving high-fives from dozens of fans and being lifted onto the shoulders of a stranger.

Maier had lost the fight for the loose ball he had knocked over the wall; Marc Jarvis, a thirty-five-year-old Connecticut man, came up with the prize. "I was at the bottom of the pile with the ball in my bare hand," Maier would say, "and I was getting absolutely pummeled."

One man kept yelling at Jeffrey that what he did was wrong, that he should not have interfered with the game, but the other adult fans were treating Maier as if he were Derek Jeter himself.

Five rows behind this chaotic scene, Bob and Fern Altman were ready to have a stroke. "It was a mob mentality," Fern said. "It was very scary to be responsible for three children in that situation."

Bob Altman pushed through a widening knot of fans to get down to the three boys and found Jeffrey on the stranger's shoulders, riding high as he pumped his arms.

"Holy shit," Bob told himself, "that guy is going to drop Jeff onto the field."

Bob immediately pulled Maier down to safety and looked the boy in the eye.

"Jeff, what happened? Did you stick your hand over the wall?" he asked.

"No," Maier answered. "I just looked up and stuck my hand out and I went for the ball."

"OK. That's your story. Stick to it."

A columnist from the *Daily News* was the first media member on the scene, followed by one from *Newsday*, and then by dozens of reporters, photographers, broadcasters, and cameramen. Security guards told the Altmans they needed to move Jeffrey out to the corridor if he wanted to conduct any interviews, and out to the corridor the scrum went.

"And then it was lights, camera, action," Fern Altman said.

Suddenly Jeffrey Maier was on NBC with Jim Gray. Wave after wave of reporters came at the Yankees' angel in the outfield, and the kid answered their questions with an innocent smile.

"I'm a Yankees fan," he said, "but I didn't mean to do anything to change the outcome of the game or do anything bad to the Orioles.

"I feel like something amazing just happened. I didn't think anything like this would ever happen to me. It's pretty cool . . . I usually make those catches in Little League. But this time, I don't care that I dropped it."

A Yankees public relations official eventually led Maier, the Altmans, and Matthew Saland to an office where all phone lines were blinking red. *Good Morning America* was on hold, and so was Letterman. The PR official asked the Altmans if they wanted to talk to the shows' producers, and Bob and Fern said they just wanted to return to their seats.

"You can't," the official told them. "The game is under protest, and we can't guarantee your safety. The best thing for everyone is if you guys left the game right now."

The official gave the Altmans a phone number, told them to dial it in the morning, and then had the party of five escorted to the Stadium exits. They started driving back to Bergen County, New Jersey, turned on the radio to catch the end of the game, and forgot that Jeffrey had given the press his parents' unlisted number.

Meanwhile, Jeffrey's father was driving home from his software job in Manhattan and listening to John Sterling and Michael Kay call Game 1 as it tumbled into extra innings. Dick Maier was on the Palisades Interstate Parkway when he heard the announcers mention that a controversial Jeter homer had made it a 4–4 game in the eighth, that a young boy had reached over the wall to steal an out from Tony Tarasco's glove.

When they identified the boy as little Jeff Maier from Old Tappan, Dick said, "I almost had a heart attack. I started going about twenty miles over the speed limit just to get home to see it.

"I mean, I'm the biggest Yankee fan you could meet. My idol is Mickey Mantle. And I'm hearing them say on the radio that my son might have helped the Yankees get to the World Series."

Soon enough, Bernie Williams hit a towering eleventh-inning homer off Baltimore's Randy Myers, whipping a crowd of 56,495 into a frenzy and leaving the Orioles to rail against the forces that conspired against them.

Johnson announced his protest was not based on Garcia's ruling — the Orioles manager knew full well he could not protest a judgment call. He said he was protesting Game 1 because the Yankees promised him that outfield fans would be blocked from getting past the railing and down to the wall.

In fact, before the game Orioles and Yankees officials met with the umpiring crew and discussed the potential for fan interference. "That was specifically covered," said Kevin Malone, Baltimore's assistant general manager. "They had issues with it in the past, and we were assured they'd be on top of it. It was bizarre. We overemphasized it in the meeting, and then it happened anyway. You think if you focused on it you'd get it right, so that was overly aggravating."

Tarasco claimed he had no doubt he would have caught Jeter's shot had Maier not beaten him to the ball. "It was like a magic trick," Tarasco said. "The ball just disappeared in midair. Merlin must be in the house, man. Abracadabra."

After watching the replay, Garcia agreed fan interference should have been called but disputed Tarasco's claim that he would have made the catch. The ump believed Jeter deserved a double and felt badly that he gave the rookie two extra bases instead.

The game had taken four hours and twenty-three minutes to play, so most of the Yankees were too tired and too frayed to embrace the notion that a twelve-year-old boy had just bailed them out. Asked about the replays of Maier's obvious interference, Joe Torre said, "Anybody see the replay of Bernie's home run? That wasn't bad, either."

For his part, Jeter said he simply saw Garcia signaling a home run and that he was not about to argue. "He should've jumped," the shortstop said of Tarasco. Jeter would eventually concede he had gotten a little help from a little friend.

"Afterward you could see there was a little interference there," he would say, "but I don't care."

None of baseball's elders cared either. Baltimore's protest was shot down, and Jeter had the first postseason homer of his career.

"And it was so huge for us because that ball was going to be caught," Yankees reliever David Weathers said. "I don't care what anyone says. We were in the bullpen, and we saw it. We saw Tarasco, who's a very good outfielder, camp under it. We were all like, 'Oh, man,' and then the crowd went crazy. It changed the whole series."

It changed Jeffrey Maier's life. He had left home that afternoon a seventh-grade athlete unknown outside the boundaries of his sleepy town, and he returned to Old Tappan that night as one of the country's most famous ballplayers.

When the Altmans pulled up to the Maier home, a stretch limo was already waiting in the driveway to take Jeffrey and his family to the Plaza Hotel in Manhattan so he could appear on *Good Morning America*. It made sense: the kid was America's most wanted man.

The next morning, with the Maiers and Altmans gathered in the ABC studio, Bob Altman assumed the role of press agent as major news media outlets jockeyed for time with Jeffrey.

Altman made it clear the family wanted lunch, limo service, and free tickets to Game 2 to grant any outlet exclusivity. "The *Daily News* comes back and says, 'OK, we'll give you two stretch limos, lunch at the All-Star Café, and after the game we'll get you into the dugout and clubhouse to get autographs from the players. We'll get you seats in the front row, behind the dugout, but it's got to be exclusive to the *Daily News*. You can't talk to the *New York Post*.'"

Altman brought the offer to Dick Maier, who accepted the terms. Jeffrey bounced from *Good Morning America* to *Live with Regis & Kathie Lee* to the All-Star Café, with photographers shooting his every step. While all this was going on, Jeffrey's grandparents were returning to their retirement community in Lake Worth, Florida. Dave and Anne Maier had no idea what had happened the previous night, so when they saw the neighbors out waiting for them, they thought a community resident had passed away.

The neighbors assured Jeffrey's grandparents that the only thing dead was Baltimore's protest.

Back at the Plaza suite, Altman called the Yankees PR office before heading to Game 2 in the Bronx. The team's director of media relations, Rick Cerrone, told Altman, "This is not going to be Jeffrey Maier Day at Yankee Stadium."

Dick Maier took the phone and informed Cerrone they already had their own tickets and would indeed be attending Game 2 as planned. Cerrone batted away one newspaper's absurd request to get Maier together with Jeter so the shortstop could be photographed thanking the boy for his help.

The Maiers ended up right behind the Yankees' dugout, also as planned, and the Orioles were furious that he was there. "We thought he got rewarded for being a criminal," said Baltimore hitting coach Rick Down.

A certain rookie shortstop did not care. Jeter made eye contact with his favorite twelve-year-old fan and threw Jeffrey Maier his wristband. This time Maier made the catch. "That was really cool," Jeffrey said.

The Yankees lost that Game 2 but regained control of the ALCS in Game 3 after Jeter's two-out double off Mike Mussina in the eighth ignited a four-run rally that erased a 2–1 deficit. Bernie Williams singled home Jeter, advanced to third on Tino Martinez's double, and then scored when Todd Zeile tried to abort a throw to second base and lost control of the ball.

Cecil Fielder dropped the hammer on Mussina with a two-run homer deep into the left-field stands, and Jimmy Key, a survivor of multiple surgeries on his left arm, had himself a masterful eight-inning, three-hit, 117-pitch victory.

Jeter had started crucial rallies in Games 2 and 3 of the Division Series triumph over Texas, and in Game 3 of this Baltimore series. So it came as no surprise that he set the tone in Game 4, leading off with a double before Williams's home run two batters later made it 2–0. Darryl Strawberry would hit two homers, Paul O'Neill would hit one, and the battered Orioles would be practically out on their feet when they took the Game 5 field.

George Steinbrenner had returned to New York after the Yankees seized the 3–1 series lead and watched Game 5 at the Stadium. His general counsel, David Sussman, received a call from a high-ranking official in Mayor Rudy Giuliani's administration who was interested in discussing logistics for a potential parade.

When Sussman brought word of the conversation to his employer, Steinbrenner nearly threw him out of his office. The Boss lived in mortal fear of jinxing imminent victory, even if it was clear Baltimore was giving him little reason to sweat.

In Game 5, the Yanks blasted Orioles starter Scott Erickson for six runs in the third inning and then spent the rest of the day hanging on. They were trying desperately to return the world's most famous sports franchise to the World Series for the first time since 1981 and trying desperately to land Torre there for the first time ever.

The Orioles cut it to 6–4 in the ninth on Bonilla's two-run, two-out shot, setting up an appropriate climax for the series. Cal Ripken Jr. stepped into the box against John Wetteland. He did not know it, but the Iron Man was batting for the final time as Baltimore's starting shortstop.

Ripken said he had been secretly hoping for another crack at the Yankees, and here was his chance to extend the series, to get the tying run to the plate, to put the fear of God in Torre.

Jeter had outplayed and outhit Ripken, batting .417 for the ALCS. Ripken carried a .263 average into this last at-bat, with no homers and no RBI. And, of course, Ripken had unwittingly and irreparably harmed Baltimore's chances of advancing to the World Series by signing Brian Altman's ball three years back.

Ripken's gracious gesture set in motion a series of events that put Jeffrey Maier in the right-field seats for Game 1. What if Altman had not put on his orange Ripken shirt that day? What if the Iron Man had not made the kid a fan for life by picking him out of a crowd?

What if it had not rained on October 8? What if Eric Saland had a lighter schedule on October 9, or a boss who would grant him permission to go to the delayed Game 1? What if the Altmans had decided to ask someone other than Maier to take Saland's ticket? What if Dick Maier had not reminded Jeffrey to be ready when Jeter was at the plate and a power arm was on the mound?

"I think about this all the time," Saland said. "If I'd gone to that game, I wouldn't have run to the fence, and my son wasn't fast enough to make it to the fence. If I go, none of this happens, and the world doesn't get to know Jeffrey Maier."

If Eric Saland had gone, and Jeffrey Maier had not, would the Orioles have won the series?

"Yes, we would have," Malone said. "If we go back to Baltimore up 2–0, it puts all the pressure on the Yankees, and momentum is so big in sports. You play differently, you manage differently, you pitch differently, you hit differently, and you think differently when you're down 2–0.

"I thought we had the better team, and we ended up with nothing to show for it."

Nothing but Ripken at the plate, ready to put the '96 Orioles to rest. This final out needed to be made before a champagne-soaked Torre could end up with half his Brooklyn neighborhood in his Camden Yards office. Before Torre's sister, Marguerite, a nun and principal at the Nativity of the Blessed Virgin Mary School in Ozone Park, could admit she was praying for Baltimore's demise.

Before the Torres could cry again over Rocco's death. Before the manager's other brother, Frank, could answer a reporter's call in his hospital room at Columbia-Presbyterian, where he was waiting for a heart transplant, and declare, "My kid brother is finally in the World Series."

Before the hate mail and a few death threats from pathetic fans and degenerate gamblers would find the Maiers in Old Tappan, compelling them to retreat from the media outlets and Hollywood agents still wanting a piece of their son.

Ripken had to close the series and an epic part of his career first, and he had to do it by hitting a ball at a kid who always looked up to him. Derek Jeter might have been a bigger fan of Barry Larkin's, the shortstop he would have ultimately replaced had Cincinnati taken him with the fifth pick of the '92 draft.

But Jeter had a tremendous respect for Ripken and his durability, and an undying appreciation for the fact that the six-foot-four Iron Man helped clear a path for the Jeters and Alex Rodriguezes by dispelling the notion that a major league shortstop needed to be a defensive-minded runt.

Only in this moment, with Ripken's grounder bouncing hard to his right, Jeter was not thinking about any debt of gratitude he might have owed his elder. He was not thinking about the fact that Baltimore could have and should have drafted him, too, and then moved the declining Ripken to where he would start the '97 season: third base.

No, Jeter was not thinking about the fourth pick of the '92 draft, outfielder Jeffrey Hammonds, and the fact that Hammonds did not even play in the postseason. Jeter was thinking only of doing precisely what he did — field the ball in the hole and unleash a throw to first base that would reach Tino Martinez before Ripken touched the bag.

Martinez would dig the ball out of the dirt just before Ripken reached the base — fittingly enough — with a headfirst slide; it was the first time anyone could recall the Iron Man diving this way into first. Ripken's last act as the Orioles' everyday shortstop was defined by his willingness to sacrifice his body, and his desperation to be great.

Rich Garcia, of all umpires, was just as definitive in ruling Ripken out as he had been in ruling that Jeter's Game 1 homer was legitimate. The rookie shortstop was the one going to the World Series, and the iconic shortstop who helped put Jeffrey Maier in the lineup was the one going home.

Derek Jeter was the leadoff man for a World Series lineup that had just been outscored 12–1 by the Atlanta Braves in Game 1 at Yankee Stadium, and he was the poor soul whose Mercury Mountaineer had just been stolen off a Manhattan street. Didn't matter. The shortstop was having no trouble relaxing at his East 79th Street apartment.

His friend and former minor league teammate R. D. Long was staying with Jeter while rehabbing from shoulder surgery. The shortstop was watching the tape ("He usually watches playoff games," Long said), watching how John Smoltz completely locked down the Yankees, watching how a nineteen-year-old from Curaçao, Andruw Jones, made the biggest rookie splash of all.

Long was struck by Jeter's placid demeanor.

"The Yankees haven't been in the World Series in a long time, and Derek Jeter's turning into the Beatles," he said. "This cat will literally be on the couch, we'll be talking, and he'll just fall asleep. He's facing [Greg Maddux] tomorrow and he just falls asleep.

"I'm sitting there looking at the cat and saying, 'You've got to be kidding me.' If I was in the same boat, do you know what I'd have to do to go to sleep? Drink fifteen beers. Derek Jeter's one of the very few I've watched do that night after night and go to sleep like a baby."

That's what struck the Yanks most about Jeter, the ice water coursing through his veins. His approach in October mirrored his approach in May. Jeter played the game with a smile and a wink, and he was forever making small talk with fans while waiting on deck.

Joe Girardi, the tightly wound catcher, a baseball player with a football mentality, marveled at how much fun Jeter would have while competing in high-stakes postseason games. "Gosh, I wish I could be like that," Girardi told himself.

"It just blew me away how relaxed Derek was," the catcher said.

So Jeter was relaxed for Game 2, even if the rest of his team was tighter than George Steinbrenner's omnipresent turtleneck. This time the Yankee offense could not generate even one run off Atlanta's starter; they allowed Maddux to go eight innings and to beat them by a 4–0 count.

In the process, a Maddux pitch hit Jeter on the left wrist, and for the balance of the World Series the shortstop would feel more pain and stiffness and have more trouble gripping the ball than he would ever let on.

This felt like a sequel to 1976, when Cincinnati's Big Red Machine steamrolled the Yankees in four. Yes, the defending champion Braves were heavily favored to win this World Series, but nobody expected their pitchers to hold the Yanks to one run in the first eighteen innings. Steinbrenner was half furious, half terrified of suffering another humiliating sweep.

The owner stopped at Mariano Duncan's locker. "Oh, you're always a very positive guy," Steinbrenner told the second baseman. "So now what's going to happen?" Duncan assured the Boss the Yankees would at least win two of three in Atlanta and return the Series to the Bronx.

After Game 1, Torre had actually told the Boss the Yanks would lose to Maddux, win three straight in Atlanta, and return to the Bronx to win the title in Game 6. "He looked at me like I had two heads," Torre said. Steinbrenner finally told his manager, "OK, go do it," but the owner was hardly a blind believer in the plan.

Torre presented the same scenario to his players in the grim wake of Game 2. "He came in and said, 'Hey, guys, Atlanta's my town,'" David Weathers said. "Joe just said, 'We're going to go down there and take three from them and win Game 6 here.'"

After landing in Atlanta, where he had been a player and manager, Torre had stronger words for his team. He knew his Yankees were doubting themselves, and he searched for another button or three to push.

"Joe said Atlanta had the champagne on ice already," Tim Raines said. "He said, 'We can do this. I know we can do it. You guys have played together all year, and now's the time to do it.'

"He mentioned the first two games and said, 'Those games are over. George Steinbrenner doesn't think we can come back. . . . Let's prove that motherfucker wrong.'"

For the sake of channeling an inner rage, Torre knew he was sending the right guy to the Game 3 mound. David Cone was there for Game 2 by accident—he was supposed to be on a flight to Atlanta, but a mechanical delay left him stuck on the runway and then parked at the gate. Cone did not have an easy time convincing the pilot to let him off the plane ("I don't even think the guy knew who I was," the pitcher said), but somehow, some way, he made it back to the Bronx.

He did not like what he saw or heard. Cone was told by a clubhouse attendant the Braves were talking trash and talking sweep, and the right-hander had not made it back from aneurysm surgery to get embarrassed on the sport's biggest stage.

"It seemed to me they were having just a little too much fun at our expense," Cone said. "People were treating us as a prop in the World Series. Everybody was looking at this Atlanta Braves team and trying to place them in history, and I was really angry about that."

Two prominent Atlanta columnists, Mark Bradley and Terrence Moore of the *Journal-Constitution*, declared the balance of the World Series a mere formality, their Yankee obituaries cutting the visitors to the bone. "No longer is this team playing against the overmatched Yankees," Bradley wrote. "The Braves are playing against history."

These words would move the Yankees the way an Atlanta sportswriter named Tom McCollister had moved a forty-six-year-old Jack Nicklaus to win the Masters ten years earlier by writing that the Golden Bear was washed up, "gone, done."

Torre knew the status quo would not prove the columnists wrong, so he benched Wade Boggs, Tino Martinez, and Paul O'Neill for Game 3 in favor of Charlie Hayes, Cecil Fielder, and Darryl Strawberry. Martinez, who had no RBI in forty-four postseason at-bats, was furious nonetheless, slamming Torre's office door after receiving the news.

The manager did not blink. Torre also put a sore Jeter in the two-hole in the lineup, behind Raines, a move that paid off in the first inning when the shortstop dropped down a bunt that moved Raines to second, setting up Bernie Williams's RBI single. The Yankees had an honest-to-God lead on the Braves when they handed the ball to Cone, going on eleven days' rest.

"To pitch in the World Series after having an aneurysm," the starter said, "I wouldn't trade places with anybody."

Cone had not won a postseason game in '96, he had missed four months of the regular season after signing his $19.5 million deal, and his failure to beat Seattle in Game 5 of the '95 Division Series still haunted him.

Cone needed to beat the Braves. He was not the pitcher he used to be, not even close, but his competitive spirit was the closest thing to an indomitable force the Yankees had. So nobody on the visiting side was surprised when Cone imposed his will on Atlanta for six innings, barely surviving a bases-loaded jam and Torre's visit to the mound by getting Javy Lopez to pop up on his ninety-seventh and final pitch.

It was 2–1 Yankees when Cone walked off, leaving it to Jeter and Williams to take care of the rest. The shortstop and the center fielder had worn out the Rangers and Orioles in the first two rounds of the playoffs, carrying an offense that offered little else, but they were a combined 1 for 12 in the two home losses to the Braves.

Matched against reliever Greg McMichael in the eighth, Jeter reached on an infield single in the hole, and Williams followed with a homer to deep right. If nothing else, their 5–2 victory guaranteed the Yankees would lose to the Braves with honor. Backup catcher Jim Leyritz would report that at least six or seven Yanks were reassuring one another with these words: "Hey, at least we didn't get swept."

After all, Kenny Rogers, the Yankees' Game 4 starter, amounted to a human white flag. Rogers was easily shaken and afraid to succeed. Few men had ever been so ill equipped to deal with the pressures tethered to a high-salaried ballplayer in New York.

Rogers surrendered five runs while recording only six outs, and this was the near-unanimous thinking in Fulton County Stadium: the Braves were back to playing against history. But with the home team holding a 6–0 lead, Jeter had the nerve to interrupt a Torre visit to the mound to tell his manager, "Don't worry. We're going to win this game."

When Jeter came to bat in the sixth, this was the narrative thread connecting the Yankees' postseason rallies: the rookie shortstop started almost all of them.

Jeter would put another right-field umpire in an unwelcome position, and it was not by coincidence. Among his many talents, Jeter consistently kept his hands inside the baseball and used the opposite field, the very reason why Dick Maier had told his son Jeffrey to be ready in the right-field stands during Game 1 of the ALCS.

Jeter did not send a ball to the wall this time; he lifted a Denny Neagle pitch foul near the right-field line. Atlanta's Jermaine Dye appeared to be preparing to catch it until umpire Tim Welke accidentally got in the right fielder's way. The ball fell to the grass as Dye went down in a heap.

The Braves were upset with Welke, but at the time they had no idea where this unfortunate twist of fate would lead. Jeter received a free do-over at the plate, and he made good on it by blooping a single — to right field, of course.

The Yankees scored three times that inning, reminding themselves how and why they had already set a postseason record by winning six straight on the road. In the eighth, the Yanks caught two major breaks — a swinging bunt from Charlie Hayes somehow stayed fair inside the third-base line, and shortstop Rafael Belliard bobbled Mariano Duncan's double-play ball and got one out instead of two.

But Atlanta still had faith in its flame-throwing closer, Mark Wohlers, who would face Leyritz with one out. Leyritz had beaten Seattle in Game 2 of the '95 Division Series with a fifteenth-inning homer in the rain, a development that did nothing to tame the backup catcher's oversized opinion of his own skill. Leyritz's extreme belief in himself helped him in pressure situations like this one.

He had never faced Wohlers, so in the dugout he called out to Don Zimmer, "Hey, what does he got?"

"Throws 100," Zimmer replied.

One hundred miles per hour. And with the World Series hanging in the balance, Leyritz had the nerve to face Wohlers with someone else's bat. The catcher's supply was running low — he had only a couple of his own left with him in Atlanta — and he was scheduled to start Game 5 as Andy Pettitte's preferred catcher. Leyritz wanted to save his bats for John Smoltz, so he asked Strawberry for a rental to carry into the biggest moment of his baseball life.

Strawberry gave him one of his brand-new bats, and off Leyritz went with a bulky pad on his left elbow to protect against that 100-mile-per-hour heat. Wohlers started him off with a 98-mile-per-hour fastball, and Leyritz fouled it straight back. The closer took that as a sign the hitter was right on his pitch and made a stunning concession, throwing two consecutive sliders for balls.

The Fox TV broadcaster, Tim McCarver, warned that Wohlers needed to get back to throwing heat. "If you get beat," said McCarver, a former All-Star catcher, "you want to get beat on your best pitch."

Leyritz fouled back another fastball, this one clocked at 99 miles per hour, before Wohlers decided another concession was in order. It didn't matter that Leyritz hadn't proved he could catch up to his best pitch. The closer unleashed another slider, one Leyritz fouled off, before making his fateful choice with pitch number six.

Another slider, designed to dive down and away from the hitter. Only this pitch looped high and out over the plate, looking more like a floating beach ball than an exploding blur of cowhide. Leyritz, wearing his lucky number 13, sent it high toward the left-field corner, high enough to clear the wall and the Atlanta phenom, Andruw Jones, who had scaled it.

The Yankees would win their seventh consecutive postseason road game, the question a matter of how, not if.

In the tenth, with Steve Avery on the mound, Jeter singled into the hole to put the go-ahead run at second. Williams was intentionally walked to load the bases, and to allow the left-handed Avery to go at the left-handed pinch hitter, Boggs, who had gone 3 for 27 in the first two playoff rounds and who had been benched after two games in the World Series.

Boggs rediscovered his greatest weapon — a set of eyes with Ted Williams vision at the plate — and drew a walk on a full-count pitch. Suddenly the Braves were suffering a severe crisis of faith. They took four hours and seventeen minutes to lose the longest World Series game ever, and to become the second World Series team in forty years to blow a lead of at least six runs.

They lost Game 4 and then lost an epic Game 5 pitching duel between Pettitte and Smoltz, punctuated by a seven-fastball battle between closer (John Wetteland) and pinch hitter (Luis Polonia). The Braves lost by a 1–0 count when Paul O'Neill — playing on a bad hamstring — ran down Polonia's potential game-winning shot to right center for the final out. The Yankee coach, Jose Cardenal, had moved O'Neill eight feet to his right before Polonia quit fouling off Wetteland's fastballs and finally ripped one fair.

Torre was proven a prophet; he had told George Steinbrenner and his players that Atlanta was his town, that the Yanks would win all three games to return the World Series to New York. In his office, Torre lit another one of his Red Auerbach cigars.

Everything was going right. Graeme Lloyd, a train wreck of a pickup, turned into a sure-thing reliever who recorded the most tense October outs. Strawberry was back to punishing the ball the way he did before he betrayed his otherworldly talent with drugs. Williams had blossomed into the kind of one-man Murderers' Row his employer, Steinbrenner, never fathomed when he ordered Gene Michael to trade him at all costs.

Torre had won in Atlanta by benching Boggs, Martinez, and O'Neill, men who were destined to retire with more than 7,000 regular-season hits combined. Torre had won in Atlanta by relying on Rivera, who could have been traded in spring training, and by relying on Jeter, who could have been demoted on the same day of that trade that was never made.

Just as the Orioles could not get past Jeter's Jeffrey Maier homer, the Braves could not get past Jeter's sixth-inning single in Game 4, right after Dye failed to catch the shortstop's foul pop.

Braves manager Bobby Cox was dragging down his team by constantly rattling on about an out that should have been made when his team had a six-run lead. "Dye couldn't get around the umpire to catch the goddamn ball," Cox grumped. "That was a big play. It was the first out of the inning. If you look at the replay, it's an easy out."

It always came back to Jeter. Before Game 6, the shortstop was asked about the wrist that required a steady application of ice wraps.

"Everybody's making too big a deal about it," he said. "It's not a problem."

Yes, it was a problem — a problem Jeter chose to ignore. Only a few knew it at the time, but despite a build that suggested he would have been better off in the non-contact arenas of tennis and golf, Jeter had a threshold for pain that would have made Vince Lombardi proud.

It was one of his greatest assets when he showed up at Yankee Stadium on October 26, 1996, wearing headphones and listening to Mariah Carey on the first day of the rest of his baseball life. Jeter was already assured of winning the American League Rookie of the Year award, but he craved only one trophy.

If the Yankees did not win the World Series, Jeter would view his first full season as a complete failure.

The Braves were giving the ball to their ace, Maddux, who made for a most appropriate fall guy. After Michael gave him a tour of suburban Jersey and took him to a showing of *Miss Saigon* following the '92 season, Maddux had rejected the Yankees' free-agent bid of $34 million to sign with the Braves for $6 million less.

In the third inning of Game 6, the city Maddux rejected was falling on top of him. O'Neill doubled. Girardi smashed a triple over Marquis Grissom's head. Jeter singled home Girardi, leaving Maddux cursing himself on the mound, and then stole second without Javy Lopez even making a throw. Bernie singled home Jeter for a 3–0 lead, and in the next inning, when Terry Pendleton hit a 3-1, bases-loaded pitch to Jeter to start a lethal double play, the Braves were done.

Thoroughly out-managed, smoke billowing from his ears, Cox got himself ejected by Welke before his team got ejected by the Yanks; it was baseball's answer to North Carolina's Dean Smith getting tossed from a lost cause at the 1991 Final Four. Those Atlanta newspaper columns that had pronounced Joe Torre's team dead on arrival could have been filed alongside the old New York newspaper column that welcomed Torre as Clueless Joe.

Torre's gravely ill brother, Frank, had received his heart transplant the day before, and Frank was strong enough to watch the game on his Columbia-Presbyterian TV. Torre's starting pitcher for Game 6, Jimmy Key, had proposed to his girlfriend before arriving at the park.

The Braves stood no chance against this unfolding fairy tale. So at 10:56 p.m., before 56,375 standing, screaming witnesses, Derek Jeter stopped in the dirt past the third-base line and threw his arms toward the night sky a split second before Mark Lemke's pop foul settled into Hayes's glove for the final World Series out.

The Yankees piled onto each other on the mound. They did a victory lap around the Stadium, the delirious fans sang along to Sinatra's "New York, New York," and Boggs ended up on a cop's horse. Finally Torre was the nice guy who didn't finish last, and for this simple reason:

The Braves had the better players, but the Yankees had the better team.

"It's just magic, magic," Jeter said as he paraded around the winning clubhouse. "Everybody wrote us off. We read in the papers that it was over [after Game 2]. We picked up the Atlanta papers and they said the Braves were going to dominate us."

Jeter was a world champion, playing the most important position on baseball's most important team. He was in a place the five prospects drafted ahead of him in 1992 could not fathom.

Phil Nevin, Houston's pick at number 1, had already been traded and had spent most of '96 in Class AA before playing 38 games for the 53-109 Detroit Tigers. Paul Shuey, Cleveland's pick at number 2, was 5-2 for the Indians before pitching poorly in the Division Series loss to Baltimore. B. J. Wallace, Montreal's pick at number 3, was 15-15 over three minor league seasons and, after rotator cuff surgery, had already thrown his last professional pitch.

Jeffrey Hammonds, Baltimore's pick at number 4, had batted .226 in seventy-one games with the '96 Orioles and did not make the postseason cut. Chad Mottola, Cincinnati's pick at number 5, batted .215 in thirty-five games with the Reds before settling into life as a career minor leaguer.

Jeter? He was partying with the beautiful people at the China Club, ignoring his early wake-up call for a ticker-tape parade in the Canyon of Heroes later that morning.

Until this night, the Monday night after the World Series triumph, Jeter had conducted himself as a perfect gentleman in every public setting he graced. But in the China Club with a number of his teammates, Jeter let his hair down for the first time.

He got carried away the way any kid who had secured rock-star fame overnight would get carried away. In all his years to come as a Yankee, this was the one and only time friends were concerned about the amount Jeter had to drink.

"Derek was on such a euphoric high that night," said someone in the bar, "you couldn't shut him down. Nothing bad happened, but he was a little out of control."

Leyritz was among the Yankees with Jeter that night, and after precious little sleep they decided to drive together to Battery Park. A building security guard told them they were crazy to try, so they jumped on a packed train and began the slow crawl south.

The fans went mad when they recognized the two new passengers on their subway car, and Leyritz and Jeter were not sure if they would make it to the parade. But make it they did, along with three and a half million of their closest friends.

The '86 Mets represented the last New York baseball team to earn a parade, and that one drew a crowd of two to two and a half million. Of the Yankees' staggering turnout ten years later, Strawberry, a member of both title teams, would say, "The extra million was for Jeter. All young girls."

George Steinbrenner did his best to try to ruin this grand New York moment, ordering the same players' wives he had banned from team flights to be banned from the players' parade floats. A couple of Yankees felt empowered enough to defy the Boss and insist their wives ride with them, "and George went fucking ballistic," one team official said. Steinbrenner directed much of his rage at Debbie Tymon, a marketing executive.

"I was looking at George," the official continued, "and saying to myself, 'Man, you can't even enjoy this. It doesn't matter that you're king of the hill in New York and in the country right now, and millions of people are here to pay homage to you. You're going crazy because the players got their way on something so silly.'

"But that's him. If something's not the way he wants it, big or small, it will set him off. And you don't want to be on the receiving end of it when George goes off."

Only Steinbrenner could not rain on this parade. Governor George Pataki was riding with Joe DiMaggio, and Mayor Giuliani's son, Andrew, was riding with his hero, Jeter.

The shortstop was wearing shades to cover his bloodshot eyes, but through them he saw an unimagined sea of humanity. "You can't explain this right here," Jeter said.

His manager gave it a shot. "I tried to count how many wedding proposals Derek Jeter had," Joe Torre said. "Everyone wanted to marry him up and down the street."

Jeter was bigger than DiMaggio that day, bigger than any ballplayer or politician on a float. He was as big as Lindbergh, MacArthur, John Glenn, and every other American lion who traveled up the Canyon of Heroes and into a blizzard of confetti, appreciation, and love.

A champion at twenty-two, the Kalamazoo kid had Broadway at his feet in every literal and figurative way.

6

Perfection

D EREK JETER WAS sitting next to his good friend Alex Rodriguez at the 1998 NBA All-Star Game, watching Michael Jordan put on a show worthy of the Madison Square Garden stage.

Jeter loomed as large as Jordan on this night, if only because he held the home court advantage. This was his town and his time.

Jordan was turning thirty-five and in the middle of his final season with the Chicago Bulls; Jeter was twenty-three, he had been chosen as one of *People* magazine's "50 Most Beautiful People," and he had appeared on *Seinfeld*.

Oh, and he was also dating the poster girl on his bedroom wall, Mariah Carey, just as he had predicted years earlier to everyone back home. Jeter and Carey had met at a Fresh Air Fund gala near the end of 1996 and ultimately started a romance when her marriage to music executive Tommy Mottola came undone.

Jeter had it all. When he left his All-Star Game seat at halftime, Jeter parted a sea of awestruck fans on his way to the men's room before one of them dared to penetrate his personal space. A hand emerged from the crowd.

The shortstop was willing to give the stranger a quick handshake on the run until he heard the young man's voice. "Derek, I'm Peyton Manning. You're having some career."

Jeter stopped to congratulate the University of Tennessee quarterback who was two months away from becoming the first pick in the NFL draft, and Manning looked as pleased as any Little Leaguer would have been to earn ten seconds of Jeter's time.

Rodriguez stood in the Garden corridor, near a concession stand, and waited patiently for his friend to return. A-Rod, as he was known, was not accustomed to playing Robin to anyone's Batman. A year after Jeter was chosen sixth in the 1992 draft, Seattle made the six-foot-three Rodriguez the first overall choice out of Miami's Westminster Christian High.

Rodriguez was an amateur prospect described by some scouts and agents as the best they had ever seen — an opinion shared by the man who drafted Jeter, Bill Livesey, and the agent who represented Jeter in his first contract negotiations with the Yankees, Steve Caruso.

"Derek's the second-best high school player I ever saw, and Alex was easily the best," Caruso said. "Alex was the same height as Derek, but his body was much more developed. With Derek, you sensed he could be a star. With Alex, you knew he'd be a star."

Caruso was among the finalists to represent Rodriguez before he lost out to Scott Boras. The teenage A-Rod was cocky, of course, "but it was an act," Caruso said. "That's what struck me about him. He did not have a lot of self-esteem. . . . You'd tell Alex, 'You're a very good player,' and he'd say, 'You think so?' He needed to hear it all the time, where Derek was more confident in himself."

During his talks with Rodriguez, Caruso found A-Rod to be fascinated with Jeter, or at least with what he would read about Derek in *Baseball America*. "Oh, man, I love Derek Jeter," Rodriguez told Caruso. Alex said he wanted to be introduced to the Yankee farmhand.

So the agent gave A-Rod's number to Jeter and had his client give him a ring. Jeter and Rodriguez met face-to-face at a Michigan-Miami baseball game during Jeter's first spring training, and one nearly became interchangeable with the other.

Over time America discovered they shared the same height, the same complexion, the same green eyes, the same short-cropped haircut, the same leg-buckling effect on women, and, of course, the same passion for being great.

"Looking at him is almost like looking in the mirror," Rodriguez would say of Jeter. "We are often mistaken for related, for brothers, when we're together. And now, we spend a lot of time together. We've grown close, to be special friends."

As major leaguers, Jeter stayed in A-Rod's Pike Place apartment when the Yankees were in Seattle, and Rodriguez stayed in Derek's Upper East Side apartment when the Mariners were in New York. In those weeks when the American League schedule makers left them miles and miles apart, Jeter and Rodriguez checked each other's box scores first thing in the morning.

Their love-love relationship was the source of constant clubhouse teasing. When Rodriguez's high school teammate Doug Mientkiewicz would run into A-Rod, he would jokingly ask him, "Are you going over your boyfriend's house?"

Jeter heard it, too. "I talk about Alex around here," the Yankee shortstop said of his home locker room, "my own teammates tell me to shut up." Jeter's teammate in '96, Jim Leyritz, confirmed as much. "We used to give Derek a hard time about it," Leyritz said of the shortstop's relationship with Rodriguez. "It was like, 'Hey, dude, he's on the other team.'"

Alex and Derek. Derek and Alex. The mention of one automatically inspired the mention of the other.

Jeter won a championship and the American League Rookie of the Year award in '96. That same season, as he was closing on his twenty-first birthday, Rodriguez became the youngest shortstop ever to make an All-Star team. A-Rod nearly won the AL MVP award (he finished a very close second to Juan Gonzalez of Texas) and became the first AL shortstop in more than half a century to win a batting title with his .358 average, a stat enhanced by his 36 homers and 123 RBI.

A-Rod had the far greater individual season — in fact, it was the greatest offensive season by any shortstop — but he already lusted for what Jeter owned in New York. "I want [a championship] very bad," he said. "I would trade everything about my year for what [Jeter] had."

They appeared together on the cover of *Sports Illustrated* in February of '97, a smiling Jeter wrapping his right arm around a smiling and kneeling A-Rod. The headline announced that the friends were heading "the finest group of shortstops since World War II."

Their numbers took something of a plunge that year, as Rodriguez lost 58 points from his batting average and Jeter lost 23 points from his. They both reached the playoffs, where Jeter hit for a higher average against Cleveland (.333) than Rodriguez batted against Baltimore (.313) and actually out-homered the more powerful A-Rod in the postseason, slamming two to Alex's one.

But like Rodriguez's Mariners, Jeter's Yankees were eliminated in the first round, and that was the way Jeter preferred to keep score. It did not matter that Mariano Rivera surrendered the big Game 4 homer to Sandy Alomar Jr., or that Bernie Williams was the Yankee star who did not come through. The Yankees failed to win it all, leaving Jeter to view the season as a waste of time.

George Steinbrenner reached the same conclusion. Already steamed over the fact that his defending champs were eliminated by his hometown team, Steinbrenner blew a fuse when he read a *New York Post* story that said his Yanks went right from their Game 5 defeat to the airport to a Greenwich Village club, where they partied through the night.

Steinbrenner immediately picked up the phone and began blasting away. David Cone had organized the boys' night out, figuring his team needed some cheering up. The Boss told Cone he was extremely disappointed in him, told him he had let down the organization. "I completely agree," Cone replied. "I apologize. It's my responsibility. I'm the one who put that thing together, and it won't happen again."

It was a fitting punctuation mark on a season shaped by none of the feel-good karma that had inspired a title in '96. The disagreeable tone was set by Cecil Fielder, who interrupted the Yankees' otherwise charmed off-season by demanding a trade, ripping Joe Torre for benching him in Game 1 of the Texas series, ignoring Torre's several phone messages, and demanding a contract extension.

The '97 team was doomed before the close of spring training. The '96 team, Tim Raines said, "wasn't concerned about 'me' and 'I.' It was a team and that's why we won the World Series. Everybody pulled for each other and the team actually liked each other, and that's hard to find in baseball because you usually have different cliques.

"You have a lot of Latinos hanging together. You've got the white guys hanging together. You've got the black guys hanging together. You've got the pitchers hanging together, the infielders, the outfielders, and there was none of that on our ['96 team]."

Jeter moved easily from group to group, clique to clique, race to race, and yet the sturdy bridges connecting the diverse clubhouse groups began to rot in '97. "We basically came back with the same team, minus John Wetteland, but we weren't a band of brothers anymore," said Brian Cashman, who would replace Bob Watson as general manager before the '98 season.

"Cecil started it off in spring training, and then Charlie Hayes and Wade Boggs were fighting like they weren't the year before. All the guys who put aside their personal interests in '96 decided it was time for me, and it really changed the dynamic of our clubhouse. So we purged our clubhouse of a lot of guys guilty of that."

Club officials wanted the Yanks built around Jeter and his team-centric goals, and they were concerned that too many players with self-absorbed pursuits would hurt the cause. So Fielder, Boggs, and Hayes were among those out, along with Kenny Rogers and Doc Gooden.

Watson was another casualty of the '97 season. He had no problem trading a left-handed starter, Rogers, for a third baseman hitting .203 in Oakland, Scott Brosius. But Watson refused to deal a left-handed first-round pick, Eric Milton, and a highly rated infield prospect, Cristian Guzman, for Minnesota's All-Star second baseman, Chuck Knoblauch, whose required wage was too rich for the Twins' small-market blood.

Minnesota initially asked for Williams and Andy Pettitte, "and I told Mr. Steinbrenner that if we waited there was a good possibility we'd get [Knoblauch] for two broken fungo bats and a bag of BP balls," Watson said. "Minnesota wasn't going to spring training with Knoblauch contract-wise, so they would've come off Milton and Guzman, too."

From afar, Steinbrenner had fallen in love with Knoblauch, and once Steinbrenner fell in love with someone else's player he would not be denied. Knoblauch had speed (62 stolen bases in '97), a little pop in his bat, and sure enough hands to win a Gold Glove. Steinbrenner saw Minnesota's second baseman as the perfect long-term partner for Jeter.

So he ordered Watson to do the deal for Milton and Guzman, and the GM refused, telling the Boss he had been hired to protect the franchise's assets. Steinbrenner would not back down, and neither would Watson.

"Mr. Steinbrenner told me someone else would make the deal, and I told him I'd have to respectfully resign," Watson said. "He had the trade made, and I packed my little box under my desk and that was it."

Watson was a burned-out mess, beaten down by Steinbrenner's relentless verbal assaults. So he stepped down, compelling the Boss to promote the thirty-year-old Cashman. The new GM was ordered to give the Twins what they wanted, and Steinbrenner got his man, a natural leadoff hitter who could move Jeter to the two-hole.

"Joe Montana," A-Rod said of Jeter, "just found his Jerry Rice."

Rodriguez had played with Knoblauch in some exhibition games in Japan. "Chuck Knoblauch is such a good player I'm not even sure New York knows what it has," A-Rod gushed. "Chuck and Derek are both Gold Glove–type guys on defense and great offensive players. I think this probably gives the Yankees the best shortstop–second base combination in the whole league."

Publicly, A-Rod was saying he wanted Jeter to forge a perfect union with Knoblauch and to watch them live happily ever after. Privately, according to a friend of A-Rod's, Rodriguez was already jealous of the off-the-charts popularity Jeter enjoyed in the world's biggest market while he was posting far superior numbers in Seattle.

The self-esteem issues identified by Caruso four years earlier fed A-Rod's Jeter envy. Rodriguez had once said of the Yankee shortstop, "He's smarter than me, though. He got 1,200 on his SATs. I got 910. My reading comprehension held me back, because we speak only Spanish at home."

A-Rod would marvel over the way Jeter handled the New York traffic and the scores of fans who approached his car to request/demand an autograph, and would suggest he could not possibly manage the same hectic pace. For his part, Jeter would say Rodriguez deserved the AL MVP award for setting an offensive standard at short that could not be touched.

"I think we bring out the best in one another," Jeter said.

At the time Jeter respected Rodriguez's opinion as much as his game, and so he accepted his February 1998 endorsement of Knoblauch as gospel. Jeter did not want to knock his previous partners, Mariano Duncan and Luis Sojo and Rey Sanchez. "But Chuck can hit, steal bases, turn a double play," Jeter said, "everything you could want in a second baseman. . . . I'm looking forward to it. We all think we have a shot at winning another championship."

A shot? As the Yankees gathered at their spring training base in Tampa, Steinbrenner did not want to believe he had made a $72 million payroll investment in a shot. The Boss thought he was paying for a sure thing.

So it was fully expected that Torre would face the kind of win-or-else mandate that came with one of those fat Steinbrenner paychecks. "When I was a football coach at Northwestern," the Boss said, "we had no materials and couldn't do a thing. When I was at Purdue we had Lenny Dawson, other horses, and we won.

"Now we've given Joe Torre the horses."

Steinbrenner said that he did not want Torre to feel any pressure, that their relationship might be the best he ever had with a manager. But the Boss also maintained he had never worked harder to put together a roster, a clear message he expected that hard work to be honored.

Steinbrenner also went public with the unnecessary reminder that he had pulled the thrice-fired Torre from the scrap heap. "When we hired Joe," the Boss said, "everyone said, 'What the hell are you doing? This guy's a loser.'"

If that comment did not dent Torre's faith in himself, Steinbrenner's guarantee that his manager would remain gainfully employed for the entire season — regardless of the Yanks' record — did not comfort him, either.

Torre understood Steinbrenner's terms of engagement. After getting eliminated in the first round of the playoffs, Torre knew only a second title in three years would ensure his return for the 1999 season.

"At least when you get fired here," the manager said, "you had a chance to win. When I got fired in St. Louis, I was told I needed to do more of this and that. Of course, it came down to the fact we didn't have the team. That bothered me. Here, you're going to get a better-than-honest chance because George isn't playing for second place."

Torre looked around his clubhouse and liked what he saw. By and large, the malcontents were going, going, gone, including Gooden, who trashed Torre on exit. Chili Davis was a likable addition and a powerful force from both sides of the plate. Knoblauch added an element of speed to a franchise often lacking it.

Torre was concerned about his starting pitching, even though he rejoiced over the subtraction of Rogers. David Cone, David Wells, and Andy Pettitte gave him a formidable top three, but Ramiro Mendoza was not a proven starter and the acclaimed Japanese pitcher acquired in a trade with San Diego, Hideki Irabu, was a proven pain in the ass.

Irabu did nothing to ease Torre's concerns about him or the Yankees' $12.8 million investment in him when the pitcher confronted a Japanese cameraman for the crime of shooting video of him, stomped on the man's foot, and seized and destroyed his tape.

"You can take that up with the gossip writers," an annoyed Torre told reporters.

Only the gossip writers had not come to Tampa to write about the overweight, overheated, and overrated Hideki Irabu.

They had come to write about Derek Jeter and Mariah Carey.

The first reports of their romance had surfaced the year before, around the time Carey split from her much older husband, Tommy Mottola, the Sony Music Entertainment president who discovered her. Jeter denied those initial reports, saying, "Man, I'm supposed to be dating everybody. First it was Tyra Banks. Now it's Mariah Carey."

Now that Carey was sitting in the Legends Field stands, fresh off her quickie Caribbean divorce of Mottola, there was no denying it anymore.

Jeter had done it again. As a child he had predicted he would grow up to become the shortstop of the New York Yankees, and talent and luck conspired to make it happen. As a teenager he had predicted he would marry Mariah Carey, and his fame and fortune and looks put him in play to become the songbird's second spouse.

Like Jeter, Carey was the child of an African-American father and Irish-American mother. But her parents went through a bitter divorce when she was three. Mariah was raised by her mother in Huntington, New York, where she said she "grew up with nothing." She encountered the same racism Jeter faced in his Kalamazoo youth, and she said she felt like an outcast in high school.

"So when I saw how great [Jeter's] family was," Carey would say, "it gave me hope. I realized that I was blaming all the problems of my life on growing up biracial. Derek's family functioned great as a unit, and I'd never seen that before. I looked at Derek, and it changed my perception."

They were very much a spring training item, and back in Kalamazoo, Jeter's old friends and teammates could not get over the news. "It was unbelievable," said Chad Casserly, one summer league teammate who had heard Jeter predict he would wed Carey. "Everything Derek said he'd do he followed through on."

Only he had not married Mariah just yet. Jeter and Carey were seen in Tampa restaurants, seen leaving Legends Field arm in arm. They had so much in common — they were young, biracial, and blessed with gifts that captivated millions. The shortstop and the songbird were falling in love, and Jeter found it hard to believe.

He used to sing Mariah's hits on minor league buses, and here she was showing up to watch Jeter perform on his stage. She would sign autographs between innings, spend a little time in the players' family lounge, and join Jeter for a dinner with Tino and Marie Martinez.

Naturally, a curious public wanted to know if the relationship had staying power. "Baseball is baseball and my personal life is separate from that," Jeter said. "I don't talk about that stuff."

Only it was not that simple. The *New York Post* was about to report that Jeter and Carey were getting married, and the *Post*'s new Yankee beat writer, George King, drew the assignment of asking the shortstop for a confirmation.

Jeter angrily denied the story. "I am not getting married," he said. He also reportedly rebuked a teammate who was teasing him about Carey before a spring training game in Clearwater.

Mariah-mania was taking its toll; the shortstop did not want to talk about his fantasy girl with his teammates or the press. "I'm here to answer baseball questions," Jeter said. "Nobody asks Tim Raines where he ate with his wife last night."

Nobody cared where Mr. and Mrs. Raines went to dinner, other than Mr. and Mrs. Raines. But Derek and Mariah represented the most fascinating Yankee romance since DiMaggio and Monroe.

Jeter was no longer the semi-famous rookie walking through New Jersey's Garden State Plaza, trying and failing to pick up an attractive brunette who did not recognize him and who told him she was not interested (to his credit, Jeter never told the woman he was a Yankee).

He had become a full-blown international celebrity, something he never desired. "That's the reason why I never want to talk about it," Jeter would say. "They say I've bought a ring. They have us getting married on an off day. It doesn't matter what I say. People start making stuff up out of the blue and write whatever they want.

"I am not engaged. I am not getting married."

Carey did what she could to help out her boyfriend. "There is no engagement," she said. "There is no ring."

Before Jeter pursued a ring of a different kind — his second championship ring — he had gotten a taste of transcendent celebrity, and he despised it. Carey? She was a blossoming diva who thrived on the fuss.

Steinbrenner was concerned his shortstop might take his eye off the ball while dating one of the few young performers in America who had a bigger and more passionate following than he did, and those fears were unfounded.

Jeter had bought a place in Tampa to put in extra conditioning work at the team's facilities, and he was known to have a commitment to excellence matched only by Steinbrenner's. His cage work and tee work were supplemented by years of fielding drills with a small Rawlings training glove he loathed, a glove Yankee instructor and minor league manager Trey Hillman forced him to use.

"He'd get all bent out of shape when I made him put it on," Hillman said. "The whole point was to try to get him to flex at the knees a bit more because his frame is so tall. He never did flex as much as I wanted him to, but he made the adjustments he needed to make, anyway."

Jeter started the 1998 season on a mission to right the individual and team wrongs of 1997, and to silence the growing chorus of voices suggesting he was the overhyped product of his market, uniform, and looks. Popular opinion had Jeter behind Alex Rodriguez and Boston's breakout star, Nomar Garciaparra, on any credible ranking of AL shortstops.

The Yankees gave him a bigger 1998 salary than they had to, anyway. Like Mariano Rivera, a third-year player eligible for arbitration in year four, Jeter took the $750,000 — a bump from his $550,000 salary in '97 — and went about his business.

Jeter had already hoped to be working on a multiyear contract. According to Ray Negron, a longtime Steinbrenner aide, Jeter approached him the previous spring in Tampa with this request:

"Can you talk to Mr. Steinbrenner about giving me a five-year contract?"

Negron did just that. Steinbrenner laughed and told Negron to have Jeter see him after a luncheon the following day. The shortstop and owner took a short walk with Negron.

"Derek, I could take advantage of you and sign you to a long-term contract," Steinbrenner told Jeter. "But I'm not going to do that to you because you're going to make a hell of a lot more money than you would in the contract I'd give you now. I'm not going to do that to you. You don't realize how much is ahead and how much money you're going to make."

"I understand. I understand," Jeter responded.

"Trust me," the Boss said. "I'm going to do the right thing by you."

No, Steinbrenner was not the same owner who wondered if the rookie Jeter could start for his team. Despite his concerns over Mariah-mania and the disappointments of the previous season, the Boss realized Jeter was a franchise cornerstone, a Yankee out of central casting.

So off went Jeter, Steinbrenner, and the rest of the New York Yankees on a journey unlike any in team history. Steinbrenner had signed a Cuban defector, Orlando "El Duque" Hernandez, to fortify his slightly suspect pitching staff, and he had in Knoblauch, Jeter, Paul O'Neill, Williams, Martinez, and Davis a top six in the order that would unnerve any opposing team's ace.

Yes, George Steinbrenner had given Joe Torre the horses. Lots and lots of horses.

But when they got out of the gate 1-4 on the West Coast, Steinbrenner forgot all about his declaration that his manager would be safe for the year, regardless of his record. Before the season started, the owner jokingly asked Torre if any team had gone 162-0.

Steinbrenner was not joking anymore. Naturally, the crushing Division Series defeat in Cleveland the previous fall had changed his relationship with Torre. So when the manager dropped the '98 season opener in Anaheim, nobody was surprised when the Boss complained to *Newsday*'s Jon Heyman, "We're behind the Tampa Bay Devil Rays in our division right now."

Three more losses over the next four games, compounded by Rivera's groin injury and Davis's ankle injury, locked the Yankees inside another crisis. Torre did not need Steinbrenner to announce he was in trouble; he had been fired enough to know the feeling. He did not need to see the walls closing in on him to know that they were.

But then his Yankees scored six runs in their very next inning, beat the Mariners by a 13–7 count, and suddenly the team Steinbrenner thought should win 162 games started looking like one that would win 100.

The Yanks ripped off eight straight, fourteen of fifteen, and twenty-five of twenty-eight. Jeter was batting .319, still seeing Mariah, and still impressing the older veterans with his ability to make a brutally difficult game look like so much fun.

Jeter's Yankees were majoring in fun. On May 17, before a Bronx crowd of 49,820, David Wells — a more imperfect man than Don Larsen could ever be — threw the second perfect game in franchise history, beating the Twins by a 4–0 count.

Jorge Posada, who was supplanting Joe Girardi at catcher, solidified his presence behind the plate; the disagreeable Wells shook him off only twice. Chuck Knoblauch, who was raising concerns about his alleged Gold Glove defense with his erratic arm, made the most conspicuous history-preserving play when he knocked down Ron Coomer's short-hop liner with a backhand in the eighth and made a sound throw to first.

The 1998 Yankees had declared themselves: at every turn they would try to expand the boundaries of human achievement. Would the Yankees win more games in 162 attempts than the '27 Yankees won in 154 (110)? Would they win more games than the 1906 Cubs, who held the record at 116-36?

Only this much was certain at the halfway point, with the Yanks at an all-time best 61-20: they thought their B lineup was as good as their

A lineup. Strawberry and Raines came off the bench, as did Homer Bush, who electrified the home crowd with his speed and his .380 batting average as Knoblauch's backup.

Among the new acquisition starters, Knoblauch was not what he had been in Minnesota, but he was good enough. Scott Brosius was a much stronger hitter in the Bronx than he had been in Oakland; he was a Clark Kent using the Yankee clubhouse as his phone booth. And the mystery man, El Duque, who claimed to have escaped Cuba on a leaky raft, combined with Wells, Cone, and Pettitte to give Torre four starters who would have been worthy aces on most staffs.

"But Derek was the centerpiece of the entire team," Cone said. "We took on his persona, which was to show up and win the game no matter what happened the day before. We never changed who we were, no matter how many games in a row we won, and a lot of that was Derek's personality.

"He was more of a leader than anyone knew. We had a relentless nature where nobody gave away an at-bat no matter what the score was, and that's who Derek was."

Jeter missed a dozen games in June with a strained abdominal muscle and still was named an All-Star for the first time, an honor that hardened his standing as a team leader at the age of twenty-four.

He was able to maintain a dignified presence while lightening the clubhouse load with his boyish energy. Jeter would tell Teammate A that Teammate B was ragging on him, almost always when Teammate B had done no such thing. Jeter freely traded playful insults with thirty-eight-year-old Raines, their routine open for all to hear, and veterans often credited the shortstop's approach for relieving the pressure as the victories and expectations mounted.

"Derek's so much more colorful inside the locker room than he is out on the field," said O'Neill, "and over the course of the year our team needed that."

O'Neill needed it as much as anyone. Beaten down by Lou Piniella in Cincinnati, tortured by his own expectations, the right fielder was forever slamming down helmets, throwing bats, and cursing the fates. O'Neill could not see a 4-for-5 day at the plate as anything other than a lost opportunity to go 5 for 5.

Like Jeter, O'Neill was angered when removed from the lineup and given a day off. Unlike the shortstop, the right fielder often ripped his manager to a coach when it happened.

In the pre-Torre days, O'Neill would be standing next to Brian Butterfield in the outfield when Buck Showalter approached with the grim pregame news. "Here comes that stumpy little fuck to give me his bullshit on why I'm not playing," O'Neill would tell Butterfield.

Showalter forgave him; he knew O'Neill's inner flame burned hotter than most. The right fielder remained the same brooding, tightly wound creature under Torre, but Torre had help his predecessor did not have, help in the soothing form of Derek Jeter.

"I never played with anybody who was able to do a photo shoot in the morning and be locked in to play at seven o'clock like Derek could," O'Neill said. "He amazed me."

Surely, subtly, Jeter grabbed his team by the throat. But the Yankees did not revolve only around Jeter; they revolved around his bond with Torre, who saw his shortstop the way John Wooden always saw his point guard — as a coach on the floor.

"Jeet believed in Joe's way," said Mike Borzello, the Yankees' bullpen catcher and Torre's godson, "and everyone kind of felt, 'If Jeet believes in it, we have to believe in it.'

"Jeet and Joe were both positive thinkers, they didn't overreact to anything, and they didn't show their emotions until the very end. It was a perfect marriage."

If the Yankees needed a buffer between manager and clubhouse, Jeter assumed the role. It made sense. Jeter always saw himself as a unifier, as someone who could reach different people because of his biracial roots. Given that he always had white and black friends, and always had people believing he was Hispanic or Italian or Jewish or French, Jeter said, "I think I can relate to everyone."

He related to the manager better than any fellow Yankee. Mike Buddie, once a Class A pitcher with Jeter in Greensboro, finally made it to the Bronx in '98 and saw veterans such as Raines, Martinez, and Knoblauch go to Jeter with matters they did not want to take straight to Torre.

Buddie saw two undisputed leaders in the clubhouse — Cone for the pitchers, Jeter for the position players. "And Derek brings out a humanity in managers that makes everybody more comfortable with them," Buddie said.

"Derek can be goofing around with Joe Torre, and instead of gasping and saying, 'Oh, my God, that's Joe Torre,' you're thinking, 'I can't believe Jeter just taped his shoes together.' Derek keeps everybody loose and honest."

Back in Greensboro, Buddie had been a college player out of Wake Forest four years older than Jeter, and he had been among the team leaders who made sure to include the teenager in almost everything they did.

By '98, Derek Jeter was famous enough to make the cover of *GQ*. His fan mail could practically fill the entire clubhouse if he let it go for a month. And yet with Buddie trying to keep his mouth shut and stay out of a juggernaut's way, Jeter returned his bygone favor and—without patronizing the spare-part pitcher—made Buddie feel as welcome in the clubhouse and at nightspots as Pettitte or Cone.

After the '98 home opener, Buddie and his wife were celebrating his first appearance in Yankee Stadium and his first major league victory when Jeter's parents approached. Charles and Dot told Buddie they were so proud of him and greeted his wife, Traci, by name.

"They hadn't seen us in years, their son's become Derek Jeter, and they even remembered my wife's name," Buddie said. "That explains why Derek's so likable, the way he was raised."

In August, Jeter became the first Yankee to collect 50 hits in a month since Joe DiMaggio's 53 in July of 1941, the very month DiMaggio saw his 56-game hitting streak come to an end. On September 9, Jeter achieved something far more dear to his heart.

He clinched another division title in a 7–5 victory over the Red Sox that improved the Yankees' record to 102-41 and their divisional lead to twenty and a half games. Jeter blasted 2 homers off Boston knuckleballer Tim Wakefield in the victory, giving him 19 for the season, 3 more than the previous high for a Yankee shortstop (Roy Smalley in 1982).

Amid the clubhouse celebration, with Heineken beer dripping from his divisional championship cap, Jeter was asked about his chances to win the American League MVP award. "It's not really something that I think about," he said.

"You can make a case for any person on this team to be MVP. It's been that type of year. Tino Martinez is having a great year, Paul O'Neill is, Bernie Williams, David Cone as well. There are twenty-five guys. You can make a case for all of them. We're playing on an MVP team."

At a time when the country was swept away by superhuman individual feats, by the home-run derby staged by Mark McGwire and Sammy Sosa at the expense of Roger Maris's single-season record, the Yankees were dominating the sport one base and one at-bat at a time. They were as perfect a team as Don Shula's 1972 Dolphins.

Williams had missed thirty-one games because of a knee injury suffered in June, and the Yankees kept winning with Chad Curtis in center. Chili Davis missed more than four months with his ankle injury and returned to find his chief replacement, Strawberry, leading the team with 22 homers.

"We had a great team, great camaraderie, great everything," O'Neill said. "If you go up and down our roster, nobody really had a bad year. We went into cities and it was like, 'Are we going to sweep these guys or take two out of three?' It got to the point where sweeping teams came naturally to us."

So did the all-for-one, one-for-all mentality that defined the Yankees — at least until the night of September 18, when David Wells acted like a horse's rump for the sake of old times. In the middle of a 15–5 rout of the Orioles at Camden Yards, Baltimore's Danny Clyburn hit a high pop between shortstop and left. When Jeter and Curtis and Ricky Ledee failed to run it down, Wells gestured in disgust, slapped his hands on his hips, and stared down his teammates.

Jeter should have caught the ball; even Torre agreed with that. The shortstop quit running for it too soon and allowed it to fall. But Wells had no right to put on this childish show, and Jeter let him know it. "Don't show me up in front of people," he warned the pitcher in the dugout.

Jeter dressed and left the clubhouse without speaking to the news media; Wells would tell reporters that his conduct was "totally unprofessional on my part." The following day, acting on a tip that Jeter had engaged in a heated confrontation with Wells over his humiliating body language, Buster Olney of the *New York Times* asked the shortstop for a comment on his source's account.

Jeter turned angry and raised his voice. "Where did you get that bullshit?" he asked. Olney tried to calm the shortstop so his competition would not hear their exchange. "You're just trying to start something," Jeter barked.

Just as Knoblauch drifted toward the conversation, Jeter sensed the living, breathing presence of an alibi.

"Hey, Buster is trying to say shit happened between Boomer and me," he said to Knoblauch, hoping his double-play partner would play along. Only the second baseman had never been mistaken for a nuclear physicist.

"Yeah, it was wild, wasn't it?" Knoblauch said.

Olney wrote what he had to write and did not hold Jeter's rare lie against him. For the shortstop, it wasn't personal, just business. He did not believe the confirmation of in-house strife was good for the business of winning.

Jeter was quite stubborn about his articles of game-day faith. He believed in being accessible to reporters, in being accountable for poor play. He was distant and guarded but was not one to be rude. Jeter did not allocate his time and attention based on the size of a newspaper's circulation, or on the coverage area of a TV station, a game played by so many star ballplayers and coaches. Jeter gave the same say-nothing answers to the *New York Times* and the *Poughkeepsie Journal*.

In a locker room culture where many multimillionaire athletes would just as soon meet a reporter's question with repeated belching and flatulence, Jeter's locker was a sanctuary of sorts. He was never going to embarrass anyone who approached his stall. He was available, benign, and cognizant of the fact that a quote from his mouth — even if it amounted to a run-on cliché — carried weight in anyone's report.

But Jeter did not believe in making his private thoughts and emotions public. So with the playoffs fast approaching, he was not about to provide details on his summer breakup with the poster girl on his bedroom wall.

Mariah Carey — and the attention she craved — wore him out, simple as that. "It was the wrong time," Carey would say of their romance. "Our two worlds were just too much for that moment."

It had nothing to do with baseball, even if some whispered that Mariah-mania was behind Jeter's early struggles at the plate. "I'm just a singer," Carey would be quoted as saying, "not some magical genie who can make or break someone's game."

Jeter said his mother and sister represented a tough screening committee for his prospective girlfriends, and his sister, Sharlee, would say Carey passed the test. "I found Mariah to be a good person," she said, "and I trust Derek's judgment. But he's my brother, and I want to keep him away from women who only care about his fame."

Carey had enough fame for the both of them. Regardless, the breakup between the singer and the ballplayer was a predictable development to the veteran New Yorkers who had watched the graceful way Jeter carried himself around the city's social landscape.

"Derek needs to write a book for the rest of us on how to do it," Cone said. "I don't know where he's hiding or what he's doing, but he stays out of the clubs, stays out of where the paparazzi hangs, and goes to the movie theater a lot, goes to dinner. If he has a drink it might be a light beer. He never puts himself in a position to be taken advantage of, not even for a little bit.

"If he's gone to clubs here and there he's gotten out early. He's found ways to get into them by the back door and then left by midnight. You'd never catch him in a club at four in the morning. With Mariah, through my connections in clubs, she didn't start her nights until after midnight, 1:00 a.m. No way Jeter was going for that."

So Derek dumped her. In fact, the dumping was decisive enough to give birth to a new street verb — Jeter. To "Jeter" someone suddenly meant to break up with a girlfriend or boyfriend in an abrupt and don't-even-think-about-getting-back-together way.

Mariah would be reportedly "Jetered" after the season, when the *Daily News* said she approached her ex at Sean "Puffy" Combs's party at Cipriani on Wall Street and flirted away, only to have the shortstop turn his back on her.

But Jeter did not say a single bad word about Carey and her high-maintenance ways, even if he was baited by his old friend R. D. Long.

"I'd be telling him, 'I told you, it's just a matter of time before she pissed you off . . . ,'" Long said. "He'd say, 'Oh, man, she's all right, man. She's OK.' . . . That's Derek. He wouldn't bash her. He doesn't bash anybody. I told him, 'You've got to find a girl who's grounded,' and he wouldn't criticize her."

Jeter was not terribly enthused about the aggressive photographers who tracked them, or the opposing fans who chanted Mariah's name, or the stadium operators who played Mariah's songs when he stepped to the plate on the road. Jeter would confess he could not adjust to the relentless attention he received as Mariah Carey's boyfriend. "It didn't bother her the way it bothered me," he would say.

In the book he would write with Jack Curry, *The Life You Imagine*, Jeter would also say the Carey relationship taught him it "would be very difficult for me to seriously date a high-profile person." Over time Jeter would defy his own words by courting an endless procession of starlets and supermodels.

But baseball was his first love, and Jeter was playing it as a precious few could. He lost the batting title to Bernie Williams over the final two weeks of the season as he swung for the fences in his failed pursuit of his twentieth homer, yet Jeter's .324 average was still a point better than Nomar Garciaparra's and 14 points better than Alex Rodriguez's.

He stole 30 bases, led the AL with 127 runs, and became the only Yankee shortstop not named Phil Rizzuto to collect at least 200 hits in a single season. Jeter had scored more runs in his first three full seasons (347) than any shortstop before him, and he would finish third in the league MVP voting.

On the other side of the ball, Jeter committed only 9 errors in 625 chances, a long, long way from his 56 errors in 506 chances in Greensboro five years earlier. His Yankees finished 114-48, the most victories in AL history. Their .704 winning percentage was the best in baseball since the 1954 Cleveland Indians won at a .721 clip (111-43).

The summer belonged to McGwire's 70 homers and to Sosa's 66, both sums mocking the standard of 61 set by Maris in '61. Only the sport would not be about the sluggers and their comic-book muscles in October.

It would be about a team that did not dress a single 30-homer hitter, a team that could not afford to go out like those '54 Indians, swept in the World Series by the New York Giants.

After the Yankees' 114th and final regular-season victory, George Steinbrenner marched into his clubhouse and announced he had been reading *Cigars, Whiskey & Winning: Leadership Lessons from General Ulysses S. Grant.*

"We're about ready to go to war," Steinbrenner said. "And I love war."

His shortstop had a far less flamboyant way of declaring the same thing.

"It makes no difference what we did in the regular season," Derek Jeter said.

On the night of October 13, in the sixth game of the American League Championship Series, Derek Jeter came to the plate in the eighth inning with a postseason batting average of .156.

He had made a big defensive play on a broken-bat dribbler near the end of Game 1 of the Division Series sweep over Texas, a play David Wells said had saved the game. Jeter had also applied his leadership skills across the first five games of the ALCS matchup with Cleveland. He had reassured his friend Chuck Knoblauch, after he had committed an embarrassing mental error in the twelfth inning of the Game 2 loss (Knoblauch blew his gum into a bubble and argued with an ump rather than chase a loose ball near first base), and he had relaxed a drum-tight Joe Torre before Game 4.

"Derek came walking down the dugout," said Torre's bench coach, Don Zimmer, "and sticks a finger in [Torre's] chest and says, 'Mr. Torre, you know this is the most important game in your life.' And everybody cracked up."

Down 2–1 to the Indians, still feeling the weight of a 114-win regular season and an overbearing owner terrified of losing again to his hometown team, Torre was bailed out by El Duque Hernandez in Game 4 and by David Wells in Game 5.

Back in the Bronx for Game 6, Torre felt good about having 20-game winner David Cone on the mound protecting a 6–0 lead in the fifth. But just like that, Cone walked in a run and Jim Thome blasted a grand slam, sending a tense night and a tense series reeling toward who knew where.

The next inning, Jeter's counterpart at short, the great Omar Vizquel, threw high to first and committed his first error in 47 postseason games and 237 postseason chances. Two batters later, with two on and one out, Jeter was a welcome sight to Cleveland reliever Dave Burba.

Jeter was 5 for 32 in the playoffs, 1 for 14 in his previous four games. In nine regular-season and postseason at-bats against Burba, Jeter had three strikeouts and one infield hit and had failed to put a single fair ball in the air. But on Burba's first pitch to the shortstop on this night, Jeter loosed that inside-out swing of his and sent a deep fly to right field that would inspire another wild, crazy, and prosperous result.

No twelve-year-old boy would define this play, just a right fielder who preferred to act like one. Manny Ramirez raced for the wall, turned his back to the ball, and never again tracked its flight. Instead Ramirez planted his spikes into the blue padding and began his dramatic, breathless climb while Jeter's shot hit the base of the wall about five feet to his left.

As the full Yankee Stadium house exploded, Jeter raced all the way to third. Two runs were in, the home team had an 8–5 lead, and the Indians would be left to listen to the crowd chant "1948"—their last championship season. Jeter robbed Travis Fryman on a grounder up the middle in the eighth, and Mariano Rivera finished off Cleveland on Vizquel's grounder back to the mound in the ninth.

The 1998 Yanks had exorcised a 1997 haunt. "It's like getting a knife stuck in your heart," Vizquel said afterward. "Your body goes stone cold."

On the winning side of the Bronx, only the champagne was stone cold. The Yanks' celebration was tempered only by the fact that Darryl Strawberry was not part of it; Strawberry was resting inside Columbia-Presbyterian after undergoing surgery to remove a cancerous tumor in his colon.

When players were not in the trainer's room talking to Strawberry on the phone, they were dousing each other in the clubhouse and trying to stay clear of George Steinbrenner, who was conducting interviews in the middle of the room. Jeter spotted the owner and made a move only he could get away with.

"Hold on, hold on," the shortstop shouted as he headed toward the bone-dry Boss. "Oh, Boss Man. Somebody's dry around here."

With that Jeter poured a bottle of champagne over his employer's head. Steinbrenner laughed and asked for someone to get him a towel. His eyes blinded by the sweetest sting, the Boss barked, "Where is that Jeter?"

On his way to another World Series parade.

As it turned out, the San Diego Padres were accidental tourists in the Fall Classic, arriving in New York as the ultimate just-happy-to-be-here props. Jeter hit a Game 1 single that helped set up Tino Martinez's deciding grand slam off Mark Langston — with a little help from plate umpire Rich Garcia, he of Jeffrey Maier fame, on a 2-2 pitch that should have been ruled a strike — and the Padres just about folded on command.

Scott Brosius delivered the crushing three-run blow against Trevor Hoffman in Game 3, silencing Qualcomm Stadium and, ultimately, nailing down the MVP award. Jeter singled and scored what would be the championship-clinching run in Game 4 — of course he did. He also worked an eighth-inning walk and scored the second run in a 3–0 victory that gave the Yankees their twenty-fourth World Series title and a staggering 125 victories in all.

Steinbrenner had been in talks to sell the Yankees to Cablevision in a potential deal that would allow him to maintain some control over the team, but suddenly he was not so eager to relinquish the brand that had made him an American titan.

Even before the first Game 4 pitch was thrown, Steinbrenner suspended all of his nagging superstitions, his maddening fear of jinxes, to answer a reporter's phone call and announce the following: "I think you have to say it now. Twenty years from now, people will look back on this team as truly the greatest of all time."

No team had ever won 125 games. "I don't see how you can say we aren't the greatest team ever," Jeter said when the sweep was complete. No, Steinbrenner wasn't letting go of that.

In the bowels of Qualcomm, the Yankees enjoyed yet another champagne bath, and Jeter — who hit .353 in the World Series — enjoyed yet another chance to dump a bottle of bubbly over Steinbrenner's head.

With the owner's familiar blue blazer and white turtleneck drenched in the victor's spoils, Steinbrenner joked that his shortstop was the only Yankee who could survive such a fireable offense.

They took a 2,800-mile victory flight home, rode in another war hero's parade, and gathered for another City Hall ceremony. Jeter led the league in marriage proposals one more time.

"I don't think there's a person in the world who's been more spoiled than I've been," he said at the ceremony.

Better yet, Jeter's luck wasn't about to turn. He was just starting a dizzying run of on- and off-field successes, one that would make him the DiMaggio and Mantle of his time.

An eighteen-year-old Jeter, a few months removed from his high school graduation, appears on the Yankee Stadium field, in Yankee colors, for the first time and receives tips from Jim Leyritz and Mike Gallego.

Richard Harbus/AP Photo

Baseball America's 1994 minor league Player of the Year holds his first trophy in the Bronx.

Mark Lennihan/AP Photo

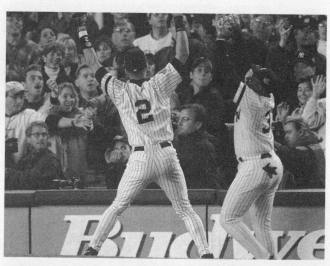

The rookie shortstop throws his arms toward the sky as Charlie Hayes records the final out of the 1996 World Series, the first of seven trips to the Fall Classic (five of them victorious) for the iconic number 2.   *Kathy Willens/AP Photo*

Derek Jeter was the one employee who could get away with pouring champagne over George Steinbrenner's head, as the shortstop did here to celebrate the 1999 ALCS victory over Boston.

Matt York/Reuters/Corbis

Derek Jeter deflates the Mets on the very first pitch from Bobby Jones in Game 4 of the 2000 World Series, homering on his way to winning the Series MVP award.

Peter Morgan/Reuters/Corbis

Perhaps the most memorable play ever made by a big-league infielder, Jeter completes his epic flip to Jorge Posada to get a standing Jeremy Giambi at the plate during Game 3 of the 2001 Division Series.

Eric Risberg/AP Photo

Mr. November wins Game 4 of the 2001 World Series with his tenth-inning homer off Arizona's Byung-Hyun Kim.

Shaun Best/Reuters/Corbis

No pain, no gain. On opening night, 2003, Jeter's devastating collision at third base with Toronto catcher Ken Huckaby left the shortstop with a dislocated shoulder.

Mike Cassese/Reuters/Corbis

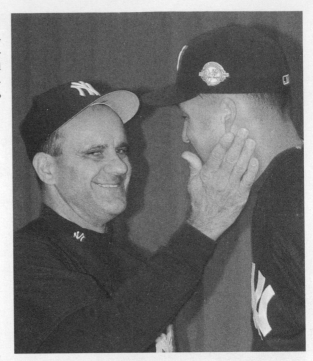

Joe Torre applies his fatherly touch to his favorite player on the day Jeter was named captain of the Yankees.
Al Behrman/AP Photo

Derek Jeter was not quite as thrilled as Joe Torre to welcome Alex Rodriguez to the Bronx in 2004. *Jason Szenes/epa/Corbis*

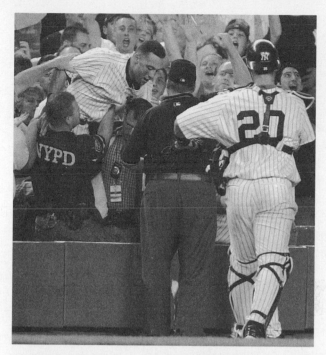

A bruised and bloodied Jeter is helped out of the stands after his catch and face-first dive against Boston in 2004.

Mike Segar/Reuters/Corbis

The shortstop's signature play — the jump throw from the hole — from start to finish.

John Angelillo/UPI

A dropped pop-up in a blowout loss in 2006 and the captain's staredown of A-Rod elevated their feud to Defcon 1.

Ray Stubblebine/Reuters/Corbis

Derek Jeter and teammates wave their caps to the crowd after Jeter delivered his postgame speech on Yankee Stadium's final night.   *John Angelillo/UPI*

The captain salutes the fans after breaking Lou Gehrig's franchise record for hits.

John Angelillo/UPI

Many longtime Jeter observers expected actress Minka Kelly to end up as the last woman standing.

Jason Szenes/epa/Corbis

Alex Rodriguez celebrates his first trip to the Fall Classic by giving his captain a champagne bath. *Anthony Causi/Icon SMI/Corbis*

A World Series champion at last, Alex Rodriguez embraces Derek Jeter as if he plans on never letting go. *Justin Lane/epa/Corbis*

The captain on his 2009 parade float with his mother Dot, his girlfriend Minka, his sister Sharlee, and his father Charles. *Anthony Causi/Icon SMI/Corbis*

7

Dynasty

DEREK JETER SAT on one side of the table, and his employer sat on the other. The shortstop and the team were much like the New York Yankees and Boston Red Sox — clearly defined enemies prepared to bludgeon each other over a singular prize.

Only this was not the American League pennant at stake, just a ballplayer's pot of gold. Jeter wanted to be paid $5 million for the 1999 season, and Yankees general manager Brian Cashman wanted Jeter to be paid $3.2 million for the 1999 season.

Either way, Jeter understood he could not lose. He was going to make more to play one year of baseball than one of his heroes, Sonny Connors, had made in a lifetime of hard labor.

At sixty-eight, Connors had died of a heart attack in January, devastating his famous grandson. Sonny was the head of maintenance at Queen of Peace in North Arlington, New Jersey, for thirty-six years, and he was so beloved in the parish that the schools were closed for his funeral.

Jeter was a pallbearer and one of nearly a thousand mourners who attended the service. At the end of the Mass, as the casket was taken out of the church, Connors inspired the kind of standing ovation often reserved for his grandson.

"I've been a priest for fifty years," the Queen of Peace pastor, Thomas

Madden, would say, "and that's the only time I've ever heard that kind of applause. It gave you chills. It was like we were honoring a saint."

Sonny was a saint to the Jeters. Derek marveled over his grandfather's refusal to call in sick, over Sonny's insistence that he show up for work regardless of circumstance. Connors was the model for Derek's own relentless commitment to his job.

"He didn't make millions," Jeter said in his clubhouse, "but he affected as many lives as anyone in this room."

Connors died with a salary of $50,000, and his grandson was hardly in the mood to fight his employer over millions of dollars. But the system said Jeter had little choice, so fight his employer he did.

They gathered in a hotel conference room in Tampa to hash it out before a panel of three arbitrators, and deep into this four-hour hearing Cashman knew he might be in a bit of trouble. An attractive attorney on the Yankees' side of the table confided she could not stop staring at Jeter.

If a member of the prosecution team was melting in Jeter's presence, Cashman figured the judges would do the same. He had seen ballplayers use their charms before, especially in the 1994 case involving a first baseman with movie star looks, Kevin Maas, who gave an autograph to an arbitrator while mentioning he had to rush to the airport to return to a pregnant wife who was almost due.

"That bothered me," Cashman said.

The Yankees won the case, but that did not make the process any more enjoyable. Arbitration was about as fun as a daylong trip to a proctologist's office, as it pitted organization against athlete and often fractured otherwise healthy relationships beyond repair.

For the first three years of a player's big league career, the team held the hammer and the ability to renew a contract on its terms. The Yankees had been generous with Jeter and Mariano Rivera in their second and third seasons, paying them wages of $550,000 in '97 and $750,000 in '98 when they could have renewed them for plenty less. The team showed good faith in their homegrown shortstop and closer, critical pieces of two championship teams, and hoped the players would do the same when submitting arbitration bids in years four, five, and six and when negotiating free agent deals after that.

But before their February '99 showdowns with the Yankees, Rivera asked for $4.25 million in arbitration (the team offered to pay $3 million) and Jeter asked for a $4.25 million raise, or an award equaling the second highest in the sport's history. Cashman did not believe his young stars were showing good faith, not after their agents promised the earlier generosity would be reciprocated down the road.

So when Jeter's agent, Casey Close, offered a midpoint settlement of $4.1 million before the hearing was about to start, Cashman shot him down. He was ready to trade heavyweight punches, and he was sure he would be the one walking out of the ring wearing the championship belt.

Cashman and Close were arbitration newcomers, young, bright, and eager to establish something of a courtroom reputation. Close had been a good enough outfielder at the University of Michigan to bat .440 and hit 19 homers as a senior in 1986, to be named *Baseball America*'s College Player of the Year, and to get drafted and signed by a Yankees scout named Dick Groch, who also signed a future Michigan recruit named Derek Jeter.

Close made it to Class AAA ball before ultimately becoming a big league agent with the International Management Group. Only a year on the job, the agent who negotiated Jeter's post-draft deal with the Yankees, Steve Caruso, got a phone call from Charles Jeter explaining the family wanted to make a change.

"And he said, 'Here's the deal. Dot's good friend is Casey Close's mom,'" Caruso said. "He felt it was a family thing, and I'm sure a part of it was you've got IMG as a billion-dollar business, and you've got Steve Caruso with a couple of employees."

Caruso did not lump in Close with the ethics-challenged agents he came to loathe; he thought his replacement had class. But if Caruso knew his firing would cost him some money, he had no idea how much.

On February 15, 1999, Close was about to start showing him. He came to the table armed with claims that Jeter was an intangible genius and good citizen whose value to the Yankee franchise brand could not be measured by stats.

Cashman figured Close was advancing a lost cause. Alex Rodriguez and Nomar Garciaparra were not even scheduled to earn a *combined* $5 million in '99. Kansas City's Johnny Damon was an arbitration loser "stuck" with a $2.1 million wage, and Cashman saw him as a comparable talent even though Jeter's stats were superior and placed him third in the MVP race.

The thirty-one-year-old general manager was in a tough spot. Jeter was sitting right there as the team's heartbeat, the face of the franchise, and it was Cashman's job to throw some heat right under his chin.

So the GM started telling the arbitrators that Jeter was a great Yankee and clutch player and all-around wonderful guy, but that he was a ninety-eight-pound weakling, too. Never mind that Jeter had just set the team record for shortstops with 19 home runs in '98 — A-Rod had smashed 42 and Garciaparra, 35.

Left unspoken was the fact that A-Rod and Nomar were playing in hitter-friendly ballparks, while Jeter was shooting at a left-center wall 399 feet from the plate. As he sat across from this contained assault, oblivious to the attractive female attorney staring at him, Jeter died a thousand deaths.

He was not a young man of many human weaknesses, but truth was, he was not any better at fielding criticism than he had been at fielding those minor league grounders in Greensboro.

"I wouldn't really say it was ugly," said Jeter, "but no one wants to sit there and listen to a team tell you how bad you are. You think you're doing a pretty good job and they tell you how bad you are."

Jeter understood that business was business, and that George Steinbrenner was not a wealthy man because he was in the habit of giving away his money. Jeter also saw how the team had fought Bernie Williams in free agency the previous fall, even agreeing to replace his bat with the one belonging to the vile Albert Belle before Belle reneged on a verbal agreement.

Steinbrenner heard Bernie's impassioned plea to remain a Yankee, and the owner agreed to give Williams $87.5 million to keep him away from the Red Sox. But both sides continued the marriage with fresh, permanent scars.

Jeter had three more seasons to go before he reached free agency, so he had no choice but to listen to the Yankees tell an arbitration panel all about his alleged small-ball approach.

"I need to hit some more home runs, it looks like," Jeter said after the hearing was complete.

"There's no dispute about the player and the talent," Cashman said. "It's just what the deserved pay scale should be."

The following day, the verdict came in. Cashman felt the orgasmic rush of sure victory; the salary figures around baseball were all in his corner. Jeter was asking for the biggest wage ever for a player with three to four years of service time, and Cashman thought Close's chief argument — his client's mass appeal was priceless in the world's biggest market — was one built to lose.

Only the final score in this hotel conference room in Tampa resonated on the ball field in the Bronx: Derek Jeter did not lose. Even when his own mighty Yankees were in the opposing dugout, Jeter found a way to win. Arbitrators Ira Jaffe, Gil Vernon, and Nicholas Zumas decreed the Yankee shortstop was most deserving of a $5 million wage.

In the days to come, Jeter would receive a stack of letters at his spring training locker congratulating him for winning the case. "Kind of overwhelming," the shortstop said.

He would playfully shout to Bernie Williams, "When will you buy me dinner? How does it feel to make $87 million?" and Williams would warn the Yankees that they had better sign Jeter to a long-term deal before his price made Bernie's $87.5 million contract look like a 20 percent tip.

Meanwhile, Jeter's arbitration triumph sent seismic waves crackling across the baseball landscape, leaving every major league executive cowering under his or her desk. Every major league executive but one: George Steinbrenner, owner of the New York Yankees.

Steinbrenner was red with rage. "I would say he is happy for Derek and disappointed in me," said Cashman, who would describe the Boss as "clearly upset."

Steinbrenner did not completely denigrate Cashman publicly, not when the winner here was everybody's all-American boy, Derek Jeter. "He is young and he is learning," Steinbrenner said of his GM. "I hope he has learned a lesson. . . . I hope it's the only thing I lose this year."

The Boss was hoping against hope. In the immediate wake of his loss to Jeter and Close, Cashman went down swinging against his closer, Rivera, who won an arbitration judgment of $4.25 million against the team's bid of $3 million. As was the case before the Jeter hearing, the player's agent approached Cashman with a settlement offer, this time at $3.9 million.

The GM had just cost Steinbrenner $900,000 by rejecting Close's compromise figure, and he could not afford to go 0 for 2. Cashman could have played it safe, agreed to pay Rivera $3.9 million, and stayed out of harm's way.

But rather than follow his survivor's instinct, Cashman followed his heart and head. He decided there would be no deal.

Cashman guessed wrong again, leaving the Yankees as the only franchise to lose in the first eight arbitration cases that were heard. By refusing to settle on Jeter and Rivera, Cashman cost his company a combined $1.25 million in the two hearings. "These were two costly decisions," he agreed.

They would not be costly just for Steinbrenner; they would be costly for Cashman, too. The Boss blistered him for losing both ends of this double-header and decided Cashman needed to pick up a small part of the tab.

"I got my World Series bonus pulled, fifty grand," Cashman said. "I didn't think it was fair, but that's life. That's working for George. Losing bothers him, and so does being taken advantage of. If he goes to a basketball game and he thinks his seat sucks, that's losing to him, and he doesn't like it."

Steinbrenner lost to Rivera after he had lost to Jeter, so Cashman would be his personal piñata for some time. Never mind that the Rivera defeat came on the same day Cashman executed only the second-biggest trade in franchise history, right behind the $100,000 purchase of Babe Ruth.

The GM had put together a megadeal with the Toronto Blue Jays that required a full meeting of Steinbrenner's cabinet. The Boss gathered his top officials at his favorite Tampa restaurant, Malio's, and asked them to vote on the proposal Cashman had before him: David "Boomer" Wells, Graeme Lloyd, and Homer Bush to Toronto for Roger Clemens.

Clemens was quite possibly the greatest pitcher of his generation and an ace Steinbrenner had been courting for years, even lifting weights with the Rocket during a recruiting visit at his home. The Boss wanted him badly, but he had built a friendship with the free-spirited Wells that compelled him to abstain from the vote.

It was unanimous — Clemens was a Yankee. "We've got a group of warriors here and we're getting a very big warrior," Steinbrenner would say. "He's a monster."

But the Yankees were a monster team in '98, and Wells had a talent as large as his gut. If the left-hander could be a high-maintenance ass, facts were facts: he was 34-14 for the Yankees, 5-0 in the postseason, and he had pitched a perfect game. Yankee fans loved him the way golf fans loved John Daly — for his Everyman body and Joe Six Pack act.

Wells had a Ruthian appetite for New York; he loved appearing on the sets of *Late Show with David Letterman* and *Saturday Night Live*. He had big plans for spending the balance of his prime bouncing from one Manhattan nightspot to the next, at least until Joe Torre — never a Wells supporter — summoned him into his office the first morning of spring training.

"I'm in the principal's office already," Wells said on the way in.

He had no idea he was seconds away from being expelled.

Wells retreated to his Tampa home, where David Cone found him to be inconsolable over a four-hour visit. "I've never seen anyone so stunned by a trade," Cone said.

It was one the Yankees had to make. When Cashman had heard what Toronto GM Gord Ash wanted in exchange for Clemens, "my knees buckled," he said. In a good way. The Yankees did not want to tinker with the karma of '98, but this was Roger Clemens, the only five-time Cy Young Award winner in the history of the game.

"We're acquiring the Michael Jordan of pitchers," Cashman said.

"Christmas in February," Torre called the occasion.

"I finally got you," the Boss told the Rocket. Nobody knew it at the time, but George Steinbrenner did not only land a pitcher who wanted to win his first championship ring as desperately as the owner wanted to win his fifth.

Steinbrenner also acquired the one player he would ultimately consider a rival to Derek Jeter for the most prestigious position in sports: captain of the New York Yankees.

• • •

When the 1999 Yankees pulled into Seattle in early August, they did so without the same aura of invincibility their predecessors wore as easily as they did their interlocking "NY." They were 64-42 and up six games in the American League East, as opposed to 78-28 with a fifteen-game lead the year before.

It had been a turbulent time for the Yankee family, starting with Joe Torre's shocking disclosure in March that he had prostate cancer and was leaving the team to treat it. Two days after Joe DiMaggio died from the effects of lung cancer, and the same day Darryl Strawberry sat in a spring training dugout to talk about his return from colon cancer, the Yankees addressed their fifty-eight-year-old manager's head-on collision with his own mortality.

"From what I understand," Derek Jeter said of Torre's illness, "it is a good cancer to have. There's no good cancer, but it is the best to have."

The shortstop had never met a negative he could not convert into a positive. But truth was, the news crushed Jeter, the Yankee closest to Torre.

"He gave me the opportunity my first year," Jeter said. "I didn't play well in the spring and he said it was my job. He doesn't embarrass you. He is one of the reasons I am here today."

Jeter's team had lost its rock, and grim bulletins were coming in from all over Yankeedom. Catfish Hunter was suffering from Lou Gehrig's disease. Mike Lowell, the likable Yankee prospect just traded to the Marlins, had been diagnosed with testicular cancer.

Chuck Knoblauch's father was suffering from Alzheimer's disease. On the day the news broke about Torre, Scott Brosius's father, Maury, would tell a reporter that his colon cancer had returned, that the doctors said he could not beat it, and that he would prefer this news not be printed before he could tell his son he was dying.

The ballpark was the Yankees' sanctuary, their place to hide. The games had to go on, and Don Zimmer, a sixty-eight-year-old bench coach with a bum knee, was the man chosen to take Torre's place until the manager returned from surgery.

Hopelessly overmatched, Zimmer waged a public battle with Steinbrenner over how he was using Hideki Irabu, whom the owner had called a "fat, pussy toad" after Irabu failed to cover first base in the spring. Zimmer mercifully handed back the team to Torre on May

18 in Boston, where the Yankees' manager returned early to a most unexpected series of sights and sounds: the Fenway Park crowd gave him a standing ovation when he walked the lineup card to the plate.

The Yankees became the Yankees again in the summer, even if Clemens could not get comfortable in his pinstriped skin. Teams still had a certain fear of the '99 Yankees — even if they were more vulnerable than the '98 team — and that respect was obvious as far back as the April 5 opener in Oakland, where rain stopped play after eight innings with the A's holding a 5–3 lead.

"Everybody was praying we wouldn't restart that game," A's general manager Billy Beane said. "The Yankees only had three outs left, and everybody in that stadium, including the general manager of the A's, thought the only way we were winning that game was if Mother Nature intervened."

The Yanks recovered from that rain-shortened defeat. Like Wells the year before, Cone would pitch a perfect game, this one against the Expos with Don Larsen and Yogi Berra in the house. (Larsen and Berra were celebrating Yogi Berra Day; the Hall of Fame catcher had finally ended his feud with George Steinbrenner and agreed to return to Yankee Stadium for the first time since his 1985 firing.)

Cone knew how to mark the occasion. "At that point we're thinking, 'We got our hands around the throat of a dynasty now,'" the pitcher said. "That's the first time that word started to creep in."

George Steinbrenner was itching to tinker with that burgeoning dynasty by shipping Andy Pettitte to Philadelphia but decided against it at the end of July, a reprieve that helped Pettitte remember how to get batters out. The Yankees opened up another comfortable divisional lead and did so without Strawberry, the recovering cancer victim who had been suspended for violating his aftercare program following his April arrest for soliciting a prostitute and possessing cocaine.

Strawberry had lectured Jeter on staying out of trouble, on avoiding the temptations that had consumed much of Strawberry's career, and to date the young Yankee had listened times ten. Just as the cloud of suspicion started hovering over baseball's home-run heroes — Mark McGwire had admitted the previous summer to using androstenedione, a steroid precursor, during his record homer barrage — Jeter had established himself as a pure, stain-free winner.

The only problem Jeter had caused anyone in baseball? He made it impossible for Little League coaches across America, especially in the New York area, to pick through the countless requests for jersey number 2 to find the kid who deserved the lucky bounce.

Jeter played the game like a boy, so boys wanted to play the game like Jeter. Right-handed kids were delaying games on ball fields in every time zone, taking that slow and familiar bowlegged approach into the batter's box.

They would stick their bat under their left armpit and readjust their batting gloves like Jeter. They would plant their right foot on the back line of the box and keep their left foot out like Jeter. They would swing their left foot into the box, drop their head toward the dirt, and stick their extended right hand toward the umpire — as if trying to put that umpire in a trance — until they were ready like Jeter.

They would look up at the pitcher and start waggling that bat like Jeter. Chances were, they would not keep their hands inside the ball like Jeter.

While taking infield practice, Little Leaguers with dreams bigger than Williamsport would try Jeter's signature play at short — the running backhand in the hole, followed by a plant of the left foot in the outfield grass, a Jordan-esque jump for the sky, and a Baryshnikov pirouette in midair while releasing a powerful throw to first.

It did not matter if the boys weren't strong enough to swing their left shoulder against their midair momentum and reach first base on the follow-through — their attempts paid tribute to the way Jeter honored the game. He ran out every ground ball. He never berated an umpire. He never betrayed the DiMaggio way of giving his all — regardless of score or circumstance — because there might be someone in the stands who had never seen him play.

Jeter lived a simple, graceful life. He ironed his own clothes and picked up his own dry cleaning. He did half-hour morning workouts in his apartment building's gym before leaving for the Stadium. He got his hair cut, in his apartment, by a friend named Mike Daddy. He ate lunch with his friend Sean Twitty and made daily pregame stops at Starbucks.

By August of 1999, Jeter was more than a role model and a complete ballplayer. He was a coveted product spokesman, too.

His long, broad face was becoming synonymous with class, virtue, and victory. Jeter was as perfect for the role of athlete endorser as the founding father, Arnold Palmer, as perfect as Michael Jordan was when the sneaker company explosion changed professional and major college sports.

Untouched by scandal or controversy, Jeter was handsome, clean-cut, and quick to sign an autograph. Almost as a bonus, the likes of established veteran Paul O'Neill were saying Jeter was the best ballplayer they had ever played with.

He was already being mentioned as a future captain of the Yankees. He dated supermodels at night and helped their grandmothers cross the street by day.

The city loved Jeter, and Jeter loved the city right back. Much like John F. Kennedy Jr., he moved about town with an elegant and digni-fied step.

Jeter and JFK Jr. were not rival princes for any throne, but after JFK Jr. perished in a July plane crash, a death that stunned and saddened Jeter and millions of fellow Kennedy admirers, R. D. Long turned to his friend as they were sitting in the shortstop's apartment and de-clared, "You are now the king of New York."

Jeter was not trying to ascend to this throne, and he certainly did not want to land there by way of a tragic turn of events. "But he knew it was something he wasn't going to be able to escape," Long said. "He assumed the role without claiming it."

If he was not the crowned king of New York, Jeter was at least the blossoming prince of Madison Avenue. He had endorsement deals with Nike, Coach leather products, Skippy peanut butter, Florsheim Shoes, the Discover Card, Fleet Bank, and Acclaim Entertainment, and he asked all of his corporate benefactors to get involved with his Turn 2 Foundation initiative to keep kids off drugs. Michael Jordan recruited him to be part of his brand and to be the only baseball player featured in a commercial starring Jordan's handpicked stable of athletes, one that included Roy Jones, Ray Allen, and Randy Moss.

Jeter turned down endorsement opportunities every week to avoid overexposure, to align himself only with companies he felt matched up with his image, and, of greatest consequence, to keep his focus on win-ning championships.

His was a life of substance over style, of dependability over drama. "Derek was the most low-maintenance star I've ever been around," said the Yankees' PR man, Rick Cerrone. "He never told us he wouldn't do something, he had no entourage, he had no special interview rules. People loved him as a baseball superstar, and women loved him as a sex symbol, but he never carried himself like that."

Cerrone received a nonstop supply of requests from parents of sick children who wanted to meet Jeter, and the shortstop met as many of those children as he possibly could. He did not offer kids a signed ball and a pat on the cap on his way to the batting cage. Jeter forever took the time to make meaningful eye contact with the boys and girls, to engage them in conversation, to give them his batting gloves, and to introduce himself to emotional mothers and fathers he addressed as "ma'am" and "sir."

"It was like the Walt Disney thing, plussing the experience," Cerrone said. "Derek Jeter always plussed the experience."

So on the night of August 6, 1999, Jeter arrived at Seattle's Safeco Field — the Kingdome's successor — as an unblemished and unchallenged baseball star. He was batting .352 with a career-high 20 homers, obliterating his employer's arbitration claims that he could barely get the ball out of the infield.

Jeter was not happy when he received the news that Joe Torre was giving him a rest; the manager thought it was a good time for a break after his shortstop had been hit on the left wrist by a Jose Paniagua pitch the previous night. But Jeter settled in and watched as his first-place Yankees carried an 11–5 lead into the bottom of the eighth.

Alex Rodriguez launched a three-run homer off Jason Grimsley to make the game interesting, just not nearly as interesting as Grimsley made it when he hit Edgar Martinez in the side two pitches later, one pitch after sailing a fastball over his head.

Grimsley was ejected by home plate umpire Gary Cederstrom, and the Yankees knew what was coming in the top of the ninth, the inevitable retribution putting their dugout on edge. Frankie Rodriguez had recently touched off a Dodger Stadium brawl by throwing at Mark Grudzielanek's head, and he was staying in the game to start the ninth as Jose Mesa warmed up in the pen.

Luis Sojo's at-bat came and went quickly without incident — he was retired on the first pitch. But baseball's code of frontier justice would have spared Sojo during a longer stay at the plate anyway, as he did not have the resumé or skill set required in the eye-for-an-eye tradeoff Seattle was seeking.

Martinez was a career .300-plus hitter coming off four consecutive 100-plus RBI seasons, and Rodriguez was not about to drill the ninth batter in the Yankee order, Sojo, who was only in the lineup to give the sore Jeter a rest.

But the leadoff hitter, Chuck Knoblauch? Now he was a worthy target, and everyone in both dugouts realized it. So on the second pitch, Rodriguez did what baseball's unwritten law told him to do. He threw a fastball that glanced off Knoblauch's rump.

Had Cederstrom ejected the Mariners' reliever right then and there, tempers might have cooled and both teams might have called it a draw and moved on. When Cederstrom did not eject Rodriguez the way he had ejected Grimsley, the Yankees started screaming at the pitcher and the ump.

Rodriguez shouted back as he left the field — Lou Piniella had taken him out of the game — and Joe Girardi, the on-deck batter, returned verbal fire, compelling Rodriguez to throw down his glove and charge the Yankee catcher.

"And now we're going to have the biggest fight you've ever seen in your life," Bobby Murcer, the former Yankee turned broadcaster, said on the air.

Rodriguez fired off a couple of unanswered punches that knocked down Girardi, and if it looked like the catcher — a devout Christian — had never before struck anyone, there was a good reason: he hadn't.

The dugouts and bullpens emptied, and it was immediately clear this would not be any garden-variety scrum. Don Zimmer fell to the ground and got trampled. Jim Leyritz and Shane Spencer and half the Yankee roster were trying to get to Frankie Rodriguez in front of the Seattle bench.

Bernie Williams slammed Mariners catcher Dan Wilson to the ground, and Chili Davis pinned Steve Smith, a Seattle coach, and wrapped both hands around Smith's throat as if he were about to squeeze the life out of him. Zimmer staggered back to his feet, but he appeared to be hyperventilating.

"It was like a war zone out there," Williams said.

And on the perimeter of this hand-to-hand combat, Derek Jeter and Alex Rodriguez were enemies acting like the best of friends. They were smiling, pretending to jab each other, just looking like a couple of guys making plans to meet up after the game. A-Rod joked with Jeter that he would come after him in the event of a second brawl.

"Those two guys aren't going to fight," Murcer's partner, Ken Singleton, said on the air. "They're probably going somewhere later."

A-Rod held his cap and slapped it twice against Jeter's chest. Just then, Seattle pitcher Jamie Moyer approached A-Rod from behind, pushed Rodriguez's mitt into his stomach, and nudged him gently while shooting him a look that screamed, "This isn't the time or place."

An umpire wedged himself between Jeter and Rodriguez, not that it was necessary, and fifteen minutes after the clash started, both teams headed back to their benches. As the Yankees spilled into their dugout, Chad Curtis, a forty-fifth-round draft choice hitting .238, decided to confront Jeter.

The teammates ran in different circles and had little in common. Curtis was a grinder, and Jeter was a star. Curtis was married and devoutly religious, and Jeter was single and a Catholic reticent about expressing his religious views outside of the on-field prayer he whispered to himself following the national anthem, when he crouched low to the field, bowed his head, asked God to protect all players from injury, and made the sign of the cross.

At the time of the brawl, the Yankees were considering putting Curtis on waivers to make room for Strawberry's return. The team saw Curtis as an expendable player, in part because he tried to impose his religious beliefs on some teammates who tired of the sell.

A man who took to wearing a bracelet marked "WWJD" ("What Would Jesus Do?"), Curtis twice approached Jeter about joining him in prayer groups and chapel services, and twice Jeter declined the invitation. "Chad was really confrontational with guys," said one Yankee official. "He'd take all the porn on the road and in the bathrooms and throw it out . . . It caused problems. You can't force all of your stuff on people."

The Yankees were concerned about rumors Chuck Knoblauch was partying too hard, and Curtis took those concerns to an extreme. "Chad used to knock on [Knoblauch's] door," the official said, "and he'd shout, 'Are you in there? Are you in there? I want to make sure you're not out.' Chad was really militant on that."

Curtis lived in a black-and-white world with no shades of gray, except when it came to fighting. With grown men rolling in the dirt and acting like silly boys in a schoolyard, Curtis suspended his religious views and let the other guy worry about turning the other cheek.

So he was appalled by the sight of Jeter and A-Rod fraternizing on the jagged edges of a frightening brawl, especially with Zimmer down and out. Curtis was as old school as Ty Cobb. He did not see a fight as the appropriate time for opposing players to renew their vows of friendship.

"You are a good player," Curtis told Jeter, "but you don't know how to play the game."

Jeter reportedly shouted at Curtis, "Get out of my face" several times and appeared a lot closer to punching his teammate than he had been to punching A-Rod or any other Mariner. The confrontation continued in the clubhouse. Curtis approached Jeter and the shortstop kept saying, "Not now . . . not now." He did not want a starring role in a tabloid spectacle.

Curtis did not listen. In full view of Yankee beat writers, Curtis again tried to explain to Jeter why he was not playing the game the right way. Jeter was desperate to end the conversation. Sojo came over to help break it up, but by then the damage was as conspicuous as the two welts on Girardi's forehead.

"He disagrees with what I have to say," Curtis said of Jeter. "I disagree with him. We're allowed to disagree."

Jeter said he would have helped up Zimmer had he seen him on the ground and conceded little else. He maintained he was merely talking to A-Rod about the Paniagua pitch from the night before and comparing that to the plunkings that led to the brawl.

"It's a situation where, hey, [Curtis] didn't know what we were talking about," Jeter would say. "Unless you know what's going on, then you shouldn't approach someone in that manner."

Curtis called his actions "a small piece of mentoring" and believed he was only helping a younger player understand the consequences of his action, or inaction. "I wasn't real mad," Curtis said. "It was just, 'Dude, you know that's not the time to go and shadowbox with your buddy.'"

In the coming days, some Yankees would privately agree that Curtis had a valid point, that Jeter acted irresponsibly given the intensity of the fight. "Chad was right, but he handled it the wrong way," Leyritz said. "I don't think Derek and Alex realized the extent of the hostility that was going on because they were pretty far away."

One of Torre's coaches, Willie Randolph, the former second baseman and captain who was instrumental in Jeter's development, scolded the shortstop for his new-school approach to an old-school fight. But David Cone, among the most respected player voices, said he had seen dozens of friendly exchanges on the fringes of brawls and thought it did not matter whether Curtis had a point.

"Chad was out of line, and he lost a little face in that situation among the leaders in the clubhouse," Cone said. "We looked at Jeter, we looked at Chad Curtis, and to me that's a no-brainer. That's an easy pick."

Curtis eventually apologized; Jeter did not see the need to do the same. He was allergic to the bee sting of criticism, and it was harder for him to forgive and forget than it was to accept an 0-for-4 day at the plate. Curtis was dead to Jeter, and there was no resurrection on the schedule.

Less than two weeks after the Seattle brawl, Jeter's reputation took another direct hit, one that could not be blamed on a backup outfielder. Jeter was so busy celebrating the twenty-eighth birthday of his good friend Jorge Posada, and enjoying the spaghetti dish cooked up by Posada's wife, Laura, that he forgot to show up for the team photo.

Joe Torre slapped Jeter and Posada with small fines and publicly moved to minimize the impact of their absence. But the manager did not leave two open spaces in the rows of players gathered for the picture, making it more difficult for a graphics designer to Photoshop the shortstop and catcher into the shot. "I'm sure they are [mad],"

Jeter said, "but nobody said anything. I forgot, that's the bottom line."

Suddenly Jeter's uncharacteristic behavior had some asking if he was fit to be the team's first captain since Don Mattingly, a role his manager wanted him to assume in the near future. Did Jeter still deserve the honor? Or did these two incidents suggest that the role model, star, and spokesman had not yet grown into the role?

Derek Jeter finished the season with staggering numbers — a .349 batting average, 24 home runs, and 102 RBI — even if he fell slightly short of the sums posted by his Boston rival, Nomar Garciaparra, who had beaten him out for the All-Star Game start at Fenway Park.

Jeter had mimicked Garciaparra's hyper batting ritual in that game to everyone's delight, but nobody was laughing when the Yankees faced the Red Sox in the 1999 American League Championship Series, the first time these ancient blood rivals had ever met in the postseason (the famous Bucky Dent game in '78 counted as a regular-season tiebreaker).

Jeter had batted .455 in the Division Series sweep of Texas, starting the clinching rally in the first inning of Game 3 with a triple to left that led to a three-run homer by Darryl Strawberry, back from his drug suspension with a bang.

The Rangers had proven to be willing postseason stooges for the Yankees, losing three Division Series to them in four years. The Red Sox? They finished with 94 victories, only 4 behind New York, and with Pedro Martinez at the very top of his game, good enough to strike out 17 Yankees in September in his most indelible start in the Bronx, the Red Sox were a wild card in every literal and figurative way.

Boston also had the batting champ, Garciaparra, to match against the two-time world champ, Jeter. And when Game 1 at Yankee Stadium was headed Boston's way, Jeter drew first blood.

Down 3–2 in the seventh, one out and a man on second, Jeter hit an RBI single to center off Derek Lowe, ultimately allowing Bernie Williams to win it in the tenth with a homer off Rod Beck. When Garciaparra responded with a vengeance in Game 2, delivering a three-hit performance that included a two-out, two-run homer off Cone, the Yanks came from behind again to win by a run.

Garciaparra exploded one more time in Game 3, exploded for four hits and three RBI on a day when Martinez was his brilliant self and Roger Clemens was reduced to an emotional and physical wreck in his return to Fenway, where fans all but welcomed him with pitchforks and torches. The Yankees lost 13–1, Jeter struck out twice in three at-bats, and the crowd let him hear about it.

Jeter was used to the abuse in Fenway, where fans chanted, "No-mar's better" and wore vulgar T-shirts mocking the Yankee star. Jeter arrived at the ballpark the next day in a relaxed state, as always, summoning the name of Boston's Game 4 starter, Bret Saberhagen, in telling as many teammates as possible, "Sabes says you've got nothing."

But in the ninth inning of Game 4, after he singled to help ignite a six-run rally that doomed the Red Sox, Jeter was finally fazed by Fenway. He saw the old ballpark turn uglier than it had ever been.

Boston manager Jimy Williams got ejected for arguing that Garciaparra had beaten out his grounder to third, Nomar threw his helmet and kicked over a water cooler, and the fans flexed their beer muscles and hurled bottles, cans, cups, and coins while the Yankees were pulled from the field.

The game was delayed eight minutes, during which time a Fenway security guard stationed at the Yankees dugout shouted obscenities at the team he was supposed to be guarding.

"Man," Jeter said, "people were animals out there. . . . It was like dodging grenades. That stuff hasn't even happened in New York since I've been here."

Jeter put the blood-lusting mob out of its misery the following night, blasting a towering two-run homer off Kent Mercker in the first inning that ensured the Red Sox would not be flying another championship banner next to their 1918 flag.

Garciaparra won the statistical battle in the series—a .400 batting average and 5 RBI to Jeter's .350 and 3—but lost four of the five games and committed critical errors in the field. Jeter produced the more decisive hits and ended up feeling about as euphoric at Fenway as one of his favorite all-time shortstops, Dent, had felt twenty-one years earlier.

In the visitors' clubhouse at Fenway, Jeter and Torre and Steinbrenner were striking their familiar champagne-soaked poses, heading back to the World Series for the third time in four years.

Someone asked Jeter about the NLCS matchup between the Mets and Atlanta, and whether he preferred a Subway Series or a sequel to the '96 Series with the Braves.

"I don't care, man," Jeter said. "Let them beat each other up."

The Yankees swept Atlanta to win their twenty-fifth championship, leaving them with victories in the last twelve World Series games in which they had played, including eight straight over the Braves. The triumph was emotional for a Yankee team that weathered Joe Torre's cancer surgery and much too much death and dying.

Paul O'Neill's father died before Game 4, and the right fielder wept as he embraced Torre amid the postgame celebration on the field. Luis Sojo missed the first two games of the Series after his father died in Venezuela, and Scott Brosius was still hurting from the death of his father in September. Once again, the ballpark was the Yankees' place to escape.

Within a baseball context, the 1999 title meant more to Roger Clemens than to anyone else. He entered Game 4 with eleven postseason starts and all of two victories to show for them. The Rocket was coming off his disastrous American League Championship Series performance in Boston, and despite carrying to the mound the luxury of a 3–0 World Series lead, he was burdened by the notion he would be the Yankee pitcher to break the streak.

"I want the Roger Clemens I used to see," George Steinbrenner had implored him. "I want the pitcher I traded for."

So Clemens out-dueled John Smoltz, surrendered one run over seven and two-thirds innings, and finally poked a pin in his ballooning reputation as a postseason choker. "I finally know what it feels like to be a Yankee," Clemens said after he had climbed on top of the home dugout to slap hands with the delirious fans.

Derek Jeter first knew that feeling three years earlier, when he had won it all as a rookie. This time around against Atlanta, Jeter turned Game 1 in the Yankees' favor when his RBI single off Greg Maddux in the eighth made it 1–1 before the Yankees scored three more. In Game

2, Jeter singled and scored in the first inning, doubled and scored in the fourth, and showed why Atlanta manager Bobby Cox was moved to say, "Derek Jeter, to me, happens to be one of the top two or three ballplayers in the game."

Jeter could not believe his own never-ending run of good fortune. "If this is a dream," he said, "don't wake me up. . . . I don't know if anyone has a perfect life, but it's close. It's getting there."

As fate would have it, the Yankee who challenged one of the top two or three ballplayers in the game would assume Jeter's role of October hero in Game 3. Chad Curtis hit his second homer of the night, this one off Mike Remlinger in the tenth, to complete a dramatic comeback from a 5–0 deficit and make the ultimate Yankee victory a matter of when, not if.

Of course, Curtis could not bask in his moment without taking a controversial stand. When NBC's Jim Gray attempted to interview him in the wake of his game-winning blast, Curtis declined. "As a team," he told Gray, "we kind of decided, because of what happened with Pete [Rose], we're not going to talk out here on the field."

Gray had come under fire before Game 2 for interrupting baseball's All-Century team festivities with an on-field interrogation of Rose, who had been banned for his alleged gambling on the game. Torre was furious at Curtis and denied the team had voted to snub Gray (the manager was unaware that such a vote had indeed taken place).

But when Curtis settled under Keith Lockhart's fly ball and ended the World Series, he had already signed his walking papers. The night he confronted Jeter was the night he guaranteed he would not be wearing pinstripes for long.

Seven weeks after he helped the Yanks repeat as champions for the first time since 1978, Curtis was traded to Texas for Brandon Knight and Sam Marsonek.

"Chad just couldn't stay around any longer because that act gets tired," a team official said. "Once he became comfortable here, he became a preacher, and it ran its course. He didn't get voted off the island simply because of Derek Jeter; there were too many other issues with Chad."

One Yankee executive said Jeter was indeed among the chief reasons Curtis was dealt, and that the shortstop — who did discuss personnel matters with George Steinbrenner during occasional off-season visits — made it clear he wanted the outfielder gone.

Either way, Curtis believed Jeter's feelings for him represented at least a contributing factor in his exit.

"Every decision has multiple reasons, and did that have one tiny part?" Curtis said. "I don't think that was *the* reason, but I think it adds in.

"Derek's the guy that, rightly so, this organization needs to empower to lead. And if I was some affront to that leadership, even if it's just a little bit, then I needed to go."

The following October, David Cone looked across the Shea Stadium field at his old friend John Franco before the start of Game 4 of the World Series between the Yankees and Mets. Cone was in the visiting dugout, flabbergasted over what he was seeing and hearing.

The Baha Men were on the field playing "Who Let the Dogs Out?," the Mets' new anthem, and Cone could not believe his former team would deface the Fall Classic with such a mind-numbing song.

Cone locked on Franco, sitting in the Mets' dugout, and mouthed the words, "Are you fucking kidding me?" Franco shrugged his shoulders and opened his palms toward the sky in what-can-I-say form.

The Baha Men were blaring their *woo, woo, woo*s, and Cone turned to face his teammate Derek Jeter. "You've got to be shitting me," he told the shortstop.

The Mets had won Game 3 of the Series to cut the Yankees' lead to 2–1, and they had two more games at Shea to play with. So the visiting side was looking for an edge, a reason to get amped up, and Cone thought the Yanks had found it in the on-field presence of the Baha Men and their dumb little song.

"It crystallized the difference between the Mets and Yankees," Cone said, "because you'd never see that at Yankee Stadium. I remember our whole bench going, 'This is bush,' because we were looking for things to grab on to use as motivation."

Cone also remembered a silent statement made by Jeter's pale green eyes. The shortstop had more to lose in this 2000 Subway Series than anyone on the active roster, Brooklyn-born Joe Torre included.

Jeter was among the leading citizens of New York. He was taking this Series personally, because he knew he would have to live with an intracity defeat every day for the rest of his life.

Torre made him the leadoff hitter for the first time in the Series; the manager did not have the luxury of a designated hitter at Shea, and he could not keep Chuck Knoblauch in the lineup, not when his throws from second were maiming women and children in the stands.

So with Knoblauch out, and with second baseman Luis Sojo more suited for the two-hole, Jeter was asked to make an opening statement against the Mets. And as the Baha Men played at earsplitting decibels in the moments before the first pitch, Cone surveyed the Yankees' best player and his bloodless gaze.

"Derek Jeter was ready for that game," Cone said. "He was ready for that first at-bat."

What a long, strange trip it had been to that Game 4 moment. Derek Jeter had made $10 million for the 2000 season, double his previous arbitration award, but only after he nearly reached agreement on a record seven-year, $118.5 million deal with the Yankees before George Steinbrenner got cold feet.

Steinbrenner decided he was against flipping baseball's salary structure onto its ear, and for doing the one-year deal that canceled a return trip to the arbitration table. But the dynamic between employer and employee had changed dramatically from that spring day in '97 when Jeter asked Steinbrenner for a five-year contract in the presence of team official Ray Negron, only to have the Boss advise him to hold out for a better deal in the coming years.

Steinbrenner bounced back with a five-year, $31 million offer in the summer of '98, a bid rejected by Jeter. Suddenly the shortstop had Steinbrenner close to breaking the $100 million barrier, at least until the Boss put off the inevitable nine-figure contract for one more year.

Down in Tampa, Jeter gladly took the $10 million and shelved his long-term financial ambitions until the following winter. He pieced together another All-Star year in 2000 by hardening his body at the International Performance Institute in Bradenton, where Nomar Garciaparra worked out. Jeter had lost weight during the '99 season, finishing the year at 185 pounds. He arrived at spring training 18 pounds heavier.

Pitcher Mike Buddie, Jeter's teammate as far back as Greensboro, said the shortstop "went from being Kevin Garnett to Shaquille O'Neal." Such physical transformations in baseball often encouraged whispers of steroid suspicion, but Jeter's integrity was never called into question, a testament to his standing in the game.

He worked his legs for the first time, strengthened the middle of his body with core exercises, and added muscle definition to his upper torso. He wanted to become a more explosive offensive force. He wanted to hit 30 home runs.

Jeter's goals would be compromised by a left abdominal strain in May, when he took too many batting practice swings in an attempt to bust out of a slump. Jeter missed a dozen games, returned to go 3 for 4 in a victory over the Red Sox, and got on with the season while his double-play partner unraveled.

For reasons unknown, Chuck Knoblauch could no longer make the most elementary of baseball throws — from second to first. He made three errant throws in the first six innings of a 12–3 loss to the White Sox on the night of June 15, stood as the loneliest man on the face of the earth — near second base — while his fellow infielders gathered at the mound during a pitching change, and finally asked Joe Torre to remove him from the game.

Knoblauch told Torre he was tired of hurting the team, and the manager sent the second baseman home so he would not have to face reporters postgame at his locker. Knoblauch had been struggling on his throws for the better part of two years, sometimes lobbing the ball, sometimes shoveling it underhanded, sometimes letting it rip without eyeing his target.

Knoblauch had suggested he might quit the game, or at least escape to the Cayman Islands or Martha's Vineyard. This time around, after Torre had someone drive him away from Yankee Stadium in the middle of a game, Knoblauch did what most lost souls do — he called his mom.

Some Yankees were concerned Knoblauch might do something rash, something more serious than quitting the team. Jeter said he was among those who called Knoblauch to offer reassurance. "By the time I talked to him," Jeter said, "he was doing OK. I knew he'd be all right. . . . We need him."

Knoblauch returned to the Stadium the following day wearing a sunshiny disposition. He joked with teammates and told reporters his mother wanted to give him a hug. While backpedaling during pregame warm-ups, Jeter gave him a playful push forward.

But some Yankees noticed there had been a recent chill between Jeter and Knoblauch. The two had been close friends and, after Knoblauch's divorce, running mates at night, but they didn't talk or tease each other nearly as much in the clubhouse anymore. It appeared the Joe Montana–Jerry Rice partnership Alex Rodriguez had predicted two years earlier was fraying at the seams.

On his return to the lineup, Knoblauch did receive a loud ovation from the fans, and Jeter did say on his behalf, "They treated him well and deservedly so. I've said before that we're not going to win without Chuck, and it's about time the fans got behind him."

Jeter had offered a mild rebuke of the very fans who adored him, and it would not be the last time he would do that in defense of a struggling teammate. Only Knoblauch's demons would not be silenced without a fight. The following day, the second baseman unleashed a throw that sailed seven rows deep into the stands behind first base, where it hit Marie Olbermann, mother of Fox broadcaster Keith Olbermann, knocking a lens out of her glasses.

Nothing came easily for Knoblauch, who would end up on the disabled list with an elbow injury before George Steinbrenner ripped him for allegedly exaggerating the depth of his pain. Nothing came easily for Knoblauch's two-time defending champ of a team, either.

Roger Clemens would nearly incite a riot by crashing a fastball against the padded head belonging to the Mets' Mike Piazza, a slugger who had his number. With a nine-game divisional lead in the middle of September, the Yankees would give their fan base a coronary by losing fifteen of their last eighteen to free-fall into the playoffs.

On the eve of that near-fatal collapse, Jeter was again reminded of his overriding good luck. The Blue Jays were in the Bronx, and they brought along a recent call-up, Chad Mottola, who had been reduced to a minor league journeyman. Mottola was made the fifth overall pick of the '92 draft by the Reds, who had traded him to Texas in '98 before watching him bounce from one Class AAA outpost to the next while the prospect they bypassed, Jeter, collected trophies like others collected lint.

Mottola's first and last appearance in Yankee Stadium would go down as an 0 for 4 at the plate with two strikeouts in a 10–2 loss; Toronto actually batted him third in the lineup. But Mottola was not resentful of Jeter. In fact, he had family members in New York who counted the Yankee shortstop as their favorite player.

"They all ended up with Jeter jerseys," Mottola would say. "They could never comprehend that I was picked before him."

Nor could Reds GM Jim Bowden, who was not in charge at the time scouting director Julian Mock decided Mottola was destined for the kind of stardom Jeter would never reach.

"Mottola didn't develop into anything and Jeter ends up one of the best players of his era," Bowden would say. "Derek Jeter became what you dream about in player personnel. He would've changed the history of our franchise."

Instead Jeter was adding to the history of the Yankees franchise while Mottola had not even earned 100 big league at-bats.

Jeter finished the 2000 regular season with a .339 batting average, but given his added muscle, he was disappointed in his number of homers (15) and RBI (73). His consolation prize? After Alex Rodriguez vacated his starting position in the All-Star Game because of the lingering effects of a concussion, Jeter became the first Yankee to be named All-Star MVP. He won the award in Atlanta, his personal gateway to World Series parades.

On their way back to baseball's biggest stage, the Yankees proved to be the most dangerous eighty-seven-win team in baseball history. They survived a tense five-game series with the Oakland A's, and then an equally tense six-game series with A-Rod's Mariners for the American League pennant. The ALCS was defined by the performance of Clemens's Yankee life, a fifteen-strikeout, one-hit shutout in Game 4 that included a near decapitation of A-Rod, who was left to watch Jeter break a scoreless tie in the fifth with a two-out, three-run homer off Paul Abbott that would give the Yankees a 3–1 series lead.

A-Rod was A-Rod against the Yanks, hitting .409 with two homers and five RBI for the series and raging against any suggestion he would someday be known as a postseason gagger. But no matter what Rodriguez did, no matter how many hanging sliders he hammered, he could not escape the sinking feeling that his dear friend Jeter was living a charmed baseball life, and he was not.

Rodriguez could not beat Jeter, or Jeter's team. He could not even skip an All-Star Game with a head injury without his friend taking his place and being named MVP. So A-Rod needed a different vehicle of retribution, a fresh plan of attack.

With an expiring contract and a representative (Scott Boras) eager to swing for the moon, Rodriguez would beat Jeter for the one title the Yankee could not win: Lord and Master of the Free Agent Universe.

Only Jeter was not thinking about the off-season arms race, not when he was about to step into the cauldron of the first all–New York World Series since the Yanks beat the Brooklyn Dodgers in 1956.

Steinbrenner used to get hot when his team lost the Mayor's Trophy Game exhibition to the Mets, so the vision of a World Series defeat at the hands of his less prominent neighbors in Queens was one colored in apocalyptic shades.

Far more than interborough bragging rights was at stake here. Steinbrenner's twelve-year TV rights deal with the Madison Square Garden Network was set to expire; it was a half-a-billion-dollar deal that helped make the Yankees the first team to hurdle the $100 million payroll barrier and helped inflate the value of the franchise to $700 million (Steinbrenner's group had purchased it from CBS for $8.7 million in 1973). The Boss had joined with the NBA's New Jersey Nets, an unworthy partner, in the hope of starting his own network.

Steinbrenner had abandoned his earlier efforts to sell the Yankees to Cablevision when its founder and chairman, Charles Dolan, refused to let him run the ball club, never mind Steinbrenner's additional request to run the Cablevision-owned New York Knicks and Rangers. When Steinbrenner entered into a July agreement with the International Management Group to form a regional cable network, MSG sued for breach of contract.

So no, this was not any time for the Yankees to lose leverage, prestige, or a seven-game series for the championship of the baseball world to the second-rate Mets.

"From a company standpoint, the city was ours," said Brian Cashman, the GM who was in the stress-induced habit of gnashing his teeth in his sleep. "The city was at stake, the television contract was at stake, the entire financial power of the business was at stake. We went into that with so much pressure, and the Mets were a good enough team to beat us.

"The Boss told me, 'You'd better win or else.' I felt like if we lost to the Mets, it would've diminished our three championships. It would've been like they didn't count. I was always proud of what we'd done, and I'd never before been scared of losing. But I was scared of losing to the Mets."

Derek Jeter was not.

"I've never been afraid to fail," he maintained. And here, Jeter said, was why:

"People put too much pressure on themselves and try to make things bigger than they really are. No matter how you look at it, whether you're in the World Series or a spring training game, it's still baseball. I've gotten a hit before. I've struck out before. I've made a play. I've made an error. I mean everything that you can think of has happened to every player. It's just a matter of, are you afraid to fail? I'm not."

This was why Jeter outlasted all the doubters and haters, including the Mets fans who used to see him around town and tell him he was no Rey Ordonez, with a profanity or three thrown in for the hell of it.

Ordonez was supposed to be the measuring stick right from Opening Day in '96, when he made that throw to the plate from his knees the day before Jeter answered in Cleveland with his homer and over-the-shoulder catch. But for all his defensive wizardry, Ordonez could not hit a lick. He had fractured his arm in May, a season-ending injury, and so he would not be presenting a challenge to Jeter in the World Series or anywhere else.

In fact, in Game 1 against the Mets, Jeter did his own little Ozzie Smith impression. Timo Perez was on first with no score and two outs in the sixth when Todd Zeile sent a blast to left that appeared to be leaving the park to every witness, most notably Timo Perez, who decided to do a home-run trot in case Zeile did not.

The ball hit the top of the Yankee Stadium wall, a couple of inches short of pay dirt, and Justice fired it into the cutoff man, Jeter. Mets third-base coach Cookie Rojas waved home Perez, who was not trotting anymore. Jeter ran toward the stands to catch Justice's throw, jumped as if he were making his signature play in the hole, and fired to Jorge Posada at the plate.

Mets officials watching from near their dugout could not believe Zeile's shot stayed in the park, could not believe how quickly Jeter got rid of the ball, and could not believe he avoided hitting Perez with the throw from his restricted angle. Mostly, they could not believe Perez was a second away from being called out at home.

"One of those Derek Jeter moments," Mets manager Bobby Valentine said.

By the time the Subway Series reached Game 4 at Shea, that seminal moment was lost in a pile of many. Paul O'Neill still had to win an epic ten-pitch battle with Armando Benitez in the ninth inning of Game 1 just to give the Yanks a shot at playing extra innings and winning on Jose Vizcaino's single in the twelfth.

The Roger Clemens–Mike Piazza heavyweight championship rematch framed Game 2, and when the overcaffeinated Rocket took the jagged remains of Piazza's bat and threw it at the Mets' catcher, it was clear this was one fight that outdid the hype. Clemens explained he thought the bat was the ball — who throws the ball at a base runner, anyway? — and Joe Torre nearly stormed out of his postgame news conference when the Rocket put him in the position of defending the indefensible.

After they were shut down by Clemens, who allowed two hits over eight scoreless innings, and after Jeter doubled and scored what would be the winning run in the eighth, the Mets recovered at home to beat El Duque Hernandez in Game 3, snapping the Yankees' remarkable fourteen-game World Series winning streak and setting up the delicious theater that was Game 4.

The pressure was all on the Yankees, as Game 5 would be played at Shea as well. "It was very easy to get away from the other World Series we played in," Paul O'Neill said. "But because it was the Mets, we couldn't get away from this one."

Steinbrenner started the day by sending a truck over the river to Shea filled with couches and chairs for the visiting clubhouse — the Yankee owner was appalled by the furniture provided his team, and he was seen lecturing Mets owner Fred Wilpon in the hours before the first pitch.

A first pitch that would leave the neighboring Yanks and Mets an entire world apart.

After the Baha Men were done screeching and the field was cleared, Derek Jeter stepped into the box with an encouraging recent history against the Mets. In nine regular-season and World Series games that year, he had hit .425 with nine runs scored.

Jeter loved playing against the Mets, he said, "just because the fans get into it, and that makes it fun. It's like you're playing in high school. I used to like playing our rivals in high school basketball games because there were more fans and excitement in the stands."

But Jeter did not have a warm spot for the leaky, creaky mess that was Shea. He could not stand the choppy infield, for one. "I'm not trying to be disrespectful," he would say. "I just didn't like the stadium. The field conditions were not good. Hitting at that stadium was a lot different than playing defense."

Jeter was not playing defense at 8:32 p.m., when he dug in against Mets starter Bobby Jones. Chuck Knoblauch had predicted in the dugout that Jeter would belt a homer, but Jones had other ideas.

"I wasn't expecting him to swing," he said of his first pitch.

Jones threw a fastball for openers, just as he had done nearly every game all year. "Bobby danced with the girl he brought to the dance," Valentine said.

The fastball tailed in on Jeter's hands, and the shortstop beat the pitch to the punch, getting the barrel to the ball and landing it over the left-field wall. Jeter blew a bubble with his gum as he rounded first base, and by 8:33 p.m. the Mets' bubble had burst. "We win Game 3, we're home for Game 4, and we couldn't even get comfortable in our goddamn chair," said Mets executive Jim Duquette. "To have it go up in smoke like that so fast, it was more deflating than the Timo play."

Jeter tripled in his next at-bat, scored to give his team a 3–0 lead, and the rest of the Subway Series was colored by inevitability. Suddenly the Yanks were not so jittery about the Mets. Cone was sitting out in the bullpen and shaking his head.

"I was looking around that Mets lineup and going, 'Man, Bobby

Valentine must be a really good manager,'" Cone said. "We had Bernie [Williams] and [Paul] O'Neill and [David] Justice in our outfield, and they had Benny Agbayani, Jay Payton, and Timo Perez in theirs. I remember thinking, 'No, they're not going to beat us. It's not going to happen.'"

Steinbrenner was not so sure. He spent the entire World Series in the Yankee clubhouse, snapping at anyone and everyone who crossed his path. He ordered Rob Cucuzza, equipment manager, to sit next to him without moving a muscle; Steinbrenner was angry that Tino Martinez had come into the clubhouse needing his ripped pants replaced and Cucuzza was nowhere to be found.

"You could see the pressure on the Boss's face," Cucuzza said. "That was the World Series he had to have."

Near the end of Game 4 a pipe burst in the clubhouse and Steinbrenner actually helped the maintenance workers and firemen bail out the water. The Boss suspected the Mets of foul play, of intentionally opening a valve to soak the Yankees' imported sofas and chairs.

No, Steinbrenner was not about to accept the explanation that a trash container fire caused the problem. On the way out of Shea, as he proudly pointed out the wet spots on his slacks, Steinbrenner said of the Mets, "I'd rather be where we are than where they are."

The following night, Jeter belted another homer, this one off Al Leiter, to make it a 2–2 game in the sixth, and soon enough Mike Piazza was driving a deep fly to center off Mariano Rivera with two outs and a man on in the ninth, Yanks up by a 4–2 count. It looked like a tie ball game, until it didn't. Williams made the catch at the stroke of midnight, Jeter jumped into Luis Sojo's arms, and the Yankees were living out a Mets fan's worst nightmare, celebrating their twenty-sixth championship on the home field of a New York team that had won only two.

"Jeter's one of the most classic winners ever to play the game," Mets GM Steve Phillips said. "Every time we said, 'OK, now we've got it going,' Jeter did something to change the game. He hits that home run on the first pitch of Game 4 and it's like, 'Oh Jesus, here we go again.'"

Jeter became the first player to win MVP of the World Series and All-Star Game in the same season. He batted .409 against the Mets and extended his World Series hitting streak to fourteen games.

On the Shea field, Jeter was wearing a champagne-soaked World Series championship T-shirt and a championship cap turned backward as he hugged his sister, Sharlee. In a chair waiting to do an ESPN interview, Jeter was wearing an Air Jordan wristband when he held up four fingers, Michael Jordan–style.

Amid the clubhouse celebration, when he was not spraying champagne, Jeter was singing a silly frat boy version of "Who Let the Dogs Out?"

At the top of his lungs, on top of the world. Derek Jeter, four-time champ, was the undisputed lord of the rings.

He had no idea how much suffering he would endure in pursuit of his one for the thumb.

8

The Flip

ALEX RODRIGUEZ HAD made a complete fool out of Texas Rangers owner Tom Hicks, siphoning $252 million out of his pocket, and suddenly A-Rod was moved to make a fool out of himself. Rodriguez had just signed a staggering ten-year contract, and for some reason he marked the occasion by turning his friendship with Derek Jeter into a contact sport.

In December of 2000, appearing on Dan Patrick's ESPN Radio show, Rodriguez was asked to identify the star he felt could break his record for fattest all-time contract. A-Rod mentioned Andruw Jones and Pedro Martinez but maintained "my talent at such a young age" would make his record hard to top.

At the time Brian Cashman was in serious long-term talks with Derek Jeter's agent, Casey Close. The ring-free Rodriguez figured he needed to protect the only title he could win.

"Even a guy like Derek," he said, "it's going to be hard for him to break that [$252 million barrier] because he just doesn't do the power numbers. And defensively, he doesn't do all those things. So he might not break the 252. He might get 180. I don't know what he's going to get. One-fifty? I'm not sure."

In one juicy on-air paragraph, A-Rod had taken his heavy lumber to Jeter's offensive ability, his defensive ability, and his leverage with

George Steinbrenner. For weeks Jeter declined to respond in public. So a columnist assigned to the New York Giants–Baltimore Ravens Super Bowl in Tampa, next door to the Yankees' minor league facility, checked in to see if Jeter finally wanted to call an all-out blitz on A-Rod.

Behind the facility, where the shortstop spent the winters honing his swing, Jeter stopped to conduct an interview he did not want to do. He had already dispatched Rob Thomson, the team's director of player development, to inform the columnist he did not have any time to give, but when Jeter emerged from the complex and saw a familiar face, he agreed to stop and talk.

That was the essence of Derek Jeter — never wanting to expose his vulnerable side to the public, but never wanting to offend, either.

Small talk about the Giants and Ravens represented the appetizer before the dreaded entrée was served. Jeter was asked about A-Rod's claim that he wasn't a $200 million shortstop, never mind a $252 million shortstop.

"I'm not trying to beat Alex's record anyway," Jeter said. "The only record I'm concerned with is Yogi's record, and that's the [ten] championships."

In two on-the-record sentences, Jeter had taken his own heavy lumber to A-Rod's obsession with winning in free agency what he could not win on the field.

"I didn't pay much attention to it because that's not my goal," Jeter continued. "I haven't been sitting around saying, 'Alex got this so let's see if I can break his record.' It's not important. I mean, I think we've been doing something right around here the last few years."

The Yankees had won four championships in Jeter's first five years, or four more than Rodriguez had won in his first six.

"You want people to remember you as a winner," Jeter said.

And not as a human hedge fund.

Jeter had returned fire on Rodriguez in a passive-aggressive way, and the shots were much deserved. A-Rod had violated an unwritten law of the big league land. Ballplayers rarely attack and marginalize each other in the middle of high-stakes contract negotiations, especially when those ballplayers are supposed to be dear friends.

Jeter did reveal that he had asked Rodriguez for an explanation, and that he had been convinced A-Rod meant little or no harm. "I don't think he had bad intentions," Jeter said. "It was probably more playful than anything else."

But in reality, the Yankee shortstop was wounded by A-Rod's jealous jabs, which picked and picked at one of his human weaknesses: his inability to forgive or forget. As Jeter drove off that day in his silver Mercedes convertible — he was finally looking to sell the old Mitsubishi with 80,000 miles on it — he was carrying a grudge in the trunk.

He had no idea A-Rod had another nuclear warhead aimed at Tampa.

Before Rodriguez escalated hostilities, Jeter had to sign his contract with the Yankees. Cashman and team president Randy Levine had started working the numbers with Close before the holidays. The Yanks wanted to avoid another arbitration showdown with Jeter, who was asking for $18.5 million to play the 2001 season, or $4 million more than the Yanks were offering.

A-Rod's ten-year, $252 million deal with Texas was signed in December (Hicks had paid $250 million for the entire franchise in 1998), just before Manny Ramirez completed his eight-year, $160 million deal with the Red Sox. Neither contract helped the Yankees' cause, nor did Steinbrenner's disposition. The previous winter, the Boss nearly signed Jeter to a seven-year, $118.5 million contract before backing out because he did not want to be the one to establish a new salary standard in the game.

This time around Steinbrenner wanted to keep Jeter's annual wage below $19 million, and so Cashman and Levine came to a tentative settlement with Close on a ten-year, $189 million commitment. The Boss let that agreement marinate for a while as he stewed over the size of the payout.

The Yankees had already given free agent pitcher Mike Mussina $88.5 million, and counting the $10 million Jeter earned in 2000, Steinbrenner was about to pay his shortstop $80.5 million more than the figure guaranteed in the seven-year deal he could have and should have signed after the '99 season.

The Boss did not care to extend lavish contract offers to players before they reached free agency; he had cost himself a lot of money by waiting until the eleventh hour to sign Bernie Williams for $87.5 million.

Jeter was one year away from free agency, but even Steinbrenner realized the waiting game was a losing proposition with his movie star at short. In his first five full seasons Jeter had four rings, the same as Joe DiMaggio. Jeter had 996 hits from 1996 through 2000, or 26 more hits than DiMaggio had from 1936 through 1940. The twenty-first century's answer to the Yankee Clipper was only getting more expensive by the game.

Finally, after one last conversation with Jeter designed to remind him who was the Boss, Steinbrenner made it official. "Derek Jeter embodies everything the Yankees are about," the owner said in a statement.

"Being the highest-paid player is not something I covet," Jeter said. "If that was the case, I would've waited another year and maximized my earning potential, so to speak. What is important is where you are and what makes you happy. . . . I never intended to look elsewhere. I couldn't picture it."

Jeter made his comments from Tampa on a late Friday afternoon conference call, and no seasoned Yankee observer with any news media savvy had to ask why. The Yankees were in the habit of throwing big news conference bashes for all of their big-ticket acquisitions, but they intentionally put the face of their franchise through a faceless exercise in the hope it would diminish the impact of the news.

Steinbrenner still believed in the power of the printed word and still saw New York as the ultimate newspaper town. Just as he had done in the seventies, the Boss knew how to run his own guerrilla campaign in the last great tabloid war in America, pitting the *Daily News* against the *Post* and vice versa.

Steinbrenner did not just understand how to deliver messages to his managers, players, and fans through the back pages. He understood everything about newspapers, including the fact that Saturday's editions reached the fewest sets of eyes.

So with commuters getting the early jump on their weekends, and with the next morning's paper scheduled to be pancake-thin, Steinbrenner decreed Jeter's latest victory at the bargaining table would come without a photo op.

"If there's any team or organization that can find a way to mess it up, it's the Yankees," said a livid Close. "They have done it. A Friday afternoon press conference? If you can sweep a $189 million contract under the rug, that's when you would do it.

"You've got the most celebrated athlete in New York. People love him. . . . It's a shame toward Derek. If anyone deserves a day of recognition, it's him."

Richer beyond his wildest imagination, Jeter was willing to move on, willing to continue calling his manager "Mr. Torre," and willing to continue chasing Yogi Berra's record of ten championship rings.

"This is the only organization I've played for, and the only one I want to play for," Jeter said. "Hopefully I'll be with the Yankees for my entire career, and this is a giant step toward that."

Jeter accepted a contract worth $63 million less than A-Rod's, and he was fine with it. Cashman? Not so much. The general manager had great respect for Jeter and found Close to be a good, tough, and smart advocate for his client.

But on this day, Cashman decided to change the way he did business with the young Yankees of the future. In his mind, Jeter and Close had pledged to reward the Yanks if they agreed to pay the shortstop more than they were required to during his second and third seasons, when the team had the power of contract renewal on its side.

Cashman felt that the Yankees were generous with Jeter, only to receive no hometown discounts on the back end. "We never got the break they said they'd give us," said Cashman, who lumped in Mariano Rivera with Jeter. "We offered above what we had to offer and they took us."

Jeter and Rivera were in the clear, but Cashman would make sure that future homegrown stars paid the pre-arbitration price. Meanwhile, if the Yankees felt like they'd been had by Jeter and Close, imagine how the Texas Rangers felt after they got through negotiating with Rodriguez and Scott Boras.

Rodriguez grew up a Mets fan, and after Jeter proved in the World Series that a world-class shortstop was the difference between the two New York teams, A-Rod seriously considered taking on Jeter in his own backyard. But Mets owner Fred Wilpon did not have the Steinbrennerian stomach for the free agent fight and never made A-Rod an offer despite all the tabloid noise that he should.

Instead Wilpon had his general manager, Steve Phillips, paint Rodriguez as a perk-crazy jerk more interested in the Mets giving him merchandise tents, marketing offices, billboards, and chartered jet service than he was in the Mets building him a championship-level team.

A-Rod was left to sign with a club that had never won a playoff series in a football-mad market that paid less attention to the Rangers than it did to its teenage quarterbacks under the Friday night lights. And for his *uber*-agent, Boras, a quarter of a billion dollars over ten seasons was not enough. No, Boras needed the extra two mil so he could brag at cocktail parties that he had doubled Kevin Garnett's record $126 million NBA deal.

"I'm almost embarrassed and ashamed of this contract," A-Rod said. Almost.

"I don't know if Michael Jordan or Bill Gates or Alexander the Great," Rodriguez continued, "I don't know if anybody is worth this money."

He sure did not believe Derek Jeter was worth the money. If that was not painfully clear in his ESPN Radio interview, Rodriguez hammered home the point in an interview published in *Esquire* magazine and in excerpted quotes that reached the New York news media in the early hours of March.

A-Rod conducted his radio and magazine interviews on December 19, so by the time he was made aware Jeter was upset over his comments to ESPN's Dan Patrick, it was too late to pull back his comments to *Esquire* and writer Scott Raab.

The Raab article was not about Jeter, and the seven deadly sentences were buried deep in a 7,000-word profile. Not that it mattered. Rodriguez was sitting with Boras and Raab in the Miami Heat's American Airlines Arena after a Heat-Lakers game, tape recorder rolling on the table, and just as clearly as Boras had walked his client into a bad deal in Texas, the agent walked A-Rod into a shit storm that effectively terminated his relationship with Jeter.

"It was Boras who added fuel to the fire that Jeter never had to carry a ball club," Raab would say. "Alex was asserting these things, but Boras was playing the role of reinforcing this idea that Alex was at a totally different level than Derek Jeter."

In the *Esquire* piece, Boras compared Jeter's 2000 power numbers (15 homers, 73 RBI) and Nomar Garciaparra's power numbers (21 homers, 96 RBI) to A-Rod's (41 homers, 132 RBI). "There's a big difference," the agent said.

And Rodriguez followed up: "Jeter's been blessed with great talent around him. He's never had to lead. He can just go and play and have fun. And he hits second — that's totally different than third and fourth in a lineup. You go into New York, you wanna stop Bernie and O'Neill. You never say, 'Don't let Derek beat you.' He's never your concern."

Armed with killer quotes, the press corps covering the Yankees advanced on Jeter's locker. The shortstop was wearing a playful, what-have-I-done-now smile when he saw the writers approach, but his face tightened into a knot when one started reading from the Book of Alex.

Jeter was stunned. Rodriguez had already assured him his radio comments had been misinterpreted, a claim Jeter did not buy. But this? *He's never your concern?*

Jeter told reporters he would call Rodriguez, but there was a better chance of Jeter volunteering to play second base than there was of a peace treaty emerging from these talks.

A-Rod immediately tried to backpedal from his comments and called Raab in a frantic bid for help. "Scott, you're killing me, man," Rodriguez told him. "I thought we were doing a nice, fun article. . . . Derek's really pissed off. He's really upset with me, really angry."

Raab heard dismay and anguish in A-Rod's voice. He offered to fax Jeter a letter stating that Rodriguez had said many positive things about him in their ninety-minute interview, too, and A-Rod took up Raab on the offer.

The writer's fax to Legends Field in Tampa read like this:

Dear Derek,

I talked with Alex on Friday night and he was understandably upset that his friendship with you might be hurt because of a few of his remarks in the Esquire article. I hope that is not the case. In the course of our interview, Alex also spoke sincerely of his professional respect and personal affection for you, and I'm sure he did not intend to sound controversial or negative.

I'm sorry for any friction the article may have created, and I wish you a healthy, successful season.

Raab never heard from Jeter; Rodriguez heard plenty. A-Rod made the ninety-minute drive from the Rangers' base in Port Charlotte to Jeter's base in Tampa. Rodriguez waited outside Jeter's home while the Yankee star — fully aware that A-Rod had made the drive — made Rodriguez wait and wait and wait until he was done eating at an area nightspot.

When Jeter finally returned home, he found an emotional A-Rod ready to beg for forgiveness from a man not inclined to grant it.

Jeter provided no details on this summit. He and Rodriguez would insist in the days to come that they arrived at an understanding, that their friendship would live on. A-Rod professed his undying affection for Jeter and his unmitigated respect for his leadership skills. "I feel like he's a brother of mine," Rodriguez maintained.

"I gave him the benefit of the doubt," Jeter said. "I don't anticipate him saying anything else. I've known him for a long time. We'll be friends after this."

Distant acquaintances? Maybe. Close friends? No shot.

Rodriguez had gotten a rare second chance from Jeter, who was not interested in the fact that A-Rod gave his radio and magazine interviews on the same day. Two interviews plus two attacks equaled one fracture that would never fully heal.

Rodriguez had earned the Chad Curtis treatment. In Jeter's unforgiving world, A-Rod had become a non-person.

"If you do something to hurt [Jeter], that's it, you're done," said Mike Borzello, the Yankee bullpen catcher who was close to the shortstop.

"Derek is a tough personality when it comes to who he lets in. And if he lets you in and you kind of screw him, for lack of a better term, hey, you were in. You had your chance."

The 2001 regular season did not come easily to Derek Jeter, not after he missed some spring training time with shoulder inflammation, and not after he started the regular season on the disabled list with a strained right quad. Jeter also was weighed down by a burden far greater than those tethered to any $189 million deal.

His sister, Sharlee, was fighting cancer.

Jeter had kept his sister's illness out of the press; he had confided in only a small number of teammates and friends. Sharlee had been watching the Yankees' playoff victory over Seattle from her Spelman College room in Atlanta the previous fall when her brother's home run made her jump so suddenly she fell from her bed and onto the floor.

Her bruised neck was initially diagnosed as a sprain, but when the swelling and pain did not subside, additional tests confirmed Derek Jeter's sister had Hodgkin's disease. The doctors believed they had caught it early, but Sharlee had to endure six months of chemotherapy treatments that caused fatigue, sleeplessness, nausea, and hair loss.

Dot Jeter called her daughter in Atlanta and sang her the same lullabies she had sung when Sharlee was a baby. "It was horrible," Dot said. "She'd be sick on a Saturday and I'd be sending her back to college from our home [in New Jersey]. I mean, she's a great kid. We prayed a lot and put it in God's hands. . . . We just knew there would be more to her life than twenty-one years."

Through the crisis, Sharlee was Jeter tough. Derek often called his sister in the middle of the night, with Sharlee in extreme pain, and she still found the strength to attend morning classes.

"Hearing I had cancer was surprising, something I never expected," she said, "but not impossible to believe. My parents always taught me to make the best out of the worst, so that's what I did."

After the chemo treatments ended in May, doctors decided radiation was not necessary. They declared Sharlee cancer-free, and her big brother approached another cancer survivor, Joe Torre, in the home dugout and said, "It's a good day today." The manager was floored when his shortstop told him why.

The extended Yankees family was already too well versed in the language of cancer. Torre's pitching coach, Mel Stottlemyre, was the most recent victim; he had been diagnosed with multiple myeloma the previous spring.

The following morning, Jeter revealed the news to reporters and assured them the experience was far more difficult for Sharlee than it was for him. He promptly went out and smashed a three-run homer in the eighth inning to beat the Baltimore Orioles.

Sharlee and her parents, Dot and Charles, were in the stands the next day, Mother's Day, and it didn't much matter that Derek booted a potential inning-ending double-play ball in the eleventh that led to a shocking Mariano Rivera meltdown and five Orioles runs.

Jeter had made eye contact with Sharlee and his parents, sitting as always on the first-base side and looking like the ultimate Little League clan. The shortstop never started a game without first finding his family members in the crowd and acknowledging them with a smile and a wave.

Sharlee was wearing a blue bandanna over her scalp to cover the hair loss, but on this game day cancer had struck out. "I don't think I've ever gotten a better Mother's Day present," Dot said of her daughter's prognosis.

This victory on a day of defeat encouraged Derek Jeter's Yankees for only so long. That night, Bernie Williams's father, Bernabe, died in Puerto Rico hours after suffering a massive heart attack. Bernie had left the Yankees to be with his hospitalized father in April; this time he arrived too late to bid his hero one last goodbye.

Williams returned to the team after missing a three-game series in Oakland and helped the Yanks regain first place at the All-Star break by lifting his batting average from .221 to .321. Jeter was hitting .292, substandard for him, and there was some doubt about whether he would be picked for his fourth All-Star Game appearance as a reserve behind Alex Rodriguez, the voted-in starter.

Jeter was already being used in television promos for the game, and he had a decided home-court advantage — Torre was the one filling out the roster. But the day before Torre revealed his picks, Buster Olney of the *Times* asked Jeter if he was comfortable with the promos, the question framed by the premise that Jeter was not a mortal lock to make the team.

"And a flash of anger came across his face," Olney said.

The following day, after Torre named Jeter among his seven Yankee All-Stars, Jeter saw Olney enter the clubhouse. "Hey, Buster," he yelled. "I guess that answers your question."

Like most ballplayers, Jeter rarely referred to writers by name, unless he wanted to make a point. Jeter had made his point.

But later that month, with his batting average still a bit south of .300, with his fielding percentage (.963) still the second-worst among

American League starting shortstops, and with his contract still the second-largest in the history of American team sports, Jeter was facing more published questions about his post-megadeal contributions to the cause.

Jeter maintained he didn't often read the papers or listen to sports talk radio. But nobody who knew the shortstop ever bought it. If Jeter did not read a critical column, his ever-protective parents read it for him and filled in the blanks.

From Muhammad Ali to Michael Jordan, Jack Nicklaus to Tiger Woods, the greatest athletes were forever motivated by their critics, and Jeter was no different. In one breath he would say, "Does [criticism] bother me? No, I don't care what somebody writes." And in the next he would concede, "I think you take criticism as a challenge."

In the immediate wake of some printed and pointed criticism, Jeter had eight hits in eleven at-bats, scored seven runs, and drove in three in a three-game sweep of Detroit. He carried a .317 average into September and helped the Yanks build a nine-and-a-half-game divisional lead before injuring his hamstring running out a ground ball.

Six days later, September 10, Jeter was testing his hamstring in some easy backpedaling drills in a rain-soaked Yankee Stadium outfield before another storm forced him inside. Jeter was not ready to return, and missing this kind of big-game event — Roger Clemens going for his twentieth victory of the year against his former team, the Red Sox — made the shortstop hurt in a way that had nothing to do with his leg.

As it turned out, Clemens's bid for his sixth 20-win season and first as a Yankee was washed away, along with a crowd of 50,000. Now up thirteen games in the American League East, Torre was not sweating the small stuff. He said he might keep Jeter benched another week, just to ensure he was ready for the postseason, and it did not matter that the shortstop was growing more anxious by the hour.

"I'm honest when I say they don't tell me anything," Jeter said of Torre and the training staff. "[The hamstring] felt good. I guess tomorrow we'll know more, I would assume."

Only tomorrow would never come for Jeter and the Yankees and the rest of baseball. Clemens was scheduled to throw his 19-1 record at the

White Sox on the night of September 11, 2001, and this time the game was not canceled by a force of nature but by a man-made event.

The Yankees knew there would be no baseball for a while the instant they started making sense of the apocalyptic scenes downtown. Jorge Posada was in the hospital with his young son, who was recovering from surgery on his skull condition, craniosynostosis, when the catcher left a message for his close friend telling him to turn on the TV.

Derek Jeter awoke to see the World Trade Center burning, to see legions of soot-covered New Yorkers fleeing the billowing clouds of smoke raging through the streets. Terrorists had flown commercial jets into the towers, and the bodies and body parts plummeting to the street began what President Bush would call "a monumental struggle of good against evil."

Hours later Jeter left his Upper East Side apartment to buy something to eat. "I felt like I was on a movie set," he said. "There were no cars on the streets of Manhattan." New York, Jeter would say, "is a ghost town."

Baseball commissioner Bud Selig would not make the same mistake made by the late National Football League commissioner Pete Rozelle, who decided against canceling games after President Kennedy's assassination and carried that regret to his grave.

Baseball was shut down, and in the days to come Jeter joined a group of Yankees — Joe Torre, Bernie Williams, Paul O'Neill, and Mariano Rivera among them — for a trip into the petrified remains of the area surrounding Ground Zero. They visited with rescue workers at the Javits Center, where cops and firefighters told the Yanks they wanted another title.

"They were asking for autographs," Jeter said, "and you felt like you should be asking for their autographs."

The Yankees comforted burn victims at St. Vincent's Hospital, and they traveled to the armory where family members waited for DNA matches to identify their loved ones. Williams told a woman it looked like she needed a hug, then gave her one.

"Nobody really talked about baseball," Torre said. "Of course, they were all asking for Jeter. There was one youngster who had lost his dad and he was looking for Jeter."

The Yankees had a visit scheduled for a firehouse, and they had given advance notice to news media outlets they would be available there to talk about the day. But Jeter balked. If he was not the official captain of the Yankees, he was the assumed future captain and current leader of the team.

And Jeter did not believe the Yankees should be publicizing their visits with exhausted rescue workers and distraught families of the injured and dead. The shortstop felt a photo op and news conference would trivialize the devastation and make it appear the team was trying to use a catastrophic event to enhance its image.

One of the Yankees' public relations officials, Jason Zillo, began going back and forth with Jeter over his stand. "This isn't about making the Yankees look good," Zillo told him. "This isn't that type of publicity. To see Derek Jeter and the Yankees out there lending a hand is inspirational, so people might say, 'I need to get off my ass and do something.'"

Jeter and Zillo maintained a strong working relationship, and this was the most heated exchange they had ever had. Jeter prevailed, as franchise players often do, and the Yankees returned to the firehouse on a day when no media outlets were given a heads up.

Jeter was among those who set a private Yankee tone for an extremely public crisis, while the local-boy Mets of John Franco (Brooklyn), Al Leiter (Jersey), and Bobby Valentine (Connecticut) joined forces with adopted Manhattan son Mike Piazza and others to practically march through the city streets playing the bagpipes behind the biggest Yankee fan of all, Mayor Rudy Giuliani.

Forever New York's secondary baseball tenants, the Mets were out front and center in the wake of this mass murder of unspeakable depths. They slapped on NYPD and FDNY caps, dared someone in the commissioner's office to try to remove them, and donated a day's pay (about $450,000) to the 9/11 victims.

Though George Steinbrenner had already publicly committed $1 million to the cause, Yankees reliever Mike Stanton responded that his team would make its donations "quietly and privately, not because you want someone to know that you're [making] them," a comment that angered the Mets and set off an embarrassing debate that bathed neither side in glory.

On the night of September 21, the Mets hosted Atlanta in the first post-9/11 game in New York, a game decided by Mike Piazza's eighth-inning homer off Steve Karsay, only the biggest swing the Mets' biggest star would ever take. "It was like Casey coming to the plate," said teammate Todd Zeile.

Three nights earlier, after a moving ceremony in Chicago, the Yankees had played their first game since the terrorist attacks and saw their own biggest star, Jeter, shake off his hamstring injury and thirteen days of rust to go 3 for 4 in an 11–3 victory over the White Sox. Jeter followed the next night with two home runs — his first multiple-homer game in three years — in a 6–3 victory that gave his team a fourteen-game divisional lead.

The Yankees staged their own emotional homecoming in the Bronx on September 25, arriving at Yankee Stadium as humbled ambassadors of their broken city. Their longtime VP of ticket operations, Frank Swaine, had lost a son at the World Trade Center, and one of the team's advance ticket sellers, Hank Grazioso, had lost one son on the 104th floor of Tower 1 and a second son on the 105th floor.

The world had changed for keeps. Police were keeping cars away from Stadium service roads, and everyone's bags were being searched on the way in, Jeter's and Torre's included.

Torre had spent enough time with pregnant widows and children of lost heroes to know the season's mission statement — win a fourth consecutive championship — had been replaced with a mission of mercy. The manager had already told his players, "We're not here to save civilization. But our job is to relieve some tension and give everyone something to enjoy."

Jeter had already done his part before the Yankees took the field. He had called ten-year-old Brielle Saracini in Yardley, Pennsylvania, a fan who had written him a letter, a girl who had told him her father, Victor, was the United Airlines pilot whose plane was crashed into the South Tower.

Brielle wanted to know why her favorite player stood up so straight when he hit; her favorite player wanted to know if Brielle and her sister, Kirsten, and mother, Ellen, would be his guests at the following night's game against the Devil Rays.

So Brielle and Kirsten talked to Jeter and Williams and El Duque

Hernandez during batting practice, and then they watched the game from the shortstop's seats behind home plate. After Jeter delivered two hits and scored a run in the 5–1 victory, Brielle and Kirsten were ushered onto the field to tap fists with the winners.

Torre gave Brielle the lineup card. "We made her smile," Jeter said. "At least for today."

The Yankees won the American League East by thirteen and a half games, and as they entered the postseason they were constantly reminded they were representing a charred, bloodstained city. New York needed something to cheer about, something to serve as a temporary sanctuary from the pain.

A long and prosperous postseason run was in order. But in the seventh inning of the third game of the American League Division Series, when Shane Spencer cut loose his throw from the right-field corner of Network Associates Coliseum and watched it sail like a child's lost balloon, the Yankees had the sick feeling their season was drifting away with it.

They were clinging desperately to a 1–0 lead over the Oakland A's, who had taken the first two games of this best-of-five in the Bronx. With a payroll of $38 million, the A's were about to sweep George Steinbrenner's dynastic $112 million champs.

Sure, Jorge Posada's homer had given the Yankees their first lead over these A's in eighty regular-season and postseason innings, and sure, Mike Mussina was painting a masterpiece in his first playoff start as a Yank.

But Oakland's precocious and gifted young lefty, Barry Zito, had held the visitors to two lousy hits. Terrence Long had just ripped Mussina's hundredth pitch for a double down the first-base line that would surely score Jeremy Giambi from first, tie the game, and ultimately leave an eliminated Torre to negotiate a new contract with Steinbrenner on the worst possible terms.

The brother of Oakland superstar Jason Giambi, the Ozzie Canseco to Jason's Jose, Jeremy Giambi had the two-out benefit of running on contact. But he was something of a lead foot and he had taken a lazy secondary lead off first.

Playing for the benched Paul O'Neill, Spencer gathered Long's laser and fired toward second baseman Alfonso Soriano, who had run onto the outfield grass as the first cutoff man, and first baseman Tino Martinez, who had pulled himself up from the dirt — he had made a failed dive for Long's shot — and stationed himself near the bag.

On release, Spencer thought he had made a good throw to the cutoff men in line with Posada at the plate. A second later, the right fielder whispered to himself, "Uh-oh."

Derek Jeter was too busy to say "Uh-oh." In the event Long tried for a triple, Jeter was positioned as a potential cutoff man on a throw to third, his head on a swivel. Jeter was watching the exaggerated arc of Spencer's throw, watching Long's stride on his way to second, and watching Oakland's third-base coach, Ron Washington, to see if he was waving Giambi home.

Almost directly behind Washington, up in his executive suite, A's architect Billy Beane surveyed the scene with great expectations. Beane had been a high school phenom drafted by the Mets in the first round, but he never amounted to more than a bit major league player. Now in the general manager's seat of a small-market, smaller-budget team, Beane used the A's as his vehicle of retribution against a sport that had denied him stardom.

Beane had three starting pitchers twenty-six or younger: Zito, Tim Hudson, and Mark Mulder. Together they went a combined 56-25 in the regular season, and they had held the mighty Yanks to four runs in the first twenty-five innings of the Division Series. The A's had a young left side of the infield in Miguel Tejada and Eric Chavez, who combined for 63 homers and 227 RBI. Meanwhile, the reigning league MVP, first baseman Jason Giambi, was carrying a .342 batting average and 38 homers and 120 RBI into free agency.

On a payroll south of $40 million, Beane had become the superstar in the front office that he could not be on the field, the maker of a 102-win team. He was the handsome, big-man-on-campus face of a movement that would forever change the way teams measured prospects, emphasizing on-base percentages over batting averages and replacing the "gut feel" of a road-weary scout with mathematical and statistical analysis of a player's contributions — or lack thereof — to his team.

The writer, historian, and statistician Bill James would name this approach "sabermetrics" as a nod to the Society for American Baseball

Research (SABR), and Beane's use of this tool to compete with Stein-brenner's budget — or lack thereof — would inspire the Michael Lewis bestseller *Moneyball*.

But as Jeter measured the developing seventh-inning situation on October 13, as the shortstop watched Spencer's sailing throw and Washington's waving arm and Giambi's chugging feet, Billy Beane was not the cool ex-jock lording over a *Revenge of the Nerds* revolution.

Beane was just another guy who thought he was watching a tied ball game, even after Jeter decided to abort his cutoff position, dash across the grass separating the mound from second base, and chase down a throw he realized was too high for either Soriano or Martinez to catch.

"I ignored Jeter's movement," Beane said. "It was like, 'Where is he going?' I was so convinced that we had scored. You're thinking, 'There's no way Jeter's connecting these dots on this play to make it work.'"

Washington had the same feeling as he moved down the line, es-corting Giambi home. Back when he had scouted Jeter in the minors, Washington was the one who decided Derek was "not no goddamn shortstop" and wrote him up as a future third baseman. If Oakland's third-base coach had long accepted the fact that he was wrong, he was about to discover just how wrong he was.

By the time Jeter caught the ball on a bounce on the first-base line some twenty feet from the plate, running toward the Yankees' dug-out and away from Posada, Washington knew he had made the right choice. Jeter's intangible brilliance was not going to overtake the tan-gibles of the play, not this time.

Momentum and time and gravity were all working against the Yan-kee shortstop. But somehow he called an audible on the fly. Jeter con-verted himself into a wishbone quarterback and delivered a pitch to the tailback that would have made J. C. Watts proud.

Jeter did not just make a backhanded flip to Posada; he had the presence of mind to flip the ball against the grain of his body, so the catcher would receive it on the third-base side of the plate. "That son of a bitch threw the ball back this way," Washington would say, "because he knew it would tail back in. He threw it so all Posada had to do was catch and tag."

Before the ball reached Posada, Ramon Hernandez, the on-deck batter, stopped begging and pleading with both arms for Giambi to slide. Hernandez's arms went slack, almost in a disgusted way. He knew Giambi was coming in standing up.

"If he slides," Posada said, "I don't have a chance."

Giambi did not slide. He was locked in on Posada, expecting the catcher to block the plate and force a collision. He should have focused on Hernandez instead.

"It would have been close either way," Giambi said.

Posada slapped the tag on his right calf a millisecond before Giambi's right foot landed on the plate, and the umpire was up to the moment. Kerwin Danley stepped into the scene with purpose, cocking his right hand and throwing a punch that would secure as memorable a play as a shortstop ever made, the infield's answer to Willie Mays's over-the-head catch on Vic Wertz's drive in the 1954 World Series.

Wearing number 7 as a tribute to Mickey Mantle, his father's favorite player, Giambi had just claimed an un-Mantle-like piece of October lore. Mussina was backing up the play, already resigned to a 1–1 score and a no-decision or worse on his record. The pitcher could not believe Posada held on to the ball or even his mitt after Giambi's left knee swung through the tag. "Holy shit," Mussina told himself. "He's out?"

Jeter usually reserved his signature fist pump in the air for series-clinching outs in the postseason, but he could not resist this time. He clenched his famous right fist and screamed as Giambi looked over his shoulder at Danley's call.

Jeter did not know it at the time, but this was a fitting moment for him to take a stand. In the coming years Jeremy Giambi would admit to taking steroids, and his brother, Jason, would testify about his own steroid use before a federal grand jury. They were both wearing the colors of a team built around sabermetrics, the analytical approach that would be used like a bayonet to puncture Jeter's standing in the game.

The disparate forces of steroids and sabermetrics collided at the plate that day, and there was no mathematical formula to explain why Jeter — patron saint of the clean ballplayer, punching bag of the sabermetric set — walked away without a scratch.

Giambi, the corner cutter who did not slide. Beane, the new-age executive who had no sabermetric chart that could evaluate this play. Washington, the doubting Thomas who had sent Giambi home.

In one artful flip of his wrist, Jeter had made believers of them all.

Across the field, A's manager Art Howe and his players were still trying to make sense of the play. Washington had smoke blowing out of his ears and nostrils, and not because Jeter had just poured a bucket of Gatorade on that old minor league scouting report.

"I walked into the dugout and everybody's patting Giambi on the back for the effort," Washington said. "And I point-blank told Giambi right there, 'You've got to fuckin' hit the dirt.' That's exactly what I said. He didn't say anything."

Up in his executive suite, Beane was locked in the same state of shock that gripped the hushed crowd of 55,861. His A's had lost a Game 5 to the Yanks the previous fall, and now they had opened the Game 3 door to the same crushing fate. "This was in the heart of the Yankee aura," Beane said. "It was a time when you were a club like Oakland, and you were playing the Yankees, at no point did you think they're not going to come back and beat you."

Mariano Rivera held the A's scoreless over the final two innings, but when general manager Brian Cashman said, "It was like Superman flying out of the sky to save the season," he was not talking about his indomitable closer.

Jeter sat at his locker, ice pack on his shoulder, and told everyone he was just doing his job. "I was supposed to be there," he said, before batting away the premature obits printed in the hours before Game 3.

"Other people may have thought we were dead," Jeter said. "But nobody in here thought we were dead."

Jeter and Torre and Don Zimmer swore the Yankees practiced that very play in spring training, with the shortstop acting as a trailer or free safety. A couple of years earlier, during a defensive drill ("We had interns running the bases," Zimmer said), a Yankee right fielder retrieved a ball from the corner, fired toward the plate, and overthrew both cutoff men.

The coaches had never seen that kind of overthrow before. "We looked at each other and said, 'What are we going to do if that happens in the game?'" Zimmer said. "Well, there's not going to be a play at second or third; what's the shortstop doing? We found a spot for him. . . .'"

But Scott Brosius put all that inside baseball talk in perspective. Of

Jeter, Brosius said, "He doesn't practice the old running-toward-the-dugout-and-flip-it-back-home play."

J. P. Ricciardi, Oakland's director of player personnel and a Boston Celtics fan out of Worcester, Massachusetts, likened the play to Larry Bird's indelible steal of Isiah Thomas's inbounds pass in the 1987 Eastern Conference finals.

Ricciardi's boss, Billy Beane? He was not angry over Giambi's failure to slide, and he was not exasperated over Danley's failure to see the play as a tie-goes-to-the-runner proposition. Beane was simply awed by Jeter's grace.

"It's almost as if Derek designed it," he said, "like, 'Hey, I've got to go into the dugout anyway.' It had to be perfect and fit right into his schedule. There were two outs, he flipped to Posada on his way to the dugout, and just sort of disappeared.

"Derek Jeter even has an elegant way of breaking your heart."

It wasn't quite so elegant on the night of Game 5, a Bronx night made possible by the Game 3 and Game 4 victories in Oakland, a night that started with Phil Rizzuto following up his ceremonial first pitch by pulling a second ball out of his pocket, trotting toward the first-base line, and then flipping the ball back to his designated catcher, Clay Bellinger, in perfect Jeter form.

The Yankee Stadium crowd loved it, and so did the eighty-four-year-old Rizzuto, who had not told a soul about his planned tribute, not even his bride of fifty-eight years, Cora.

"You're stealing my thunder," Jeter told the Scooter as they met in the dugout.

Jeter stole it right back in the top of the eighth, Yanks leading 5–3 with one out and Oakland's Eric Chavez on first. Terrence Long, the same batter whose Game 3 double led to Jeter's forever flip to Posada, lifted a high foul ball behind third base, and the shortstop chased it the same way he chased Shane Spencer's errant throw.

Jeter looked at the ball, the stands, the ball, the stands, and the ball again. At the time, he had already driven home what would be the winning run on a sacrifice fly, and at age twenty-seven he had already collected his eighty-sixth and eighty-seventh career postseason hits to break the record held by Pete Rose.

Beane was not in his seat to watch Jeter break Rose's record or give the Yanks a 4–3 lead; he had left the Stadium after his A's went up by a 2–0 count in the second inning, too tormented to watch. Beane jumped on a train to Manhattan and tried to forget about the game. He closed his eyes and fantasized about popping back into the Stadium in the ninth inning to watch the A's win.

"I didn't want to go through the hell of watching them beat us again," Beane said. "I figured if I disappeared at that point in the universe, something crazy would happen and we'd win."

While Beane was riding the subway, Jeter was going over the rail. He went head over spikes and crash-landed flat on his back against the cement floor of the photographers' pit. The crowd of 56,642 gasped when Jeter disappeared from view, fearing serious injury and an extended at-bat for Long.

There would be neither: Jeter suffered only a cut on his elbow. Of greater consequence, he had caught the ball. Scott Brosius grabbed it out of his glove and fired to second, but Chavez had already tagged up and beaten the throw. It didn't matter; the A's were pronounced dead on the spot.

"Got beer spilled on me," Jeter said. "Nobody caught me. I think people were just reaching for their drinks."

As Jeter wiped at the spilled beer and climbed back over the rail and onto the field, the fans chanted his name. Not since 1996 had the shortstop heard the Stadium sound half as loud as this.

"It felt good," Jeter said of the chant. "But really, I'm not kidding when I say my first thought was, 'We have to score more runs.'"

New Yorkers were using this Yankee playoff run as a reprieve, using the Stadium as a place to go and forget the worst weeks of their lives. A month and four days after the Twin Towers collapsed into a smoldering heap, the city needed a diversion and one of the surest signs that everyday normalcy was within reach — the Yankees winning games in October.

Their best player, Jeter, had plunged into the stands and emerged with the Division Series in the webbing of his glove. Beane made it back for the final two innings, made it back to watch the Yanks become the first team to lose the first two games of a best-of-five at home and then win the series.

Rivera again pitched the final two scoreless innings. "It was so psychological to know he was out there; you knew you weren't going to beat them," Beane said. "You had no chance. You knew Rivera had the sickle in hand ready to get you."

But Jeter was the one who delivered the fatal stab. He batted .444 in the series and saved the Yankees from near-certain elimination with his glove and feet and instincts in Oakland, where the shortstop who shared a birth date with Abner Doubleday (June 26) invented a new way of playing the game.

"We definitely win the series if Jeter doesn't make that flip play," Ricciardi said. "But with the Yankees it's like a mob hit. When they tell you the guy's killed, you've got to see the body in the coffin to believe he's dead."

In victory, Joe Torre talked about the look in Jeter's eye, the same look he saw in the eye of the Tiger — Tiger Woods — when the manager first met Jeter's friend. The look of purpose and fearlessness. The look of an athlete who does not sweat the potential consequences of putting his body in peril or his big-game reputation on the line.

"It's a look that you don't teach," Torre said.

George Steinbrenner was weeping when assessing the performance that validated Jeter's look. "I've never seen any athlete dominate a sport — football, basketball, or baseball — the way he did in this playoff series," the Boss said.

But the most poignant praise came from Rizzuto, the Hall of Fame shortstop on seven Yankee championship teams. "I couldn't carry his glove," he said of Jeter.

Rizzuto called him the best shortstop he had ever seen, and a figure worthy of comparison to the most graceful and instinctive Yankee of them all, Joe DiMaggio.

"Derek is very comparable to DiMag in that they both have that sixth sense," Rizzuto said. "They both play the game so naturally and beautifully. Never out of place and always heading to the right spot. Joe never made a mistake and Jeter doesn't, either.

"I mean, the kid has a gift. Joe's gift."

In the tenth inning of Game 4 of the 2001 World Series, Derek Jeter stepped to the plate with a .067 batting average against the Arizona Diamondbacks. Since the start of the five-game American League Championship Series victory over Seattle, Jeter had gone 3 for 32.

He had taken far more punishment on that Game 5 fall against Oakland than he ever admitted, and so Jeter was a shell of his Division Series self against the Mariners, a team that had won a record 116 games in the Year 1 A.A. — After Alex.

Curt Schilling and Randy Johnson had plenty to do with Jeter's struggles in the first thirty-six innings of the World Series, but the shortstop's body ached — his hamstring, his shoulder, and his back. The ice packs strapped about his torso and limbs said it all: this was not Derek Jeter trying to win a fourth consecutive title as much as it was the mummified remains of Derek Jeter trying to win again.

"My whole thing has always been, you either play or you don't play," Jeter would say. "If you play, I don't think people want to hear about what's bothering you or what's hurting you. I think that is a built-in excuse. . . . It didn't feel good, but I was all right to play."

Jeter's pain threshold was the Yankees' best friend, and their longtime trainer, Gene Monahan, ranked the shortstop among the toughest players he had ever treated, right there with Thurman Munson and Graig Nettles.

After his fall into the photographers' pit in the Game 5 victory over the A's, Jeter was "hobbling around pretty good," Monahan said. "He had trouble putting his shoes on. He had trouble getting dressed. You could see the pain, and it was a tough time for him. But he's never going to entertain any thoughts of not playing. His mindset was, 'This is only going to hurt me for a couple of hours, and I've got the night to feel better tomorrow.'"

Through the Seattle series and the first three games of the World Series, Monahan did everything he could to try to piece Jeter back together. "We used a lot of ice, a lot of contrasting back and forth, hot and cold," the trainer said, "and pretty much when he was at the ballpark we wouldn't let him do a lot of work on the side. We just saved every ounce of whatever energy and health we could for the innings of the ball game. We got him off his feet, put him up in the training room, and elevated his legs."

But Jeter needed an off-season more than he needed a training table or a tub. At the time he stepped to the tenth-inning plate in the final moments of Halloween night, Arizona holding a 2–1 World Series lead, Jeter's biggest contribution to the Yanks had come in the roles of Game 3 host and adviser to the president of the United States.

George W. Bush landed at John F. Kennedy International and flew to Yankee Stadium by helicopter (he touched down on an adjacent ball field). September 11 had changed the terms of engagement, so the Stadium was a police state complete with 1,500 cops, sharpshooters on the roof, bomb-sniffing dogs in the clubhouses, hazmat specialists in the ballpark's bowels, and an armed Secret Service agent in the umpires' locker room, dressed for the part.

Scheduled to become the first sitting president to throw out the ceremonial first pitch at a World Series game since Dwight Eisenhower, Bush headed to the batting cage to warm up his right arm. He did not want anyone — countrymen, terrorists, anyone — to see the president of the United States show any sign of weakness.

Bush said he wanted to throw the pitch "with a little zip. I didn't want people to think that their president was incapable of finding the plate." Bush was wearing a New York Fire Department sweat jacket over a bulletproof vest when Jeter arrived on the scene to shake his hand.

"I hear you're throwing out the first ball," the shortstop said. "Are you going to throw the first pitch from the mound or in front of the mound?"

"I think I'll throw from the base of the mound," Bush said.

"I wouldn't do that if I were you, Mr. President. You'd better throw from the mound, otherwise you're going to get booed. This is Yankee Stadium."

"OK. I'll throw from the mound."

Jeter started to walk away to get ready for Game 3 before he stopped, looked over his shoulder, and told the president, "Don't bounce it. They'll boo you."

Bush suddenly did not feel as relaxed as he had five minutes earlier. "The great Derek Jeter, don't bounce it, they'll boo you," the president would say. "All of a sudden the pressure mounted."

Bush was in the dugout when Yankee Stadium's iconic public address announcer, Bob Sheppard, introduced him to the full house in his voice-of-God way. The president waved to the crowd, stood tall on the mound behind the rubber, and threw back his head and shoulders in a pose of certainty and strength. A burned and tattered flag found at the World Trade Center site hung above the scoreboard façade behind him. Bush gave the thumbs-up sign to the masses, then fired a perfect strike to backup catcher Todd Greene.

The crowd chanted, "USA . . . USA" as Bush walked off, and then Roger Clemens outperformed the other big sporting act in town, Michael Jordan, who had emerged from retirement to make his Washington Wizards debut at Madison Square Garden. Jordan lost to the Knicks, the Diamondbacks lost to Clemens, and now Jordan's favorite baseball player — his handpicked Nike heir — had a chance to even the World Series with one swing of his Game 4 bat.

Jeter was given that chance by Tino Martinez, who batted with two outs and one on in the ninth, Arizona up 3–1 and closer Byung-Hyun Kim on the mound. Martinez had nearly been traded to Atlanta the year before, a trade supported by Joe Torre and other club officials before Brian Cashman killed it. The GM decided Martinez was too valuable in the clubhouse and in the lineup to part with, and the first baseman was about to make Cashman a prophet.

Martinez had watched Kim throw first-pitch fastballs in the eighth before turning to his slider. "So I was going to look for that first fastball and hammer it," Martinez said.

Hammer it the first baseman did, nearly bringing down the Stadium as he rounded the bases. Rivera pitched a 1-2-3 tenth, and the Yankees' leadoff hitter for the night, Jeter, made a dramatic claim.

"Derek came back to the dugout, put down his glove, and said, 'This game is over,'" Martinez said. "He didn't say, 'I'm going to hit a home run and end it.' He just meant he was going to find a way to win the game."

Kim retired Scott Brosius and Alfonso Soriano before Jeter stepped in, the scoreboard flashing his .067 World Series average in big, bright lights. In the dugout, with Torre holding his bat for good luck, Jeter had made a playful reference to Torre's contract — due to expire at 11:59 p.m., October 31.

"This is the last time I have to listen to you," the shortstop said, "because once it turns midnight you don't have a job."

It was still October when Jeter was getting set in the box. He fouled off the first pitch, the clock struck midnight, and Jeter shot a half smile at the manager he still called Mr. Torre. The scoreboard announced, "ATTENTION FANS: WELCOME TO NOVEMBER BASEBALL," and Jeter and Kim engaged in the longest duel of the night — nine pitches, four foul balls, and a full count.

As he fought to stay alive in the at-bat, Jeter represented the battered state of the Yankee offense. Paul O'Neill and Scott Brosius were planning to retire, Martinez was approaching free agency and the realization the Yanks weren't bringing him back, and the benched Chuck Knoblauch knew he was done in the Bronx, too.

This was a dynasty running on fumes, trying to sputter its way home one last time. So the shortstop who had been hearing his mother implore him to "do something" all week finally did something no major leaguer had ever done: he hit a home run in November.

At 12:04 a.m., Kim's 3-2 pitch had landed on the other side of the 314-foot sign in right, not far from Jeffrey Maier–ville. The Giants' Barry Bonds had belted a record 73 homers in the regular season, and none of them packed a wallop like this Jeter shot that cleared the wall by a matter of inches.

A fan held up a sign that read "Mr. November," and as Jeter approached the plate and the manic pile of teammates surrounding it, he decided to take the kind of lunar leap Bobby Thomson took to punctuate his Shot Heard 'Round the World half a century earlier; Jeter had better hang time.

"It was the only showboating thing I ever did," Thomson had said.

Jeter could have made the same claim. One of his biggest fans, John Wooden, who likened Jeter to his championship point guards at UCLA, watched from his California home and said he was surprised that baseball's most selfless superstar engaged in this celebration of self.

"Joe DiMaggio would've just rounded the bases and touched the plate," Wooden said.

Jeter joked that he nearly broke his foot on the plate, but he had his reasons to fly. "I've never hit a walk-off home run," he said. "Not even in Little League."

The following night, Brosius did in Game 5 exactly what Martinez had done in Game 4: hit a two-out, two-run homer off Kim in the ninth to send the Yankees barreling into extra innings, and to ensure this edition would go down among the greatest World Series of all time.

The remarkable Brosius homer was sandwiched between the Stadium chant for the retiring O'Neill when defeat seemed imminent, and Soriano's RBI single in the twelfth (after his diving, bases-loaded catch in the eleventh) when defeat seemed impossible to fathom. Under a full moon, Torre called this absurd event "Groundhog Day."

The Diamondbacks were as devastated as their closer, Kim, who appeared intent on winning as many World Series games for the Yankees as Whitey Ford did. Before the Series, when asked about the Yanks' dominance, Schilling said, "When you use the words *mystique* and *aura*, those are dancers in a nightclub."

Mystique and aura were appearing nightly, read the classic Game 5 sign in the Bronx, and when the Yankees boarded their plane for the Arizona desert, they were safe bets to bring another title to a city in dire need of something to celebrate. Jeter was going to separate himself from Nomar Garciaparra, the two-time batting champ, and from Alex Rodriguez, who had smashed 52 homers in the first year of his record $252 million deal.

The ring-free A-Rod and the ring-free Nomar could gorge themselves on individual stats. Jeter? He was about to win his one for the thumb.

Somehow the Yankees had the ninth-inning lead in Game 7. Somehow they had handed Mariano Rivera the ball with three outs to go and the bottom of Arizona's lineup on deck.

It all started going wrong before Game 6, before Andy Pettitte tipped his pitches and the Diamondbacks teed off on him in a 15–2 victory, leaving the Bank One Ballpark operators to play Sinatra's "New York, New York" in jest. Bernie Williams had shown up late for pregame warm-ups, very late, and as the Yankees were stretching, Jeter turned to a teammate and said, "Where the hell is he?"

Jeter was furious by the time Williams finally arrived, asking him, "Where the hell have you been?" The center fielder offered a dog-ate-my-homework answer, and Jeter jumped all over him. "What do you think you're doing here?" the shortstop shouted at Williams. "We're trying to win a championship, and this is unacceptable. . . . There's no more important place for you to be than right here with your team for this game."

This wasn't the only time Jeter had to rouse Williams out of his oblivious state. "It was Bernie being Bernie," one team official said, "and I think Derek got sick of it."

Jeter was not one to chastise teammates in front of others, or even to speak up much in team meetings. Only this time he ripped a page out of the book George Steinbrenner once gave him, a book titled *Patton on Leadership: Strategic Lessons for Corporate Warfare* and inscribed this way: "To Derek. Read and study. He was a great leader as you are and will be a great leader. Hopefully of the men in pinstripes."

Jeter was not the team captain, even if the conversation about his candidacy had been carried on for a couple of years. But as the Yankees' de facto captain, Jeter felt the need to go after Williams behind closed clubhouse doors, even if some were looking on.

No news media members were present, and Jeter did not mean for it to become public knowledge. "I don't think it's necessary for people to know about things publicly," the shortstop would say when asked about his confrontation with Williams. "That's just the way I've always handled it."

Once Jeter was done rebuking Williams a second time near the clubhouse bathroom, all that mystique and aura were flushed down the drain. The Yankees came undone in Game 6 and were losing by a 15–0 count in the fifth inning when Torre applied his own mercy rule and removed Jeter, Tino Martinez, and Jorge Posada from the game.

Jeter ended up in the trainer's room when he overheard reliever Jay Witasick say, "Well, at least I had fun." Witasick made this remark after allowing Arizona nine runs, eight earned, while recording all of four outs, inspiring Jeter to give him the Bernie treatment times two. The shortstop had never been angrier.

"Fun? I can't relate to it," Jeter would tell *Sports Illustrated*'s Tom Verducci. "I really can't relate to it. I'll never forget that. At least you had *fun*? I'll never understand it. I don't want to understand it."

Their nerves frayed, their faith no longer as blind as it had been in the Bronx, Jeter's Yankees were left to face the 22-game winner, Schilling, in Game 7.

It was a tense struggle between Schilling and Roger Clemens, the

20-game winner who had ten years earlier showered his opponent with tough love, warning Schilling he needed to work harder and stop wasting his outsized skill. The Yankees were trailing the Diamondbacks by a 1–0 count before Jeter singled and scored in the seventh, and before Soriano homered in the soft desert rain to lead off the eighth.

The bullpen doors ultimately opened for Rivera and Randy Johnson, the Game 6 winner who had so memorably emerged from the Seattle pen in '95 to eliminate Buck Showalter's Yanks. Rivera survived the eighth and was a prohibitive favorite to survive the ninth.

Arizona's Mark Grace opened with a single before David Dellucci pinch-ran for him, then Damian Miller dropped down a bunt that headed the closer's way. Rivera fielded the ball and fired to Jeter at second, but his throw tailed in left to right, two-seamer form, and the shortstop tried in vain to stretch his sore, stiff body for the ball while keeping his foot on the bag.

Dellucci crashed his spikes into Jeter's left ankle as the throw skipped off the shortstop's glove and into center field, allowing the Bank One Ballpark crowd to dream this impossible dream: Rivera losing his streak of twenty-three consecutive postseason saves in a winner-take-all game.

A wincing Jeter pulled himself to his feet, limped to the mound for Torre's conference with Rivera, and hobbled back to his position. Only three innings earlier, Jeter had made another breathless defensive play, leaping high to catch Williams's relay throw on Danny Bautista's RBI double, and cutting down Bautista's attempt to make it an RBI triple with a release that was Dan Marino quick.

Jeter was no longer physically capable of making such a dramatic play. His body was shutting down, and there were still three outs to go.

Rivera got one of them on Jay Bell's sacrifice bunt, throwing to third to get Dellucci. Even that sequence hurt the Yankees' cause; Brosius had a shot at a double play but did not throw to first.

Tony Womack followed with the game-tying double into right field, breaking his bat the way Grace had broken his on the leadoff single. Rivera was sawing wood with his cutter, just as he always did, and it did not matter. By the time the closer hit Craig Counsell to load the bases, the Diamondbacks were looking like the Yankees, and the Yankees were looking like the '98 Padres, the '99 Braves, and the 2000 Mets.

Luis Gonzalez had blasted 57 homers in the regular season, yet he came to the plate as if he were a slap-hitting middle infielder, choking up for the first time all year. Rivera had struck him out in the eighth, and this time Gonzalez just wanted to get a piece of the ball.

Rivera's second pitch was a cutter that broke Gonzalez's bat; of course it did. The ball normally would have taken a benign path into Jeter's glove, but there was nothing normal about this night. The infield was playing in, so millions of viewers took in a most stunning scene:

Derek Jeter lifting his glove for the hell of it, lifting it the way he would a white flag.

The Diamondbacks mobbed Gonzalez between first and second, and Jeter looped around them and onto the outfield grass to avoid crashing their party on his way to the dugout. Head down, Rivera trudged in the same direction as "We Are the Champions" blared on the speakers. The Yankees did a zombielike stagger off the field while Torre watched from the rail.

Jeter slumped on the dugout bench as the Diamondbacks celebrated November the way he had always celebrated October. Over his first six seasons, Jeter had played in sixteen out of a possible eighteen postseason series, and this was only his second series defeat.

"You expect it to be over when Mo comes in," Jeter said. "Ninety-nine percent of the time, it's over."

Rivera was blaming himself for the loss, blaming himself for the throw that got past Jeter, as the shortstop sat in the corner of a clubhouse as still as a confessional booth at midnight. Torre had already addressed his players, told them they should be very proud of their efforts. The manager noticed that Jeter looked more pissed off than anyone in the room.

Mayor Giuliani hugged George Steinbrenner and told him, "Everyone in New York appreciates what you guys did for us." Hopelessly burdened by his superstitions, Steinbrenner had been enraged late in the game when the Fox TV crew entered the Yankee clubhouse to set up for a celebration that would never come.

The Boss composed himself and promised his team would bounce back stronger than ever, even if that team would not include O'Neill, Brosius, Martinez, and Knoblauch.

The shortstop would return; Steinbrenner knew that much. And as he limped into the trainer's room, a World Series loser for the first time, Derek Jeter had no idea he was beginning the second phase of his Yankee career, one that would not be half as charmed as his first.

9

New Guys

IN THE WAKE of his crushing World Series defeat, Derek Jeter wore his torment well. Talking in front of people "always scared me to death," Jeter said, yet he agreed to host *Saturday Night Live* and even to dress up in one skit as Alfonso Soriano's wife.

It was a clutch at-bat that notarized Jeter's standing as a performer who did not fear the consequences of failure, no matter the forum. The shortstop always fell back on his preparation and forever remained ready to keep his head in the event everyone around him lost theirs.

In many ways, Jeter was still the same consistent, low-maintenance Yankee he had been for years. He was still the son who lived in mortal fear of hurting or disappointing his mother and father. He was still the star player who never asked for special clubhouse privileges, who never so much as asked if his parents could tour the Yankees' inner sanctum.

He was still the New Yorker who gave his time to the children of 9/11 victims, including Kate Mascali, the young daughter of a lost firefighter Jeter invited onto the field during stretching exercises while her mother, Lori, wept over the scene.

He was still the guy buying his daily cappuccino at Starbucks. He was still the Yankee using his black Louisville Slugger P72 bat, still swinging 34 inches and 32 ounces at the plate, still using his Rawlings glove, and still wearing his uniform to a certain fit — not baggy or tight, but just right.

"Most guys make changes in how they wear a uniform over the years," said Yankee equipment manager Rob Cucuzza. "Derek Jeter has worn his uniform exactly as he's worn it from day one."

Millions of Little Leaguers were trying to wear his number 2 with the same grace. Jeter was not beloved merely because he was a four-time champion who delivered big October hits, patented that running flip play at the plate, and made those acrobatic midair throws from the hole.

He was beloved for signing autographs for as many kids as he could accommodate, for playfully asking fans from the on-deck circle if he should swing at the first pitch, for never disrespecting an authority figure, and for making sure he had fun on the playing field.

In 2001, Jeter's former teammate, David Cone, returned to the Bronx as a member of the Red Sox and tried to ignore Jeter while the shortstop approached the plate in the first inning. But Jeter tilted his head sideways and shot a crooked stare at the mound, announcing to Cone that he would not step into the box until the pitcher lost his game face and acknowledged him.

"So I finally looked at him," Cone said, "and Jeter gave me this goofy face. It was utterly disarming. And I was like, 'Come on, don't do that.'"

Jeter ripped Cone's first pitch for a double to right and went 5 for 5 for the night.

Parents read and heard about the way Jeter carried himself, saw it with their own eyes, and they passed down their admiration to their children. Truth was, Jeter "got it" at a time in professional sports when those who "got it" were in dangerously short supply.

He understood the power of Yankee tradition and mythology, so it was no surprise that Jeter was a steady guardian of the empty locker next to his, the one that belonged to Thurman Munson, the catcher and captain killed in a 1979 plane crash. Sometimes visitors to Jeter's stall in the far left-hand corner of the cramped Yankee clubhouse would forget the space next door was a shrine, and they would stand right there, or drop a piece of equipment or a bag right there, before the shortstop asked them to show a little courtesy and respect.

On Old-Timers' Day, even with some of the living pinstriped legends eager to spend time around him, Jeter was careful to avoid over-stepping his bounds. He summoned the nerve to talk to Joe DiMaggio only one time, in the dugout, and the shortstop was shaking in his spikes.

"I heard a lot about you," DiMaggio told him.

"Nice to meet you, sir," Jeter replied.

And that was it. Jeter quickly moved past the Yankee who projected a forbidding aura, the Yankee who wore a Do Not Disturb sign around his neck, and got himself ready to play the game.

"I admired him from afar," Jeter said. "I didn't get an opportunity to know him, but I wish I would have."

DiMaggio and Jeter were linked first and foremost as the great-est Yankees of their generations, but also as men fiercely protective of their privacy despite relationships with high-profile starlets the likes of Marilyn Monroe and Mariah Carey.

It was easier in DiMaggio's day to maintain an air of mystery; Jeter had to navigate an exploding media environment defined by never-ending coverage of celebrities, outlets multiplying by the hour, and technological advancements just starting to put camera phones in the hands of trigger-happy bar patrons.

But somehow, some way, Jeter negotiated the electronic jungles of Manhattan and Tampa without getting photographed in compromis-ing positions, alcoholic beverage in hand. By 2002, he had already dated more beautiful women than Hugh Hefner could count, his list of significant others including Miss Universe Lara Dutta, actress Jordana Brewster, and singer Joy Enriquez, who was reportedly introduced to Jeter by none other than a smitten Alex Rodriguez at the 2001 All-Star Game.

Jeter was said to have stolen Enriquez's affections away from A-Rod, who, of course, had it coming to him. The Jeter-Enriquez relationship "has my total blessing," Rodriguez would say, though A-Rod's blessing was not one Jeter was actively pursuing.

Regardless, as New York's most eligible bachelor, Jeter was a player without scars. "He almost never gets photographed out," said Jim Ley-ritz, his friend and former teammate, "and think about all the high-profile girls he's dated. None of them come back and say he's a lousy lover, he's not good in bed, he's cheap, he doesn't pay for this. You don't hear any of that. He's either real smart, or there's nothing bad about him."

Jeter was smart enough to keep his circle of confidants tight, a circle that defied the celebrity entourage prototype. He remained close with a grade-school friend and aspiring golf pro from Kalamazoo, Doug Biro, and with a former minor league teammate, Sean Twitty, both salt-of-the-earth types. Jeter spent time out with Rafael Oquendo, his personal trainer. Another former minor league teammate, R. D. Long, was the resident good-natured hellion of the group, serving in the role of Derek's alter ego.

Out on the town, Jeter understood he had an image to protect. He never snapped at fans or waiters who approached for autographs in the middle of dinner, even if the request was made as his forkful of chicken parm was halfway in his mouth.

By all accounts, Jeter never turned away kids; sometimes he would ask an overbearing adult to return when he was finished eating. His behavior stood in stark contrast to that of DiMaggio and Mickey Mantle, who could act boorishly when dealing with fans of all ages.

Billy Martin, of all people, repeatedly rebuked DiMaggio for "treating people like shit," according to Ray Negron, the batboy turned team official. Mantle's former driver, Mark Dymond, was once walking with the Mick toward an elevator at a Florida fantasy camp when a boy of about eleven years of age approached.

"Mr. Mantle, can I have your autograph?" the kid asked.

"Fuck off," Mantle barked.

Jeter was leaving no such trail of shocked, heartbroken worshipers. "And I like that as a friend of his," Tino Martinez said, "because I've been with other players who rejected people in restaurants, and you go, 'Oh, man.' It brings you down. With Derek it's always just a matter of when he'll sign. He'll sign for the entire restaurant if they want, the cooks, the waiters, everybody."

As it was, Jeter often chose to stay in and watch movies. When he did go out he preferred clubs with roped-off areas for VIPs in search of a little distance and peace. His brushes with troublemakers were kept to a minimum, but his fame, fortune, and team affiliation made some incidents unavoidable.

During his early years with the Yanks, Jeter was out with Martinez when approached by a nervous stranger who kept asking him, "Do you have any candy? Do you have any candy?"

"No, but I've got some gum," Jeter responded. Martinez had to inform his teammate the man wasn't looking for M&M's, but drugs.

"In Boston, first three or four years of Derek's career," Martinez said, "no matter where we went guys would get loud and shout, 'Nomar's better than you. Nomar's the man.'

"They were always trying to get Derek fired up and say, 'Go fuck yourself,' but he wouldn't do it. Derek would just say, 'Hey, you're right. It's cool. Nomar's a great player.' And it would defuse the situation."

Jeter had a way of minimizing the chances of a confrontation. Jorge Posada, his close friend, marveled over the way the shortstop could apply the same instincts that framed his flip play in Oakland to a crowded nightclub.

"He's always looking around," Posada said. "He knows if that lady's standing right there and she looks, he knows that lady's coming about ten, fifteen minutes later to either say hello or do something. He sees the whole room. He's unbelievable, how he can scan out people and really read them.

"We'll be out and there will be a situation that puts us in a spot, and he'll know to take off right away. He analyzes things before they happen, which is what he does on the field."

Sometimes Jeter would cause a problem just by showing up in a restaurant. Martinez was a dinner partner of Jeter's at times when roomfuls of women were angering their boyfriends and husbands by staring at the shortstop.

"You hear their comments, and you know they've had a few drinks," Martinez said. "Derek's not looking at the girls, it's not his fault, but I'd just tell him, 'It's not good here. Let's get out of here.'"

Not that the shortstop spent his off-field life fleeing the advances of attractive women. Jeter thoroughly enjoyed the spoils of his looks and stardom when it came to the opposite sex, though he was careful to avoid women he felt were more interested in his celebrity standing than they were in him.

Jeter's mother and sister reviewed the candidates, and they represented a tough judge and jury. "Divorce is not an option," Sharlee would say. "We have those traditional values that, you get married, you're in it for the long haul . . . [Derek] keeps saying, 'I've got to be with a girl for five years before I marry her. I've got to make sure this is the one.'

"Our parents are still madly in love with each other after all these years, and that's how we want it to be. So we're not going to marry the first person that we think is great, and oh, if it doesn't work there's always a way to get out of it. That's not an option for us."

With the stakes so high, Jeter did not rely solely on his sister and mother. If he thought a relationship was possible, he would run his girlfriends through a quiz that resembled the one Eddie gives his fiancée, Elyse, in the classic scene in the movie *Diner*.

Only Jeter would not ask his date/contestant about the Baltimore Colts, or the New York Yankees for that matter. He would pose hypothetical, what-would-you-do-in-this-situation questions to get a read on a woman's moral compass. "It's usually about how she would handle a certain situation," Jeter's friend and former teammate Gerald Williams would say. "He's trying to find out if she would lose her cool and rant and rave, or stay calm and keep her dignity. He's not looking for someone who exhibits extreme behavior. . . ."

Mariah Carey passed a few of these tests along the way but flunked the final exam. "She was much more boisterous than Derek wanted," said one Yankee official. "He likes women in the background, and she was the opposite."

Jeter was not receptive to aggressive come-ons, whether the aggressors were female fans running onto the field — one would race out to Jeter at short to hand him her phone number — or supermodels gracing the covers of the most prominent fashion magazines. "I've seen a supermodel at the top of her game try to get to Derek," R. D. Long said, "and it never happened. Just how she tried to do it didn't work for him."

Enough women were smart enough, conservative enough, and classy enough to catch Jeter's eye, win his affections, and contribute to his standing as a ladies' man extraordinaire. Teammates who were close enough to Jeter to get away with it occasionally teased him about the parade of women forever marching his way.

Bernie Williams watched music videos with Jeter in the players' lounge, and whenever an attractive singer or dancer appeared on screen, the center fielder pushed the shortstop's buttons.

"Do you know that girl?" Williams would ask. "I know you know that girl." Sometimes Jeter would confess he did.

In his dealings with the news media, Jeter reacted to questions about his personal life the way he would react to a four-strikeout day at the plate. He occasionally showed up with a girlfriend courtside at Madison Square Garden for a Knicks game, but he did what he could to prevent photographers from the *Daily News* and *Post* to provide a running visual commentary on his love interests in their gossip pages.

"If he's dating a girl," Martinez said, "it's dinner and a movie, and no drinking until four in the morning. Maybe when you win the World Series, but other than that, no.

"I mean, he's a normal guy, and the girls he dates usually are pretty normal. And when they're not, or they want the big party scene, then they're gone."

Discretion was of utmost importance to the shortstop. One woman who briefly dated Jeter would tell a story of the time she and a girlfriend were invited to the shortstop's home for a small party. Jeter answered the door and politely asked his guests to remove any cell phones or cameras they were carrying and place them on a table, explaining that he wanted to protect his privacy.

When out in a club, Jeter would often ask a wingman, teammate, or staffer to approach a woman he would like to meet and extend an invitation on his behalf. If Jeter and the woman were interested in taking the evening elsewhere, they would often leave separately, through different doors. Sometimes Jeter would leave a club in a separate car while his driver transported the woman to their next meeting place.

Image wasn't everything, despite Andre Agassi's claim to the contrary in the Canon ad, but it still meant a lot even to a ballplayer defined by his substance-over-style core. One late night on a West Coast trip, a witness spotted Jeter pulling up to the team hotel in a cab with two female passengers. The witness stayed in the shadows and watched the scene unfold.

Jeter emerged from the cab first and made his way to the hotel elevators. A few minutes later, one female passenger stepped out and followed in Jeter's footsteps. A few minutes after that, the second female passenger stepped out and took the very same path.

It did not matter whether these women were Jeter's dates, or his friends, or his Scrabble partners looking for a game at 3:00 a.m. What mattered was his concern over appearances, even in the middle of the night.

Jeter never made a mistake in public, and there was a good reason why. From the spring training fields of Florida to the big league hotels of California, Jeter never forgot Don Mattingly's warning the day the veteran first baseman told the kid shortstop to run it in:

You never know who's watching.

Derek Jeter knew 2002 would be a different season even before Ruben Rivera, Mariano's cousin, was literally caught stealing one day in March — stealing a glove and bat from Jeter's locker.

Once regarded as a Mantle-like prospect, Ruben had a deal to sell the items to a memorabilia dealer for $2,500, a curious move for an outfielder with a million-dollar wage. "A rookie mistake," Ruben called it, even though his rookie season had come and gone six years earlier.

"He had six or seven gloves; I didn't know he would be that mad," Rivera would explain. Oh, Jeter was mad. "I have no comment on the whole situation," the shortstop said. "There's no need to add fuel to the fire."

That fire was an inferno. Jeter often sold his game-used bats and gear through Steiner Sports Memorabilia and committed more than $250,000 a year in proceeds to his Turn 2 Foundation and its programs designed to keep kids drug- and alcohol-free.

But Jeter never sold his gloves. "I know those gloves are very personal," said the head of the memorabilia company, Brandon Steiner.

Only this wasn't just about the glove, among Jeter's favorites. His space and his standing as unofficial team captain had been violated.

Rivera was released by the Yankees, who likely would have released Mariano's cousin even if he had swiped the glove belonging to the twenty-fifth man on the roster. But with Jeter as the victim, Rivera's admission and apology never stood a chance. Brian Cashman agreed to a $200,000 settlement on Rivera's contract and bid the disgraced Yankee farewell.

This was still very much Jeter's team, even if George Steinbrenner had given Jason Giambi a seven-year, $120 million deal to restore the Yankee offense to a championship level (and allowed clubhouse access to the Oakland slugger's personal trainer, Bob Alejo). Giambi was given the full news conference treatment on arrival — as opposed to Jeter's quickie conference call announcing his $189 million deal — and was fully expected to use Yankee Stadium's inviting right-field porch to match or surpass his 38-homer, 120-RBI final season with the A's.

Giambi had shaved his goatee and cut his biker-boy hair in accordance with Steinbrenner's clean-cut mandates, and he picked number 25 because the digits added up to 7, the number worn by the Mick, his father's favorite player.

"I know I'm replacing a great Yankee," Giambi said of Tino Martinez, who had replaced a great Yankee in Don Mattingly. Martinez understood the lure of Giambi's league-leading .477 on-base percentage and .660 slugging percentage, but he was wounded by the fact that the Yanks did not re-sign him after a 34-homer, 113-RBI season, and by the fact that Roger Clemens was among the teammates who helped recruit Giambi.

Jeter was the one prominent Yankee who made it clear he would not help the team replace his friend, who wound up in St. Louis. "He was the only one who wasn't afraid to stand up," Martinez said.

No, Jeter was not afraid to make a stand for a friend. But when it came to social or political issues, even those directly related to the business of baseball, Jeter defaulted to the Michael Jordan, Republicans-buy-sneakers-too approach.

In May of 2002, if soaring home-run totals and bulging biceps had not already made it clear baseball had a major steroids problem, Ken Caminiti stamped the plague official in an explosive interview with *Sports Illustrated*'s Tom Verducci. Caminiti acknowledged having used steroids when he won the National League's Most Valuable Player award for the Padres in 1996 and said of his sport: "It's no secret what's going on in baseball. At least half the guys are using steroids. They talk about it. They joke about it with each other."

Jose Canseco would put the number of steroid users at 85 percent. "There would be no baseball left if they drug-tested everyone today," Canseco said.

At the time 50 percent appeared to be the more credible figure, and one approved by the likes of Curt Schilling. Some players were adding thirty to forty pounds of muscle, and they were having trouble finding batting helmets to fit their swelling heads.

Steroids represented a legitimate health crisis in America, as young athletes were in the habit of imitating their big league heroes. Mark McGwire's admission of androstenedione use in '98 inspired so many teens to buy andro, a steroid precursor, that fitness stores could not keep it in stock.

Players were using performance-enhancing drugs, and clean teammates were feeling the pressure to use them to keep up with the cheaters. This dangerous dance could not go on forever.

Giambi called Caminiti's claims "ludicrous" and said he bulked up after McGwire introduced him to his weightlifting program in Oakland. But Murray Chass of the *New York Times* would later report that Giambi's agent, Arn Tellem, had the Yankees remove steroid-related language from their $120 million contract before his client signed it.

"There is no miracle thing to this game," Giambi said. "You either have talent or you don't. Steroids can't help you hit a ball, that's for sure."

Barry Bonds, who broke McGwire's single-season home-run record after his body all but doubled in size, echoed Giambi's sentiment. "If you're incapable of hitting [a baseball]," Bonds said, "it doesn't matter what you take. . . . I think [steroid use] is really irrelevant to the game of baseball."

Irrelevant? Players would soon find out that nothing was more relevant to their sport than performance-enhancing drugs. Mike Stanton, the Yankees' player representative, said drug testing was among the issues on the negotiating table between the union and the owners. It was the perfect time and opportunity for Jeter and other clean players to implore the union to agree to strict testing and penalties to weed out the cheaters and protect the health of the membership.

Jeter was a four-time World Series champ, a star with enough clout to host *Saturday Night Live*. He could have made a difference if he wanted to. Only when asked about Caminiti's 50 percent figure, Jeter said, "I guess I am the other half. You can't say half the players unless you know every player in the game."

His stance grew weaker by the quote. "The bottom line is they don't test for it," Jeter said, "so it's not something that concerns me."

The shortstop even suggested steroids did not help players drive baseballs over the outfield wall. "Look at [Alfonso] Soriano," Jeter said of the lean second baseman. "He's not the biggest or strongest guy, but he's hitting more home runs than anybody."

Jeter was like Jordan and Tiger Woods; it just was not in his DNA to lead a cause that had nothing to do with winning titles. He once declined an offer from John F. Kennedy Jr.'s *George* magazine to write one of its "If I Were President" columns because he did not care to make any political statements.

In 2002, Jeter's only concern was finding a way to win at the old October clip with a new cast of actors. Giambi had replaced Martinez at first, and Robin Ventura had replaced Scott Brosius at third. Paul O'Neill, Chuck Knoblauch, and Luis Sojo were out; Raul Mondesi, Rondell White, and John Vander Wal were among those in.

As it turned out, Jeter's numbers dropped a bit from his 2001 levels; he batted .297 with 18 homers and 75 RBI. But he did become only the third player since 1900 to score at least 100 runs in his first seven seasons, joining Earle Combs and Ted Williams, and his Yankees did win 103 games and another division crown. Giambi was the 41-homer, 122-RBI, .435-on-base-percentage horse he was hired to be, and Mike Mussina and the reacquired David Wells combined to win 37 games at the top of a staff stacked with the usual assortment of aces.

Joe Torre had no reason to believe he would not be managing in his sixth World Series in seven years, especially after his team won Game 1 of the Division Series against the Anaheim Angels at Yankee Stadium, won it with Jeter opening the scoring on a homer in the first, with Bernie Williams finishing the scoring on a homer in the eighth, and with Giambi delivering a two-run shot in between.

But Torre would not be making a return trip to the Fall Classic. In fact, Game 1 would be recorded as his final victory of 2002.

As championship teams go, these newfangled Yankees had the requisite hitting and pitching. They were about to find out they did not have the requisite heart.

It all started to unravel in the eighth inning of Game 2, after El Duque Hernandez surrendered back-to-back homers to Garret Anderson and Troy Glaus to give the Angels the lead. With the Yankees down 7–5, bases loaded and two outs, Jeter stepped to the plate with a home crowd of nearly 56,695 fully expecting something magical to happen near the right-field wall.

Jeter had hit his second homer of the series in the third inning, after all, and this was his situation, his building, his month. Angels closer Troy Percival worked the count to 1-2 before throwing a pitch the shortstop did not like.

Jeter thought it was ball two. The umpire called it strike three.

The Yankees actually led by a 6-1 count early in Game 3 in Anaheim, only to watch Mussina go down with a groin injury before Jeff Weaver, Mike Stanton, and Steve Karsay failed to protect a 6-4 lead. If nothing else, the Yanks were making a star out of the Angels' twenty-year-old rookie reliever, Francisco "K-Rod" Rodriguez, who had made all of five regular-season appearances and yet had earned his second consecutive playoff victory by striking out four in two perfect innings.

In the losing locker room, Jeter was reminded his team had survived four Division Series sudden-death games with Oakland over the previous two seasons. "It's a different group," the shortstop said. "Some of us have [won sudden-death games], the ones that have been here. But this is a new group. So we'll find out."

Reporters were surprised Jeter drew a line in the infield dirt between the new guys and the core guys. It did not sound like him — "You have to build up a history with this team," Jeter said — but then again, his Yankees had never been in a first-round series where they looked so overmatched.

None of it made sense. The Angels were paying $61 million in salary, or some $80 million less than George Steinbrenner was paying. The Yankees' roster entered the series with 543 games' worth of postseason experience; the Angels entered with a grand total of 2, the 2 belonging to Kevin Appier from his time in Oakland.

Anaheim was a faceless lot, but it was also by far the superior team. With men on second and third in the fifth inning of Game 4, no outs and the score at 1-1, Jeter sent a deep fly to left field that Anderson caught on the run, honoring the fifty-fifth anniversary of Al Gionfriddo's catch of Joe DiMaggio's shot in the World Series.

DiMaggio kicked the dirt back then, about the only time he reacted emotionally to a play made against him. Jeter did not kick the dirt, but his grimace and slap of the hands amounted to a rare show of on-field negativity. "Garret Anderson really pulled the plug on us," Torre said.

In the bottom of the fifth, the Yankees gave in as they never had. David Wells allowed a leadoff homer to Shawn Wooten and a couple of one-out singles before Darin Erstad lifted a short fly between Williams and Soriano. Williams quit on the ball, Soriano could not reach it, and Wells — undefeated as a Yankee postseason pitcher — suddenly decided he was not going to try any harder than Bernie did.

The Angels mowed right over Wells, just as they had mowed over the previous three Yankee starters, Roger Clemens, Andy Pettitte, and Mussina. When Anaheim was done in the fifth, done with Wells and Ramiro Mendoza and El Duque Hernandez, it had become the first postseason team since the 1929 Philadelphia A's to rack up ten hits in one inning.

"It seemed like it lasted forever," Jeter said.

The Angels were leading 9–2, leaving the Yankee starters with a 10.38 ERA for the series, the same opposing starters who formed what Torre called the best staff he ever had. The Yankees were not coming back from that. The final out came in the form of a Nick Johnson pop-up, and as the winners mobbed one another the way the Diamondbacks had the previous November, Jeter watched stone-faced from the dugout, his chin planted on the green-padded railing and his arms dangling down toward the dirt.

Fireworks exploded out of the fake rock formation in left center as photographers moved in to capture this stunning image of Jeter. After a few minutes the shortstop grabbed his cap and glove and headed for the tunnel and the quickest postseason exit of his big league life.

"It's not a good feeling," Jeter said. "I mean, you have one goal, and that's to get to the World Series and win a championship. You shouldn't accept losing."

To a man the Yankees accepted the fact that Anaheim was the superior team. Torre said the Angels reminded him of his '96 champs. The Angels scored 31 runs on 56 hits in the four games, and the Yanks could not get the ball to Mariano Rivera after Game 1.

"We've changed our personality a little bit," Torre said.

For the worse.

There was a small-picture moment in Game 4 that made a big-picture statement about what had become of the dynastic Yanks. Tim

Salmon hit a tapper to Wells in the fourth inning, and the left-hander turned and fired to first, his throw low and inside.

Giambi had a choice: go for the ball and a possible catch while getting pancaked by Salmon, or let Wells's errant throw sail away while the runner headed to second base.

Tino Martinez? Every veteran Yankee knew what choice he would have made. But the hulking Giambi — who had a good series at the plate — chose to preserve his body and let the Angels have their way.

Anaheim did not score in the inning, but that was not the point. The old Yankees always went for the ball, regardless of the consequences, and Giambi's Yankees did not.

"They wanted it more than us," Jorge Posada said of the Angels. "It seemed like some of [our] guys were just acting like we lost a regular-season game. I can't understand that."

Neither could Jeter. He became the first man to collect 100 post-season hits, and he batted .500 for the series, but he was not asking anyone to spray him with champagne over that.

The Angels had never won a playoff series and had gone 2,527 games without appearing in one, and yet, "No team has ever played better against us than that team has," Jeter said.

"They did everything better than we did . . . I don't see anyone beating them."

Jeter was right. The Angels would defeat the Giants in a seven-game World Series classic the Yankee shortstop could not bring himself to watch.

After the Game 7 loss to the Diamondbacks the previous fall, Steinbrenner barked, "I believe in what Ernest Hemingway said. The way to be a good loser is to practice at it. And I ain't going to be practicing."

Suddenly Steinbrenner and Jeter and the rest of the Yanks were practicing how to lose. They would get damn good at it, too.

George Steinbrenner was not going to absorb any humiliating defeat in silence. This was not the programming he had in mind when he launched his own TV station, the YES Network, in March. The more he thought about the money spent on the 2002 Yankees and the different ways the no-frills Angels had dismantled his team, the more Steinbrenner stewed.

The Boss needed a suitable forum, and he got one in a wide-ranging December interview scheduled to mark the thirtieth anniversary of his purchase of the Yankees on January 3, 1973. Given the opportunity to discuss his three decades of ownership with Wayne Coffey of the *Daily News*, Steinbrenner teed off on figures past and present, but especially present.

He pointed out that Joe Torre had been fired three times before he became a certain Hall of Famer with the Yankees, and that Torre had come so far "because of an organization, and he's got to remember that." Steinbrenner also fired a hard jab at Don Zimmer and the rest of Torre's staff, saying he wanted the coaches "to understand that just being a friend of Joe Torre's is not enough."

Only the Boss did not become the Boss by taking on managers and coaches. The old Big Ten football man was never afraid to sack his star quarterbacks, a truth discovered the hard way by the likes of Reggie Jackson, Dave Winfield, and Don Mattingly.

So Steinbrenner blitzed Derek Jeter from the blind side.

Never mind that Jeter had batted .500 against the Angels, or that Jeter had 101 postseason hits at age twenty-eight. Steinbrenner cared only that his shortstop had not won him a title since the Boss guaranteed him $189 million of his hard-earned cash.

Jeter had gone from winning his fourth title and signing the monster contract to losing in the World Series and then losing in the first round. Jeter had gone from hitting .339 and signing the monster contract to hitting .311 and then .297. Naturally, Steinbrenner was not paying nine figures for this.

Asked if he saw Jeter as a strong candidate to become the team's first captain since Mattingly, whom the Boss once ordered to get a haircut, Steinbrenner actually questioned the shortstop's focus, declared that Jeter didn't need to do as many commercials as he did, and worried aloud about his late-night habits.

"When I read in the paper that he's out until 3 a.m. in New York City going to a birthday party, I won't lie," Steinbrenner told the *News*. "That doesn't sit well with me. That was in violation of Joe's curfew. That's the focus I'm talking about.

"Jeter's still a young man. He'll be a very good candidate for the captaincy. But he's got to show me and the other players that that's not the right way. He's got to make sure his undivided, unfettered attention is given to baseball. I just wish he'd eliminate some of the less important things and he'd be right back to where he was in the past."

Jeter was stunned when he read Steinbrenner's comments. The very essence of what he believed himself to be — an athlete devoted exclusively to winning — was being debunked by his own employer.

Steinbrenner's criticism of Jeter's endorsement load made little sense, as the shortstop and his agent, Casey Close, turned down more sponsorship deals than they ever accepted. Jeter spent most of his off-season a long way from Madison Avenue, in Tampa, so he could work out at the Yankees' facilities. He was a lot more concerned about his bat speed than he was about his portfolio.

Close also wanted to avoid overexposure, and to pick corporate partners that best matched up with his client's image. In fact, at least one prominent marketing expert criticized the strategy for failing to fully capitalize on Jeter's earning power.

Sonny Vaccaro, who fired the first shot in the sneaker company revolution by signing Michael Jordan for Nike, said Close erred when he agreed to put Jeter under the Jordan brand umbrella and group him in a commercial with lesser lights such as the NBA's Ray Allen, the NFL's Randy Moss, and boxing's Roy Jones.

"Derek Jeter was good-looking, articulate, free of scandal, a champion, and he played for one of the greatest brands in sports," Vaccaro said. "Jeter was a premier guy and he allowed himself to become second fiddle, ancillary."

But just as Jeter was not trying to break Alex Rodriguez's salary record, Close was not trying to drive Jeter past Jordan and Tiger Woods on the endorsement front. Jeter's goals were to protect his image and win as many championships as possible, and not in that order.

The Yankees had not won since 2000, a drought of biblical proportions in Steinbrenner's world. Jeter believed that was the primary reason the Boss bashed him.

So he met with Steinbrenner and left the sit-down believing he had sufficiently explained to the Boss that the gossip pages often printed bogus information about his nocturnal travels, and that he had no interest in becoming another Broadway Joe.

But the shortstop grew angry again in February after his quote in the *Daily News* following Steinbrenner's controversial remarks — "I'm not going to change. Not at all" — inspired the screaming back-page headline "PARTY ON." Jeter believed the line was taken out of context, and that the headline gave fans the impression he was more interested in carousing than he was in making sure the Yankees did not suffer another first-round defeat.

Jeter had not been this angry about a tabloid headline since the *Post*'s "SHORTSLOP" in '96, and he decided to punch back at all New York metropolitan-area outlets that covered him on a regular basis. A day after assuring the Yankees' beat writers gathered at the team's minor league complex that he would address the Steinbrenner controversy when he reported to camp, the Associated Press ran an interview with Jeter that covered all the bases in a way the shortstop never did.

"He's the Boss, and he's entitled to his opinion, right or wrong, but what he said has been turned into me being this big party animal," Jeter told the AP's Steve Wilstein in the interview arranged by Close. "He even made a reference to one birthday party. That's been turned into that I'm like Dennis Rodman now.

"I don't think that's fair. I have no problems with people criticizing how I play. But it bothers me when people question my work ethic. That's when you're talking about my integrity. I take a lot of pride in how hard I work. I work extremely hard in the off-season. I work extremely hard during the season to win. My priorities are straight."

Jeter said the *Daily News* "PARTY ON" headline sent fans a message that "couldn't be farther from the truth" and repeated his claim to Steinbrenner that the gossip pages were putting him in clubs and bedrooms he had never visited.

"I'm not a hermit," Jeter said. "It's not like I'm locked up in my house.... They've got me dating everyone imaginable. A lot of it I wish I would have."

The writers who regularly covered Jeter were upset he chose to give his side to the AP, and to a columnist he did not know. Jeter was not apologizing. He said Steinbrenner's remarks had gone national — Jeter was pestered about them at the Super Bowl in San Diego — and so he decided to go national, too.

Upon arriving in camp on February 17, Jeter met with close to a hundred reporters in the Yankees' dugout at Legends Field and acknowledged he was concerned his pristine reputation had been splattered with mud for the first time.

"Image is important, because that's who I am," Jeter said. "It's not like I have this false image. I don't want Yankee fans to think I don't care if we win or lose, that I'm caught up in the New York nightlife."

Of course, there was one sure-fire way to prove that to any fan inclined to doubt Jeter's commitment for the first time — win. Win it all. To help Jeter toward that end, his most prominent critic, Steinbrenner, opened his vault again and signed Cuban pitcher and defector Jose Contreras to a four-year, $32 million deal and signed Japanese slugger Hideki Matsui to a three-year, $21 million deal.

The Yankees outlasted the Red Sox in the pursuit of Contreras, a development that inspired Boston's new boy-wonder GM, Theo Epstein, to take out his frustrations on the furniture in his hotel room and compelled team president Larry Lucchino to tell the *New York Times*, "The evil empire extends its tentacles even into Latin America."

And Japan. Matsui was not just a star with the Yomiuri Giants; he was, in the words of Yankees general manager Brian Cashman, "the Tom Cruise of his country," a claim that Yankees assistant GM Jean Afterman, a major player in the Matsui recruitment, called an understatement.

"When Tom Cruise goes to a London premiere," Afterman said, "he's not carrying the hopes and dreams of a nation like Hideki. He's carrying the hopes and dreams of Warner Brothers."

As a Yankee, Matsui would help Jeter carry the hopes and dreams of George Steinbrenner, who would not start the season in a good mood, not after he fined David Wells $100,000 for writing in the released galleys of his upcoming autobiography, among other things, that he pitched his perfect game in 1998 while "half-drunk."

The controversy irreparably harmed the close relationship Steinbrenner had with Wells, who would refuse to appear with the owner and the rest of his high-profile pitching staff on the cover of *Sports Illustrated*. The flap also began tearing at the relationship between Torre and management.

Steinbrenner gathered his manager and team executives in a Legends Field conference room, with team president Randy Levine on speakerphone. The Boss told Torre to demote Wells to the bullpen, and Torre argued that Steinbrenner should simply fine the pitcher. In the middle of the heated back-and-forth, Levine tried to interrupt before Torre snapped, "Randy, shut the fuck up," making himself a new blood enemy in the highest corner of Steinbrenner's cabinet.

In a subsequent meeting between Steinbrenner and Rick Cerrone, senior director of media relations (Levine and chief operating officer Lonn Trost were on speakerphone), the Boss made it clear he was livid that the New York sports talk radio team of Mike Francesa and Chris Russo were scheduled to do their popular *Mike and the Mad Dog* show live from the Yankees' facility, and that the show would surely focus on the Wells book.

Steinbrenner called for a vote to decide whether the Yankees should cancel the on-site appearance, and Levine and Trost voted with Cerrone to keep the show scheduled. The PR man gave some players advance warning that Francesa and Russo would likely pepper them with questions about Wells's galleys, which included jabs at Mike Mussina and Roger Clemens and assertions that steroid and amphetamine use was rampant in baseball.

Jeter was among the players Cerrone warned. "You just worry about Wells," the shortstop said. "I'll be fine."

Even after the made-in-tabloid-heaven mano a mano he waged with Steinbrenner, Jeter was reestablishing the fact that he did not need any PR help. Jeter acted as his own senior publicist, almost always saying and doing the right things.

He could have used a big season, though, the kind of season he had in 1999. Jeter could have used the kind of season he had when the Yankees were ripping off titles, the kind, Reggie Jackson said, "where Jeter didn't lead the league in anything except victories. People looked at him as the best player in baseball even though he didn't have the best skills, which is a very hard thing to pull off."

A lingering shoulder injury had helped drag Jeter's numbers back to the pack, not that he would ever admit it. Jeter refused to be defined by his stat sheet, anyway. When a New York–based columnist told Jeter he was planning to write that the shortstop had not been playing up to his $189 million deal, Jeter defended himself this way:

"But I don't look at it as living up to my contract. When I signed that deal, they didn't tell me I had to start hitting 50 homers with 120 RBI. I was told to continue doing the things I've always done.

"Personally, things weren't as good last year as they were in other years, but I'm still scoring runs and doing whatever it takes to help this team win. If [Alfonso Soriano] is hitting 50 doubles batting leadoff, I'm going to move him over. I'll make sacrifices to help this team.

"You can't win a championship by yourself. You can be the best player in baseball and, unless you have good people around you and a good team, it won't matter. . . . I couldn't care less about numbers. I'd love to hit .380 with 40 homers and 150 RBI; anyone would. But that's not what winning is about. I'm my own biggest critic, so I have no problem with criticizing my play. I know I can do better. A lot better."

The same New York–based columnist told Steinbrenner he agreed with him that Jeter had not been a $189 million ballplayer since signing the $189 million contract, and the Boss replied, "You're not the only one. But I know the young man will come through for me this year."

Truth was, Jeter could not wait to get the 2003 season started, could not wait to shut up the Boss and the *Daily News* and anyone else painting him as a frat boy in pinstripes.

On opening night in Toronto, Jeter had already managed a double, a run scored, and a walk after his first two at-bats. He was standing on first base when the Blue Jays' infielders shifted a quarter mile to their left to defend against the Yankees' lumbering pull hitter, Jason Giambi.

As he took his lead off first, Jeter made a mental note that the third baseman, Eric Hinske, had planted himself at shortstop and left his bag wide open. So when Giambi grounded Roy Halladay's 3-1 pitch back to the mound, Jeter decided the time was right to make a play only Derek Jeter could make.

This would be his baserunning answer to the flip play to the plate against Oakland in the 2001 playoffs. When Jeter saw Halladay throw to first for the easy out, he hit second base the way an Olympic sprinter hits the final turn in the 400. The shortstop was going to race all the way to third.

Just Jeter being Jeter, eyeing the free base the shift was offering and forever seizing upon the smallest of openings in an opponent's defense.

But this time two of the ten athletes on the field, not one, were seeing this play one frame ahead of everyone else.

Toronto catcher Ken Huckaby was a twenty-second-round draft choice of the Los Angeles Dodgers in 1991, and he was briefly a Yankee farmhand during his twelve-year minor league odyssey. He would play a total of 161 big league games for five teams over six seasons, batting .222 along the way.

On March 31, 2003, Huckaby was supposed to be a mere tourist passing unnoticed through Derek Jeter's world, a holiday shopper strolling by Macy's window before going on his way.

But Huckaby did not want to go back to the Crash Davis existence he had known in the minors. He needed to make an impression, needed to make a play, needed something that would convince Toronto's front office — any front office — he was worthy of a major league job and major league hotels and major league meal money.

Huckaby saw his opening when Hinske shifted for Giambi, and when Giambi hit the ball back to Halladay. The Toronto ace threw to first baseman Carlos Delgado, and suddenly Huckaby was struck by the same thought consuming Jeter: nobody was covering third.

Yes, this was Crash Davis's big chance. His big break. He was going to win a race with the great Derek Jeter. He was going to outsmart the game's smartest player.

He was going to make *SportsCenter* lead with this play.

He was going to win an ESPY with this play.

Some 215 pounds in full pads, Huckaby started trudging up the third-base line. "He just looked like the catcher," said Torre, the former catcher, "like he was running after a school bus."

Or like he was pulling a school bus with a rope tied to his waist.

Across the field, Delgado was making like a quarterback waiting for his tight end to complete his crossing route and find a soft spot in the middle of the zone. Finally, Delgado fired the ball to where he thought his intended target would be.

The throw to third base was high, nullifying any shot the graceless, unathletic catcher had of making a graceful, athletic play. Once Huckaby left his feet, all bets were off. There would be no swipe tag, no aesthetically pleasing climax to match the one defining Jeter's flip to the plate in Oakland.

Huckaby made the grab, and as Jeter made a headfirst dive into the bag, the catcher awkwardly crash-landed into him, his left knee and shin guard blasting into Jeter's left shoulder. "He sort of jumped on me," the shortstop would say.

Jeter immediately clutched his shoulder with his right hand and rolled off the bag as his helmet flew off, his face betraying the excruciating pain, the veins in his forehead appearing ready to explode. Huckaby applied the tag, and the umpire who had called Jeter safe, Paul Emmel, suddenly called the runner out.

For the first time in his baseball life, from Little League to the Bronx, Jeter did not care about the umpire's call. He had dislocated his left shoulder — actually, Huckaby had dislocated it for him — and Jeter was writhing in pain in the dirt, adding injury to Steinbrenner's insult.

From the looks of it, Jeter's 2003 season was over before it began. "The kid never shows any pain," Torre said. "But this was something he couldn't hide."

Torre, Yankees trainer Gene Monahan, and two Blue Jays doctors ran out to Jeter, who was surrounded by grim-faced teammates. The shortstop had felt something pop. He wondered if he had broken his collarbone, and he was afraid to look at it. The thought of missing the entire season flashed through his head.

A cart was driven onto the field and a stretcher was prepared to take him off, but as the SkyDome crowd applauded, Jeter was helped to his feet and loaded onto the cart without the stretcher's aid. An endorphin rush kicked in, and Jeter's agonized expression was replaced by a blank mask as he was transported off the field after a twelve-minute delay.

His shoulder was returned to its rightful home inside the clubhouse, and then Jeter was sent to the hospital for x-rays. Meanwhile, on the Yankees' bench, at least one newcomer was cursing the fates. John Flaherty, who had been catching in the majors for eleven years, including the previous five with the god-awful Tampa Bay Devil Rays, had waited this long to play with the mighty Yanks only to see the injury-proof Derek Jeter fail to make it through three innings.

"I'm sitting there like, 'This is just great. Perfect. I make this team for the first time and here he's out for a couple of months,'" Flaherty said. "But I remember the whole team on the bench, not to say it wasn't a big deal, but everybody was like, 'All right, we'll find a way.'

"I couldn't believe what I was seeing, but Andy Pettitte was just sitting there without emotion like, 'We'll find a way. It's all good.' And so coming out of that I thought, 'Wow, that's why this team is always so good, because they find a way to keep going.'"

The Yanks won, 8–4, after Enrique Wilson filled in at short, Hideki Matsui delivered an RBI single on the first pitch he saw as a Yankee, Soriano belted a grand slam, and Roger Clemens pitched six scoreless innings. Only nobody could talk about a win afterward when all the questions were about a devastating loss.

Wilson called Huckaby's action "a dirty play," and other Yankees grumbled that the Toronto catcher had gone too far in knocking Jeter off the bag. The shortstop had returned from the hospital, his arm in a sling, to appear in a SkyDome interview room and field questions about the injury and the play.

Jeter needed to get an MRI done before he had a clear timetable on his rehab and return, but the early word was that he would be lost from one to four months, four being more likely than one. Asked if he thought Huckaby was guilty of a dirty play, Jeter said, "You will have to ask him."

For his part, Huckaby was telling everyone and anyone that he never intended to hurt Jeter, that the high throw put him in a bad position, and that he felt terrible about the result. The following day the Toronto catcher swore he left a message on Jeter's cell phone to express his regret — Huckaby said he got the number from someone close to the shortstop — but Jeter insisted he never received the voice mail. "He doesn't have my phone number," Jeter said.

Either way, Huckaby appeared to be guilty only of playing through the whistle the way Jeter did. "He was hustling and I was hustling," the catcher said. "It was just two guys meeting at the wrong time."

Jeter maintained he was not angry at Huckaby — "I'm angry that I'm going to miss a long time. It doesn't do much good to sit here and be angry at him" — but few observers found it a convincing claim, Huckaby included. So two days after the collision, the catcher decided he needed to make the long and lonely walk to the visitors' clubhouse during batting practice.

Huckaby took a deep breath, pushed through the door, and walked right up to Jeter and shook his hand. He told Jeter that he did leave a voice mail, that maybe he had the wrong number. "I hope you're all right," Huckaby told him. "I didn't know where the base was when I was looking for the throw. It wasn't on purpose. I didn't know where I was on the field. It was just unfortunate we were at the same place at the same time."

Huckaby told Jeter he was sorry about the injury and waited for a response, a nod, a facial expression, something, anything, to loosen the suffocating knot in his gut.

Jeter gave him nothing but a cold, bloodless stare. Not a single word or even a discernible grunt. Finally, Huckaby said, "I just turned around and walked out."

Jeter was back to his one-strike-and-you're-out policy, the one he had applied to Chad Curtis. One team official thought Jeter's behavior in the matter was unbecoming.

"I was surprised, but he's human," the official said. "He's almost perfect. So when you run into something like that it's so surprising because he's almost perfect."

Almost.

The year before, Jeter had hardly been thrilled when Cleveland's John McDonald rolled into him hard at second and injured his knee, but that collision cost him a couple of games.

This one threatened to ruin the season. Jeter was so hell-bent on making this a season to remember, too, a season that would silence the Boss and the critics forevermore. If someone was going to stop Jeter from attaining his goal, a journeyman catcher did not make for a worthy candidate.

"People say, well, I treated him wrong and I shouldn't have acted like that," Jeter would say. "He never called. He came over the last day and said something, [but] it wasn't a situation where I thought the guy did it on purpose, or I refused to call him, or I was being a bad guy. But no, he never called, regardless of what he said.

"I see all these things, 'Oh, I treated the poor kid wrong.' He's older than me. . . . I don't think he purposely hurt me, but I thought it was a little out of control."

Jeter would miss thirty-six games and return to the lineup on May

13, hoping to put the nightmares of winter and spring behind him. Three weeks later, his phone would ring with word of a reprieve.

George Steinbrenner had a new title for his shortstop, and it was not party animal.

Derek Jeter was named captain of the New York Yankees on June 3, 2003. The announcement came out of left field, in Cincinnati, where Joe Torre acknowledged he was not even consulted on George Steinbrenner's appointment.

Not even six months after he publicly questioned whether Jeter was fit to be captain, and whether Jeter partied too much for his own good, Steinbrenner had cut against his own grain for the sake of old times. He was firing and rehiring Billy Martin all over again.

"It's something I'll always treasure," Jeter said of the captaincy, "and I'll do it to the best of my ability."

Strangely enough, entering spring training, Steinbrenner had floated Roger Clemens as his possible choice for captain to a couple of people inside the organization. Clemens over Jeter would have been a terrible judgment call, as the Rocket had established himself with the Red Sox and was not an everyday player. But the Boss adored Clemens's John Wayne swagger. The thought did not gain any traction, and the homegrown Yankee was left as the logical choice.

Steinbrenner's off-season rip job on Jeter led to a commercial offer from Visa that was — surprisingly enough — accepted by the owner and shortstop. In the ad, the Boss summoned Jeter into his office and asked how, as the starting shortstop, he could afford to spend so much time out dancing, eating, and carousing with his friends. Jeter pulled out his Visa card, and the commercial showed him bouncing from one nightspot to the next before the shortstop and Steinbrenner ended up on the same conga line in a club.

It was a cute spot, and one that suggested the Boss and Jeter were back to being amicable business partners. But naming Jeter the first captain since Don Mattingly retired in '95? Without telling Torre? After four full years of media speculation that Jeter would get the nod? In the Great American Ball Park in Cincinnati?

"I know the timing was strange," Steinbrenner said, "but I felt the team . . . needed a spark."

So the Boss bestowed upon Jeter the most prestigious title in American team sports because his team needed a spark in early June? Longtime Yankee observers saw something more sinister in the move.

They saw Steinbrenner rebuking Torre with the Jeter promotion, suggesting the manager needed help in leading his team. The Yankees were not the Yankees who had started the season 23-6 without Jeter. Yes, they had won four of five entering this series with the Reds, but they had lost twelve of fifteen prior to that. Steinbrenner was upset over the way Andy Pettitte and Jeff Weaver were pitching, and over the way Jason Giambi and Hideki Matsui weren't slugging.

The owner was also down on Rick Down, the hitting coach, and on Don Zimmer, the bench coach, who had picked yet another public fight with Steinbrenner on behalf of Torre and the staff. The Boss had decided three nights earlier, after Weaver's loss in Detroit, that he needed to make a move. Torre was among the last to know; he got the news from Brian Cashman.

That's how Jeter finally became captain. "This is an honor that's not thrown around too lightly here," the shortstop said.

Steinbrenner did not attend the press conference; he sent his son, Hal, and son-in-law, Steve Swindal, in his place. Nobody could understand why the Boss did not wait until the following week, when the Yankees could have thrown Jeter a fitting coronation in the Bronx, rather than this rush job in a modest interleague setting on the road.

Jeter insisted he did not care. "An honor is an honor regardless of where you get it," he said.

If teammates always saw Jeter as their unofficial captain, they remained curious over how he would carry the official label. Many assumed he would take the Mattingly approach and continue to counsel players privately, rather than call them out in front of the group. Jeter had loudly reprimanded Bernie Williams and Jay Witasick before and during Game 6 of the 2001 World Series, but Mattingly had occasionally aired out a teammate, too, especially Paul O'Neill.

"O'Neill would hit a ball hard right at somebody and he'd be whining halfway to first," former Yankees manager Buck Showalter said, "and Mattingly would jump his ass and say, 'Oh, big fuckin' O'Neill, grow up. You think these people give a shit that you hit the ball on the nose at the right fielder. I don't want to hear it when you hit one off the end of the bat and it corkscrews over the third baseman's head.'"

Like Mattingly, Jeter was not one to pull a Knute Rockne in team meetings, though a couple of weeks earlier in Boston, after three straight losses to Texas, he had told players in one meeting he did not see the same fire in them he had seen when he was injured and watching on TV.

That period of watching and waiting positively killed Jeter, who had never played in fewer than 148 games. He was going stir-crazy inside the home he purchased in 2001, a $12.6 million apartment in the upper reaches of Trump World Tower. On one visit, Jeter's sister, Sharlee, found Derek stripped down to his boxer briefs, batting helmet on, his Louisville Slugger planted on his bare shoulder as he prepared to swing at an imaginary pitch. Jeter would run around his 5,425-square-foot place as if he were racing from first to third, yelling at his sister, "I'm back, I'm back."

Jeter made it back in time to play 119 games, to collect his 1,500th career hit in August, and to lift his batting average to .324 — 2 points behind batting champ Bill Mueller of Boston. Jeter would finish his eighth season without earning his first Gold Glove — the award would go to Alex Rodriguez for the second straight season; Omar Vizquel had won it the previous nine years — and the sabermetricians were closing hard on him, presenting more and more numbers that placed Jeter among the very worst defensive shortstops in the game.

But he always had October as his counterclaim. And after feeling the full force of George Steinbrenner's mouth and Ken Huckaby's knee, Jeter wanted this October like none before it.

By the eighth inning of Game 7 of a classic American League Championship Series against the Red Sox, Derek Jeter was a physical wreck. His left shoulder still ached from his opening-night collision with Ken Huckaby in Toronto, and his left thumb had been rendered useless by a ruptured tendon suffered on a Game 1 dive for a ground ball.

Of course, Jeter and the Yankees did not disclose the severity of the thumb injury, and when reporters inquired about the omnipresent ice wraps, the shortstop said, "It's no big deal."

Dislocated shoulder aside, no bruise or sprain or strain had ever stopped Jeter from playing a regular-season game, never mind a Game 7 against the Yankees' defining opponent on the other side of the greatest rivalry in sports.

Jeter was always getting hit by fastballs on the hands and wrists, the result of his dive-into-the-pitch style and the prevailing opposing strategy of working him inside. So he was used to getting by with swollen knuckles and mangled fingers.

"He couldn't even hold the bat one time," Jorge Posada said. "He didn't tell Joe Torre and he was hiding it from the trainers, and he told me, 'Hey, I've got one hand. I can find a way to get a hit with one hand.'"

Again, Jeter's threshold for pain was one of the Yankees' most valuable assets. But when word spread internally after Boston's Game 1 victory that the shortstop had ruptured a tendon in his thumb, some Yankees thought Jeter was done and the series was over. Neither was the case.

If Jeter was not the same hitter who had batted .429 in the first-round triumph over Minnesota, he was a relevant figure and the ultimate survivor in a series displaying all the hostilities and haunts that had shaped Yankees–Red Sox for decades.

Jeter had homered off Pedro Martinez to tie the score in the third inning of Game 3, a game that would see a brawl featuring the thirty-one-year-old Martinez throwing seventy-two-year-old Zimmer to the Fenway Park ground, Pedro plunking the Yanks' Karim Garcia, Manny Ramirez charging Roger Clemens, and a Red Sox employee battling Garcia and Jeff Nelson in the bullpen. "We've upgraded it from a battle to a war," said losing Boston manager Grady Little.

A ghostly white Zimmer ended up postgame on a stretcher and in an ambulance after his mad, bulls-of-Pamplona dash at Boston's pitcher, who took a little too much delight in putting the old man down.

So the series and the teams looked as discolored as Jeter's thumb late in Game 7, Red Sox up 5–2 and five outs away from a trip to the World Series and a shot to win it all for the first time since 1918. Boston had knocked around Clemens for a 4–0 lead before Mike Mussina made the first relief appearance of his career and kept his team within reach by escaping a two-on, no-out jam in the fourth and by pitching two more scoreless innings beyond that.

Giambi, the $120 million designated hitter demoted to seventh in the lineup, hit two solo shots off Martinez, and David Ortiz responded with one off David Wells. Little sent Martinez out for the eighth, a move that surprised his starter and his team for this reason: Pedro had finished the seventh by striking out Alfonso Soriano and then pointing a punctuating finger toward the night sky.

With one out, the bases clear, and an 0-2 count on Jeter in the bottom of the eighth, the Yankees looked beaten, anyway, at least until Jeter ripped the next pitch to right field, a corner of the Stadium almost as kind to him as it had been to Babe Ruth. Trot Nixon took an unfortunate path to the ball, which sailed over his head and into a whole new ball game.

Bernie Williams singled in Jeter, and Little came out to remove a spent Martinez — or so it seemed. The Boston manager left the mound after he left the ball in Pedro's right hand. On his way to the dugout, Little crossed the line between blind faith and career suicide.

Hideki Matsui did what Jeter did — doubled on an 0-2 pitch — and Little did not do a damn thing about it, other than watch Jorge Posada hit a bloop that half the Red Sox roster chased and could not catch. The game was tied, Little removed Martinez, and the Curse of the Bambino felt as real as it had inside Shea Stadium in 1986, the night the ball rolled through Bill Buckner's legs.

The Yankees and Red Sox were destined to go extra innings. They had already played twenty-five times in 2003, including this ALCS, the Yanks winning thirteen, the Sox winning twelve. Each team had scored twenty-nine runs in the sixty-three innings of regulation in the series, and given the devout fatalism passed down from New England generation to New England generation, there was little question which team would score the magical thirtieth run.

So who was going to assume the role of Bucky Dent? And when would that Yankee assume it?

Aaron Boone had come to New York from Cincinnati in a trade-deadline deal to replace third baseman Robin Ventura, who was sent to the Dodgers. Over the final two months of the regular season, Boone's new captain had made a hell of an impression on him.

"When I came over from the National League," Boone said, "I was under the impression Derek Jeter was a very good player. But when I got to play with him, I had no idea he was that good. I was blown away by how good of a player he is."

So when Jeter said something, Boone listened.

"Like in the first inning he'd come back and I'd ask him how the pitcher was," Boone said. "And Derek always said, 'This guy fucking sucks,' every single time. That was always his scouting report."

Jeter had another scouting report for Boone, this one about Yankee Stadium.

"Every now and then in the regular season the ghosts will come out," Jeter told him. "But they come out in October all the time."

Boone came to bat in the eleventh inning of Game 7 with all of two hits in the series, and five hits in thirty-one postseason at-bats for a .161 average. "You stink right now," his older brother, Bret, the Seattle second baseman and World Series broadcaster, had told him the night before.

"Do something tomorrow," Bret continued, "and everyone will forget all about that."

Tomorrow had finally come, and only because Mariano Rivera pitched three scoreless innings in relief, and only because Boone — benched in favor of Enrique Wilson — pinch-ran for Ruben Sierra in the eighth. He was leading off the eleventh against knuckleballer Tim Wakefield, who had pitched a 1-2-3 tenth and had been MVP brilliant all series.

Willie Randolph reminded Boone that he was his pre-series sleeper pick, his choice to be the hero. Torre told the third baseman to bring a certain plan to the plate. "Stay through the middle of the field," the manager said. "It doesn't mean you won't hit it out, but stay through the middle."

Boone told himself to take a pitch, then changed his mind as he approached the batter's box. If that first Wakefield knuckleball looked good, he decided he was going to swing.

Boone was hoping and praying for a single. "But like Derek told me," he said, "the ghosts will show up eventually."

At 12:18 a.m., Wakefield's first knuckler floated over the plate; Boone raged into it, sent it sky-high to left field, and landed it deep in the seats as the crowd of 56,279 made Yankee Stadium as loud as it had ever been. He knew it was gone on contact. As he ran around the bases, Boone told himself to look around and take it all in.

Wakefield marched off the field, grabbed his jacket in the dugout, and headed for the tunnel as the Yankees mobbed Boone around the plate. Rivera collapsed on the vacated mound as if he had seen some immaculate vision. Jeter stepped away from the scrum near the plate and did his signature pump of the right fist for the crowd. Wearing a gray hooded sweat jacket on the losing side, Pedro Martinez sat on the bench and wore a mask of sheer disbelief.

The Curse of the Bambino lived on. "I believe in ghosts," Jeter said in the winning clubhouse. "And we've got some ghosts in this Stadium."

The Yankees partied deep into the night, leaving their clubhouse in its old champagne-soaked state. Mussina and the bullpen catcher, Mike Borzello, were the last men in there while Stadium workers were vacuuming the champagne and beer out of the carpet. Mussina and Borzello were sitting in a corner at 3:00 a.m., asking each other the same questions over and over.

How did we just do that? How did we ever win that game?

Earlier, in the losing clubhouse, the Red Sox were in desperate need of grief counselors. "If you told me somebody just came in here and shot half my teammates with an AK-47," said Boston pitcher Bronson Arroyo, "by the looks on people's faces I would've believed it."

Arroyo was struck by the presence of the anti-Jeter, Nomar Garciaparra, a great shortstop who hadn't won a title. "Nomar stood up and talked and he was crying," Arroyo said. "He was saying, 'Everyone else other than the twenty-five guys here will never understand what it's like to play in this uniform, and not being able to get over the hump, and what it's going to do to us this entire off-season. . . . Don't let it get to you. We're all going to have to deal with this shit, and nobody else knows what it's like.'"

On the somber plane ride back to Boston, some players had to listen to utility man Lou Merloni, a Red Sox fan while growing up in Framingham, Massachusetts, rail about the fact that he would spend the winter locked up in his own little prison.

"You guys are going home to Florida, man," Merloni barked at his teammates. "You don't have to deal with this shit. I live here. I can't go to Blockbuster without hearing this shit. Why didn't Grady take [Martinez] out of the game? I might not come out of my house for two months."

It would be another long and cruel winter in New England. But as much as it would shock the Red Sox and the rest of baseball, Boston was nine days away from receiving this glorious bulletin from the south:

It would be another long and cruel winter in the Bronx, too.

Florida Marlins phenom Josh Beckett struck out Derek Jeter in the first inning of Game 3 of the World Series, and back in the Yankees' dugout Luis Sojo heard Jeter give the kind of scouting report the shortstop often gave Aaron Boone.

"Derek comes in and says, 'I'm going to get him. I'm going to get this guy. I'm going to kill him. Just kill him,'" Sojo said. "Then he gets the only three hits [Beckett] allows.

"Jeter's always saying he's going to get this guy or kill that guy. I've never seen a player with as much confidence as he has. It's amazing. I think that's what makes him a winner."

Jeter scored three runs in that 6–1 victory, giving the Yankees a 2–1 World Series lead and injecting his heavily favored team with the kind of confidence only its captain could provide. The Marlins were expected to roll over on command; they were spending $120 million less on payroll.

But in Game 4, Florida scored three first-inning runs on Roger Clemens, who was at the end of his alleged retirement tour. The Marlins weathered Ruben Sierra's tying two-run triple with two outs in the ninth and beat the Yanks' Jeff Weaver on Alex Gonzalez's leadoff homer in the twelfth.

Jeter had been a big proponent of the Weaver acquisition the year before, and yet the pitcher had been a complete bust, his sagging shoulders suggesting a constant crisis of faith. Weaver did negotiate a 1-2-3 eleventh, retiring the Marlins on eight pitches. But Joe Torre's decision to push his luck with Weaver rather than summon Mariano Rivera turned the World Series against him.

The Yankees' season began to crumble in the hour before Game 5, when Jason Giambi nodded at a columnist talking to Torre behind the batting cage, silently asking for a word with his manager. Giambi would tell Torre he needed to be scratched from the lineup because his bum knee would not allow him to play first base.

One Yankee coach said he believed Giambi begged out because he could not make the throw from first to second, and because he was afraid David Wells's pickoff move would put him in the embarrassing position of having to make that very throw.

Whatever. One inning deep into his start, and one day after he joked about his firm lack of commitment to fitness, Wells followed Giambi's lead and pulled a *no más* with his bad back. The Marlins carried a 6–2 lead into the ninth and held on as a Yanks rally — featuring a pinch-hit homer from none other than Giambi — fell short.

Jeter contributed three hits, two runs, a walk, and an RBI to the lost cause, and given his own history of playing in pain, he was furious Giambi had begged out of the lineup on a night he was healthy enough to hit a home run.

Asked if players were upset with Giambi, one Yankee said, "It was more like rage, and Jeter was hotter than anyone. It was like, 'Are you fuckin' kidding me? It's the World Series and you're pulling yourself out because you're afraid their guys like Juan Pierre and Luis Castillo will bunt all over the place?' Jason actually made it worse for himself by hitting that home run. My first thought was about Derek, and how sitting would never even cross his mind. He'd go out there at 25 percent feeling he'd find some way to beat you."

Game 6 in the Bronx was a damning indictment of the Yankee offense. The formula for victory was in place: Andy Pettitte went seven strong innings, Jeter made one of his signature jump plays in the hole, and Florida sent out a twenty-three-year-old pitcher going on three days' rest for the first time.

And yet Josh Beckett dominated the Yankees in his complete-game performance. The Yanks managed five lousy hits, struck out nine times, and lost, 2–0. Yankee batters were terrible all year with runners in scoring position, and that proved to be their undoing against Florida, as they were 7 for 50 in the Series.

Three foundation players — Jeter, Pettitte, and Posada — made mistakes in the Game 6 field that allowed the two Florida runs. Posada missed a tag, Pettitte threw to the wrong base, and Jeter committed his first World Series error since 1996.

But this defeat was not about defense or pitching; it was about hitting. In the eighth inning, after Soriano opened with a single, Jeter brought the full house to life by battling Beckett to a full count. Everyone was waiting for Jeter to create some of that same old magic near the right-field wall; instead he ripped a pitch to center field. Once Juan Pierre settled under it, Torre and everyone else on the Yankee side knew it was not meant to be.

The hundredth World Series game played in Yankee Stadium ended with the Marlins in a dog pile, with their catcher, Pudge Rodriguez, firing his mask into the sky. "It makes you sick," Jeter said of the fact that another team was celebrating a title in his ballpark. "How else can you feel?"

Marlins players, wives, and kids ended up on the field. The team owner, Jeffrey Loria, did an amateur-hour run around the bases, looking like some yahoo banker who had just won a fan contest.

Jeter sat at his locker in full uniform, hoping reporters would keep him there all night so he would not have to take off his jersey for the last time. Players were leaving the building, and Jeter was still sitting there trying to make sense of it all.

"They just played better than us," he said. "There's no sugarcoating it. They pitched better than us, they had more clutch hits. People need to stop saying it's a big shock."

The Yankees had been beaten by the smaller-market Marlins a year after they were beaten by the smaller-market Angels and two years after they were beaten by the smaller-market Diamondbacks. No, George Steinbrenner did not share the glee of the commissioner, Bud Selig, who embraced the virtues of league-wide parity championed by the late NFL commissioner Pete Rozelle.

Steinbrenner began hunting for scapegoats, and his hitting coach, Rick Down, was in his sights. Don Zimmer, bench coach, had already signed his walking papers by trashing Steinbrenner one last time on his way out of the Stadium, and by promising to never again work a day in the Boss's employ. Mel Stottlemyre, pitching coach, said he was considering stepping down because he felt "personally abused" by Steinbrenner.

But Down wanted to return. As the hitting coach walked out of the Stadium the day after the Marlins' conquest, Torre wrapped an arm around him, kissed him on the cheek, and said, "You've got nothing to worry about. I love your passion for the game."

As Torre walked away, another Yankee coach, Lee Mazzilli, started laughing.

"What's so funny?" Down asked.

"Do you know who that is?" Mazzilli responded.

"Yeah, that's my manager."

"No, that's the Godfather, and that was your kiss of death."

Sure enough, Brian Cashman phoned Down the next morning to tell him he had been fired. When Torre called to express his regrets, he explained to Down, "I couldn't buy a new house, but I can rearrange the furniture."

Suddenly Down was a frayed love seat moved out to the curb, ultimately replaced by Don Mattingly. But the Yankees were not only going to hire a new hitting coach.

They were going to hire a new infielder, too, one who would forever alter the franchise and every aspect of Derek Jeter's baseball life.

10

♦

Alex

ALEX RODRIGUEZ THOUGHT he had found an exit strategy in the Boston Red Sox, who were miles apart in contract negotiations with Nomar Garciaparra, scheduled to be a free agent at the end of the 2004 season.

A-Rod's Texas Rangers had finished dead last in the American League West for three consecutive years, and the $252 million man wanted out. He was desperate to win. Desperate to get out of Arlington, Texas. Desperate to avoid finishing his career without a parade to call his own.

Boston had deals to send Manny Ramirez to Texas for Rodriguez and Garciaparra to the White Sox for Magglio Ordonez. The Red Sox needed to clear one hurdle — they wanted to lower the average annual value of A-Rod's contract, and the Players Association was more inclined to allow random, unlimited steroid testing than it was to allow a megastar player to give back a pile of guaranteed cash.

A-Rod wanted to go to Boston, the Red Sox and Rangers wanted A-Rod to go to Boston, and Commissioner Bud Selig wanted one of his most marketable players to go to Boston, or any place other than Texas, where the reporting date for punters and kickers is bigger than the one for pitchers and catchers.

But the union and the Red Sox could not agree to agree on the amount of the contract reduction, leaving Garciaparra stuck with a franchise that did not want to pay him, and leaving A-Rod stuck with a market and a manager (Buck Showalter) he could not stand.

Until the Yankees' home-run hero from the 2003 triumph over Boston, Aaron Boone, blew out his left knee in a pickup basketball game. Suddenly the Yankees needed a third baseman, and Drew Henson, the two-sport star at Michigan and $17 million bust with the Yanks, was busy escaping to the NFL. The remaining candidates included Enrique Wilson, Erick Almonte, Tyler Houston, and Miguel Cairo, and nobody was singing a Sinatra tune over them.

Brian Cashman ended up on the phone with his counterpart in Texas, John Hart, in an attempt to scoop up Boston's fumble and, against all odds, lateral A-Rod over to third base. "I didn't tell anyone about it," Cashman said. "I didn't even tell my owner I was working on that deal."

His owner, George Steinbrenner, had collapsed in December while attending the memorial service for NFL great Otto Graham, and the Boss had retreated from public view. But Steinbrenner was still the principal owner, still the one in charge. He had personally signed Gary Sheffield to a $39 million deal (against the wishes of Cashman and team president Randy Levine) before his collapse, and even though he was speaking through statements released by his publicist, Howard Rubenstein, Steinbrenner remained active in a much less visible way, fully committed to the same old mission statement of winning it all.

Hart advised Cashman to seek permission from the commissioner's office to talk directly to Rodriguez and his agent, Scott Boras. "I'm not talking to Boras," Cashman said. "He will try to extract something from us. You guys have to tell Alex he's got to waive his no-trade clause, and that he's got to play third base. If you put the Yankees on the phone with Scott Boras, he's going to smell leverage, and I don't want to be in that position."

Cashman hoped to keep the trade talks confidential, as the public nature of Boston's negotiations with Texas helped prevent the Red Sox from landing A-Rod. "But Alex told a friend of his who's a real estate tycoon in Miami," Cashman said, "and that guy happened to be a friend of Randy Levine's. So I got nailed there and was put in an uncomfortable position.

"Randy calls me and says, 'Hey, I got a call from a buddy of mine in Miami who said we're on the verge of getting Alex Rodriguez. Is that true?' And I was like, 'Oh, shit,' because I hadn't presented our side yet."

The talks hit the papers, but there was no killing this trade. Cashman had the Rangers tell Rodriguez that there was zero chance the Yankees would unseat Jeter at short, that it was third base or nothing at all. Cashman and other club officials discussed whether it made any sense to move Jeter to third and arrived at a quick consensus that the incumbent had to stay put.

It did not matter that Rodriguez was the superior physical talent; Jeter was the captain and the soul of the team. The Yankees did not want to diminish him in any way.

And besides, Rodriguez would have agreed to become a catcher if it meant escaping his own Arlington cemetery and resurrecting his championship hopes in New York. So A-Rod willingly surrendered his cherished position — and any future claim as the greatest shortstop of all time — while Rangers owner Tom Hicks agreed to take Alfonso Soriano and to cover $67 million of the remaining $179 million of A-Rod's deal.

Selig still had to approve the deal, and the commissioner was concerned that the move would leave the Yankees with a staggering talent and payroll advantage over the rest of creation. But Selig was no dummy. Send his biggest star to the brightest lights of Broadway? Yes, it was worth the sacrifice of competitive balance.

In a statement released on February 16, 2004, the commissioner warned that he would not let money deals of this magnitude become the norm. "However," Selig said, "given the unique circumstances, including the size, length, and complexity of Mr. Rodriguez's contract and the quality of the talent moving in both directions, I have decided to approve the transaction."

Steinbrenner, the ultimate star collector, was ecstatic over the news. A-Rod would not just improve the Yankees' chances of winning another title, at least theoretically, but he would be a brand-new TV star for Steinbrenner's YES Network. If the Yankees were a sitcom, Rodriguez would be expected to have a *Seinfeld*-like impact on ratings and advertising revenue.

Steinbrenner merrily agreed to bid farewell to a $5.75 million player at third (the Yanks gave Boone only thirty days of termination pay, as he violated language in his contract forbidding him to play basketball), and to absorb the $112 million fee for A-Rod, who would be the fourth Yankee with a nine-figure contract (Jeter had signed for $189 million, Giambi for $120 million, and newcomer Kevin Brown for $105 million with the Dodgers).

Few cared anymore that David Wells was gone, that Andy Pettitte had signed with the Astros, and that Roger Clemens had emerged from his fifteen-minute retirement to do the same. The A-Rod trade represented another Christmas in February, as Torre had called the 1999 acquisition of Clemens. Everyone marveled over the new toy under the tree. Everyone except the captain of the team.

On a cold, sunny day, Cashman was driving southbound on I-95 between Darien and Stamford, Connecticut, when he called Jeter with the big news. The general manager knew the history of bad blood between the captain and Rodriguez. He knew Jeter would have preferred it if the Yankees had signed Chad Curtis out of retirement and traded for Ken Huckaby rather than deal for A-Rod, but in the end, Texas made an offer Cashman could not refuse.

The GM rarely called players about trades that did not involve them, but this was different, much different. Cashman did not want a member of the media to break the news to Jeter, and to ask the shortstop if he was concerned Rodriguez might take his job.

Cashman needed to assure Jeter up front that he would remain at short. So the GM got the captain on the phone and without pause told him, "I just want you to know we just acquired Alex Rodriguez."

"Really?" Jeter said.

Really.

Cashman explained his reasoning, explained that Rodriguez understood there would never be any quarterback controversy at short. Jeter absorbed the information that was coming at him like a truck, paused for a moment of deliberation, and said, "This sounds pretty cool."

Pretty cool. Under the circumstances, "pretty cool" was the best answer the Yankees could have hoped for.

To present a united front, Steinbrenner told Jeter he should appear at A-Rod's Yankee Stadium press conference — the kind of press conference Jeter did not get for his $189 million deal — and appear Jeter did. Not only did he show up at the Stadium, but Jeter agreed to fly with Rodriguez from Tampa to New York.

On that flight, A-Rod told Jeter he was committed to third base for the long term. "I'm going to stick close to you," Rodriguez told Jeter, "ask your advice on many issues. I need your support and mentorship."

The peace-in-the-Middle-East-sized press conference in the Stadium Club was attended by three hundred reporters. Never had baseball seen anything like this. Joe Torre had become Chuck Daly at the Barcelona Olympics, coaching Jordan, Magic, and Bird. Or Magic and Bird, anyway, forming their own Dream Team on the left side of the infield.

"Derek has four world championships," Rodriguez said, "and I want him to have ten. That's what this is all about."

Ten rings, the same as Yogi?

"Let's work on making it five first," Jeter said.

A-Rod wore a pinstriped tie to go with his new pinstriped jersey. He would get number 13, the number Jeter first coveted as a rookie, the same number Jeter's father wore at Fisk University. Rodriguez was not paying any tribute to a father who had abandoned him as a child; the former Miami high school quarterback wanted to wear the number of his favorite NFL player, Dan Marino.

Before the cameras and notebooks, with Steinbrenner watching on TV in Tampa, Rodriguez kept deferring to Jeter, kept calling him the leader, kept saying he just wanted to be "one of the guys." Of course, if Rodriguez was a man of many talents, being one of the guys was not among them.

A-Rod was the American League's Most Valuable Player, a two-time Gold Glove winner, and a shortstop considered by most baseball observers to be a better defender than Jeter, who had yet to claim his first Gold Glove. So the question had to be asked:

Why was Rodriguez the one being asked to move to third?

"That's a non-issue," A-Rod claimed.

"I know you're going to be enjoying this issue for as long as we're playing together," Jeter told reporters. "There's always a spin on it. I'm playing short. That's my job here. His job here now is to play third."

Remarkably enough, Cashman made the decision that A-Rod would be the one to move without consulting Torre. The general manager had explained that "you go with the man that brought you to the dance. . . . We have, arguably, the best left side of the infield in the history of baseball, and this is what it's going to be: Derek Jeter at shortstop, Alex Rodriguez at third base."

Torre would have made the same call Cashman did, and the GM knew as much in advance. In many ways, Jeter had made Joe. Jeter had helped turn a retread manager into a Hall of Famer, and Torre was not about to betray him now.

But in defending Jeter's honor, Torre conceded Rodriguez had greater natural talent. "There are things that go beyond ability," the manager said. "And I've said this about Derek in the past. He can't hit with A-Rod, maybe can't throw with him. Can't throw with Garciaparra, can't do this with Garciaparra.

"But what I know is I wouldn't trade him for anybody. There is something special about Derek Jeter. What is it about him that makes him what he is? It's something that you can't put down on paper."

When they were young big leaguers who slept in each other's homes, Jeter and Rodriguez talked about finishing their careers together. That dream died a painful death on the pages of *Esquire*, leaving Jeter and A-Rod to answer questions about their breakup.

"The worst thing that could happen for the media, I think," Jeter said, "is for me and Alex to get along. I think everyone wants us to disagree, to battle over who's doing this and who's doing that. But that's not the case."

Yet during this only-in-New-York media event, Jeter said more with his expressions than he did with his words. He looked like he would rather have spent the day getting a few boils lanced from his rump.

Jeter surveyed the scene and understood the game had changed for good. With Pettitte in Houston, only four teammates remained from the glory days — Mariano Rivera, Jorge Posada, El Duque Hernandez, and Bernie Williams — and Williams was in a fight for his center-field life with Kenny Lofton.

The Yankees had all but kicked Pettitte to the curb in free agency, they were closing in on Bernie, they were letting Torre enter the final year of his contract without an extension, and they were giving the keys to the kingdom to an athlete, Rodriguez, who represented everything Jeter was not.

"The measuring stick is how many championships you win," the captain said, as if reminding A-Rod that none of his monstrous home runs took his zero off the October scoreboard.

Rodriguez had endured a wild winter, nearly landing in Boston before showing up in the Bronx. Worn down by all the negotiating, by all the back-and-forth between owners and agents and union officials, Rodriguez's wife, Cynthia, turned to Jeter on the flight up from Tampa and said, "I'm glad this is all over."

The captain smiled. "The party has just begun," he said.

If Jeter was in a partying mood, at least for public consumption, his friend and former minor league teammate and roommate, R. D. Long, killed the mood in private.

Years earlier, in his first meeting with the Class AAA Columbus manager, Stump Merrill, Long was reminded of his true identity within the Yankee organization. "He called me into his office once and said, 'You're Jeter's buddy, right?'" Long said. "Not R.D., but Jeter's buddy."

Jeter's buddy walked away from baseball in 1997, at age twenty-six, when he realized he was through chasing the big league dream. But even though Long was out of the game, nobody tracked Jeter's career more closely than Jeter's buddy.

And with the Rodriguez acquisition announcing the start of a new era in the Bronx, Jeter's buddy wanted Jeter to know that the Yankees had just made a huge mistake.

"I told Derek the minute A-Rod [joined] his team," Long said, "told him that day, 'The championship run is over. You will not win a championship with Alex Rodriguez on your team unless your karma is bigger than his. . . . You won't win another one with this guy. You'd better get rid of him some kind of way.'"

Derek Jeter greatly appreciated George Steinbrenner's willingness to spend whatever it took to surround his shortstop with championship-grade talent. Hours after Andy Pettitte had reached a deal with the Astros, Jeter was sitting with Jay-Z at a high school basketball game at Fordham University when informed of the news.

Jeter said a few complimentary things about his longtime teammate and friend but basically handled the bulletin with the greatest of ease.

"I'm sure we'll get someone else," the captain said.

"You already did," a reporter told him.

The Yankees were finalizing a trade with the Dodgers for Kevin Brown, sending back a package that included a Jeter favorite, Jeff Weaver, who had flopped in the Bronx. To offset their considerable personnel losses, and the second-place finish to the Red Sox in the race for Arizona ace Curt Schilling, the Yankees acquired, among others, Brown, Javier Vazquez, Gary Sheffield, Kenny Lofton, Tom "Flash" Gordon, and Paul Quantrill.

And Alex Rodriguez.

With his budget knowing no bounds, Steinbrenner was forever giving Jeter a chance to win titles, even if the captain would have preferred a less aggressive approach when it came to trading for A-Rod.

"I hope all the writers lay off on this thing, A-Rod versus Jeter," Steinbrenner told reporters while sitting in a golf cart at Legends Field. "It has no part. It really doesn't. Let them go about playing baseball. It's going to be tough enough as it is in the American League East."

Asked if he planned to take Rodriguez to dinner, Steinbrenner responded, "Jeter should take him to dinner." The Boss had just read a *USA Today* column explaining how another Yankee captain, Lou Gehrig, learned how to thrive in the shadows of Babe Ruth and Joe DiMaggio.

Steinbrenner said Jeter should find a way to deal with the new Ruthian presence in his life, just as Gehrig did. "He'll show that kind of great leadership," the owner said. "I would bank on it."

Of course, Gehrig's mother once criticized an outfit Ruth's daughter was wearing, and the Yankee stars did not speak to each other for six years.

Jeter and A-Rod would never get away with that, not in this electronic age of 24/7 scrutiny, even if they represented the most fascinating intrasquad feud since Thurman and Reggie.

As spring training opened, Rodriguez finally disclosed his three-year-old secret: after his *Esquire* comments were published, he had made the loneliest ninety-minute drive of his life from the Rangers' Port Charlotte camp to Jeter's Tampa home in an attempt to save the very friendship he had torpedoed.

"From that day on," Rodriguez told a few reporters, "I thought it was over."

He thought wrong. A-Rod conceded the two shortstops "haven't been as tight the last three years," a claim everyone in Yankeedom knew to be a gross understatement.

"We had that discussion," Jeter said, "and in my mind that was the end of it. In my mind it's a dead issue, in [Alex's] mind it's a dead issue, so we just move on from there. . . . We don't have problems. Let's get that out there."

As much as Jeter cited Rodriguez's marriage and the players' off-field demands as the cause of their altered friendship, and as much as he compared their differences to those of brothers who argue and make up, the captain knew this ship was not sailing.

Their relationship would remain under constant observation, something A-Rod would acknowledge in a spring training interview with Matt Lauer on the *Today* show.

"He's like a brother to me," Rodriguez said of Jeter. "I mean, we've been out to lunch this week three or four times already. And I think they have to see us hold hands and go to a movie so they know that we've made up. When we're fifty years old, they're going to say, 'Well, Alex and Derek, are they arguing? Are they best friends? Are they brothers?' We're just having fun with it now."

Jeter was having no fun with this story. He knew people were going to study the vibe between the shortstop and third baseman a lot more closely than they would study the out-of-town scoreboard.

As it turned out, that vibe helped take Derek Jeter right out of his element. In a season-opening loss to Tampa Bay in Tokyo, his first game as Rodriguez's teammate, Jeter grounded out four times and struck out in five at-bats; A-Rod fared only a bit better, twice striking out looking, popping out, and doubling and scoring a run in four at-bats.

Jeter and Rodriguez were dreadful for much of April; A-Rod went 0 for 16 in a series at Fenway Park, a development all of Boston met with considerable glee. But Jeter seemed to be the one more adversely affected by this tense and awkward pairing on the left side of the infield, as he descended into the worst slump of his life.

With the Red Sox looking to finish a three-game sweep in the Bronx on April 25, Jeter struck out three times in a 2–0 loss, extended his hitless streak to twenty-five at-bats, and actually heard the home crowd of 55,338 turn against him. Booing Derek Jeter? "I never thought I'd hear that," said Boston's Kevin Millar, who called the Yankee fans "ruthless."

Of course, Jeter would never admit that Rodriguez's presence was unnerving him; the captain would not even use the word *slump* to describe his, well, slump. But several teammates said they thought A-Rod's arrival was a contributing factor, if not an overriding factor, in Jeter's struggles at the plate.

"Derek had the whole city to himself," said one teammate, "and Alex represented a threat to that. It was like Derek was trying to protect his home from an invasion."

Rodriguez had been stepping to the Stadium plate to music from *The Natural*, and by the end of the home Boston series he had managed to lift his batting average to .257 with three homers, or 75 points and three homers higher than Jeter's totals.

The shortstop was jumpy in the box, shifting his weight too quickly to his front foot and flailing away at pitches he should have taken. The fans adored him, yes, but they were tired of watching it and decided to let Jeter know it.

"I would boo myself, too," the captain said. "I wouldn't want to play on a team where if you're playing bad, they don't care."

Jeter quickly shot down any suggestions that his shoulder and thumb injuries from 2003 were keeping him down. He also made sure to remain available to reporters, and to maintain his even-keeled approach with them.

Jeter did not change his in-game persona, either. If the twenty-fifth man on the roster put down a productive sacrifice bunt, Jeter remained the first Yankee on the top step of the dugout to congratulate him.

The captain did not want any teammates or fans to sense that he was panicking, or that he was growing angry over the boos. Jeter even joked that his parents were not waiting around for him after games anymore. "If your parents walk out on you," he said, "you know you're not doing too well. They're probably getting booed, too."

Oakland came in on April 27, and Jeter's 0 for 3 left him 0 for 28. The fans reacted differently this time, as if making up for the unforgiving Sunday crowd. They stood and cheered for the shortstop when he batted in the seventh inning, trying to will him to a hit.

Jeter grounded into a force play.

The following night, the fans gave the shortstop standing ovations in his final two at-bats—"Let's go, Jeter," they chanted—before he walked and grounded out, extending his hitless streak to 32, doubling A-Rod's 0 for 16 in Boston and establishing the longest Yankee run of futility since Jimmy Wynn's 0 for 32 in 1977.

Just before that closing groundout, Bubba Crosby had whiffed on a feeble swing and then stopped on his way out of the box when the crowd erupted in cheers. Crosby thought the umpire had somehow ruled it a ball, at least until it became obvious the crowd was only responding to the hitter on deck.

"That's what happens when you bat in front of Jeter," Crosby said.

That's what happens when four championships and more than eight years of dignity and class are rewarded with clemency for thirty-one consecutive failures at the plate.

"The fans have been great," Jeter said. "They've been cheering for me going up, but afterwards they haven't had anything to cheer about."

On the night of April 29, for the third and final game of the series against Oakland, Jeter took extra batting practice and listened as the human good luck charm, Yogi Berra, told him he once went 0 for 32, too.

Jeter had heard advice from teammates, friends, people on the street. He had engaged in private lessons with the new hitting coach and former captain, Don Mattingly. The 0 for 32 had cost Jeter 2 full points from his lifetime batting average, which fell to .314, and had left fans actually feeling sorry for him.

"A streak like that," Jeter said, "you wouldn't want to wish on anyone, even other teams. Guys on other teams even have been giving me support."

When the Yankees' leadoff man dug in against Oakland lefty Barry Zito, he absorbed a louder ovation than any .161 hitter had ever heard in the first inning of a game in which his team was already trailing 2–0. The Yankee Stadium crowd was back on its feet, trying to do what it could to help. Only this was Jeter's burden to bear.

Zito owned one of the best curve balls in the game, but he decided to open with a fastball. On his end, Jeter decided to open with a cut that released all of his mounting pressures and frustrations, like a volcano blowing its top. The ball traveled well over 400 feet, over the left-center wall, into Monument Park. Jeter's first homer of the year left the Stadium shaking to its core.

Jeter did a slight fist pump as he rounded first, but his face remained expressionless. "I was smiling on the inside," he confessed. Jeter had his first hit since an infield single against the White Sox nine days earlier, and he was so haunted by the drought, he figured his home-run ball might crash into a bird in flight and fall into an outfielder's glove.

The shortstop touched home with the fans chanting his name. Jeter lost himself in a procession of high-fives near the dugout, and when he found his manager, "he kind of head-butted me in the chest," Joe Torre said. Jeter took his curtain call, liberated at last. "It was like the world was off his shoulders," Torre said.

Jeter did not care that his first hit of the night would also be his last. "It's like a bad dream is over with," the captain said. He was batting .165 and loving every precious second of it.

On July 1, Derek Jeter proved himself to be the toughest shortstop and the toughest man in the toughest rivalry.

He had rediscovered his stroke to hit .400 over June and blast an A-Rodian nine homers in the month, driving the Yankees to a seven-and-a-half-game lead in the American League East and a potential series sweep of the Red Sox.

With two outs and runners on second and third in the top of the twelfth, Trot Nixon at the plate, the Yankees and Red Sox had already played a game right out of the 2003 ALCS. Boston was burning to win once in New York, to avoid leaving town with an insurmountable eight-and-a-half-game deficit.

Pedro Martinez made the early statement by hitting Gary Sheffield between the numbers with a pitch in the first inning, after Sheffield had the audacity to step out and call for time with Pedro starting his delivery. Sheffield shouted at Martinez and took a few steps toward the mound, but the Red Sox were going to fight for this one.

Twenty-four of them, anyway.

Nomar Garciaparra had missed the first fifty-seven games of the season with Achilles tendinitis but had returned to the lineup on June 9 and played in the first two games of this latest Yankees series. Only on this crucial night in the Bronx, Garciaparra told manager Terry Francona his right Achilles was too sore to go.

Garciaparra started stretching the tendon in the ninth inning to see if he could at least enter as a pinch hitter, yet he said he could not get it loose enough to play. As it happened, Garciaparra's Achilles was as frayed as his relationship with the team.

If Nomar had been as beloved in Boston as Jeter had been in New York, the Red Sox star was mortally wounded by the off-season pursuit of A-Rod and by what he considered a low-ball contract offer from management. Garciaparra had become distant, cold, lost in his own isolated world. But the brooding and the growing disconnect between player and team had largely been secrets contained within the walls of Boston proper until the witching hour of July 1.

Few outside those walls had ever questioned Garciaparra's work ethic and Jeter-like commitment to excellence, at least until this night, until this game, and until this little pop fly Nixon had hit over A-Rod's head in the twelfth. Garciaparra was on the bench, and Jeter was on the run. In a matter of seconds, Nomar would be No-more.

Rodriguez had given up on the play; he went through the motions on a trot toward the plunging ball. Meanwhile, Jeter was flying for the left-field line and tracking the ball with his glove hand extended. The shortstop had been playing the left-handed Nixon to pull the ball, so he had a long way to go. It looked like two runs for the Red Sox and a round of applause for the captain for giving it the ol' college try.

Only Jeter made the catch just inside the line, drawing a late October sound from the midsummer crowd. There was only one problem: Jeter did not have time to hit the brakes. He had two full strides to make a pick-your-poison choice: crash into the low wall knees first, or take flight and take his chances.

Jeter decided to dive headfirst into the crowd with the same speed and ferocity of Pete Rose diving headfirst into third. The captain figured his landing would be cushioned by the beer-stained lap of some overweight fan stuffed inside a T-shirt bearing the Jeter name and number.

"When I fell into the stands in the playoffs against Oakland," Jeter would say of the 2001 Division Series, "I landed in the photographers' pit and it was all cement. So I thought on this one I would try to jump over the photographers' pit and run into somebody, but there was nobody there."

Millions of Yankee fans would have killed to get close to Jeter, to touch him, to be in his presence for even a nanosecond. In midair, realizing there was no canceling this flight, Jeter needed just one of those fans to be there for him.

In a crowd of 55,265, not a single soul was there to save Jeter from himself.

Having given no thought to the shoulder he had wrecked the year before, Jeter went face first into a vacated chair three rows back, his legs and spikes kicking up toward the sky on impact. "I always get a laugh out of it when people say, 'You could've stopped,'" Jeter would say. "No, you can't stop. I was running full speed and I caught it like three feet from the wall."

The fall in Game 5 of the Oakland series actually hurt more and caused a drastic decline in Jeter's performance across the balance of the postseason. "In the Oakland one," Jeter said, "a lot of things hurt."

But this regular-season dive against Boston was not just about pain. It was about a $189 million captain risking his million-dollar smile to make a play pretty boys are not supposed to make.

As Jeter was helped to his feet in the crowd, Rodriguez reached in, put his right hand on his forehead, and then started waving for the trainer with his left. A-Rod saw the blood on Jeter's chin, the blood splatter on his jersey, and the growing mouse under his right eye.

"He looked like he got punched by Mike Tyson," Rodriguez said.

With photographers firing away, Jeter was helped by a couple of fans and a couple of cops. He put his right hand to his mouth to feel for blood, then closed his lips and rolled his tongue to make certain his teeth were intact. He stepped on top of the wall, rising above the applauding fans, before lowering himself to the field and wobbling away with Jorge Posada on one side and the trainer, Gene Monahan, on the other.

Jeter dabbed his sweatband against his mouth, checking again for blood, and the crowd gave him a standing ovation as he crossed the field. Monahan held a towel to Jeter's chin, and before the shortstop went down the dugout steps he flipped the ball to a kid. Of course he did.

Just as Manny Ramirez was homering in the top of the thirteenth, an ambulance beyond the left-field wall flashed its red lights before it transported the Yankee captain to Columbia-Presbyterian. But whenever Jeter made a play like the one he had just made, the Yankees knew they could not lose.

With the Yanks down to their last strike, Miguel Cairo doubled in the tying run before John Flaherty delivered the game winner four hours and twenty minutes after the first pitch was thrown. A-Rod and others said it was the best game they had ever played in, and their moods were brightened when the team disclosed that x-rays on Jeter's battered cheek were negative. The captain was diagnosed with a lacerated chin, a bruised right cheek, and a bruised right shoulder.

"He took off like a 747," Rodriguez said. "If they had said he'd broken his shoulder, you wouldn't be surprised. If they had said he'd broken his jaw, you wouldn't be surprised."

A-Rod actually finished the game at shortstop, his old position, but only after he turned a remarkable double play on a bases-loaded, no-out smash from Kevin Millar in the eleventh, finishing the play with a throw to the plate from one knee.

Nonetheless, Rodriguez was humbled by the physical sacrifice Jeter had made. "Greatest catch I've ever seen," A-Rod said. "It was unbelievable. He's just so unselfish. He put his body in a compromising spot. It was hard to watch."

Even as the handsome face of baseball, Jeter was willing to take a punch. He was the full-scholarship player with a walk-on's approach. So once he got inside with the medical and training staff, Jeter needed to make one thing perfectly clear.

"We're trying to organize the injury," Monahan said, "and the first thing out of his mouth to the doc and myself was, 'I'm playing tomorrow.' That was the epitome of toughness right there."

On the losing side of the Stadium, the Red Sox were shaking their heads over the way Jeter gave up his body to record an out in a regular-season game his team did not need to win. Curt Schilling was sitting at a table in the Red Sox clubhouse when he was approached by the *Boston Herald*'s Tony Massarotti, who made a remark about Jeter's play.

"You know what," said Schilling, pointing to the fingers of his left hand, "that's why he's got four of those big fucking rings right here."

At that moment in time Jeter had a higher standing in the Red Sox clubhouse than Nomar did.

As a former member of the 2001 Oakland A's, Boston center fielder Johnny Damon had not gotten over Jeter's Division Series flip to the plate before watching the Yankee shortstop batter and bloody himself on his dive.

Damon said the respect for Jeter inside the Red Sox clubhouse grew with each team-first move the Yankee made. "Not one player on any of my Boston teams ever had a single negative thing to say about him," Damon would say.

The Red Sox GM, Theo Epstein, had his first brush with Jeter's greatness as a young San Diego Padres official during the '98 World Series. "You hear all the glowing things said about him and your natural inclination is to think that it can't be all true," Epstein would say, "and that he's built up by the media. . . . You come and see him play twenty times a year against you and you realize, hey, he's the real deal. He's earned every bit of his reputation . . . You'd want your kid, if he grows up to play ball, to be that type of player and person."

If Jeter was baseball's most respected figure even before Trot Nixon lofted that ball over Alex Rodriguez's head, Garciaparra was not far behind. But something changed forever the moment Jeter made the catch and turned his landing into an X Games stunt gone wrong.

A television camera caught Garciaparra alone on the bench, with the rest of his teammates on the dugout rail, while Jeter was risking life and limb. For a franchise and a fan base waiting some eighty-six years for a championship, the juxtaposition was impossible to ignore.

"It was just straight superstition that Nomar always sat in a certain place in the dugout," Boston pitcher Bronson Arroyo said. "And our fans were like, 'Look, Derek Jeter's diving into the stands and busting his face up, and Nomar's sitting on the goddamn bench and not even cheering for the team.' It was just one of Nomar's superstitions, and he got ripped for it."

Just as Jeter had millions of kids holding up their right hands to plate umpires as they stepped into the box, Garciaparra had every Little Leaguer in New England adjusting and readjusting his batting gloves after he stepped out of the box. Nomar was the Ted Williams of his day.

But Garciaparra's defensive abilities were in serious decline, along with his passion for remaining in Boston. Red Sox management confronted a question Yankee management never wanted to answer: How do you trade an iconic shortstop?

On July 2, as promised, Derek Jeter reported to work at Shea Stadium to open a series against the Mets, a team he positively owned. "Like Chipper Jones," former Mets GM Steve Phillips said, "Jeter was captain of the Mets killers."

Only the hyped-up intramural competition with the Mets did not draw Jeter to the ballpark — his willingness to play hurt against all comers did. Jeter confirmed as much when asked if the rivalry with the Red Sox inspired him to go flying into the crowd.

"When you compete," he said, "I don't think it makes a difference who you're competing against. I still want to win. Definitely there's more excitement in the stands when we're playing Boston, but I'd like to think I'd make that play against anyone."

Jeter arrived at Shea with a large purple welt under his right eye, and a bandage over a gashed chin that required stitches. "I'm fine," he declared.

Jeter made an impressive backhand stop in the hole in the first inning and later ignored his condition by stealing a base with a headfirst slide. The Yanks lost by an 11–2 count, but Jeter won just by showing up.

Down in Atlanta that same night, while Garciaparra proved healthy enough to get three hits, influential *Boston Globe* columnist Dan Shaughnessy was up in the press box writing a column that opened like this: "Trade Nomar."

Shaughnessy called Garciaparra's absence in the thirteen-inning loss to the Yankees a "ridiculous day off" and cited Terry Francona's pregame comment to Yankee broadcaster Jim Kaat — "I gave him every opportunity [to play]" — as evidence the manager wanted and expected Nomar in the lineup that night.

Four weeks after that column appeared, and two minutes before the trade deadline, Garciaparra was dealt to the Chicago Cubs in a four-team deal that brought shortstop Orlando Cabrera and first baseman Doug Mientkiewicz to Boston. In one bold move by Epstein, the Red Sox had upgraded their team defense and their team chemistry.

Nomar's decision to sit out the thirteen-inning game was not the primary reason he was traded. It was merely on the list of reasons that made a deal sensible.

"It was weird," Jeter said of Boston's reaction to Nomar's no-show on July 1, "because I didn't think Nomar deserved to be treated the way he was. I thought that was bad."

It was now official: Jeter had outlasted the most conspicuous challenges to his shortstop throne. Rey Ordonez, who was supposed to battle him for New York supremacy, had long been traded by the Mets and had already played his final big league game. Alex Rodriguez had surrendered the position to join a winner in the Bronx. And Nomar Garciaparra had been shipped out of the rivalry and out of the American League, out of sight and out of mind.

If the lasting image of Nomar would be his Yankee Stadium sit-in, the lasting Red Sox sounds of that night would belong to other prominent figures. As his players headed into the clubhouse, Francona made a big show of congratulating them for their efforts, offering handshakes and pats on the back.

This was not your standard major league scene, not on the losing side of a ballpark. Once the door to their room opened for the news media, the Red Sox spoke optimistically of a second-half surge, of fighting their way back into the playoffs.

But with Jeter's Yankees dominating the division, and with the Red Sox cooked before any Fourth of July barbecues, one particular quote from the losing side came off as absurd.

"We still believe we will win the World Series," Johnny Damon said.

The Game 4 ball was in Mariano Rivera's right hand, and the Yankees were going to sweep Boston in the American League Championship Series. More than that, they were going to crush the Red Sox with their new weapon of mass destruction — Alex Rodriguez.

Painful as it was to lose Game 7 of the 2003 ALCS on the indelible homer hit by Aaron Boone, that Red Sox team could retreat into winter knowing they were one swing and/or one Grady Little brain freeze away from advancing to the World Series. In addition, the 2003 Red Sox could find solace in the firing of Little and in the hiring of Curt Schilling.

The 2004 Boston team showed up as a free-spirited lot that grew fond of calling itself a band of Idiots. The Red Sox thought they would finally defeat the Yankees this time around, even if a fateful pickup basketball game in the off-season turned Boone into Rodriguez.

Boston had grown to detest A-Rod with every fiber of its being, in part because he did not close the deal to join the Red Sox, in part because he did close the deal to become a Yankee, and in part because he got into a fight with catcher Jason Varitek, a team leader in the Mark Messier mold, after Bronson Arroyo hit him with a pitch in July.

But at the time Rivera took the mound in the ninth inning of Game 4, ready to finish off a 4–3 victory after pitching a scoreless eighth, A-Rod was batting .388 in the series with eight runs scored, five runs driven in, and two homers, including a two-run blast on this night to open the scoring in the third inning. Rodriguez was making the uppercased Idiots look like lowercased idiots.

In fact, his performance in the postseason mocked any notion he was destined to become known as a big-game choker of Greg Norman proportions. He had batted .421 in the four-game Division Series triumph over the Twins, and as a Mariner he had batted .409 with 2 homers and 5 RBI in the 2000 ALCS loss to the Yanks.

The numbers said A-Rod was a lethal postseason force. Starting with his first playoff appearance as a full-time player in '97, and ending at the point where Rivera stood three outs away from returning the Yanks to the World Series, Rodriguez was batting .375 with 6 homers, 16 RBI, and 16 runs scored over four and a half series.

This was what general manager Brian Cashman had in mind when he made the trade with Texas: A-Rod and Derek Jeter overcoming their personal differences to win championships together, just like Ruth and Gehrig did, just like Thurman and Reggie did.

Jeter was thirty, A-Rod twenty-nine, so they had a number of prime years ahead of them, an alarming thought in Boston. Cashman's combustible experiment was working. After Jeter launched himself into the stands against the Red Sox, Rodriguez said, "I told him recently, 'You're a greater player than I thought you were, and I thought you were a great player.'"

A-Rod and Jeter had done enough as a tandem to lead the Yankees to their third consecutive season of more than 100 victories and their seventh consecutive division crown. To the rest of baseball, it seemed another simple case of the Yankees steamrolling the competition with their checkbook.

Forbes estimated the franchise that had sold for less than $10 million in 1973 was worth $832 million thirty-one years later — $300 million more than the second-most-valuable franchise, the Red Sox. The small-market teams did not care that the Yankees had paid out $60.6 million in revenue sharing and luxury tax fees in 2003.

They were screaming bloody murder over the absurd payroll disparity between George Steinbrenner's and everyone else's. The Yanks were laying out $184 million in wages, almost $60 million more than the second-highest payroll (Boston's) and at least $150 million more than four other teams. In 1996, the year of their first title under Joe Torre, the Yanks' payroll of $52 million and change was not even $4 million greater than the second-highest payroll (Baltimore's).

But the money train did not make for an easy ride to the ALCS. The trouble started in March, when the *San Francisco Chronicle* reported Jason Giambi and Gary Sheffield had received steroids from Barry Bonds's trainer, Greg Anderson, who had been indicted by the federal grand jury investigating the Bay Area Laboratory Co-operative, or BALCO, a sports nutrition and supplement lab in Burlingame, California run by a man named Victor Conte, who also was indicted.

Sheffield put up monster numbers, anyway, while Giambi suffered through the worst year of his career. First the Yankees eliminated access to his personal trainer, Bob Alejo, as part of the sport's crackdown on nonessential personnel. Giambi was later diagnosed with a parasite, and then with a benign tumor, though neither the slugger nor the team would disclose the location of the tumor (later identified as the pituitary gland) for fear it would harden suspicion of steroid use despite Giambi's denial ("This is absolutely not related to steroids at all . . . ," he had said).

The cloud of suspicion hovered over the Bronx and all of baseball, as players were tested for performance-enhancing drugs — for the first time under the possibility of penalty — after 5 to 7 percent of them ignored advance warning and turned up positive during survey testing the year before.

The Yankees had other problems, too. Kevin Brown's season was almost as grim as Giambi's, as he, too, was diagnosed with a parasite (the team said it found no connection to Giambi's condition) before he broke his left hand punching a clubhouse wall in frustration. Brown was supposed to help offset the losses of Andy Pettitte, Roger Clemens, and David Wells, but the same teammates who saw him as a brooding loner did not forgive his selfish act of playing tough guy with the wall.

But the Yankees made it through. In the end, Rodriguez compensated for his drop in batting average (to .286) with 36 homers and 106 RBI, and Jeter compensated for his drop in batting average (to .292) by piecing together his first Gold Glove season.

Jeter and A-Rod would be major contributors to the Yankees' first victory of the postseason, a breathless 7–6, twelve-inning triumph over Minnesota after the Twins had taken the Division Series opener. Jeter opened the home team's scoring with the first postseason homer into the center-field black by a Yankee since Reggie Jackson landed one there to punctuate his epic three-homer game against the Dodgers in the '77 World Series.

Rodriguez also homered among his four hits against the Twins that night, and he lashed a tying, ground-rule double off closer Joe Nathan in the twelfth. Jeter would score the winning run on Hideki Matsui's sacrifice fly, making a daring dash to the plate before sliding and leaping for joy as the ump called him safe.

The Yankees had the look and feel of champions even before Jeter produced three hits and three RBI in Game 3, even before Rodriguez doubled, stole third, and scored the series-winning run on a wild pitch in the eleventh inning of Game 4.

The ALCS started out as another study in Yankee dominance. A-Rod had done most of the damage in the first three games against Boston, especially in the 19–8 Game 3 romp that saw him score five runs and drive in three. It appeared the Yankees' victory over Boston in the off-season hunt for Rodriguez would be the difference in the series, not Boston's victory over the Yankees in the off-season hunt for Curt Schilling.

But a far less compelling acquisition changed the ALCS in a way nobody could have imagined, a way that defied more than eight decades of history. On the same day he traded Nomar Garciaparra, Theo Epstein dealt minor leaguer Henri Stanley to the Dodgers for outfielder Dave Roberts, who was not even making a million bucks.

Roberts was a .250 slap hitter with one distinct big league skill: he had speed. Roberts had 118 stolen bases in two and a half years in L.A.

So in the ninth inning of Game 4, with Rivera and the Yanks three outs away from the World Series, Roberts pinch-ran for Kevin Millar, who had led off with a walk. The former Dodger knew he had to get into scoring position as quickly as possible, as Rivera was far more likely to get three broken-bat outs with his cutter than he was to give the Red Sox two base hits.

Roberts ran on the first pitch to Bill Mueller, ran as if his middling career depended on it, and barely beat Jorge Posada's throw and Jeter's tag. Jeter did not react. His team did not react. This steal would be nothing more than a benign footnote to the inevitable Yankee conquest.

Until Mueller's single sent Roberts racing home and sent the game into extra innings. Until David Ortiz belted a two-run homer off Paul Quantrill in the twelfth, leaving the Red Sox fans in a temporary state of grace. They were reveling in the fact that there would be no sweep.

On the losing side of Fenway Park, the Yankees did not look or sound overly concerned. "We know they're not going to give up," Jeter said. "But we're exactly in the position we want to be in."

Pedro Martinez was the Boston starter in Game 5, and Pedro had already admitted he was afraid of the Yankees after a loss in September, when Terry Francona took a surreal stroll down Grady Little lane and stayed with Martinez too long.

"What can I say? Just tip my hat and call the Yankees my daddy," Pedro had said then. "I can't find a way to beat them at this point. . . . I wish they would disappear and not come back."

A full Yankee Stadium house had showered Martinez with "Who's your Daddy?" chants in Boston's Game 2 loss, and few believed the friendlier sounds and sights of Fenway would make a difference.

For spiritual Game 5 guidance, the Red Sox summoned Massachusetts-born Olympic hero Mike Eruzione, captain of the 1980 Miracle on Ice hockey team that upset the Soviets' Big Red Machine. Eruzione delivered the game ball to the mound, and Lake Placid highlights were shown on the video board before this message was posted for the crowd:

"Ladies and gentlemen, it has happened before."

The scene felt forced, especially when Jeter turned Martinez's hundredth pitch into a two-out, three-run double in the sixth inning, giving the Yankees a 4–2 lead. Yes, this would play out as expected. The Red Sox had secured their little moral victory, and now they would allow the Yanks to win in five.

Martinez reloaded the bases and watched helplessly as Matsui ripped a liner to right, the dagger that almost surely would have finished off the Red Sox, at least until it somehow landed in the glove belonging to Trot Nixon, who made the catch from his knees.

Without notice, the Yankees' momentum died right there. Their bullpen failed again in the eighth inning, when Tom Gordon surrendered a homer to Ortiz, a walk to Millar (Roberts pinch-ran for him, just as he had in Game 4), and a single to Nixon.

Joe Torre turned to Rivera, who could not hold the lead for the second consecutive night. He allowed Varitek to hit a fly ball far enough to score Roberts and turn Game 5 into the most tense Boston Marathon the commonwealth had ever seen.

It lasted five hours and forty-nine minutes in all, with each side threatening in extra innings before the drama ended at 11:00 p.m. Esteban Loaiza, the pitcher the Yankees had acquired on the same trade-deadline day the Red Sox dealt for Roberts, had quietly put down the Red Sox in the twelfth and thirteenth innings and was one out away from escaping the fourteenth.

But the Game 4 hero, Ortiz, was at the plate, trying to win it for the Game 7 goat in 2003, Tim Wakefield, who had been brilliant over three innings, allowing one hit and striking out four. With Johnny Damon representing the winning run at second base, Loaiza battled the Boston slugger across an epic at-bat. Ortiz fouled off pitch after pitch before he sent Loaiza's tenth offering into center field, the ball dropping safely in front of Bernie Williams.

"One of the best at-bats I've ever seen," Boston general manager Theo Epstein called it.

Damon came roaring around third, his shoulder-length hair flapping like a racehorse's mane. "Damon coming to the plate," Fox announcer Joe Buck said on the air. "He can keep on running to New York. Game 6 tomorrow night!"

The Red Sox had just survived back-to-back sudden-death games at Fenway that covered twenty-six innings and lasted ten hours and fifty-one minutes. Boston had won a Game 4 that featured eleven pitchers, and a Game 5 that featured fourteen.

"Nothing surprises me at this point," Jeter said. "Something always seems to happen. . . . We put ourselves in a perfect position two days in a row; we just didn't win the games."

Now the Yankees were afraid. Very, very afraid. Suddenly they were locked inside a nightmare that even a Red Sox fan named Stephen King would not have wished upon them: Boston was halfway home to perhaps the greatest comeback in sports history.

The Red Sox arrived in New York feeling like they were the ones with a 3–2 series lead. They did not believe the Yankees could stop them, but they did worry that Schilling's injured right ankle could.

Battered for six runs over three innings in Game 1, a hobbled Schilling needed something of a medical miracle to push the series to a Game 7. He had a ruptured tendon sheath in his ankle, and the plastic brace used in Game 1 did not offer enough support. Team doctor Bill Morgan performed fifteen minutes' worth of experimental surgery on Schilling, inserting six sutures in an attempt to stabilize the tendon and keep it from snapping over the bone.

Neither Morgan nor anyone else knew if the procedure would work, or if it would even hold up for a single inning. But it was October and it was the Yankees, which meant it was worth a shot.

Schilling pulled his own Willis Reed in New York, dragging his zombie film of an ankle out to the Game 6 mound. At that moment, Schilling was every bit as valiant as Reed was in 1970, when the Knicks' center hobbled down the Madison Square Garden tunnel to conquer Wilt Chamberlain's Lakers in Game 7.

"[Schilling] will be a king and a hero if they can win a World Series in Boston," Arizona Diamondbacks owner Jerry Colangelo had said upon dealing his ace.

Schilling went 21-6 for the Red Sox, beat the Angels in the Division

Series, and showed plenty of nerve when, on the eve of the ALCS, he declared, "I'm not sure I can think of any scenario more enjoyable than making 55,000 people from New York shut up."

If Schilling failed to accomplish that mission in Game 1, he did not in Game 6. His right sock soaking up blood, Schilling out-pitched Jon Lieber and shut down the Yanks just as he had in the World Series, allowing four hits over seven innings and handing a 4–1 lead to Arroyo in the eighth.

Suddenly the Jeter-Rodriguez partnership began showing signs of wear and tear. Jeter followed Miguel Cairo's double with an RBI single, leaving Rodriguez with a chance to tie it on one Herculean cut. This was A-Rod's moment, the reason he had been hired. One perfectly timed swing here would make him an instant Yankee legend.

And on the sixth pitch he saw, the mighty Alex took his shot. Maybe he would land the ball in the upper deck in left. Maybe he would drive it the opposite way and hope some twelve-year-old kid from Jersey would reach over the wall and carry it home.

Or maybe Rodriguez would do exactly what he did: produce a sorry-looking roller down the first-base line.

Arroyo fielded the ball, tucked it away, and moved toward the chugging Rodriguez. Cornered and acting on a survivor's instinct, A-Rod raised his left hand and slapped at the pitcher's glove. The ball kicked free, and all hell broke loose in the Bronx.

While the Red Sox chased the fumble, Jeter ran all the way around to score and Rodriguez headed off to second base. Most in the crowd were too delirious to notice or care that Boston manager Terry Francona had scrambled onto the field to protest A-Rod's slap. The Yankees had cut the Red Sox lead to 4–3 and Gary Sheffield was about to bat with one out, all because Rodriguez had made the kind of resourceful postseason play patented by Jeter.

But Francona persuaded the umpires to huddle. Randy Marsh, the first-base umpire, acknowledged he did not get a good look at the play before Joe West, the plate umpire, said he had it all the way. West ruled that Rodriguez should be called out for interference, for using his arms to commit an unsportsmanlike act.

Informed he was out as he stood on second base, A-Rod slapped his hands on top of his helmet and shouted, "What?" Torre came out to argue in vain, and enraged fans threw bottles and debris and let loose with a profane chant, forcing police in riot gear to prepare to line the field.

"I don't know what the ruling was, or what the rule was," Jeter said. "I saw the umpires talking about it, and I don't think I was going to change anyone's mind."

The run came off the board, A-Rod was sent back to the dugout, and Jeter was sent back to first. "If Alex doesn't do that," Arroyo would say, "Derek's standing on second base and it's a different mindset for me with Sheffield up and a runner in scoring position."

When order was restored, Sheffield popped out and left every last witness in Yankee Stadium believing the unbelievable: the Red Sox were now in strong position to advance to the World Series.

Boston closer Keith Foulke walked Matsui in the ninth with two outs, then recovered to strike out Tony Clark on a full-count pitch to stamp the Red Sox as baseball's first team to force a Game 7 after losing the first three. In the wake of a third consecutive defeat, Torre had to explain why he did not bunt on the badly injured Schilling, and A-Rod had to explain what he was thinking when he tried to karate-chop his way onto base.

"Looking back," Rodriguez said, "maybe I should've run him over."

Schilling decided to run over A-Rod instead, this while helping Jeter to his feet. Before Game 7, the winning Game 6 pitcher went on ESPN Radio and said this of A-Rod's decision to slap at Arroyo's glove:

"That was freakin' junior high baseball at its best. Let me ask you something: Does Derek Jeter do that? . . . You know for a fact he doesn't because Derek Jeter is a class act and a professional, that's why."

All of New England had ridiculed Rodriguez over the Varitek fight in July, over the photo from that tussle that showed A-Rod's contorted face buried in Varitek's fingers and mitt. But as far as material went, the Slap trumped it by a country mile.

Rodriguez, who had called his failed off-season talks with the Red Sox "a huge blessing in disguise," found himself in the wrong dugout at the wrong time. The Red Sox were about to deliver the most devastating blow a Yankees team had ever taken, and A-Rod was the face of this disaster, the star of his own Shakespearean tragedy.

Never mind that the Yanks could not overcome the losses of Andy

Pettitte, Roger Clemens, and David Wells, that Mike Mussina was their only reliable starter, that the staff was built around older right-handers who could not get the Red Sox out.

A-Rod was the one with the $252 million contract, the one who nearly landed in Boston, the one who was supposed to help Jeter find his way to a fifth parade. Rodriguez needed an ace to save him, a Schilling, but Torre did not have one available.

It was Kevin Brown or Javier Vazquez — a choice between the electric chair and lethal injection — and Torre picked Brown.

Before Game 7, Jeter saw general manager Brian Cashman addressing reporters in the dugout. "You going to make any acquisitions before tonight's game?" the shortstop yelled.

"Don't need any, babe," Cashman answered.

The GM had never been so wrong.

The Yankees had brought in Yogi Berra for the occasion, and not simply because Yogi had approached Bernie Williams before the '99 ALCS victory over the Red Sox to tell him, "We've been playing these guys for eighty years; they can't beat us."

Yogi was the official mascot, and people would have been surprised if he was not there. But the Yankees embarrassed themselves by asking Bucky Dent to throw out the ceremonial first pitch, a decision that only threw a brighter spotlight on their desperation. As it turned out, Dent's strike to Yogi Berra looked better than anything Brown would throw to the plate.

The fans chanted "1918," and one took the time to dress up as Babe Ruth's ghost. Nothing worked. Jeter tried to single-handedly stop the tidal wave of momentum raging in Boston's favor in the first inning, taking a relay throw and nailing Damon at the plate. "The dugout went from a complete high to a complete low," Boston's Doug Mientkiewicz said. "We were like, 'Dammit, that might've changed everything,' because you always worry about one play or one pitch changing the momentum."

On the very next pitch, Brown eased all Red Sox fears by surrendering a two-run homer to David Ortiz.

The Yanks were dead men walking. Brown was booed off the mound — booed as loudly as any Yankee had ever been — after loading the bases in the second inning, leaving Vazquez to try to prove he should have been the man Torre selected for this apocalyptic start.

Damon stepped to the plate; he had dragged a .103 series batting average into the night. "I knew the curse was still living," he said.

The Curse of the Bambino.

Damon had decided he had looked at too many pitches in Oakland, where he had been taught by Billy Beane to play the on-base-percentage game. Damon wanted to become a more aggressive hitter in 2004, and after grounding into a critical double play in Game 7 of the 2003 ALCS, he wanted to make sure he put something from Vazquez in the air.

So Damon put the first pitch from Torre's starter turned reliever in the air, over the right-field wall, into a forever corner of Red Sox lore. The grand slam did not officially end the series like Aaron Boone's homer ended it the year before, but it ended this ALCS in every other way.

The most profound scene of Yankee anger and dismay came in the third inning, after Jeter singled home Miguel Cairo to make it a 6–1 game. As Rodriguez left the on-deck circle, the captain screamed at him from first base.

Jeter was not encouraging A-Rod as much as he was scolding him. Rodriguez answered that scolding with a predictable squibber back to the pitcher, Derek Lowe, and after his final two at-bats — a groundout and a strikeout — the fans gave him the Kevin Brown treatment.

A-Rod finished the series 0 for 7 with runners in scoring position. Rodriguez was 2 for 17 overall in the four losses, and fans could not let go of his defining ALCS at-bat, a one-out strikeout in the eighth inning of Game 5 after Jeter had bunted Cairo over to third with the Yanks holding a 4–2 lead.

But the entirety of this defeat could not be stuffed inside Rodriguez's locker. A-Rod's was a broken team, a team with a $120 million slugger (Jason Giambi) who could not even make the postseason roster.

The Yanks were beaten by Lowe, going on two days' rest. They were beaten by four home runs, three on the first pitch, including a second from Damon off Vazquez punctuated by an upper-deck landing that would have made Ruth proud.

More than anything they were beaten by a better team. When it was over, when Ruben Sierra grounded out to second and the 10–3 final was frozen in history's lights, frozen at 12:01 a.m., the 2004 Boston Red Sox had joined the 1975 New York Islanders and the 1942 Toronto Maple Leafs as the only North American professional teams to recover from a 3–0 series deficit.

The winners mobbed each other under the surreal sounds of Sinatra. They would end up celebrating on the Yankee Stadium field, spraying champagne on the Boston fans who had gathered around the visitors' dugout, fans who were filling the Bronx night with chants of "Let's go, Red Sox."

Epstein, Boston's young and dynamic architect, held a cold Budweiser in his clubhouse and dedicated the victory to all Red Sox players and coaches who had fallen to the Yanks in the past. On the other side of the Stadium, Epstein's counterpart, Cashman, shook his head over this remarkable event. "All year long," the losing GM said, "Boston was kind of like Jason from [*Friday the 13th*] or Freddy Krueger."

A-Rod said he was embarrassed. At Jeter's locker, the captain's face was an unruly brew of anger and pain. He called the defeat "shocking" — Jeter never, ever used words like *shocking* — and conceded the pain was greater because Boston made history at his expense — Jeter never, ever made those kinds of concessions.

A week later, the unwashed and unworthy Red Sox finished off a sweep of the Cardinals and won their first World Series title since 1918. Edgar Renteria made the final St. Louis out, and he was wearing Ruth's number, 3, when he did.

Back in New York, the Yankees' number 2 remained livid that the curse had been reversed on his watch. "I'm not going to forget it," Jeter promised on the night he was eliminated.

The shortstop made something else crystal clear to the reporters in his midst, to those wondering what had become of the Yankees' endless run of magical October nights. "It's not the same team," Jeter reminded them. "I've said it time after time, it's not the same team."

As Jeter's buddy R. D. Long had predicted, A-Rod's karma was taking hold of the Yankees, a truth that could mean only one thing for the captain:

There was a lot more postseason pain and suffering around the bend.

11

The Great Divide

A SIMPLE AUGUST POP-UP in the middle of a blowout loss to the Baltimore Orioles announced that the Yankees' shortstop and third baseman were participants in a chemistry experiment gone wrong.

Baltimore designated hitter Jay Gibbons sent a Mike Myers pitch high into the afternoon sky, a ball Alex Rodriguez figured was his. But infield protocol said the shortstop took control whenever he deemed it necessary, and this was one of those occasions when the captain deemed it necessary.

Derek Jeter was calling for the ball as he drifted to his right and into A-Rod's territory, the two superstars looking up and tracking this routine sixth-inning pop. A-Rod, the $252 million third baseman, planned to catch it. Jeter, the $189 million shortstop, planned to do the same.

Only the ball glanced off Rodriguez's glove as Jeter bumped him, and then it landed behind the shortstop. Miguel Tejada would score to give Baltimore a 10–2 lead, and Jeter? Jeter did not even bother to retrieve the ball.

He was too busy shooting A-Rod the kind of stare armed troops often gave each other from opposite sides of the 38th parallel.

The fans had been shredding Rodriguez; the 2005 American

League MVP was having a rough 2006 at the plate and in the field. The fans had been chanting "MVP" for Jeter, who was enjoying one of his best seasons — enjoying it, at least, when reporters were not asking him why he never gave those fans a captain's order to back off and cut A-Rod a break, the same captain's order he had given the year before on behalf of Jason Giambi, admitted steroid cheat.

After the *San Francisco Chronicle* reported Giambi had told a federal grand jury he used steroids and human growth hormone, and after Giambi delivered a bizarre public apology, expressing contrition for a sin he would not identify for fear of jeopardizing his contract, the fans lost their patience with the slugger's problems at the plate. Giambi was no longer a $120 million bust as a first baseman and designated hitter; he was also a $120 million pharmacological hoax.

But when the fans turned ugly in the Bronx, Jeter told them to knock it off. "If you're a Yankee fan and you want us to win," he said, "we need Jason to do well. They should be cheering him."

Only a year later, the shortstop was not campaigning for any such clemency for A-Rod. Rodriguez was drowning and the captain refused to pull him in. The fans were taking out their past postseason frustrations on A-Rod. He was the face of the disastrous 2004 loss to Boston and the slugger who delivered 48 homers and 130 RBI in the 2005 regular season before batting .133 with no homers and no RBI in another Division Series loss to the Angels, a performance that compelled A-Rod to admit he had "played like a dog."

Rodriguez was the enduring symbol of a $203 million payroll ousted in the first round. "We can win three World Series," A-Rod said, "and with me it's never going to be over."

Yankee fans were just hoping for one World Series title from A-Rod, and when he struggled in 2006, the Stadium crowds were no more forgiving of him than they were of Giambi. Only Giambi had an influential teammate in his corner.

Alex Rodriguez did not.

"I can't tell the fans what to do," Derek Jeter said.

He told them what to do in Giambi's case. In fact, when the Stadium crowd had cheered for struggling second baseman Chuck Knoblauch years earlier, Jeter remarked that "it's about time the fans got behind him."

Rodriguez was on his own, and Brian Cashman was fed up with it. So after the August 17 pop-up fell to the ground in the 12–2 loss to Baltimore, after Jeter gave A-Rod a look that could maim, if not kill, and after A-Rod was roasted by the fans for popping out in his final at-bat, the general manager decided to take the issue head-on.

But first Joe Torre would address Jeter and Rodriguez in the clubhouse. If Torre, an accomplished former player, was not crazy about singling out Yankees in front of the team, he did it when he had to.

He had first shown a willingness to criticize a Yankee before a full and captive clubhouse audience in 1996, when he ripped Paul O'Neill for not hustling after a fly ball. "You're better than that," Torre barked, "and I expect more out of you. I don't want to see that again." O'Neill did not say a word in response.

Ten years later, Jeter and A-Rod were bigger stars than O'Neill, bigger than their combined salaries of $45 million. Torre had no choice but to confront them anyway, with the rest of the team looking on.

The clubhouse doors were shut to the media, and the manager stood before the hushed Yankees, fixing his glare on the two heavyweights among them. "I don't know what happened out there," Torre told the left side of his infield, "but that fuckin' ball's got to be caught. I don't care who catches it, but somebody had better catch it."

Now that Torre had confronted Jeter and Rodriguez, Cashman decided it was time to confront Torre. The manager was partial to Jeter, the team-centric winner who made Torre a four-time champion. Jeter never would have been pictured in the *New York Post* sunbathing shirtless in Central Park before a game the way A-Rod had been the previous month (before going hitless and committing three errors in a game for the first time in his career).

Rodriguez had not won for Torre, and he brought to the clubhouse a level of narcissism not seen in the Bronx since the days of Reggie Jackson. A-Rod was worth two diva dramas a week, at least, and so naturally Torre did not connect with him the way he did with his shortstop.

But Cashman saw in Rodriguez a nine-figure corporate asset that had to be protected. For that reason, the GM wanted Jeter to appeal to the fans to support A-Rod just as he had appealed to them to support Giambi.

To date Jeter had declined. The botched pop-up upped the ante, inspiring Cashman to make his move. He asked his manager to order Jeter to end his cold war with A-Rod for the betterment of the team.

Torre did not believe it was necessary. "I'm not going to bring that up with them," he replied. "If you want something done on that, you handle it."

So Cashman handled it, face-to-face with a captain who hated criticism almost as much as he hated losing.

"Listen, this has to stop," the GM told Jeter. "Everybody in the press box, every team official, everyone watching, they saw you look at the ball on the ground and look at him with disgust like you were saying, 'That's your mess, you clean it up.'"

Jeter responded by summoning the Cuba Gooding Jr. character in *Jerry Maguire*.

"Show me the video," he told Cashman. "Show me the video."

The GM told Jeter to look for himself and reiterated that the captain's body language had screamed to the world he had no use for A-Rod. Jeter maintained again that Cashman and the rest of creation had it wrong.

"If that's not what you meant, fine," the GM said. "But perception is reality, and that's what people perceive it to be. . . . You've got to do a better job with Alex as far as embracing him."

Cashman asked Jeter to do a "self-test" on the Rodriguez issue, to go home and question himself about whether he was doing enough as a captain and teammate for A-Rod, and the conversation ended. Meanwhile, the Yankees were heading off to play five games over four days in Fenway Park while holding only a one-and-a-half-game divisional lead, and all the news media wanted to talk about was a Little League mistake made by two men who had combined to win the last four American League Gold Glove awards at short.

"When it was hit, I was calling it," Jeter explained. "I guess he didn't hear me."

"Just a goofy play, that's all," Rodriguez said. "He called it. I called it. We didn't hear each other."

The official scorer, Howie Karpin, originally assigned the error to Rodriguez, which would have given the third baseman — plagued earlier by throwing problems — a league-leading 22. On further review, Karpin decided the shortstop had impeded Rodriguez's ability to catch the ball and reassigned the error to Jeter, whose total increased to 10.

Told he had been stuck with the bill on the pop-up, Jeter said, "That wasn't my error, buddy." Assured he had been assessed the error, the captain said, "I was? Really? I didn't touch it. Wow. . . . I don't care."

Only Jeter did care. In his eighth year as a scorer, Karpin had never been approached by the shortstop to question one of his rulings. But Karpin went down to the clubhouse in case Jeter wanted to talk, and the captain did indeed call him over.

Karpin explained that after reviewing the play, he decided Jeter's slight contact with the third baseman from behind caused the ball to drop. "Derek was cordial," Karpin said, "but the ruling definitely seemed to bother him."

Before he left for Fenway and five games his team would win, Jeter spotted Karpin in the Stadium hallway and approached a second time in an attempt to persuade him to hand the bill back to A-Rod.

"I think you may want to look at it again," the shortstop said.

"I think *you* may want to look at it again," Karpin responded. They went back and forth for a few minutes, neither party raising his voice, and then Jeter boarded the bus.

No, Jeter and A-Rod were not another Kobe and Shaq, superpowers who openly feuded and criticized each other in the press. They were too smart to engage in a shouting match or fight in front of teammates, who would undoubtedly leak word of any such confrontation.

But the tension between them was real enough for Cashman to approach Jeter several times about the need for the shortstop to build a bridge to third base. Jeter maintained he had spoken with A-Rod on more than one occasion and was trying to improve the relationship, and when Cashman asked Rodriguez if this was indeed the case, the third baseman confirmed the captain's account.

Jeter never lied about team business. If he said he did something, he did it, and Cashman respected him for that.

Only there was a problem: those conversations between Jeter and Rodriguez did not thaw out the sheet of ice that separated their lockers, which, fittingly enough, were across the room from each other, Jeter's on the left and A-Rod's on the right.

One friend of Jeter's who agreed with Cashman's take tried to persuade the shortstop to make more of an effort to bring A-Rod in from the cold. "Now you're sounding like everyone else," Jeter told the friend. "Don't you think I've tried? I try, and sometimes I've just got to walk away and come back and try again, but you know I've tried. And every time I try, he'll do something that pushes me away."

Don Mattingly, hitting coach and former captain, told Yankee officials he tried giving Jeter the same advice. Mattingly could not stand teammate Wade Boggs, once his chief rival in Boston.

"But I faked it with Boggs," Mattingly said he had told Jeter. "And you have to fake it with Alex."

It was a tough sell. One Yankee official said he was afraid to approach Jeter on the subject of his relationship with A-Rod "because it would've been the last conversation I ever had with Derek. I would've been dead to him. It would've been like approaching Joe DiMaggio to talk to him about Marilyn Monroe."

Truth was, Jeter did not hate A-Rod. He just hated being A-Rod's teammate.

More than five years later, Jeter was not hung up on the *Esquire* comments as much as he was hung up on Alex's me-first antics. Jeter's idea of the perfect teammate was Rivera, Pettitte, or Posada from the glory days, or Hideki Matsui from the current group.

Matsui was quiet, dignified, chiseled from stone, ready to play every day. If he had been raised in Iowa instead of Ishikawa, Matsui would have been Jack Armstrong, everyone's all-American boy.

The Japanese slugger appreciated Jeter's kindness when he first arrived in the States ("It was huge to me," Matsui said), and Jeter appreciated the same toughness and selflessness in Matsui he saw in the dynasty keepers.

Matsui broke his wrist trying to make a catch in May and then apologized to his fellow Yankees for being unavailable to help them.

"I had never seen that before," Jeter would say. "He's been one of my favorite teammates I've ever played with."

Rodriguez was the anti-Matsui, an insecure wreck who constantly craved positive reinforcement, and who cared much too much about what was written and said about him in the newspapers, on the air, in a media culture spawning a new invasive platform every hour, on the hour.

Jeter was hardly the only Yankee who noticed. One teammate of both who did not count himself as a member of Jeter's camp or A-Rod's camp — if A-Rod even had a camp — offered this agenda-free scouting report on Rodriguez's standing in Yankeeland:

> Alex isn't a bad guy, but he's just very phony.
>
> I was taken aback by how insecure a person he is. He's very cognizant of how other people were reacting to him. He would walk into the clubhouse, and he knew immediately who was where. You could tell he'd be asking himself, "Are they acknowledging me? Are they looking at me?" In batting practice he'd tell people, "Hey, I'm going to put on a show for you today," and when he did, he'd say, "Did you see that? Did you see that?"
>
> It amazed me how he'd walk from the parking lot to the clubhouse and see the same people every day and not give them the time of day. I made that walk with him, and I was disgusted by the time I got to the clubhouse. Alex gave those people nothing, walked right by them as if they weren't even there, and I was embarrassed by it. You've got to try pretty hard to be that mean.

Derek Jeter was rarely, if ever, rude or dismissive to the minions in his midst, which raised a question about A-Rod: If the third baseman was so obsessed with the shortstop, why didn't he do a better job of following his lead?

And yes, one team official said, Rodriguez was indeed obsessed with the captain. "Alex," the official said, "would constantly ask, 'Is Jeter doing this? . . . Is Jeter doing that? . . . Did you talk to Jeter last night? . . . Is Jeter involved in this charity thing?' It never stopped."

Rodriguez should have walked around wearing his own "WWJD" bracelet ("What Would Jeter Do?"). People told Rodriguez to stop comparing himself to the captain, if only because A-Rod had no chance of ever measuring up. Rodriguez was not born with Jeter's spectacular talent for doing the right thing at the right time. All the time.

A-Rod would walk past kids in the dugout before a game, oblivious to the fact that they were there for a reason (often because they were battling a serious illness). Jeter did not need to be told. If he saw a kid in the dugout, near the bat rack, he almost always stopped to chat, tousled the kid's hair, and made the kid's month. "Do you have a girlfriend?" he would ask the boys. "Do you have a boyfriend?" he would ask the girls.

Jeter was once filing out of an event at the Yogi Berra Museum & Learning Center in New Jersey when an official spotted a boy of about seven or eight walking in front of the shortstop, blissfully unaware of who was behind him. Jeter planted his hands on the boy's shoulders and shook him playfully before starting a conversation with him.

"Most athletes in that situation," the official said, "would've been telling themselves, 'Oh, God, please let this kid walk another ten feet without turning around.'"

Rodriguez was one of those athletes.

A-Rod did not get it, off the field or on. While Jeter was a master of shrinking the biggest moments, Rodriguez often made them too big to handle, and the Division Series loss to the Angels the previous fall had offered ample evidence of that.

Jeter batted .333 with two home runs and five RBI in the series, and in the sudden-death fifth game, on the road, he had three hits, including a homer in the seventh inning and a single to lead off the ninth with the Yanks down 5–3.

Rodriguez finished the series with two hits in fifteen at-bats, finished hitless in Game 5, and all but killed the Yanks' last chance by following Jeter's ninth-inning single with a ground ball double play before, of course, likening himself to a dog.

A-Rod wanted badly to become a made man in a pinstriped suit, to win like the former three-peat champ at third, Scott Brosius, a World Series MVP whose talent could fit inside one of A-Rod's shoes. If he could not win a title, Rodriguez would at least settle for the kind of signature October moment seized by his predecessor, Aaron Boone.

Jeter had reached out to the homer hero of 2003 after he tore up his knee, clearing the way for Rodriguez. "I think the way Derek put it to me, I wouldn't repeat," Boone said. "But it was appreciated by me. . . . I think he felt bad about the situation."

Jeter was not a hard captain or teammate to please. He demanded hard work, accountability, and a willingness to place team ahead of self. Sometimes Jeter even embraced those whose commitment to the cause did not match his.

He buddied around with Jeff Weaver, a bust and a mope. Jeter came to like Giambi, who had lost a lot of respect in his clubhouse when he pulled himself out of Game 5 of the 2003 World Series. Jeter believed that Giambi partied too heavily, and that he did not take losing half as seriously as the first baseman he replaced, Tino Martinez, also Jeter's friend.

But through his actions and words of support, Jeter gave the fun-loving Giambi his papal blessing. The defrocked slugger was liked by star teammates and low-level staffers alike, especially those staffers who benefited when Giambi demanded in a postseason shares meeting — against the wishes of established Yankee veterans — that they receive full shares instead of the reduced bonuses they had been getting.

Giambi showed leadership in that 2003 case, and there was no doubting his standing as the tattooed leader of the renegade Oakland A's teams that challenged the Yanks. Only Giambi was not that dynamic force anymore. He was a fading player who had been exposed as a cheat, and so Jeter did not see him as a threat to his standing with the team and fan base.

Rodriguez? The magnitude of his talent, contract, stardom, and personality made him a natural threat. So Jeter was not beyond taking an occasional poke at him, as he did the time two female reporters who happened to be wearing pink shoes stopped at his locker.

Jeter mentioned the matching shoes, and when one of the reporters playfully asked him where his pink shoes were, Jeter said, "I don't have any." He then rolled his eyes toward A-Rod's locker and joked, "He might."

It was clear Jeter and Rodriguez needed a Kissinger-like mediator the way Reggie Jackson and Thurman Munson did. Back in the day, the simmering Jackson-Munson feud was settled — or tempered, anyway — when backup catcher Fran Healy and clubhouse attendant Ray Negron persuaded the two stars to meet inside a hotel restaurant in Detroit.

The gruff and grumpy Munson was an unmade bed; Jackson was a polished, self-celebrating star made for Hollywood. "When Reggie would put on a uniform," Negron said, "he would say, 'This is my cosmetic touch.' Everything had to be right, including his socks, or he wasn't ready to play the game. Thurman? He was just like, 'Let's go, motherfucker.' He was a monster."

On arrival in the Bronx, Jackson had his own *Esquire* moment — he was quoted (erroneously, he swears) in *Sport* magazine as saying, "I'm the straw that stirs the drink. Maybe I should say me and Munson, but he can only stir it bad."

Munson was just as furious with Jackson's remarks as Jeter would be with A-Rod's nearly a quarter century later, but the two eventually got past it and won a couple of championships together before Munson died in a plane crash.

"Thurman is Jeter and Reggie is Alex, and I've told Jeter that," said Negron, who became an adviser to George Steinbrenner. "Jeter is more to himself like Thurman was, and Alex is more outgoing like Reggie."

Jackson was among those who tried to improve relations between Jeter and A-Rod. He spoke to Rodriguez and Jeter separately, telling A-Rod about his own isolation in Munson's and Billy Martin's clubhouse, and advising Jeter on his responsibilities as a team leader.

"I spoke to him as a captain, not as Derek Jeter," Jackson said. "I told him what I thought was needed, and I think he took pieces of what I said that he agreed with and didn't take the pieces he disagreed with.

"I certainly hope Derek and Alex can win together like I did with Thurman. Alex has a good heart, but sometimes he doesn't express himself well, and he tries to express himself too much. If he would say less and let his bat do the talking, no one can talk like him with a bat. But when he tries to say the right things, it just doesn't work."

Joe Torre did not believe he needed to talk to the left side of his infield about forming a unified front, as he reasoned Jeter and Rodriguez knew each other before either had met Torre and would figure it out between themselves. But Torre was concerned enough about A-Rod's tenuous place in the clubhouse to dispatch others to talk to him.

"Joe Torre asked me to talk to him all the time," Gary Sheffield said. "In talking to [Rodriguez] it was more about giving of yourself, Alex, because if you want to win a championship you have to be in a team concept rather than as an individual.

"I didn't go to him and say, 'You've got to be about the team,' and this and that. I just let him know that I was asked to come talk to him. This was nothing I thought was an issue; other people said it was an issue . . . I was just doing what my manager asked me to do."

If nothing else, no Yankee was ever asked to talk to Rodriguez about his game-day preparation. A-Rod's sweat-soaked routine was a blur of indoor batting practice, outdoor batting practice, infield practice, long toss, and medicine ball exercises. Only Roger Clemens's pregame intensity matched A-Rod's, and Rodriguez was not merely pitching one out of every five days.

His teammates were not blind to Rodriguez's near-maniacal work ethic, which was one reason some believed Jeter should have done more to help him. As much as A-Rod could be his own worst enemy, he did bust his ass in his attempt to be the best ballplayer he could be, a truth those teammates felt should have counted for something with the captain.

But as far back as spring training 2005, Jeter had clearly established he would not be stepping in front of any freight trains heading Rodriguez's way. One by one, the Red Sox were taking the lumber to A-Rod's good name, or what was left of it, their venom inspired by an interview Rodriguez gave Bob Klapisch of the *Record* in New Jersey. In it A-Rod made this self-serving declaration about his commitment to fitness: "I know there are 650 or 700 other players who are sleeping this morning. Either that, or they're taking their kids to school. But there's no way they're going to be running the stairs or doing what I'm doing."

Trot Nixon took the first cuts of spring, saying of A-Rod, "Well, I'm not a deadbeat dad, you clown." Nixon also said that when people asked him about the Yankees, "I tell them about Jeter and Bernie Williams and [Jorge] Posada. I don't tell them about Rodriguez."

On cue, Jeter was asked to respond to Nixon's verbal assault on his teammate. "I'm not getting into a war of words with them," the captain said. "That's between Trot and Alex."

Sensing an opening, realizing Jeter had not protected his third baseman when Nixon attacked, or when Schilling had attacked in the past, the Red Sox announced the opening of hunting season on A-Rod.

Everyone got a free shot. Bronson Arroyo, Jason Varitek, Keith Foulke, Kevin Millar, and former Yankee David Wells fired away without fear of retribution. They mocked A-Rod's little Game 6 squibber, and his little slap at Arroyo's glove. They mocked his ten bare fingers, too.

None of the Yankees who had supported a steroid user, Giambi, stepped up in Tampa to return fire on Boston's Fort Myers base. Including Jeter.

Especially Jeter.

The Red Sox kept praising the Yankee captain at A-Rod's expense, kept calling him a pure winner, a team player, as professional as anyone in the game. "Derek Jeter, he's a Yankee, period," Millar said. "Alex Rodriguez's salary doesn't dictate that he's a Yankee. Just because he's making $25 million doesn't mean he's a Yankee."

Jeter did nothing about it.

"As long as I've been here," he said, "we've never been a team that talks a lot. I don't think it's necessary. Really, I'm indifferent to it."

When Wells, Boston's latest recruit, threw his usual assortment of misplaced jabs the Yankees' way, including one aimed at Rodriguez for acting like he was part of the dynasty years, Jeter merely responded that he did not have any problems with Wells, and that his former teammate had even sent him a Christmas card.

Again, Rodriguez was on his own. He could choose to defend himself or simply let this Boston tee-off party go on forever. And if it were up to Steinbrenner, Rodriguez would have told the offending Red Sox where they could stick their championship rings.

The Boss had met with A-Rod weeks earlier and ordered him to stop trying to fit in, to stop deferring to Jeter and everyone else and assume a leadership role. It was virtually the same conversation Steinbrenner had with Clemens when the Rocket could not get comfortable in his pinstriped skin during his first season in the Bronx.

But Rodriguez played dead as the Red Sox piled on, his only sign of life coming in the form of a slight of Arroyo, whom he referred to as "Brandon." Finally, Boston's self-styled band of Idiots let it go, leaving A-Rod to answer the question that had more lives than a cat, Freddy Krueger, or the 2004 Red Sox:

How's your relationship with Jeter?

"Very good," Rodriguez said.

"As good as ever?" he was asked.

A-Rod laughed. "I don't know. I think it's good."

Rodriguez was proven wrong as the season unfolded. And for every teammate who thought the captain was obliged to cover Rodriguez's back, whether he wanted to or not, there was a teammate or two who felt A-Rod was the only Yankee required to bail out A-Rod.

"A lot of guys just felt, 'Hey, if you don't want to get booed, go out there and play better,'" one teammate said. "We never really looked at it as something Derek should've done. When you sign up to play for this team, you know if you don't play well you're going to get booed. And Alex was the one in control of that."

This was a point hammered home to Rodriguez by his friend Mike Borzello, the bullpen catcher and Torre godson who was not afraid to get in A-Rod's face. "You don't need anybody," Borzello told him. "Your bat should be bailing you out of whatever mess you're in with the fans. They don't boo you after you hit a home run. They boo you when you stink."

Yet when Alex Rodriguez did stink, the easy default position for media members, for fans, even for teammates, revolved around a single question: Did Jeter's cold shoulder have something to do with it?

Everyone knew Jeter loathed the Brangelina-like scrutiny of his relationship with A-Rod, so it was a subject a precious few people were willing to raise with him. Cashman had no choice but to be among those precious few.

He was in charge of a payroll that had cleared the $200 million barrier, a mark once considered as unreachable as Joe DiMaggio's 56-game hitting streak. Cashman needed to protect Steinbrenner's massive investment, even if it meant confronting Jeter after the dropped August pop-up, or pushing him on A-Rod in a couple of other conversations.

The GM would tell Jeter he had to "fake it" with A-Rod, repeating Mattingly's line. "You can't lead twenty-three guys out of twenty-four," Cashman would say. "You've got to lead them all, the ones you like and the ones you don't like."

The captain was being asked to repair something he did not break. A-Rod was the teammate who led the league in saying and doing dumb things. A-Rod was the opponent who said Jeter's presence in a lineup was "never your concern."

Funny, but other Yankees had made similar comments about Jeter, only never laced with the jagged-edged jealousy that defined A-Rod's. Many of them mirrored the thoughts of Aaron Boone, who said he had no idea Jeter was as good as Jeter was until he played with him.

Mike Mussina, who pitched against Jeter across five seasons in Baltimore, said he understood the point Rodriguez had clumsily tried to make.

"When you read the scouting report and you're preparing to play the Yankees," Mussina said, "Derek isn't the one who stands out. Yeah, it says Derek Jeter in the lineup, but if you're concerned about somebody driving in four runs or beating you late with a home run, he's not the first name that comes to mind. . . . But he's going to beat you with three singles to right, two of them with two outs and a guy in scoring position, or maybe he's going to give you a tough at-bat against the closer and draw a walk."

Jeff Nelson, a longtime teammate of Jeter's who also played for three different American League clubs, said he had to convince fellow pitchers that the Yankee shortstop was a dangerous hitter.

"Everyone took it for granted," Nelson said. "Not that they were relaxed about pitching against him, but they'd say, 'Oh, well, this is not one of the guys that we're worried about.'"

So in 2001, Rodriguez was not some lone voice of dissent when it came to Jeter's place in the Yankee lineup. Only there was no absence of malice in A-Rod's voice. He was the close friend, the sleepover pal, the guy who likened himself to Jeter's brother. Rodriguez was supposed to be the last man in the world who would try to hurt Jeter's leverage in contract negotiations in a radio interview, and who would try to hurt Jeter's feelings in a magazine interview.

But there was no way to erase those errors from the score book. With the Yankee Stadium fans booing their third baseman, Rodriguez and Jeter would have to live with the fallout.

Derek Jeter was having a bigger year in 2006 than he'd had in 2005, when he hit the first grand slam of his career (in a June victory over the Cubs) after 5,770 at-bats and hit consecutive game-winning solo shots (in August victories over the Texas Rangers).

The '05 season was an especially draining one, as the team watched Boston's historic ring ceremony at Fenway Park, started 11-19, and struggled when new acquisitions Randy Johnson, Carl Pavano, and Jaret Wright failed to give Brian Cashman the dominant staff he craved.

Johnson was not quite the terminator he had been when he eliminated the Yanks in the '95 and '01 postseasons, and his introduction to New York — he got rougher with a TV cameraman on a Manhattan street than he would with the Angels in the Division Series — represented an ominous forecast of things to come.

Beyond the pitching, Bernie Williams was in a deep state of decline, and one of the new recruits, Tony Womack, was equally ineffective on both sides of the ball.

At 95-67, the Yankees won the division from the Red Sox on a tie-breaker, and if Jeter did not match his 2004 power numbers, he did add 17 points to his batting average to finish at .309. But it was a bumpy journey on the way there.

In June, with his team having already lost seven of nine games on a tour of middle America, Jeter was caught on a YES Network camera throwing a cup and yelling in his Busch Stadium dugout after the Cardinals scored five runs in the third inning in the Yankees' first trip to St. Louis since the '64 World Series.

Jeter had never been caught on or off camera throwing anything other than a ball, but he was as angry over the Yanks' effort as Torre, who was embarrassed on this return trip to the town where he was last fired.

Torre ripped into several players in the clubhouse, and in a rare public rebuke, Jeter chastised his team to the reporters who surrounded him. "We were just going through the motions," he said. "It seems like we don't care."

One of those players Torre ripped, Gary Sheffield, was later quoted in *New York* magazine as suggesting that he was the team leader and the Yankee hitter opposing teams needed to stop, and that the media portrayed Jeter and Alex Rodriguez "in a positive light, and everyone else is garbage."

The Yankees moved past it. Besides, Sheffield had admitted to using a couple of BALCO potions that later proved to be steroids — unbeknownst to him, Sheff insisted. The slugger had his own problems.

The same could be said for Jeter in September, after the disclosure of a racially charged threat the shortstop had received in the Yankee Stadium mail. The threat said he would be "shot or set on fire" if he continued dating white women, and the FBI and the New

York Police Department's hate crimes unit were moved to investigate.

Jeter appeared more upset that the issue went public than he was by the letter, and he tried to downplay its impact. "It was just a stupid letter," he said. "I've gotten stupid letters before."

The son of a black father and white mother, Jeter never wanted to give a racist satisfaction by reacting to bigotry and hate in an emotional way. He never wanted to show vulnerability to anyone, whether he was subjected to the ignorance of strangers, or merely to the hard opinions of fellow athletes who did not see greatness in his game.

In 2006, early in what would be one of his best seasons, Jeter was named baseball's most overrated player in a *Sports Illustrated* poll of 470 of his peers. The shortstop did not welcome criticism that was constructive, never mind criticism that wasn't, and human nature said this poll had to hurt.

Only Jeter did not show it. "I don't care," he said. "I guess anything I do now is a plus."

Torre said he could understand A-Rod's third-place finish in the poll — people were jealous of his landmark contract, the manager reasoned — but could not see how Jeter was anywhere near the top. One respected longtime veteran, Brad Ausmus, explained that Jeter was merely a victim of his marketplace.

"Before I ever played against him," Ausmus would say, "I thought he was overhyped because of the New York media. . . . But after playing against him, I think he's one of the best players of his generation. I think the players in the anonymous poll who said he was overrated are probably the same people like me, who didn't know until you played against him. Many times New York players are overhyped, but not in Jeter's case."

Yet major league clubhouses were filled with players who were not as enlightened as Ausmus. Tino Martinez found out the hard way when he ended up in St. Louis and then in Tampa Bay, places where he had to constantly defend Jeter to teammates.

"They did have an appreciation of Derek, but they were really jealous of him," Martinez said. "You know, like, 'What does he do that's so spectacular?' And you have to explain to them that you have to play with this guy every day to see how great he really is. You see him in a game or two and you're not going to know."

Martinez was asked to name the most popular misconception about Jeter that existed in these other clubhouses. "Probably that he's cocky," he said, "that he thought he was better than everyone else. That was way off track.

"He wants to win the World Series every year. He's not worried about hitting 30 home runs or who he's going to date and how many commercials he's going to get. I'd tell them that stuff comes to Derek in the off-season, that he does none of that stuff during the year. His whole focus during the year is to win, and when that's over he'll do a commercial or two. But [the jealousy] goes along with winning the World Series and all the awards and all the beautiful women he's dated."

Yes, the beautiful women. By 2006, Jeter's lineup was more impressive than the '98 Yankees'. To the previous roster of Mariah Carey, Miss Universe Lara Dutta, actress Jordana Brewster, and singer Joy Enriquez, Jeter had added Brazilian supermodel Adriana Lima, model Vida Guerra, MTV personality Vanessa Minnillo, and the two acting Jessicas — Alba and Biel.

Yet Jeter was almost never photographed with a high-profile girlfriend — or low-profile girlfriend, for that matter — in a nightclub. "That's why the Vanessa thing didn't work out," said Jeter's former teammate Jim Leyritz. "He didn't want to be seen out. . . . The only [picture] I ever saw was when he went on a trip with Jessica Biel to Puerto Rico."

Jeter grew weary with the fascination over his love life, and some of the tabloid tales were priceless. One woman claimed Jeter bought her an island (he did not even buy her a drink), another wrote about her night with Jeter (he only posed for a picture with her), and two others claimed he did not pay for their parking after an overnight romp in Miami (he said he was not in Miami).

One time Jeter walked into the Yankee clubhouse, threw down a newspaper with a measure of disgust, and asked the PR man, Rick Cerrone, "Can you explain to me why every woman I've ever dated is in the paper?"

Cerrone quickly scanned the article and photos in question and asked Jeter, "You really did date Scarlett Johansson?" The shortstop did not fill in the blank.

For the record, Johansson denied she dated Jeter, though it was not what anyone would call a vehement denial. It would not be long before actress Gabrielle Union also refuted reports she was dating Jeter, though her denial said it all.

"Trust me," she said, "if I were dating Derek Jeter, I would hold my own personal press conference to announce it to the world."

To the average red-blooded, testosterone-fueled American male, Jeter was living out the ultimate fantasy. During a road trip, one teammate walked into a nightclub and found Jeter and another Yankee in a private room surrounded by fifteen to twenty women. Turned out the shortstop had sent an associate into the crowd of clubbers to pick out the most attractive women and invite them to the party.

If Jeter looked like a judge backstage at a beauty pageant, it was not the first time. He could not get away from the hopefuls if he tried. When Jeter allowed *Sports Illustrated*'s Rick Reilly to open his fan mail, only to have Reilly discover a letter, a revealing photo, and a more revealing cell number from a Miss Universe, the baseball star who had ditched Dutta actually said, "No way, dude. I'm not going down that Miss Universe road again."

This was the life. Fame, fortune, a lavish apartment in Trump World Tower, and enough attention from assorted starlets and sexpots to tell a Miss Universe to go find another solar system.

But something critical was missing in Jeter's vision of a perfect world. Winning. October winning. World Series winning.

Jeter had gone five full seasons without seizing a fifth title, and it was eating him alive. On the flight home from Anaheim after the Division Series loss to the Angels, Jeter sat in the back of the plane with the veteran pitcher Al Leiter, who was ending a nineteen-year career.

"Derek was completely dejected and down," Leiter said. "We were in the last row, alone, and I was trying to pump him up. I was telling him he had a good year, but he said, 'You don't understand. It's about winning a championship,' and it was totally genuine. That really is all it's about to him."

In his short time with the club, Leiter had noticed the impact of A-Rod's presence on Jeter even before their broken friendship became a constant talk radio topic. "I know it wasn't comfortable," Leiter said. "It was pretty obvious after what Alex said; he betrayed Derek. . . . If you have your captain and your big [acquisition], it was probably uncomfortable enough to have had an effect on that team."

But Jeter was doing everything in his on-field power to move beyond an invasive public conversation he could not escape. On his way back to the playoffs and another division title in 2006, Jeter became the second-fastest Yankee to reach 2,000 hits, making it in his 1,571st game (DiMaggio secured number 2,000 in his 1,537th game).

With Sheffield and Hideki Matsui missing big portions of the season, and with Pavano gone for the entire year because of a bizarre run of injuries, Jeter did not allow the Yankees to fall apart. His three-run double on the eighth pitch he saw from Boston reliever Mike Timlin, who had owned him, allowed for the five-game sweep in Fenway, as did the tying two-out bloop in the ninth off closer Jonathan Papelbon two nights later.

The following week, after the Yanks lost the first two games of a three-game series in Anaheim, leaving players, coaches, and fans to wonder if they would ever beat the Angels, Jeter closed out that series with two homers and one of his traditional high-jump throws from the hole in an 11–8 victory. Rodriguez went 1 for 15 with 10 strikeouts in those three games, picking up right where he had left off in the Division Series.

The captain pieced together a 25-game hitting streak, the Yankees' longest since Joe Gordon's 29-game streak in 1942. Jeter finished with a .343 batting average, 97 RBI, 118 runs, a career-high 34 stolen bases, and a .381 average with runners in scoring position. According to the Elias Sports Bureau, Jeter became only the fifth man in seventy-five years to hit at least .340, drive in at least 90 runs, and steal at least 30 bases in a single season (Willie Mays, Jackie Robinson, Ellis Burks, and Larry Walker were the others). And no stats were needed to validate Jeter's standing among the very best and brightest base runners in the game.

Jeter would be good enough to win a third consecutive Gold Glove award, his first Silver Slugger award as the best offensive player at his position, and his first Hank Aaron Award as the best hitter in the league. But he would not win his first Most Valuable Player award; he would lose a close vote to Minnesota's Justin Morneau.

In September, Jeter had swatted away the claim by Boston designated hitter David Ortiz that he was not MVP-worthy. The eventual third-place finisher in the MVP derby, Ortiz praised the shortstop but channeled his inner A-Rod by adding, "Jeter is not a 40-homer hitter or an RBI guy. It doesn't matter how much you've done for your ball club, the bottom line is, the guy who hits 40 home runs and knocks in 100 [Ortiz would hit 54 and knock in 137], that's the guy you know helped your team win games."

The Yankee captain would not take the bait, of course, even when hearing Ortiz's challenge that he should "come hit in this lineup, see how good you can be." Jeter responded that he did not have to hit in Boston's lineup, and that he was not focused on individual awards.

That much was true: Jeter never focused on individual awards. But he did want to win the MVP, a lot; it just was not his top priority at season's end.

That priority would be winning a first-round playoff series, something the Yankees had not done the previous year. And on October 3, before 56,291 fans in Yankee Stadium, Derek Jeter looked as ready to win a first-round playoff series as he had ever been.

In the third inning, against Detroit's Nate Robertson, Jeter doubled to center to move the first-year Yankee Johnny Damon over to third, before another first-year Yankee, Bobby Abreu, doubled both home. Jason Giambi's two-run homer two batters later made it 5–0, and afterward the 8–4 winners savored their near-flawlessly executed game plan.

Damon, the former Red Sox leadoff man and center fielder signed as a $52 million free agent, had scored two runs. Abreu, acquired from Philadelphia at the trade deadline, had driven in four. Chien-Ming Wang, the 19-game winner with a cruel sinker, had held the Tigers to three runs over six and two-thirds.

Jeter, batting behind Damon, had delivered five hits in five at-bats. He had homered, scored three runs, and knocked in one. Everything was perfect about a lineup that bottomed out with twenty-three-year-old second baseman Robinson Cano, who hit .342 and, according to Elias, became the first player ever to bat ninth in a postseason game after finishing among his league's top three hitters.

"Murderers' Row and then Cano," Detroit manager Jim Leyland called the Yanks.

Everything was ideal about that lineup, except this little $252 million quirk: Alex Rodriguez was batting sixth, behind Sheffield and Jason Giambi.

Rodriguez was about the only ballplayer in history who could hit .290, slam 35 homers, and drive in 121 runs and then feel the need to apologize for it. Torre could not hide the obvious: he was losing faith in his third baseman.

Game 2 was postponed by a late-night rainout, and when the Tigers showed up a little bleary-eyed at the Stadium — they had scrambled to find Manhattan hotel rooms after checking out of the Grand Hyatt — they gave off a Jack Lemmon vibe from *The Out-of-Towners*.

The tourists were down 3–1 after Damon's three-run blast in the fourth inning, inspiring thoughts of a sweep. The Tigers had all but imploded at the end of the regular season and appeared anxious for a long winter's nap.

Only Mike Mussina could not hold the Game 2 lead, allowing a Carlos Guillen homer and a Curtis Granderson RBI triple in a 4–3 loss that cost his team a chance to put the Tigers on the brink of elimination.

But Mussina was not the story. Alex Rodriguez — now he was the story.

Justin Verlander struck him out looking with the bases loaded in the first inning, and Joel Zumaya struck him out swinging on four pitches in the eighth, the last three clocked at more than 100 miles per hour. A-Rod said he did not see those pitches and claimed he did not hear the boos that followed each of his three strikeouts.

"The playoffs aren't over," Rodriguez reminded. "This is just getting started. . . . My chin is up. My chin isn't going anywhere."

On his way out of Yankee Stadium, George Steinbrenner was asked for an assessment of A-Rod's performance, or lack thereof. "I didn't like him that well," the Boss responded.

Torre didn't like him that well, either. But since Sheffield was struggling at the plate and at a position that was practically foreign to him, first base, where he moved like a Sunday beer leaguer, Torre decided to bench Sheffield, put Giambi back at first, insert Bernie Williams as the DH, and try to revive A-Rod by promoting him to cleanup.

Even though forty-three-year-old starter Randy Johnson was going with a herniated disc in his lower back and had not pitched since September 23, this one looked like a two-foot putt. Kenny Rogers, forty-one, was starting for the Tigers, and this fearsome Yankee lineup had a .391 batting average against him.

Rogers had not beaten the Yanks in more than thirteen years, and he came across as a Charmin-soft October opponent. He had never won a playoff game, and he was an unmitigated disaster while pitching for the Yanks in the '96 postseason, and again for the Mets in the '99 postseason, when he walked in the run that sent the Braves to the World Series.

Rogers had been chased out of New York not once, but twice, and he certainly did not forget what Torre had said about him in a bygone book. In *Chasing the Dream*, published after the Yanks won the '96 title despite Rogers's wretched pitching, Torre wrote that the left-hander "could not seem to conquer his anxiety" and that he wished doctors could put confidence in liquid form and "hook up some device to his left arm and just inject it."

Upon making his first spring training appearance after the book's release, Rogers said, "If I read it I'd probably just throw it in the trash."

All these years later, before 43,440 screaming people inside Comerica Park, Rogers did not need any injection of faith. He was tired of pitching passively against the Yanks, tired of bringing a knife to a gunfight.

So he attacked the strike zone and dared the world's greatest lineup to attack back. "I wanted this game as much as I wanted any in my life," Rogers would say.

It showed. As he drew strength from the Detroit crowd, Rogers allowed the Yanks only five hits over seven and two-thirds scoreless innings. He struck out eight and walked two. As he left the mound to a standing ovation, to the sounds of fans chanting his name, Rogers tipped his cap and touched his heart.

"That's not the Kenny I remember," A-Rod would say.

Rodriguez was not the Alex whom Kenny remembered, either.

Johnson could not keep up with Rogers in this duel of forty-somethings, and the Yankees lost by a 6–0 count, running their scoreless streak to fourteen innings. But again, the Big Unit was not the big topic. Rodriguez had gone 0 for 3 to stand 1 for 11 in the series and 4 for 38 in his last eleven postseason games, without a single RBI to his name.

A-Rod likened the suddenly new and improved Rogers to Sandy Koufax and admitted, "There's tension in this clubhouse." Yes, it revolved around third base.

Rodriguez was batting .091 in this Division Series; Jeter, .583. Something had to be done. Torre's attempt to lift A-Rod's spirits by lifting him in the order did not take; Rodriguez's lone contribution came when he was hit by a pitch.

A-Rod was going down, and it appeared he was taking the entire lineup with him. The Tigers entered the series hoping to keep it close; if they were allowed, they would have run Dean Smith's old four-corners offense to bleed the clock.

And now? Now all they had to do was beat Jaret Wright at home to advance to the American League Championship Series.

"That's why you don't go on numbers, you don't go on the past," Jeter said. "You don't play the game on paper. You've got to go out there on the field and perform. . . . I'm confident we can get back to New York. We have to find a way."

The next morning, Torre thought he had found a way. He spent the moments after Game 1 in the Yankee Stadium interview room talking about Jeter's fearlessness in the postseason, talking about how his shortstop "seems to just relish this atmosphere." Jeter would show up in the same room that night and disclose his simple October game plan.

"You have to try to treat the postseason like a regular-season game," he said.

Teammates marveled over Jeter's ability to maintain a May pulse rate in the all-or-nothing October tournament. John Flaherty, a Yankee from 2003 to 2005, recalled a dreadful swing Jeter took in a playoff game in the Bronx, at a crucial moment in that game, and then the sight of Jeter staring into the dugout "and laughing his ass off.

"I'm stressed out just watching, and he's laughing, and I'm thinking to myself, 'How can any human being be that relaxed in that spot?' And then the next thing you know it's, boom, base hit. Derek just believes he's the best player on the field, and it doesn't matter that a lot of the time he's not the most talented. He knows he's going to beat you anyway."

If only Rodriguez could carry the same mentality to the postseason plate. A-Rod treated the first inning of every Game 3 of the Division Series like the fourth quarter of a tied Super Bowl. Worse yet, he was more concerned about the perception of his performance than he was about the performance itself.

So Torre figured he needed to try something drastic. He came up with a beauty.

He posted a Game 4 lineup with Alex Rodriguez batting eighth.

Eighth. One team official who thought Torre did not grasp the impact of this move was itching to approach him and ask, "Do you realize you've just decided to bat Babe Ruth eighth?" The official thought better of it.

Torre was incredulous when questioned about the A-Rod move by the media and claimed he was "just trying to win a ball game." But this would be the equivalent of, say, Tony Dungy demoting Peyton Manning to the position of long snapper in the AFC playoffs.

"That was the end of Alex and Joe," one team official said.

That was the end of the Yankees, too. Detroit steamrolled them again, taking an 8–0 lead before the doomed visitors scored three garbage-time runs. Wright was awful, this as Wang waited in New York so he could pitch a Game 5 on full rest, a Game 5 that had been called on account of hubris.

The Yanks were completely shut down by a twenty-three-year-old kid, Jeremy Bonderman, whom the Tigers acquired in the three-way deal that landed Jeff Weaver in the Bronx, with a thud. Torre's team could not even get a man on base until the sixth inning and made it twenty consecutive innings in the series without a single run.

Just as A-Rod did not respond to batting cleanup, he did not respond to batting eighth. He grounded out in his first at-bat, grounded out in his second at-bat, and flied out in his third. So once more, the Yankees allowed an underdog playoff opponent to bathe itself in champagne.

How could this have happened? George Steinbrenner was spending more than $200 million on salaries, and he had finally given Cashman the control over baseball operations he needed. The franchise was flourishing, the YES Network was feeding the beast with more and more cash, and hardhats in the Bronx were moving the earth across the street for the construction of a new Yankee Stadium.

How could this empire have been toppled by the likes of Kenny Rogers and Jeremy Bonderman?

"They annihilated us," Rodriguez said.

A-Rod did not just go 0 for 3; he also made a critical error in the field. Rodriguez finished the series 1 for 14 (.071), leaving him 3 for 29 (.103) in the Yanks' last two first-round losses, and 4 for 41 (.098) in his last twelve playoff games, with no RBI.

Naturally, after Steinbrenner had gone six seasons without a title, after the Boss had spent almost $1 billion on wages along the way, and after he had watched the Mets sweep the Dodgers on the same day his Yanks were eliminated, the hunt for scapegoats was on.

Cashman maintained he would not trade A-Rod, who swore he wanted to remain a Yankee unless "they're dying to get me out of here." Publicly, Rodriguez took responsibility for his plunge to eighth in the order. "I've got no one to blame but myself," he said.

Privately, he felt betrayed by Torre, who he rightfully believed would have never pulled the same humiliating stunt with a struggling Jeter.

No, A-Rod was not rooting for Torre to be retained. The manager had only one year left on his contract, and as much as Steinbrenner clashed with Don Zimmer, the Boss did notice that Torre had not reached a World Series since his bench coach quit following the 2003 loss to the Marlins.

An old pitching staff came undone on Torre's watch, and the big-name mercenaries hired by Steinbrenner and Cashman buckled while the one blue-chip recruit they decided against signing, Carlos Beltran, was leading the Mets to the NLCS.

In a statement Steinbrenner called the defeat in Detroit a "sad failure" and barked, "This result is absolutely not acceptable to me." None of it sounded good for Torre, who was being fired in a *Daily News* story that claimed A-Rod's manager in Seattle, Lou Piniella, would be the next Yankee manager, a report Torre would survive.

Jeter was about the only Yankee who escaped this first-round loss unscathed. He had a great statistical series, enhancing his legacy as a clutch October player. The manager who beat him, Leyland, would later call Jeter "the ultimate person. . . . Every man would like to have a son like that. Every guy would like to have somebody like that marry his daughter.

"He's a dream player, that's what he is. I don't think anyone in the history of the Yankees has handled New York any better than Derek Jeter."

But as the shortstop stepped toward another winter of his discontent, his ability to handle New York as easily as he would a hanging curve was about to be tested to the max.

Eight days after *Post* baseball columnist Joel Sherman wrote that Jeter's refusal to support A-Rod for the good of the team should cost him the league MVP award, *Daily News* baseball columnist John Harper wrote that Jeter hurt his team's chances of winning a title by freezing out A-Rod and wrote it under the headline "Yanks' Captain Abandons Ship."

Sherman and Harper were widely respected voices in the city, so their rebukes did not go unnoticed. But Jeter was like most athletes — criticism from players, especially teammates, hurt more than criticism from credentialed media members paid to deliver it.

So when Darryl Strawberry, friend and former teammate and big-brother figure, chose to publicly implore Jeter to do the same thing columnists had been telling him to do for months, the captain officially became a casualty of the first-round flameout in Detroit.

"I hope Jeter [will] embrace [Rodriguez] this year, in spring training, and bring him into the full circle as a part of the Yankee family," Strawberry said. "If Jeter does it, I think everybody else will respond."

Strawberry would later say, "I just wanted Derek to accept him more in the clubhouse. I wanted Derek to put their differences aside and accept Alex so they can move forward and play well as teammates."

Jeter was being squeezed from all sides, and some team officials were hoping the public pressure would make the captain crack. But before Jeter could consider adjusting his approach, Rodriguez had a little surprise for him.

A-Rod was tired of living the lie, tired of batting eighth, tired of everything that went with being a ring-free megastar on Derek Jeter's team.

Rodriguez was ready to take the fight to the captain, once and for all.

12

◆

Moment of Truth

DEREK JETER CLAIMED four championships in his first five years and played in five World Series in his first six, and he did it largely with teammates he believed placed winning above all else.

Jeter wanted those days, and that group, to live on forever, to disprove the notion that clubhouse karma and harmony in sports did not matter, and to allow him to run down Yogi Berra's record of ten titles. Jeter joked about that record with Yogi, telling the Hall of Fame catcher his total was inflated by the fact that there were no playoffs bridging the regular season to the World Series back in the day.

"You were born at the wrong time," Berra would shoot back.

Jeter would laugh and slap down the oversized cap on Yogi's head. But make no mistake: the shortstop was as serious about chasing Yogi's record as his friend Tiger Woods was about chasing Jack Nicklaus's record of eighteen major titles.

So Jeter was hurting and bleeding in the months before the start of spring training in 2007. He had gone six full years without a parade, and he was starting to wonder if R. D. Long's prediction that he would never win a ring with Alex Rodriguez as a teammate was slowly morphing into prophecy.

A-Rod was ruining the Yankee experience for Jeter, though the third baseman was hardly the lone reason the Canyon of Heroes — once as regular a stop for Jeter as the local Starbucks — suddenly seemed a million miles away.

Jason Giambi was another living symbol of everything gone wrong. He was a bloated one-trick pony whose trick was enhanced by steroids, a lumbering base runner and brutal defensive player who pulled himself out of the only World Series he appeared in. Replacing Martinez with Giambi was the beginning of the beginning of the end.

After the signing of Mike Mussina, Brian Cashman kept acquiring pitchers who were missing that distinct gene needed to thrive in New York under win-or-else conditions. Jeff Weaver. Jose Contreras. Kevin Brown. Javier Vazquez. Carl Pavano. Randy Johnson. Jaret Wright. None proved to be strong enough, mentally or physically, to do what the Cones and Pettittes and El Duques and Wellses did for Joe Torre when it mattered most.

And Torre himself had lost that human touch he so deftly applied to his dynastic teams. Big-name position players who were brought in after the championships dried up — Giambi, A-Rod, Gary Sheffield, Kenny Lofton, Johnny Damon — never believed they could build up the gravitas with Torre enjoyed by Jeter and his fellow dynasty keepers.

Asked if Torre could have done something specific to avoid the postseason failures that started piling up like soiled laundry on a locker room floor, Sheffield said, "I think believing in what you have, more than anything. It's easy to do when you have Jeter and Mariano and Posada on the main stage and you're just focusing on those guys and thinking they've done it before and they're going to do it again, as opposed to embracing the guys that just came in and believing in them also.

"We have track records also. We know how to win. . . . You want to make the guys who just got here feel like part of the family, too, and I don't think that was established enough."

Sheffield was traded to Detroit a month after the Tigers eliminated the Yankees, and though his accessibility made him popular with many reporters who covered him, the slugger's outspoken nature and history of semi-plausible claims left him labeled as a loose cannon.

But on the issue of Torre and how the manager had different strokes for different folks, one team official confirmed Sheffield was shooting straight.

"Players would come in with All-Star or Hall of Fame credentials," the official said, "and they were always on the outside looking in."

Of course, nobody embodied that truth more than A-Rod.

"There was just always a tension, and you could just see it," the official said, "and then in small ways Torre would promote it, too, because he would never call out Jeter on anything but he'd have no problem doing it to Alex. With Jeter, he'd never bat him eighth, but he'd do it to Alex.

"So Joe would treat Derek one way and Alex another, and you've got to treat all of your best players the same. Your twenty-fifth man, you can treat any way you want. But that's why the clubhouse went offline, because there were rules for some, and rules for others."

One name player who left the Yankees, and left them unhappily, put it this way: "I wasn't in the club. I wasn't in Joe's club."

The Yankees were a fractured lot, and their lack of cohesion showed up in the postseason, when younger, cheaper, leaner, and meaner opponents whipped them with an underdog's carefree, nothing-to-lose approach. Despite their overwhelming firepower, the Yanks ended up hoist by their own petard.

The captain was sick of it, too.

"In the off-season he wouldn't knock individual guys," Martinez said of Jeter, his fellow Tampa resident, "but he felt the team wasn't there to win a World Series. He thought they were more there to have fun and collect a paycheck and go home, and that really drove him crazy.

"When the season was over, he'd come to Tampa and he wasn't the same. He was always a little bit flustered. He wouldn't go out. He'd go out to eat, but he wouldn't go out to have fun. He was always thinking about trying to make the team better, who we should get, that type of attitude."

Jeter could talk to his friend Martinez because Tino represented what he wanted to recapture. Those Yankees were team players, gamers, legends of the fall.

"When we played together," Martinez said, "David Cone would pitch with a broken arm. We all had aches and pains in the postseason, but we never wanted a built-in excuse for not playing well, and we didn't want to give the other team an advantage.

"I hated it when [Paul] O'Neill didn't play because he was hurt, he hated it when I didn't play, we both hated it when Bernie [Williams] didn't play, so we all played hurt together."

No Yankee ever played hurt more than Jeter, and the captain felt he was surrounded by players who did not have the same toughness he had, the same toughness his old teammates had, physically or mentally.

"Derek would just say, 'It's not the same. It's not the same as it was when we played when everybody wanted to win,'" Martinez said. "I would tell him, 'You've just got to keep playing hard every day like you do. You can't control the whole team. You can't control guys' attitudes and wanting to win or not. You're not going to convince them to want to win.'

"I'd tell Derek, 'You've got to get to guys who you think are driven to win and pull with those guys and see if you can corral the other guys and get them to come with you.' But the playoffs would come, and all of a sudden guys you relied on had fake injuries, or all of a sudden they had injuries and they couldn't play."

Martinez was not naming names; it wasn't the Yankee way. But Jeter clearly was enraged when Martinez's successor, Giambi, begged out of the lineup before Game 5 of the 2003 World Series.

"I think they lost that feel of guys wanting to be really out there when the pressure's on and failing and dealing with the media," Martinez said. "I think after we left certain guys came in with more of a let's-have-fun-off-the-field mentality. If we win or lose today it's no big deal because we'll have fun tonight wherever we go.

"It's that type of mentality that drove [Jeter] crazy. Guys were laughing after losses. It's not that we were a morgue in there when we lose a game in June or July, but you don't want guys laughing or joking around like it's no big deal."

Jeter's scouting report alone did not inspire these conclusions. Martinez saw it for himself when he returned to the Yanks in 2005, after spending two seasons with St. Louis and one in Tampa Bay.

"Everybody was on different pages, guys were out, and it was a mess," Martinez said. "I knew I had a year to come back, maybe two, and I wanted to win the World Series again, get that whole experience, get another parade. But it just wasn't the same feeling."

Mike Stanton reached the same verdict when he also returned to the Yanks in 2005. The reliever had a great appreciation for Jeter, especially after he thought he had nearly ended the shortstop's career years earlier.

Stanton was part of a Nike commercial shoot before a Subway Series against the Mets, an ad pitting the Yanks against the Mets in a stickball game. With Jeter on first, Stanton swung his broomstick and ripped a pitch from John Franco right into the shortstop's lower stomach, inches north of his groin. As Jeter doubled over, gasping for air, Stanton thought to himself, "Oh, my gosh, there goes my Yankee career."

Jeter survived. Stanton remained gainfully employed and ended up as a vital part of three championship teams under Torre. On his second go-around in the Bronx, Stanton believed the 2005 Yanks had title-worthy talent.

"You had an All-Star from another team at every position, not the homegrown guys," he said, "but it was completely different.

"We had a great team on the field, but we just didn't have the cohesiveness as we did in the past. I think we had the same commitment to winning, but not the same commitment to being a team. You had guys going in different directions, and when we were winning championships everybody put the team in front of ourselves. In 2005 it was more about playing for the three-run homer and making sure you got your ERA down or your batting average up."

The 2006 season offered more of the same, and the most conspicuous source of tension in Yankeeland — the awkward public dance between Jeter and Rodriguez — was still a hurdle the entire franchise could not clear.

Their extreme differences went far beyond A-Rod's habit of watching as much televised baseball as he could, and Jeter's refusal to watch any game in which he was not playing. Rodriguez finally decided to do something about his relationship with the shortstop. Emasculated by Torre in the Detroit series, burdened by the probability that 2007 would be his final year as a Yankee, A-Rod chose to put Jeter on his heels.

As tired as Jeter was of all that October losing, Rodriguez was just as tired of seeking the captain's approval in vain. The third baseman was tired of tiptoeing around Jeter, tired of swearing their friendship was intact, tired of carrying all that baggage to the plate.

So he dumped it right in Jeter's lap. Rodriguez reported to spring training, took a seat in a Legends Field dugout, and while Jeter was taking his physical, A-Rod became the first known major league player to announce a divorce from a teammate.

"Let's make a contract," Rodriguez said to reporters. "You don't ask me about Derek anymore, and I promise I'll stop lying to all you guys."

As much as they loved this story A-Rod was telling, the gathered reporters were not ready to make that trade.

"The reality is there's been a change in the relationship over fourteen years and hopefully we can just put it behind us," A-Rod continued. "You go from sleeping over at somebody's house five days a week, and now you don't sleep over. It's just not that big of a deal."

Oh, this was as big a deal as the opt-out in A-Rod's contract, the clause he could exercise at season's end to become a free agent. Rodriguez was done speaking from the scripts he had run past focus groups.

This cathartic exchange explained why Rodriguez walked into camp as if he were arriving for a weigh-in before a middleweight bout. He had shed about fifteen pounds, reduced his body fat from 18 percent to 10 percent, and lowered a two-ton issue from his shoulders.

"People start assuming that things are a lot worse than what they are, which they're not," Rodriguez said. "But they're obviously not as great as they used to be. We were like blood brothers. . . . I think it's important to cut the bull."

A-Rod was as free as a bird. Yes, he lied about Torre, saying he blamed only himself for the embarrassment of batting eighth against Detroit. One Rodriguez friend maintained there was a better chance of Jeter forgiving A-Rod for his sins than there was of Rodriguez forgiving Torre for his.

But Rodriguez liberated himself on the more critical front, the Jeter front, and when the shortstop heard about A-Rod's little stunt he did not do a handstand. "Why does he keep running his mouth off?" Jeter asked a team official. "Why doesn't he just shut up?"

The day after Rodriguez's confession, Jeter sat in the same dugout and, per the captain's policy, refused to feed the media beast.

"I don't have a rift with Alex; let's get that straight," Jeter told reporters. "Like Alex said yesterday, when we're on the field we support each other, we're pulling for each other, and that's all that matters. What we do away from the field really has no bearing on us playing baseball."

Jeter was asked to characterize his relationship with Rodriguez. "How would I characterize it?" he said. "I would characterize it as it doesn't make a difference."

The captain revealed he'd had a conversation with Rodriguez about his perceived lack of support, and that A-Rod did not believe what reporters and columnists were writing — that Jeter needed to do more to make his former best friend feel at home in the Bronx.

"From day one, I've said I support Alex," the shortstop said. "The only thing I'm not going to do is tell the fans what to do."

Even if he told them what to do when they were jeering Jason Giambi.

Jeter said that he and A-Rod laughed about the dropped pop-up against Baltimore, that media members were analyzing their relationship without knowing all the closed-door facts. Rodriguez swore his only desire was to win a championship with Jeter at his side, and to be there in 2009 for the opening of the new stadium across the street.

But with Rodriguez a potential free agent, with Torre in the last year of his contract, and with Jeter desperate to win after six years of postseason losing, something would have to give in 2007. The Yankees were not going to crash and burn in another Division Series and make it to 2008 with their core figures intact.

The conflict within the organization was not limited to the left side of the infield. Steinbrenner had almost fired Torre after the loss in Detroit, and ownership and management no longer viewed him as the manager with the Midas touch. One constant issue was Torre's use, or overuse, of certain members of the bullpen, the most recent and obvious case represented by the dangling right arm belonging to Scott Proctor, who had pitched 102 1/3 innings over 83 games in 2006.

Over the winter, Brian Cashman consulted with members of Torre's coaching staff and arranged for an intervention. Cashman called in bench coach Don Mattingly, third-base coach Larry Bowa, first-base coach Tony Pena, and bullpen coach Joe Kerrigan. Most, if not all, shared the general manager's opinion that Torre needed to adjust the way he used relief pitchers and do a better job of protecting valuable arms. Cashman did not bother inviting Ron Guidry, the pitching coach, because the GM saw Guidry as a blind follower of Torre's who would never cut against the manager's grain.

Once the meeting started and Torre figured out its agenda, he got so defensive that the coaches turned stone-cold silent, hanging Cashman out to dry. Suddenly a group intervention became a face-off between the GM and Torre.

It did not go well, and after the meeting ended, Kerrigan, Bowa, and Mattingly apologized to Cashman for, in effect, chickening out. But if Torre needed another reason to believe he could not lose in the first round of the playoffs for the third straight year, he had gotten one.

Torre would have to make do without Bernie Williams, who was not brought back, and again without Carl Pavano, who answered teammate criticism of his lack of commitment and availability (Mike Mussina put an on-the-record face and voice to that criticism) by making two starts, including one on Opening Day, before going down for the season with a ligament tear in his elbow that required Tommy John surgery.

A far more reliable Yankee, Andy Pettitte, was back on Torre's side after three years in Houston, making the manager feel a bit more secure about his staff. That was the good news surrounding Pettitte's return. The bad news?

Pettitte found that balls his Houston shortstop, Adam Everett, used to reach were getting by Derek Jeter for base hits. Pettitte would never consciously show up his friend and captain; the first and last time Pettitte did big-time Jeter, the two were minor leaguers in Greensboro and the left-hander was watching the teenage shortstop botch a series of ground balls.

But veteran Yankee observers noticed that Pettitte's body language occasionally screamed, "How did that get through?" when grounders — especially those to Jeter's left — were bouncing into the outfield. If Pettitte was silently asking that question, others were asking it out loud.

The sabermetric crowd was ganging up on Jeter, the three-time Gold Glove winner who was number 1 in the hearts of Yankee fans, number 2 in their game programs, and number 30 or so in the sabermetric rankings of everyday shortstops.

Bill James, one of the godfathers of the movement, a widely respected author and statistician hired by the Red Sox as a senior adviser after the 2002 season, wrote a piece for *The Fielding Bible* comparing Jeter to Everett based on data provided him by John Dewan and his fellow sabermetricians at Baseball Info Solutions.

"One of their conclusions," James wrote, "was that Derek Jeter was probably the least effective defensive player in the major leagues, at any position."

James watched video of the best twenty plays and worst twenty plays made by Jeter and Everett in 2005, film that showed the Yankee shortstop playing shallow and rarely setting his feet, and the Astro shortstop playing deep and almost always setting his feet. James also studied charts and summaries of every 2005 play Jeter and Everett did and did not make.

He concluded that Everett failed to make 41 plays that "given the vector, velocity and type of play, the expectation that the shortstop would make the play was greater than or equal to 50%," while Jeter failed to make 93 such plays. James also concluded Everett did make 59 plays one would not expect a shortstop to make (expectation of less than 50 percent), while Jeter made only 19 such plays.

James allowed that Jeter was a superior offensive player to Everett, and one who was responsible for creating 105 runs in 2005 against Everett's 61. But the author of the annual *Baseball Abstract* books argued in *The Fielding Bible*, "It makes intuitive sense that Derek Jeter is the worst defensive shortstop of all time. . . . The worst defensive shortstop in baseball history would *have* to be someone like Jeter who is unusually good at other aspects of the game."

Mathematical equations and statistical analyses had long been suggesting Jeter was a below-average fielder despite his soft hands and his unmatched ability to come in on slow grounders and to run down pop flies over his head. In 2003, a Monmouth University mathematics professor named Michael Hoban wrote a book, *Fielder's Choice: Baseball's Best Shortstops*, that ranked Jeter as the worst in the game at his position because of the dramatic decline in his range. In 1997, Hoban wrote, Jeter's range was 39 points above the league average; by 2002, his range "had fallen to a disastrous 75 points below the league average."

Dewan's plus-minus rating, based on a computerized study of every chance and designed to identify the number of plays a fielder made above or below the average defender, left Jeter with a wretched minus 34 in 2005.

Shane Jensen, a professor at the Wharton School of the University of Pennsylvania, led a group of researchers who studied every ball put in play from 2002 through 2005. Jensen concluded that Jeter was costing the Yankees 13.81 runs per season, and that Alex Rodriguez was saving the Rangers 10.40 runs per season before leaving for New York. Jensen would say his statistics suggest "the Yankees have one of the best defensive shortstops playing out of position in deference to one of the worst defensive shortstops."

Of course, the sabermetricians could not account for the fact that Jeter played hurt as often as any other position player in the game. Despite the flip play against Oakland, despite the relay throw to get Timo Perez at the plate in the Subway Series, despite those Jordan-esque jumps from deep in the hole, their exhaustive studies showed what they showed — Jeter helped the Yankees with his bat, but not with his glove.

"Jeter gets more outrageous and patently false praise than any other player," James would say.

But the sabermetricians rarely, if ever, argued that Jeter was not a good to great player. Asked if he would want Jeter on his team, knowing what he knew about the shortstop's abilities, good and bad, James did not let his printouts or his Red Sox paychecks get in the way of his response.

"Oh, absolutely," he would say. "Jeter is a tremendous player, for reasons that I shouldn't have to explain."

Jeter did not feel the need to explain them, either, not when confronted with sabermetric data suggesting he was a liability on one side of the ball. The captain took great pride in his defense. He wrapped his entire baseball identity around the only position he ever wanted to play.

Jeter also spent entire winters protecting his claim to that position. He worked out with his trainer, Rafael Oquendo, and logged more hours at the Yankees' minor league facility in Tampa than any veteran player.

So at his locker, Jeter offered no warm welcomes to reporters who wanted to ask about a possible position change in the future. On a day A-Rod was getting rested, goes a story Mattingly told, the coach once asked Jeter — half-jokingly — if he would consider playing third base.

"Ain't happening," Jeter answered.

He came in as a shortstop, and he wanted to go out as a shortstop, even if he knew that was not a realistic proposition. Cal Ripken Jr. had to move to third base full-time in 1997, at thirty-six, and Jeter was approaching his thirty-third birthday.

One day during spring training, Jeter had baseball mortality on his mind when he came across Gene Michael, the Yankees' longtime executive and scout.

"How much longer do you think I can play shortstop?" Jeter asked Michael.

"One year," Michael joked.

"One year? Nah, I'm serious. What do you think?"

"How long do you want to keep doing this?"

"I want to play another ten years."

"Ten years? Not at shortstop."

"I can DH later. . . . Or I'll just move over to first base. I'll have a good on-base percentage and I can hit with a little power there."

"Well, don't you have anything else you like to do besides play baseball?"

"No, I don't. That's what I love to do."

Jeter added that he wanted to own a team someday but made it clear he planned on extending his playing career into his forties. The captain was not vacating his shortstop position one day before he absolutely had to, and he was not allowing his sabermetric critics to convince him that day should come sooner rather than later.

"You can't mathematically figure out how everybody plays defense, otherwise you're just playing Nintendo," Jeter would say. "You're playing on a computer. You can't mathematically figure that out. That's impossible to do, so I don't care."

Jeter said he did not pay attention to sabermetric rankings, and he was incredulous when asked why.

"A *computer*?" he said. "I don't know anything about it. I haven't learned about it, and I really don't care to learn about it. . . . I think it's literally impossible to do that, because everybody doesn't play in the same position and doesn't have the same pitcher. The ball's not hit to the same spot, and you don't have the same runner. . . . One day he's got a leg problem, the next day he doesn't.

"You just can't do it. There are too many factors that go into it."

Only it was not just the computer. Even the most ardent Jeter fans were seeing a slower and less supple version of the shortstop's former self in the field.

One was his former teammate and coach Joe Girardi, National League Manager of the Year in Florida who was fired by Marlins owner Jeffrey Loria in a clash of stubborn personalities. Girardi had become an analyst for the YES Network, and he thought as much of Jeter's tangible and intangible skills as any teammate the captain ever had.

Girardi saw Jeter as a baseball player who could beat you eight days a week. But as he watched his old teammate cheat to his left to compensate for lost range up the middle, watched him get to fewer ground balls than he used to, Girardi told a couple of friends something he took no delight in saying.

"I feel sorry for the next Yankee manager," he said, "because he's the one who's going to have to tell Jeter he can't play shortstop anymore."

Joe Torre's Yankees were on the verge of total collapse in Toronto in the final days of May, which meant Joe Torre was likely on the verge of being fired. His team was 21-29 and a staggering fourteen and a half games behind the Red Sox in the division. Torre's pitching was terrible, and the free agent signed a few weeks earlier to save his staff, Roger Clemens, was closing hard on his forty-fifth birthday.

The season opened with a historic burst of power from Alex Rodriguez, who became the fastest man to collect thirteen and fourteen homers in a season by hitting them in his eighteenth game. The predictable story line went like this: A-Rod was a new man after telling the truth about his broken relationship with Derek Jeter, who conceded Rodriguez was playing a game with which he was not familiar.

"You enjoy it and you appreciate it," Jeter said. "I can't relate to it. You'll never see me do it. . . . He's as hot as I've ever seen a player."

Jeter was not driving balls over the wall at any such rate, and he was not fielding his position the way he had the previous season. The shortstop committed six errors in the first eleven games; in 2006, he did not commit his sixth until the fiftieth game.

But near the end of May, Jeter was still hitting .350 with an on-base percentage of .425. He was not the problem. A-Rod was not the problem, either, even if his .371 batting average on May 1 had plunged below .300 four weeks later.

Rodriguez had 19 homers and 44 RBI, and he also was making a concerted effort to stay out of trouble, to field baseball questions only and to keep his interaction with the news media to a minimum. Larry Bowa, a blunt, tough-love type hired as Torre's third-base coach before the 2006 season, asked Rodriguez why he kept making silly comments in the press, and wasn't satisfied with the third baseman's answer.

So Bowa and Mike Borzello came up with their own penal system. "Every time you make a stupid comment you've got to give us a hundred dollars," Bowa told A-Rod, who did not fight the plan.

"We got about three or four hundred dollars from him," Bowa said, "and then he realized, 'Hey, I'd better stop making these stupid statements.' And he stopped."

Rodriguez was helped by the presence of Doug Mientkiewicz, his teammate and friend from Westminster Christian High in Miami. Brian Cashman had signed the first baseman — and the member of the 2004 championship Boston team who recorded the final historic out of the World Series sweep of St. Louis — knowing Mientkiewicz could serve as a buffer between A-Rod and Jeter and the rest.

Mientkiewicz wasn't afraid to tell Rodriguez what he did not want to hear. "I've never called him A-Rod in my life; he's always been little Alex to me," Mientkiewicz said. "I never got wrapped up in the aura. As soon as he walked in the clubhouse door I'd scream at him, 'Cheer up. It's not about you. Every day you don't come to the yard with a smile on your face I'm going to kick you in the nuts. You think the game is hard with your talent level? Try playing it with mine.'

"It made Alex smile. [Jorge] Posada told me, 'We should've brought you over here a long time ago,' because I helped everybody else see Alex in a different light. Alex let some of his guard down and let the guys see he's human."

Only a humanized A-Rod and a productive Jeter could not prevent the Yankees from coming unglued. Torre called a team meeting on May 28, before the first game of the Toronto series. Jeter had already been on record as far back as April trying to disarm those calling for Torre's head, saying after a lost series to the Red Sox, "There shouldn't be any questions. He's in no way responsible. . . . You should never talk about his job. It's unfair and it should stop."

Of course, it did not stop. The Yankees were not helping their manager with their play or their preparation, and Torre thought it was time to drop the hammer. He ripped into his players for a general lack of effort and focus, and nearly all veteran witnesses agreed it was the angriest Torre had ever been.

"There were some fired-up people in that meeting," Mike Mussina said. "Even Derek was fired up, more than the standard, 'We're not doing this, we're not doing that.' . . . It was about as serious a meeting as I was involved in in my years as a Yankee."

It lasted some fifty minutes, and Jeter was not the only player who spoke; Andy Pettitte was among those who delivered their own impassioned pleas. But Jeter was the captain, so he had the E. F. Hutton effect on his teammates.

"Now is when you find out what kind of player you are," Jeter barked in the meeting.

The captain did not get up in front of the group unless there was something to say. Sometimes he spoke when Torre called on him, and sometimes he thought the manager had already covered what needed to be said.

"Sometimes in those meetings," one Yankee said, "you didn't want to talk after Joe because Joe was so good at it. And sometimes players would say things and you're like, 'You're the person Torre was talking about.' From past years, Kenny Lofton comes to mind. And you're sitting there saying, 'Just shut up.' Gary Sheffield, on the other hand, he was straight to the point and a lot of times said things we needed to hear."

Following Torre was a tough act, no matter who you were. Jeter was very careful in picking his spots. He grew more willing to speak up after his appointment as captain in 2003, but he did not believe in wasting anyone's time.

"If Derek said something," Mussina said, "we knew he was frustrated or upset or bothered by what was going on. . . . He wouldn't pick out anybody. It was *we* are not getting guys over. *We* are not working counts like we do when we're successful. *We* are not playing good defense. Derek understood that he had to talk like the manager, that it had to be *we* and not *you*."

Jeter's leadership was a popular subject in and around the Yankee clubhouse. The debate over whether the captain should have shielded Rodriguez from the storm of fan abuse often fueled the discussion, but there were sidebar issues that had little or nothing to do with A-Rod.

No right-minded teammate or observer ever doubted Jeter's lead-by-example work ethic, his willingness to play in pain, and his talent for playing big in the biggest games. But if there were a few Yankees who thought Jeter should have imposed his will on the team in more of an in-your-face way, whether by being more vocal and demonstrative or by telling a pitcher he needed to hit an opposing batter to retaliate for a downed Yank, Jason Giambi was in that group.

Giambi had tremendous respect and affection for Jeter, who had publicly backed him at his lowest point. Yet even though he was a steroid cheat, a party boy, and a guy who had benched himself for a World Series game, Giambi fancied himself capable of filling a leadership void.

"I can really help this team," Giambi had told one teammate. "There are things that need to be said, and I can't say them. This is Derek's team. I can't be the guy to go out there and say it. In Oakland, I could kind of run that ship and get on guys and send a message, but I feel like I have to hold back here."

Jeter always felt as if he did more leading and guiding and captaining than even his teammates knew. When it came to individual admonishment or advice, the captain almost always preferred to deliver it in a quiet corner, his rebukes of Bernie Williams and Jay Witasick in the 2001 World Series notwithstanding. Jeter would take aside the young, impressionable likes of Robinson Cano and Melky Cabrera and sternly remind them to hustle at all times.

Asked how often he pulled players aside who needed direction or a kick in the butt, Jeter said, "A lot more than you think. . . . I don't think you have to do it through the media. I don't think you have to do it when you have a camera in your face, so that people say, 'Oh, look what he did.' Why would you do that? I never understood it, so I'll never be that way. . . . If I had a problem with someone or had a problem with what someone said, I'll tell him. I don't think it has to be a bigger story than necessary by going through the media."

If Torre did not want to confront a player, or if he felt that player would better respond to a peer, the manager often asked Jeter to deliver his message. "I've seen Joe go up to Jeet many times and say, 'You wanna handle it?'" Bowa said. "And Jeet would always say, 'I'll take care of it,' and he would."

As a team leader, Jeter had a strong record of making low-profile newcomers feel at home. Nick Green, a utility infielder who played all of forty-six games for the 2006 team, said Jeter treated him "like a friend you've known forever that you've never met."

Aaron Small, the obscure pitcher who somehow went 10-0 with the 2005 team, recalled Jeter introducing himself to him in spring training, eating lunch with him, treating him as if he were David Cone. A few weeks after he had met Small, Jeter insisted the two come up with the kind of personal secret handshake the captain had with other teammates.

No, Jeter did not have to speak to lead. He performed one of his jump throws from the hole during Small's first Yankee Stadium start, and the journeyman pitcher stood there on the mound, mouth agape. "Just like a kid watching it on TV," Small said.

Ron Villone, the much-traveled relief pitcher, spoke of how Jeter would come to the mound and express his appreciation for the number of innings he had thrown. "Derek would give me an energy boost, a mental boost on the mound," Villone said. "I watched him for years do that with other pitchers, and that confidence in his voice really helped me."

Mientkiewicz remembered Jeter sitting him down on arrival in Tampa and telling the first baseman he was available to answer any questions about New York, the Yanks, the media, whatever. Jeter then went about needling Mientkiewicz every day, with Posada's help, calling him Pete Rose ("I have no idea why," Mientkiewicz said) and making him feel comfortable. "He'd already accepted me into that clubhouse," the first baseman said.

Mientkiewicz recalled Jeter showing necessary leadership "by playing when he could barely walk" and by validating the new recruit's presence even when that recruit overstepped his bounds.

"In one meeting when we were losing I basically called everybody out, and I was hitting .205 or something," Mientkiewicz said. "I said, 'You know what, guys, you always had a swagger that made me want to kill you. Jeet, I've got a picture of me trying to break up a double play in 2003, and my foot is above your belt and I'm trying to kill you. You guys had swagger. Where is it? You're not stapling my name to the first team that doesn't make the playoffs in Joe Torre's tenure.'

"And Jeter came up to me after and said, 'Coming from you that got the attention of a lot of people.' I was a newcomer, a small piece of a big machine, and Jeter took it to heart."

Off a poor feed from Robinson Cano to start a potential double play against Boston, Jeter would bounce a throw to Mientkiewicz, who was kneed in the head by the hitter, Mike Lowell, as he tried to scoop the ball. The first baseman ended up face first in the dirt and landed in the hospital with a mild concussion and a fractured wrist.

"And Derek was the first guy on my phone to say how sick he felt," Mientkiewicz said. "He felt awful, and I told him it was just part of the game. But just hearing his voice meant something to me."

The stories of Jeter taking in new Yankees and young Yankees far outnumbered the one relayed by Ricky Ledee, who told people Alex Rodriguez was more helpful to him in Texas than Jeter had been in the Bronx. For the captain, it always came back to Alex, somehow, some way.

Following their blowout meeting in Toronto, the Yankees lost their next two games to the Blue Jays and then woke up to the very last thing any of them needed — Alex Rodriguez pictured on the front page of the *New York Post* with an attractive woman not his wife.

"STRAY-ROD" screamed the headline, and A-Rod was left to explain to his spouse, Cynthia, why he was in the company of a woman later identified as stripper Joslyn Noel Morse. Inside the Yankee clubhouse, word of a player caught fooling around on the road was met with a Captain Renault–like reaction: teammates were shocked, *shocked*, to find that adultery was going on in here.

Either way, Rodriguez was brought to his knees. His quest for a season of pure baseball, and pure baseball only, had been shot to hell. One member of the Yankees' traveling party even tried to convince A-Rod that someone in Jeter's camp had tipped off the *Post* photographer.

It was a positively absurd suggestion, as Jeter would be the last athlete to have endorsed such a devious plot. But this potentially divisive claim underscored the notion that the A-Rod–Jeter armistice was a fragile one.

Did Jeter and Rodriguez engage in open hostilities? Shouting matches? Shoving matches? No, even if one false report had them squaring off in Ali and Frazier form.

Truth was, even if Jeter and Rodriguez almost never entered or exited the clubhouse side by side, they did occasionally lunch together on the road. In the past A-Rod had wanted more than that, of course, because he was an emotionally needy star who craved positive reinforcement and Jeter's full approval. But the captain would extend himself only so far for the third baseman.

"Jeet never said one negative word about Alex to me, ever," Bowa said. "I don't think they're ever going to dine together or go on vacations together, but I don't think they hate each other."

Mientkiewicz echoed Bowa's sentiments and said age created distance between Jeter and Rodriguez. "Grown men don't have sleepovers and order pizza and rent movies from Blockbuster," Mientkiewicz said. "Alex never said anything negative about Derek, and with Alex having such a phenomenal year, Jeet would just sit there and shake his head and say, 'That's just not normal. What we're watching right now is just not normal.'"

Nothing was ever normal about A-Rod. Hours after the *Post* ran its Stray-Rod story, Rodriguez was running out Posada's two-out pop-up in the ninth with the Yanks holding a two-run lead. As Toronto's Howie Clark settled under the ball and prepared to end the inning, A-Rod yelled "Ha" as he passed Clark, who backed away from the play under the assumption that his shortstop, John McDonald, had just called him off.

The ball fell, the Yanks added a run to their lead, and McDonald and an entire roster of Blue Jays wanted to choke the life out of A-Rod. Blue Jays manager John Gibbons told Rodriguez his was a bush-league play and summoned the spirit of Curt Schilling and the 2004 Red Sox when he said, "That's not Yankee baseball."

The chief representative of Yankee baseball was asked for his reaction. "I don't know; you will have to ask [Rodriguez]," Jeter said. "I wasn't out there."

Torre initially backed his third baseman, saying catchers trying to run down pop-ups near enemy dugouts hear "I got it" all the time. But after realizing A-Rod was getting trashed all around baseball — and the Stray-Rod story and photo sure did not help Rodriguez in this case — Torre decided Toronto had a point.

"It was probably something he shouldn't have done," the manager said a couple of nights later. "It was probably inappropriate to do it at the time he did it."

Suddenly Rodriguez had another reason to feel isolated. A year after Jeter would not shield him from the fans, Torre would not shield him from the Blue Jays.

George Steinbrenner and front-office officials were upset that their manager did not do more to protect Rodriguez. "Alex made a good, smart baseball play," one team official said. "It was gamesmanship that paid off and helped us win. The old-timers would say they did that stuff all the time, and good for Alex, he got away with it.

"But Torre got to a point where his image was more important than the Yankees. He backtracked because public opinion said Joe Torre's a good man, and that's cheating, and how could he feel that way. He left Alex out in the wind to get pummeled, and he never would've done that to Derek."

No, Torre never would have done that to Derek. Of course, Derek never would have put Torre in a position to defend his captain for yelling "Ha" at an opposing infielder.

Nevertheless, if the manager had a flaw or three in his approach, he remained a master at guiding a team through a 162-game season. The great basketball coach Chuck Daly used to say a head coach's job is to navigate the turbulence of an endless regular season and find a way to land the plane.

No coach or manager knew how to land the plane like Joe Torre.

"There's only one manager in baseball who would've let us make the playoffs that year, and it was Joe," Mientkiewicz said. "And there was only one captain who would've let us make the playoffs that year, and it was Derek. That's because neither one ever panics.

"We had some real knock-down, drag-out meetings, but Jeter never worried and always believed. He always said, 'We're one pitch or one play away from reeling off eighteen of twenty, and if you believe it, it's going to happen.'"

The night Rodriguez yelled "Ha" in Toronto marked a turning point; including that victory, the Yanks would finish the season 73-39, would nearly erase Boston's entire fourteen-and-a-half-game divisional lead, and would seize the wild card to give Torre a dozen postseason appearances in a dozen years on the job.

Along the way, A-Rod would crack his 500th homer, and Jeter would pass Joe DiMaggio on the career hit list with number 2,215. Jeter would also complete a remarkable stretch that started the previous August in which he hit safely in 59 out of 61 games, becoming the only major leaguer since 1900 not named DiMaggio to have no more than two hitless games over a span of 56 or more, according to Trent McCotter of the Society for American Baseball Research.

But Jeter never measured himself by his numbers, no matter how impressive they were. One number defined him — four — his collection of World Series championships, and the shortstop would have gladly given back his captaincy if it meant upgrading that defining number to five.

The Yankees were down 2–0 in their best-of-five Division Series with the Cleveland Indians, George Steinbrenner had threatened to fire Joe Torre if he did not win three straight sudden-death games from his hometown Indians, and Derek Jeter responded to the pressure the way any self-respecting captain would.

With a prank.

This was two days after a plague of Lake Erie midges descended on Jacobs Field in the eighth inning of Game 2, leaving the Yankees' bullpen phenom, Joba Chamberlain, looking like a helpless grade-school camper who had walked into a beehive.

Jeter and Alex Rodriguez and Doug Mientkiewicz were among the Yankees who were swatting at the bugs with their hands, gloves, and caps, but Chamberlain was the lead victim in this Hitchcock horror. The Yankee trainer, Gene Monahan, went out to spray him with repellent, but Monahan might as well have covered Joba in honey.

The bugs attached themselves to Chamberlain's eyes, face, and neck. Joba's vision and focus were impaired long enough for the setup man to set up his team's demise, unleashing his second wild pitch in ten pitches, allowing the tying run to score, and ultimately allowing the Indians a chance to win in the eleventh.

Torre should have tried to stop the game; even Roger Clemens, his forty-five-year-old Game 3 starter, would say as much. But the Yankees managed all of three hits in that 2–1, eleven-inning loss, and Rodriguez went 0 for 4 with three strikeouts, extending his postseason hitless streak to eighteen at-bats and ending up 4 for his last 50 in the playoffs without a single RBI.

So it was not just the midges. It only seemed that way.

"I've never seen anything like it before," Jeter said. "It was like someone let them go."

The next day, a workout day in the Bronx before Game 3, the day before the Yankees faced the possibility of a third straight first-round exit, Mientkiewicz found humor in his team's desperation, referencing the captain's personal brand of cologne.

"The joke around the guys is that we all had Derek Jeter's 'Driven' on," Mientkiewicz said. "That's why all the bugs were attacking us."

Jeter woke up to the quotes the following day, game day, and decided Mientkiewicz would regret that remark. Rome was burning, Steinbrenner was blustering, and Jeter was busy proving that no situation was too alarming to make him forget he was a man playing a boy's game.

In the clubhouse before Game 3, Jeter made a point of completely ignoring Mientkiewicz, who returned to his locker after batting practice to find a letter resting on his chair, a letter supposedly from Macy's.

The letter read something like this:

Dear Mr. Mientkiewicz. Thanks to your comments to the media, we've had to pull 12.2 million bottles of Derek Jeter's Driven off the shelves. You've cost my company and Mr. Jeter millions of dollars. I hope this turns out well for you.

Mientkiewicz nearly passed out. He thought that he was done as a Yankee, and that he would be sued for everything he had.

"I was crushed, and my stomach was in knots," Mientkiewicz said. "Derek wouldn't even look at me. And then right before he takes the field for the game, he runs by me and says, 'That letter was bullshit. It was a joke.' I'm bent over, hands on my knees, going, 'You're an asshole. I know this playoff thing is easy for you and it's another game for you, but it's not for me.' And Derek's over there giggling his ass off."

Laughing before an elimination game. This was the essence of the postseason Jeter, never sweating the stakes.

Two years earlier, with the Yankees five minutes away from playing the Angels in the Division Series, Aaron Small had found himself sitting next to a completely relaxed Jeter in the dugout. "Don't you ever get nervous?" Small asked.

"Ah, man," Jeter said. "We're just playing a game."

Postseason, regular season, it did not matter: everyone called baseball a game of failure, but Jeter refused to let the failure get in the way of his fun.

The shortstop loved exchanging banter with teammates, opponents, fans, even himself. "The only thing he's negative about is himself once in a while," Mientkiewicz said. "He tells himself he sucks, in a funny way that shows he's human. Sometimes he'd have conversations with his front foot. He'd scream at himself, 'Get the foot down,' and some fan in the front row would yell, 'Jeter, you suck.' And he'd be like, 'I know I suck. I'm trying my best.'"

When Jeter was not engaging in a good-natured back-and-forth with the fans from the on-deck circle, he would playfully shout at his coaches from the batter's box. Mientkiewicz said Don Mattingly was a favorite target, especially after Mattingly reported in a pregame meeting that an opposing pitcher topped out at 92 miles per hour, only for that pitcher to throw a fastball by Jeter at 94 miles per hour.

"Jeter would look into the dugout," Mientkiewicz said, "and he'd mouth, 'Hey, Don-ehhh. You stink.'"

It was all said and done with a wink. Jeter never disrespected umpires, coaches, or any authority figures, never mind a former Yankee captain who carried himself the way Jeter did, before Jeter did.

The shortstop just never saw the need to make the game more serious than it had to be. At least until his team ended up on the wrong side of the final score. Jeter saw no fun in losing. He saw no redeeming qualities in seasons that did not end in a parade.

"After we got eliminated in the playoffs," one teammate said, "I didn't sense him being disappointed or devastated. I sensed him being pissed off. That was usually his mood."

In that context, Jeter worked for the right man. Nobody in the history of American sports got more pissed off over losing than George Steinbrenner, who had won six World Series titles but had spent an ungodly amount of money in a vain pursuit of his seventh.

At seventy-seven, Steinbrenner was not the Boss of old anymore, not with his health in a state of steady decline. He did not attend games, did not fire employees, did not call up writers to rip this bum or that one. Steinbrenner was speaking through statements released by his publicist, Howard Rubenstein, who swore to everyone who asked that the Boss remained a vigorous leader with an ample supply of fire in the belly.

Rubenstein's pitch did not jibe with the sad and pathetic portrait of an incoherent man in his midafternoon pajamas painted by *Portfolio* writer Franz Lidz, who arrived at Steinbrenner's home unannounced and accompanied by the Boss's longtime friend Tom McEwen of the *Tampa Tribune*.

Had Steinbrenner suffered a stroke? Was he locked inside the dark prison of dementia? The Yankees' owning family decided the answer was not for public consumption, but the word in early October was that Steinbrenner was having good days and bad days, with the good sometimes outnumbering the bad.

The Boss was feeling strong enough to attend Game 3 of the Division Series and make his first Yankee Stadium appearance since Opening Day, and so a columnist from the *Record* of New Jersey called his Manhattan hotel room to see if Steinbrenner was having a good enough day to talk. Turned out he was.

In what would be his final interview, his last blast from the past, Steinbrenner laced into umpire Bruce Froemming, the Game 2 crew chief, for not stopping the game on account of midges. "It was terrible," the Boss barked. "It messed up the whole team, Jeter, all of them."

Steinbrenner claimed that his health was fine, that he still maintained full control over the team, and that he planned on re-signing Rodriguez. But as far as re-signing Torre, that was an entirely different matter.

"His job is on the line," Steinbrenner said of the manager making $7.5 million. "I think we're paying him a lot of money. He's the highest-paid manager in baseball, so I don't think we'd take him back if we don't win this series."

Torre and the front office were blind-sided by the quotes, and team officials were scrambling to find out how the columnist's phone call made its way to the Boss. Meanwhile, the Yankees went out and played inspired baseball for a manager under siege, surviving a terrible performance by Clemens, who ended the last start of his career in the third inning, limping away with a strained hamstring. The Yanks recovered from a 3–0 deficit, ripping off eight unanswered runs, three on a homer from Johnny Damon. A-Rod actually got a couple of hits, and Torre lived to manage another day.

"The Boss is the Boss," Jeter would say. "He's going to say what he wants to say. This is just a regular day in New York."

The Yankees had momentum at home, but that momentum would die in the right hand of Chien-Ming Wang, the 19-game winner going on three days' rest in Game 4. Though Wang had been hammered in Game 1, he had won 38 games over two seasons for Torre, who no longer believed in his fully rested alternative, Mike Mussina.

As it turned out, Wang would give up four runs on five hits — including a leadoff homer to Grady Sizemore — while recording only three outs. The sinkerballer sank the Yanks, who were down 6–2 in the sixth inning when their big chance to get back in the game arrived in the form of their captain.

Jeter had hits in his first two at-bats, including an RBI single in the second, and this time he had runners on the corners, one out, and lefty reliever Rafael Perez on the mound. As Jeter worked the count to 2-1, the sellout crowd stood and stomped and chanted for the shortstop to do something dramatic.

Jeter grounded into a double play instead. Cleveland won, 6–4, to advance to the next round.

"We've done it so many times," the captain would say. "I thought we were going to do it again."

Rodriguez would homer in the seventh for his first postseason RBI since Game 4 of the 2004 ALCS, and he finished the series with back-to-back two-hit games. Finally, A-Rod had done just barely enough to funnel the toughest post-series questions toward another locker.

Derek Jeter's.

The shortstop batted .176 over the four games and had no walks, four strikeouts, and one RBI. A lifetime .314 postseason hitter entering the series, Jeter grounded into three double plays in the last two games.

He made no excuses when it was over, just said he did not get it done. But Jeter did not have to defend himself as much as he had to defend the only manager he had known as an everyday shortstop.

"Everyone knows I love Mr. T.," the captain said. "He's the best, in my opinion. It seems like every season you're asking if this is his best year, and this by far is his best year. It goes without saying I support him."

With Steinbrenner again in the house, the fans had supported Torre, too, chanting his name when he went out to the mound. It did not sound like a crowd trying to save the manager; it sounded like a crowd saying goodbye.

"Whatever the hell happens from here on out," said a choked-up Torre, "I'll look back on these twelve years with great, great pleasure. The twelve years just felt like they were ten minutes long, to be honest with you."

In the end, the Yankees would make Torre a reduced-rate offer designed for him to refuse, and refuse it he did. The manager could have taken a one-year deal for $5 million in salary and $3 million in postseason incentives, but he knew the Steinbrenners and team president Randy Levine did not truly want him back, and he felt Brian Cashman's support — once unconditional — had waned.

Torre walked away, A-Rod was thinking of doing the same, and

Steinbrenner was finally relinquishing control of the team to his sons. The franchise was being rocked by seismic change, and Cashman was trying his damnedest to hold it together.

But as the general manager considered candidates to replace Torre, considered the amount of money required to keep A-Rod, and considered how strange it would be answering to Hank and Hal Steinbrenner instead of the Boss, Cashman also pondered a move that would be among the more difficult of his front-office career.

Cashman had to tell one veteran employee his job performance needed to improve. After seven years of postseason losing, after three years of failing to reach the second round, Cashman had to inform this lifer that the status quo was not good enough.

So here was the question the GM kept asking when he was all alone with his thoughts:

How do you tell the great Derek Jeter he needs to pick it up?

Even by New York Yankee standards, it would be a turbulent off-season. Joe Torre left in a huff and ended up with the Los Angeles Dodgers, forcing Brian Cashman to choose between an iconic Yankee, Don Mattingly, and a decidedly noniconic Yankee, Joe Girardi, whose approach would stand in greater contrast to Torre's.

Cashman picked Girardi.

On muscle memory, Alex Rodriguez played the fool when his agent, Scott Boras, announced in the middle of Game 4 of the Boston-Colorado World Series that his client was opting out of his contract. Officials all over baseball roasted Boras and Rodriguez for trying to upstage their signature event, and the Boss's more volatile and impetuous son, Hank Steinbrenner, declared there was "no chance" he would bring back A-Rod after warning him against opting out (a move that would cost the Yanks the $21.3 million subsidy from Texas on Rodriguez's existing ten-year deal).

But after A-Rod begged and pleaded and apologized, and after the slugger put Boras on the bench, Hank would take him back for $275 million over ten years, plus another $30 million in the event Rodriguez broke baseball's career home-run record.

Hours after A-Rod spoke about his new deal and conceded the timing of the opt-out was "inappropriate," former Senate majority leader

George Mitchell concluded his investigation into steroid use in baseball by releasing a report that identified eighty-six players, including twenty-two current or former Yankees. The undisputed star and ace of the Mitchell Report was Roger Clemens, who was alleged to have used steroids and human growth hormone provided by Brian McNamee, the pitcher's former trainer and the former Yankee strength and conditioning coach.

Rodriguez was not on the list, a fact that stunned the juicer turned accusatory author Jose Canseco, but suddenly the Yankee brand was in the same company as Barry Bonds and Mark McGwire — linked forevermore to what would go down as the sport's Steroid Era.

Only before this would prove to be an issue that would haunt the Yankees over the long haul, Cashman had a more pressing on-field problem with a player who was not among George Mitchell's traveling all-stars: Derek Jeter. His defense was hurting the Yankees, and Cashman decided to do something about it.

Jeter had made his eighth All-Star team, had won his second straight Silver Slugger award, and had become the first major league shortstop ever to collect six 200-hit seasons. But the sabermetric police had hauled in Jeter again, charging him with a number of fielding felonies.

John Dewan of *The Fielding Bible* slapped Jeter with another minus 34 in 2007 (he made 34 fewer plays than the average shortstop), and the captain's score from 2005 through 2007 added up to a league-worst minus 90 (Houston's Adam Everett led baseball over the same period at plus 92). Jeter's 2007 Ultimate Zone Rating, according to FanGraphs.com, checked in at minus 17.9, meaning his defense cost the Yanks 17.9 runs the average shortstop would have saved.

Not that Cashman discovered Jeter's defensive deficiencies in any statistical chart; his eyes told him the shortstop hadn't lost one step, but two. So he invited Jeter to dinner and met him in an Upper East Side restaurant. The captain had no idea he was scheduled to be the main course.

In Jeter, Cashman knew he had the near-perfect player. Near-perfect in the way he carried himself, in the way he competed, in the way he won, in the way he respected his elders and embraced his role-model responsibilities to the kids.

The kids. Jeter was always great with the kids, regardless of the circumstances. One day after he had retired from baseball, Chad Curtis, the old Jeter antagonist, showed up at Comerica Park in Detroit with twenty-five students from NorthPointe Christian High School, where the former Yankee outfielder worked.

Wearing shorts and a backpack and looking like he was ready to climb Mount Everest, Curtis made his way to the field and over to Jeter while the shortstop was doing his pregame stretching. Five minutes later, Jeter was near the stands and shaking hands with every single one of Curtis's twenty-five students.

"If you had a daughter, you'd want her to marry Derek Jeter," Cashman said. "He's a great person."

Great, not perfect.

Jeter could be overly sensitive to criticism, and Cashman had that figured out going into this dinner. Some who knew the shortstop suspected this weakness was rooted in the racism he faced in his youth, and to the fact that his African-American father and Irish-American mother shielded their son and daughter from the ignorance of others by wrapping them in a warm blanket of nurturing and love.

Others felt Jeter was overly sensitive to criticism for the simple reason he was so damn good at everything he did, he wasn't used to receiving it.

And those who did criticize the shortstop could feel the sting of Jeter's River Avenue freeze-out. "One of Derek's standards," said longtime *New York Post* baseball columnist Joel Sherman, referring to club personnel and not journalists, "is if you burn me once you'll live outside my igloo forever, and if you freeze to death that's your problem."

One teammate who was friendly with Jeter recalled mocking the shortstop — in a joking way — in front of a small group of Yankees. Jeter glared at the teammate, turned away, and ignored him for two weeks.

"I didn't understand it, because we'd kidded each other all the time," the teammate said. "But then I realized: that was the first time I did it in front of teammates, and as the captain he didn't appreciate having that done in front of others."

Nor did Jeter appreciate less than glowing critiques from any corner of his athletic past. Told one of his former youth summer basketball coaches recalled he had likely been dunked on more than anyone in the state of Michigan — if only because Jeter hustled so much to get back on opposing fast breaks — the shortstop said, "I don't know about getting dunked on. Power lay-ups, maybe."

Jeter had a long memory, too. In 2001, teammate David Justice was talking with *Newsday* baseball columnist Ken Davidoff when the writer mentioned he was the sports editor of the University of Michigan school paper who had assigned a piece on Jeter to another writer when the shortstop enrolled there in the fall of '92.

Justice yelled over to Jeter, "Hey, Jeet, this guy wrote about you at Michigan." Expressionless, Jeter replied, "The story said I played football. I didn't play football."

Yes, Jeter had a low tolerance for real or imagined slights. He rarely deviated from his one-strike-and-you're-out policy, as his old friend from his days as a minor leaguer in Greensboro, Earl Clary, could attest. Clary adored Jeter and opened up his home to him, but recalled their relationship changing over a chance meeting in a Baltimore restaurant.

Clary was entertaining a customer when they stumbled upon Jeter sitting with some Yankees at a table. The customer grabbed two bags of souvenirs and rushed over to the shortstop to have him autograph each item.

"I'd never asked for anything from Jeter, but it was my fault; I should've told the jackass not to do that," Clary said. "I can't express what a great guy Jeter is, but he used to call me back right away and it was never the same after that night. He was cool to me after that night."

Jeter could be cool and distant and suspicious. "If you knock on his door," said the YES Network's Michael Kay, "he'll talk to you for four or five hours through the screen, but you'll never get invited in."

Jeter's buddy R. D. Long was among the precious few who had been welcomed inside the screen door. But getting inside did not mean full trust was offered without careful inspection.

"Fame and fortune can make you very paranoid," Long said, "to where I have the sense he's unsure what my intentions are as his friend sometimes, and that bothers me. . . . Derek's always feeling, 'Somebody may be taking advantage of me.'"

The founder of a nonprofit college prep program for student athletes in the Rochester, New York, area called Mind, Body & Soul, Long invited his former minor league teammate to his wedding in 2004. "Derek flew in on a Thursday night and flew out on a Sunday night and stayed the whole time for my wedding, all aspects of it, like a normal person," Long said. "He bought eleven suits, $2,000 apiece, for my groomsmen and the fathers, from Michael Jordan's tailor in Chicago.

"Instead of those suits, he could've written a $22,000 check to me for my program, but he's not going to do that. He doesn't know exactly where the money's going. It comes with the territory."

Long said he still loved Jeter the way he would a kid brother, still saw him as a man with almost no character flaws. But even as he looked at Jeter's world from the inside out, Long understood the shortstop often lived behind impenetrable walls.

"Derek," he said, "is the iciest non-icy person I've ever met."

So when Brian Cashman sat down with Derek Jeter to tell him he needed to improve his lateral movement on defense if he wanted to remain at shortstop, the GM knew he would be standing outside of Jeter's locked screen door at the start of their dinner, and quite possibly freezing outside of Jeter's igloo at the end of it.

Cashman had little choice but to play the bad guy here. He could not ask Girardi to confront his former teammate in his first significant act as manager, even if Girardi had already confided in friends that Torre's successor ultimately would be the man to tell Jeter he would have to change positions.

The GM could not risk destroying the manager-captain relationship before it ever had a chance. Besides, Cashman had held a few conversations with Torre about moving Jeter to center field as far back as 2005, when the Yankees were dissatisfied with the aging Bernie Williams and Tony Womack.

Torre told Cashman he would run the idea past Jeter, who was so reliable on pop flies the Yanks believed he could make a Robin Yount–like transition to center. When the GM later asked Torre what had come of his talk with Jeter, the manager said the captain wanted to stay put.

So as dinner began, Cashman reminded Jeter that Torre had spoken with him about a move to center. Only Jeter swore he'd had no such discussion with Torre. In fact, despite Torre's claim to Cashman that he had spoken with the shortstop about improving his range, Jeter maintained his manager never once mentioned that his defense was an issue.

Cashman nearly fell face first into his soup. He could not believe what he was hearing. Was it possible Derek Jeter had become so big and so iconic that a fellow icon and four-time champ and future Hall of Famer and living New York institution such as Joe Torre was afraid to coach him?

Jeter said Larry Bowa did tell him to shade toward third base, as if to cover for Alex Rodriguez, but that no other coach suggested he needed to improve his own play. Cashman countered that A-Rod was playing at a Gold Glove level, and that if there was a weakness on the left side of the Yankee infield, it was not at third base.

The stunned shortstop and the stunned GM were at a stalemate. The relationship between employer and employee could have detonated on the spot.

Cashman knew there were coaches who did not want to risk their standing with a superstar player by criticizing him. Jeter, a three-time Gold Glover, knew the Yankees were now suggesting his defense was among the reasons the team had not won a title in recent seasons.

Man, it had been a long year, and it had nothing to do with the fact that New York tax officials were maintaining that Jeter owed them three years' worth of unpaid taxes as a state resident. (The shortstop claimed he was a Florida resident who kept an apartment in the city, and the case was ultimately settled.) The sabermetric crowd was buzzing about this declining range factor and that declining zone rating, Gary Sheffield had hurt him in an HBO interview by saying the biracial Jeter "ain't all the way black," the Yankees had lost again in the first round, and Torre had left for L.A.

This dinner could have turned into the ugliest of food fights, yet Cashman could not turn back. He had been taught by Gene Michael to speak his mind, with feeling, just as he did as an assistant GM in the spring of 1996, when he voted to keep the rookie Jeter in the starting lineup.

Right here, right now, Cashman would show his own extreme talent as an executive. He would show why he helped the Yankees win multiple championships.

He would make a critical stand nobody else in the organization had the nerve to make. It was up to the captain to decide how this game would end.

And on this night, with the Yankees telling him for the first time his best was not good enough, Derek Jeter rose above his human frailty, above his allergic reaction to criticism, and put his beating champion's heart right on the table.

"You mean to tell me we were trying to win a championship every year," Jeter told Cashman, "and there was a way for me to get better to help us do that, and nobody told me?

"I'm only going to play for so many years, and if you're telling me there are things I can do to make us better and put us in a better position to win, why wouldn't someone tell me this? . . . I want to do everything I can to get better. It makes me wonder how good we could've been and how many more championships we might've won if I'd dealt with this."

It was the perfect response. It was the winning response.

It was Jeter revealing the essence of his greatness.

The captain was not angry at Torre; he could not get angry with the manager who had meant so much to him. "I was with him since I was twenty-one years old and I pretty much grew up with him," Jeter said.

But the shortstop was incredulous that the manager and those on his staff never mentioned that he needed to work on his defense. As it turned out, Jeter was more coachable than his bosses had given him credit for.

"I don't think you should have a problem with trying to get better," Jeter would say of his dinner meeting with Cashman. Asked if he was completely on board with the GM's suggestion that he needed to improve defensively, Jeter said, "Why wouldn't I be? It's important to get better and to be willing to listen."

Yes, the ultimate team player was going to take one for the team. The Yankees had a new fitness trainer in mind, one recommended by Jeter's agent, Casey Close. The Yanks thought the trainer might make a thirty-three-year-old ballplayer a more explosive lateral force, and the shortstop agreed to give it a shot.

The general manager and the captain shook hands. In the middle of a Manhattan restaurant, even if Derek Jeter did not realize it, the prince of the city was reborn.

13

◆

Rebirth

"EXCUSE ME, EXCUSE ME," Derek Jeter pleaded with the last crowd ever to set foot inside Yankee Stadium. The captain lowered his chin as he held a microphone in his right hand while tugging on the bill of his cap with his left.

Jeter was standing on the field, surrounded by teammates, cameramen, and photographers. A few soundmen on the perimeter reached over the mob with their boom mikes as some 54,610 people stood and waited for the shortstop to speak.

Excuse me, excuse me. Jeter sounded like a schoolboy poking his head into a conference room full of teachers, looking for directions to the bathroom. The only son of Charles and Dorothy Jeter was closing down the most famous ballpark on earth, trying to settle a night crowd in the city that never sleeps, and still he was careful to mind his manners.

Jeter did not want to make this address, if only because public speaking ranked somewhere between a playoff loss to the Red Sox and not making the playoffs at all on his list of things to avoid like the plague.

Jason Zillo, the Yankee director of media relations, had been bringing it up for about two weeks. "Do I have to do it?" Jeter asked with a knowing smile. "Absolutely not," Zillo answered.

"You should, though. You're the captain and the face of the franchise."

They talked about it almost every day, if only to fill the conversational void left by this cold, hard truth: it was clear Jeter would not be playing in the postseason for the first time in his charmed career. Tampa Bay, of all teams, had emerged as a divisional powerhouse, and Boston had remained steady enough to claim the wild card.

The Yankees? They were defined all year by the tense and distant approach of their first-year manager, Joe Girardi, who seemed less comfortable following Joe Torre than Gene Bartow did following John Wooden. In stark contrast to Torre, Girardi struggled in his daily dealings with the news media and had difficulty telling the truth — or an acceptable version of the truth — when giving injury updates.

Torre also exuded calm; even the unshakable Jeter said his relaxed manager relaxed him. But at times Girardi could be one big bulging vein, wearing out his players by treating every game as if it were week 15 of the NFL season.

Girardi did not have Torre's people skills, either, did not have his talent for working a room. That was never more evident than on a road trip in early September, a trip the Yankees started twelve and a half games out of first place. Girardi told his players they were not hustling and walked up to a table in the middle of the visitors' clubhouse in Detroit, a table most observers thought was about to get flipped. Instead of turning it over, Girardi ran around the table three or four times at a cartoonish speed.

When he finally stopped, a sweating, panting Girardi told a clubhouse full of stunned and silent Yankees, "That's how you hustle." One witness said the stunt was among the most embarrassing things he had seen a manager do. A second witness said, "Joe tried something, and it fell flat. It looked like he was losing it a bit."

The Yankees played better in the final weeks of 2008, but theirs was a garbage-time run. If one positive development came out of this lost season, it was this: Yankee Stadium would have a definitive goodbye, rather than one clouded by the uncertainties of a postseason series.

In the days leading up to the September 21 farewell game against the Baltimore Orioles, Jeter told Zillo he would indeed speak to the crowd. "No one would've made Derek do it," the PR man said. "But he had to do it. He had to hold the microphone that night and say some-thing to the crowd."

The Saturday before the big Sunday night, Jeter was nailed by a pitch on the left hand. He said he would play in the final Stadium game even if the hand was broken (it wasn't), reasoning he could always try to work out a walk. "It's kind of selfish to say it," Jeter said, "but at least for one day I can try and be selfish."

He entertained Reggie Jackson in his apartment Saturday night, and Mr. October and Mr. November shared their favorite ballpark memories. Sunday morning, Jeter lost himself in televised highlights of the greatest Stadium moments, many of his own making.

On his drive into the Bronx, Jeter was hit hard by the reality that this would be it, his last pilgrimage to a baseball landmark being sac-rificed at the altar of greed. Jeter had played more than a thousand games at the Stadium. He adored the old place, and truth be told, he did not see the need for a new place across the street. He did not see why the House That Ruth Built had to be replaced by the House That Ruthless Men Built.

Jeter loved taking his bat to the weight room door and banging it hard for good luck, while scaring everyone inside half to death. Jeter loved the walk from the clubhouse through the tunnel to the dugout, loved reaching up to touch the sign carrying the Joe DiMaggio quote, "I want to thank the Good Lord for making me a Yankee."

Just as the old ballpark had been magic to his grandmother, the ballpark renovated in the mid-seventies was magic to Jeter. "Playing at Yankee Stadium," he said, "it's sort of like performing on Broadway.

"It seems like every time you play at Yankee Stadium, the lights are a little bit stronger here. It seems like you're just performing on stage. I've always dreamt of doing it. I didn't know what to expect. It's above and beyond anything I've ever dreamt of. You just don't realize how special this place is."

No matter how many hundreds of millions of dollars were being poured into the new place, "I still can't picture being over there," Jeter said.

It was hard for him to believe there would be no October goodbye for his beloved Stadium, no postseason baseball for the first time in his Yankee life.

"It's like when you were a little kid and your parents don't let you go outside and play," Jeter said, "and you've got to sit at the window and watch because you got grounded."

Only in the Stadium's final hours, the captain was under one strict order from his parents: enjoy the ride. Charles and Dot Jeter told their son that he should step back, look around, soak it all in. They wanted to be sure Derek celebrated his record for hits at the eighty-five-year-old Stadium (he passed Lou Gehrig on September 16 with number 1,270), and celebrate it Derek did.

"Records are made to be broken," he said, "but this one at least will never be broken."

The Yankees put on a hell of a show for the September 21 night game, making it another Old-Timers' Day. Yogi Berra was behind the plate. Don Larsen, David Cone, and David Wells — the only three Yankees to pitch perfect games — were on the mound. Phil Rizzuto's widow, Cora, joined Jeter at short, and Mickey Mantle's son, David, and Bernie Williams ended up in center, not far from Roger Maris's son, Randy, who stood with Reggie Jackson and Paul O'Neill in right. Babe Ruth's daughter, Julia Ruth Stevens, would throw out the ceremonial first pitch hours after the fans were let in early and allowed onto the warning track and into Monument Park.

Jeter was the last Yankee in the clubhouse. "OK, Jeet, time to get out there," Zillo told him.

The shortstop rose from his locker and jogged out the door and down the ramp. He reached up to touch the DiMaggio sign for the last time on this side of the street and received the final honor awarded in the Stadium, a Waterford Crystal bat for breaking Gehrig's record.

Every significant Yankee figure had a place on the field or on the video board, everyone except the not-so-dearly-departed Joe Torre and the disgraced ace of the Mitchell Report, Roger Clemens. The Yankees proceeded to beat the Orioles, 7–3, with Andy Pettitte claiming the victory and Mariano Rivera securing the final three outs. Derek Jeter was pulled off the field with two down in the ninth, replaced by Wilson Betemit so he could bask in one last standing ovation.

The sound of affection was deafening. Jeter came out of the dugout for a curtain call, too, and soon enough he was back on the field, in a scrum, with a microphone in his hand. Police in riot gear surrounded the scene, and some officers were on horseback in the outfield grass.

Excuse me, excuse me, Jeter said into the microphone, and the crowd turned still. "I was always scared to death talking in front of people," Jeter would say of this moment. It was too late to turn back now.

The captain was standing near the base of the mound, with rows of teammates standing at attention behind him. Flashbulbs exploded throughout the hushed Stadium crowd. The encroaching photographers in front of Jeter snapped away and threw flickering light across the captain's face.

His speech would last ninety-nine seconds, pauses and all, and it went like this:

For all of us up here, it's a huge honor to put this uniform on every day and come out here and play. [Pause for cheers; Jeter tugs on the bill of his cap.] And every member of this organization, past and present, has been calling this place home for eighty-five years.

There's a lot of tradition, a lot of history, and a lot of memories. Now the great thing about memories is you're able to pass it along from generation to generation. And although things are going to change next year — we're going to move across the street — there are a few things with the New York Yankees that never change. That's pride, it's tradition, and most of all, we have the greatest fans in the world.

And we are relying on you to take the memories from this Stadium, add them to the new memories that come at the new Yankee Stadium, and continue to pass them on from generation to generation. So on behalf of the entire organization we just want to take this moment to salute you, the greatest fans in the world.

With that, Jeter lifted his cap high off his head, pointed it toward the fans on the first-base side, then pointed it to all corners of the Stadium while his teammates did the same. The captain put an arm around Girardi, patted him on the back, and then led the Yankees on a slow victory lap that started on the third-base side and continued past a dozen cops on horseback.

As he walked toward the left-field corner, his teammates falling in behind him, Jeter extended his cap high toward the fans in the upper deck. The captain was reaching out over the barriers to touch the people.

His final night inside Yankee Stadium was also his finest.

Jason Riley checked his phone. It was Joe Girardi, calling out of the blue.

This was before the 2008 season, and Riley was the director of performance of the Athletes Compound, a training facility at Tampa's Saddlebrook Resort. He was the man who was going to make Derek Jeter reach all those ground balls Brian Cashman told the captain he needed to reach.

Cashman kept Girardi away from that Upper East Side dinner with Jeter, kept him away from a potential confrontation with the most important Yankee in his clubhouse. But the new manager had to involve himself at some point, so he called the trainer Cashman and Jeter's agent, Casey Close, agreed could do the job.

"Joe asked about the program and how it would be geared toward Derek," Riley said. "He only cared about Derek's defense and his mechanics; he didn't care about anything else. Joe wanted him to play defense better, and I told him I had the program to make that happen."

Cashman so wanted Jeter to go through the program, the Yankees told their shortstop they would pay for it. Riley did not come cheap, either.

Jeter first showed up at the trainer's facility the week before Christmas 2007 and asked, "What do you have for me? . . . How is this going to work?" Riley walked him through his program of speed and agility drills and worked out the shortstop from early January through spring training, conducting early-morning sessions before Jeter had to report to camp.

The captain had brought along his longtime personal trainer and friend, Rafael Oquendo, for the first few weeks. "And then one week Rafy didn't show up," Riley said. "I said, 'Where's Rafy?' and Derek said, 'Rafy doesn't need to come anymore.'"

Jeter had replaced Oquendo with Riley. "Just making adjustments," the shortstop said. As always, Jeter moved to downplay the significance of those adjustments.

"I think any time you go through a season," he said, "you're going to have some issue that you have to address in the off-season. You have a leg problem one year, you do something to help out your leg. You have an arm problem, you do something to help out your arm."

Only Jeter did not have a leg problem or an arm problem as much as he had a position problem. He wanted to remain at shortstop for as long as he possibly could, and if his range continued to diminish as dramatically as it had, he would end up in left field before he knew it.

Girardi had the requisite admiration for Jeter, his teammate on three championship teams. But Girardi did not have the same blind loyalty to Jeter that Torre had. If the new manager thought a different shortstop would better his chances of winning, earning some job security, and enjoying the kind of extended run Torre had enjoyed in the Bronx, a different shortstop would be in play.

"What we discussed with Casey [Close] and Joe," Riley said, "was the need to improve the length of Derek's career. If he's going to get injured and slow down, there won't be many years ahead of him where he can play at the level he wants to play. Maybe he can be a DH, but not a shortstop.

"We needed to improve Derek's performance and length of career, and to accomplish that through injury prevention. We had to keep him on the field, and ultimately that could help him get a contract extension."

Jeter did play better defense in 2008, and did improve his sabermetric scores (his Plus/Minus went from minus 34 to minus 12, and his Ultimate Zone Rating went from minus 17.9 to minus 0.3). But his body needed time to adjust to the new routine, and a quad injury limited the improvement in his range.

In the months leading up to the 2009 season, a healthier Jeter was throwing himself into the workouts as never before. Riley had worked with Ryan Howard, Ryan Zimmerman, and Joey Votto on the baseball side, and Maria Sharapova on the tennis side, but Jeter's work ethic was off his charts.

"I've been in the industry for fifteen years," Riley said, "and I've never come across anyone like Derek."

At thirty-four, Jeter already knew he wanted to take his career into his forties. "Derek said it may not be eight to ten years at shortstop," Riley said, "but that he wanted to play that long."

So Riley focused on Jeter's agility and first-step quickness to the ball. The shortstop needed to become more flexible and explosive in his side-to-side movements, and toward that end he would show up before 7:00 a.m. to get in his extra work.

Riley found what most Yankee coaches, players, fans, and beat writers already knew: Jeter had the most difficulty when moving toward second base. "That was something Girardi really stated," Riley said. "Derek's defensive mechanics to his left were something Girardi really wanted to improve."

Like many right-handed players, Jeter had much better mobility and flexibility in his right ankle and hip than he did in his left ankle and hip. Riley had Jeter perform a wide array of drills to loosen up his left side.

The trainer wanted to reeducate Jeter's brain to improve its communication with his nerves and muscles. Riley had his student do a series of resistance drills, running at full speed with a belt around his waist and covering five to seven yards with twenty to thirty steps, recoaching that first step over and over so Jeter could create more force in the direction he wanted to go.

Riley had the shortstop doing shuffle drills from cone to cone, dropping him into a low defensive stance — as if he were guarding a point guard on the perimeter — and using resistance to build a more powerful lateral move.

"I think he hated doing those drills at first," Riley said, "because it's almost like reeducating a little kid. An accomplished athlete is like, 'I don't want to do this because it makes me look stupid.' And then suddenly, Derek was killing those drills.

"One day we're doing crossover movements for base-stealing mechanics, and at the end of the workout he was close to getting it right, but not quite. I told him to shut it down for the day, but he said, 'No, I can tell you're not happy about it.' We ended up doing another ten or fifteen sprints before I had to stop him for fear he'd injure himself."

No, Jeter was not giving up his position, his identity, without a fight. But just in case a new trainer with a new fitness program produced the old 2007 results in 2009, Jeter had put his fallback plan in place.

"Derek mentioned something to me about DH at the end of his career," Riley said. "If he realizes he's a detriment to the team playing at a certain level, he would take that role as DH. He'll do it to help the team out."

Derek Jeter's buddy R. D. Long posted a blog dated September 19, 2008, under the headline "A-Rod Represents the Collapse of an Empire."

Of course, back in 2004, Long was the man who told Jeter he would not win a title with Rodriguez as a teammate, and that he should try to find a way to get rid of him. In the 2008 blog Long stated that Rodriguez's presence had sent the great Yankee franchise downhill.

"If anyone thinks this amuses the Captain, Derek Jeter," Long wrote, "you couldn't be more wrong. Derek has the unenviable task of watching Alex chase the HR record by piling up meaningless HRs that tend to help only his stats, not the win column for New York. . . . These sentiments have been felt from the day Jeter presented him with that so unlucky #13 [at Rodriguez's introductory news conference]. This has to represent one of the worst days of Jeter's career.

"It's hard to imagine Derek Jeter finishing his career with a bunch of meaningless baseball games while he approaches the 4,000-hit mark."

It would grow harder to imagine Derek Jeter finishing his career with a megastar teammate who had confessed to being a chemically enhanced fraud.

In February of 2009, Alex Rodriguez was outed as a steroid user by *Sports Illustrated*'s Selena Roberts, outed as a name on the list of 104 players who turned up positive in survey testing. Rodriguez had no choice but to address the report. After a dreadful attempt to come clean in an interview with ESPN's Peter Gammons, A-Rod agreed to take a mulligan in a February 17 press conference outside Tampa's George M. Steinbrenner Field, formerly Legends Field.

Rodriguez's personal life had taken some turbulent turns in 2008. His marriage ended in divorce after he reportedly had a love affair with none other than Madonna ("It was more of an infatuation," one Rodriguez friend maintained). Now A-Rod's professional life was unraveling at the same breakneck speed.

Fittingly, this circus was held under a tent, and it was attended by Joe Girardi and Brian Cashman, who sat with the man of dishonor, and by thirty of A-Rod's teammates and coaches, who were gathered off to the right. Mariano Rivera, Andy Pettitte, and Jorge Posada sat in the front row of that group with the grim-faced captain. Dressed in jeans and a hooded shirt, Jeter slumped in his chair and rested his clasped hands in his lap.

Rodriguez started by reading from a crumpled piece of paper, and he choked up and needed to pause for thirty-seven seconds when he reached the part of the script where he was to thank his teammates for their show of support.

The year before, Andy Pettitte had confessed to using human growth hormone to expedite his recovery from injury. But even if Pettitte was not telling the whole truth, people wanted to believe him. He was a neighborly, low-maintenance Yankee and a four-time champ.

Nobody wanted to believe A-Rod, and on that front the third baseman did not disappoint. Rodriguez's story was impossible to believe.

He said a cousin he would not identify injected him with a substance called "boli" that they obtained in the Dominican Republic. As Rodriguez was reported to have tested positive for the steroid Primobolan and testosterone, it was believed "boli" represented a street name for Primobolan.

But A-Rod claimed he was not sure what he took, or if it had any positive impact on his play, in general, and on his home-run total, in particular. The man with 553 homers and three MVP awards said he took this mystery potion over three years as a Texas Ranger without knowing if his mystery cousin knew how to administer it.

"It was really amateur hour," Rodriguez said.

A-Rod claimed the "boli" was always injected, never taken orally, and yet when Rodriguez admitted he realized he was doing something wrong, he used an oral visual ("I knew we weren't taking Tic Tacs") to make his point.

The news conference was broken up after thirty-two minutes, before Rodriguez could further embarrass himself. The slugger worth $305 million, including his tainted $30 million homer bonus, left the tent a shattered man.

"If this is Humpty Dumpty," Cashman said, "we've got to put him back together again and get him back up on the wall."

The general manager acknowledged that the news conference did not end anything, that Rodriguez would have to deal with the fallout for the balance of his career. A-Rod was not alone.

Jeter would have to deal with it, too, and he wanted to wait a day before addressing Rodriguez's not-so-venial sins. For a while, anyway, A-Rod had to go this one alone. The captain was smart enough to wait the twenty-four hours.

When he spoke with reporters on February 18, the captain also was smart enough to stay clear of the tent. Jeter was a baseball player, and a clean one. He would conduct his briefing in the dugout.

Jeter did not come to George M. Steinbrenner Field on this day to throw a figurative arm around A-Rod. Separation — or a greater degree of separation — was on the captain's agenda.

"One thing that's irritating and really upsets me a lot," Jeter told the gathered reporters, "is when you hear people say it was the Steroid Era and that everybody is doing it, and that's not true. Everybody wasn't doing it."

Jeter had his theme for the day, and he wasn't veering off message. The third baseman was a cheater ("I think he cheated himself," Jeter said), and the shortstop was not.

"I never took performance enhancers," Jeter said, "and I never took steroids. . . . I understand a lot of big names are coming out. But that's not everybody. . . . That's the thing that's most upsetting to me."

The captain said he was disappointed in Rodriguez, and in the parade of former teammates who showed up in the Mitchell Report. "It really has given the game a bad name," he said.

Only Jeter was not as disappointed in the steroid cheats as he was in the notion that all players were presumed guilty by association, a fact that raised a tough question for the captain to answer:

Why didn't you use your considerable clout and unmatched public platform to pressure the Players Association into accepting a tougher drug-testing plan?

Jeter had long been the living symbol of the clean ballplayer, the one superstar who would have been voted by the fans and his peers as the least likely major leaguer to end up on the wrong side of a steroid bust. Whenever asked, the shortstop explained that his father was a drug and alcohol abuse counselor who taught his children to stay clear of illegal substances.

"Me and my sister were always educated on that," Jeter said, "pretty much all the time growing up."

Asked if he was ever tempted, even a little bit, to dabble in performance-enhancing drugs to keep up with the Joneses (and the McGwires and the Bondses), Jeter said, "No."

"Why?" came the follow-up.

"It's a little different when your dad is a drug and alcohol abuse counselor, you know what I'm saying?" he answered. "I'm not saying I'm any better than anybody else. I've just been educated on that, and there are side effects, too. Eventually, I think you're making a deal with the devil."

So Jeter refused to make a Faustian deal for the sake of another ten to fifteen homers a year. He believed in working on his body and game the old-fashioned way, and besides, he was never obsessed with individual numbers. Jeter realized early in his career he would never be a big home-run hitter, so why risk destroying his good name and legacy to inflate a stat that would not define him anyway?

But Jeter also remained silent when the union resisted drug testing at every performance-enhancing turn, in effect doing more to protect its dirty members than its clean ones.

"You never know what somebody's doing," Jeter would argue. "You can't sit here and speculate and guess, because I think it's unfair to them. So it wasn't like I sat down and said, 'I think this guy's doing this or that guy's doing that.' I've always given people the benefit of the doubt."

Only the Mitchell Report and the BALCO case made it painfully clear the Yankee clubhouse was a place where the benefit of the doubt went to die. Asked if it would have been hard for a Yankee to spend season after season in that clubhouse without suspecting steroid use among some teammates, Mike Mussina said, "I would have to say yes."

Given Jeter's intelligence and awareness, he had to have strong suspicions teammates were not just doing their pushups and taking their Flintstone vitamins to remain at an elite competitive level. Jeter also had to know the entire sport was rotting at its core, its integrity compromised in murky underground labs.

Baseball had long been reduced to a battle of pharmacology, with one simple rule of engagement: it's your back-room chemist against mine. Confronted by this reality, Jeter declined to take a public stand even though his voice would have resonated like no other in the game.

This was a four-time champion, an iconic Yankee, a Madison Avenue heavyweight, and an athlete with enough mass appeal to host *Saturday Night Live*. Yes, before the feds went after BALCO, before Congress started swinging its heavy lumber, and before the players flunked their survey testing, Jeter would have had a better chance of moving an immovable union than Bud Selig had.

But the shortstop was not any more eager to go after the cheats than he was to tell Yankee fans to stop booing A-Rod. "Who am I to assume somebody's doing something?" Jeter would maintain. "How would you know?

"I mean, how am I supposed to know? Do you think if somebody's doing something they're going to come tell me? I was never at a meeting, like a big group or a Players Association meeting. . . . I don't ever make assumptions on what somebody's doing or not doing."

Jeter no longer had to worry about assumption when it came to Alex Rodriguez. A-Rod admitted he had crossed over to the dark side, and it looked like the third baseman and shortstop were a million miles apart.

Jeter had to be thinking his buddy R. D. Long had been right after all: he would never win a World Series title with Rodriguez as a teammate.

Only Long had a little surprise for the captain in February of 2009, one Jeter welcomed. Long said he believed A-Rod's steroids admission would deflate the slugger's aura and allow Jeter's to have a greater positive impact on the club.

"So for the first time since A-Rod arrived," Long said, "I changed the way I was looking at it.

"I told Derek, 'You've got another ring coming, buddy.'"

As the 2009 season unfolded, the Yankees were defined by the new Stadium, the new recruits, the new Joe Girardi, the new Alex Rodriguez, and the old Derek Jeter.

The Stadium was a $1.5 billion monstrosity, the Steinbrenners' answer to the Mall of America. A cavernous clubhouse was only the gateway to a labyrinth of fitness rooms, rehab rooms, meal rooms, and other restricted hideaways to allow the players to flee the advancing New York news media.

Tickets were wildly overpriced, running up to $2,500 a pop, giving the new place too much of a wine-and-cheese personality and not enough of the beer-and-pretzel intensity that made the old Stadium a forbidding house to the visiting side. Pop-ups kept riding some mystery jet stream over the outfield wall in right and right center, turning the new Stadium into a homer-happy Little League field and mocking the fact that its dimensions were identical to those of its predecessor.

Soon enough the ticket prices were reduced, the home-run rates were tempered, and the public's focus was returned to the Yankees' improved product on the field. Brian Cashman had spent $423.5 million of the Steinbrenners' money on three free agents — CC Sabathia, A. J. Burnett, and Mark Teixeira — and traded for free-spirited right fielder Nick Swisher, moves the GM made to ensure the Yanks never again missed the postseason under his watch.

As a legitimate ace, Sabathia was the key to the off-season plan. He had concerns about the Yankees that extended beyond the fact that they played 3,000 miles away from his California home.

"CC's main concern was our clubhouse, and how people got along," Cashman said. "We had a reputation for not being together. We had a reputation of fighting each other, and that was a big concern there.

"I told him the truth. 'Yeah, we are broken. One reason we're committing [$161 million] to you is you're a team builder. We need somebody to bring us all together.'"

Sabathia knew all about the Jeter–A-Rod divide, so Cashman had to throw more than money at the extra-large lefty with the gregarious personality and easy smile. He took a top-secret flight to Sabathia's home and told him he could be the grand marshal of the Thanksgiving Day parade, told him about the eclectic nature of the tristate area, told him he could own the town in a New York minute.

"I had to be John Calipari," Cashman said. He had to get this blue-chip recruit to sign the Yankees' letter of intent.

"CC's like Santa Claus," the GM said. "He lights up an entire room."

Cashman thought his broken team needed that positive life force. And as much as Sabathia's generosity of spirit, and Swisher's nonstop goofiness, and Burnett's pie-in-the-face celebrations altered the dynamics of the clubhouse, the dramatic changes made by the incumbent manager and third baseman were no less important.

Girardi was pressed by Cashman and the PR man, Jason Zillo, to lighten up. The GM handed Girardi a magazine profile on Giants coach Tom Coughlin, who had softened the jagged edges of his personality on the way to his epic Super Bowl upset over Bill Belichick's unbeaten Patriots. "You need to read this," said Cashman, a former roommate of Coughlin's son.

Girardi read it, thought about it, then thought about it some more. On the eve of training camp, he invited Zillo into his office, closed the door, and showed the PR man a yellow legal pad full of notes to himself, notes on how he wanted to change. They spoke for ninety minutes before the meeting broke up and Zillo called Cashman.

"There's been a breakthrough," the PR man reported.

Girardi canceled a spring training practice for a billiards tournament, just as Coughlin had canceled a training camp practice for a bowling outing. The manager eased the disconnect with his players and was not as quick to deceive the press. His bosses believed his user-friendly style was showing up in the box score.

They felt the same way about Alex Rodriguez's decision to reinvent himself one more time. A-Rod was not just humiliated by his own steroid confessions; he was a physical wreck going into his March surgery to repair a torn labrum in his right hip. He feared his career might be over, or at least permanently impaired.

"I'd hit rock bottom," A-Rod would say.

Around the same time *Details* magazine published a piece on Rodriguez that included a photo showing A-Rod in a muscle shirt, kissing his own reflection in the mirror. So after Rodriguez rehabbed from surgery, and before he rejoined the team in early May, A-Rod would be dragged to a Tampa diner, Mom's Place, by two people close to him — Zillo and longtime friend Gui Socarras.

Rodriguez had surrounded himself with an ever-growing circle of advisers and crisis counselors, including Madonna's manager, Guy Oseary, John McCain's strategist, Ben Porritt, PR man Richard Rubenstein, and, of course, Scott Boras. But none of these suits had the nerve to piece together an intervention quite like this: Zillo and Socarras shouted down A-Rod over ninety minutes, ordering him to shed his self-serving skin for keeps.

"I'm glad I had two friends that were very honest with me," Rodriguez said of the ambush.

Two days after this breakfast meeting, A-Rod hit the first postsurgical pitch he saw for a three-run homer in Baltimore. Of greater consequence, he maintained a relatively humble demeanor over the course of the season and, in his words, "divorced myself from any personal achievements."

Rodriguez would say he had spent more time with his teammates off the field — at dinners and backyard barbecues — than he had in his first five Yankee years combined. Although A-Rod did not say so publicly, it was obvious Derek Jeter had embraced him as never before.

For one, Jeter had given up trying to understand why A-Rod could not be more like him. For two, Jeter realized an emasculated A-Rod was someone worth giving another shot.

The captain saw A-Rod was making a legitimate attempt to curb his high-maintenance ways. More often than in the past, Jeter was seen engaging Rodriguez in small talk in the clubhouse, in the dugout, around the batting cage. They acted less like business partners with competing agendas and more like teammates with a common goal.

"Alex really believes that for us to win a championship, he needs to have a good working relationship with Derek, and vice versa," one team official said. "I think they have it now. I think they've found enough common ground where Derek can laugh off some of the stuff about Alex in the newspapers.

"I think it took Derek a long time to get that point, where it would frustrate him so much for so long. Derek used to be like, 'Why can't you just get this shit right? It's easy. Don't say anything. Say what I say, which is nothing.' Now Derek's able to slough it off rather than re-create Alex into somebody who's always going to say and do the right things."

Yes, it was a monumental struggle for Jeter to understand Rodriguez, the attention-starved boy abandoned by his dad. At thirty-five, Jeter was still very much his parents' son. He still sought their approval on a daily basis. He remained, in effect, afraid of his mother and father, or at least afraid of hurting them, which was one of many reasons he did not turn to steroids.

Just as they'd never imposed on their son's youth baseball and basketball coaches, Charles and Dot Jeter never so much as asked for permission to enter the Yankee clubhouse after a big victory. When the Yankees opened the 2004 season in Japan, *New York Post* beat writer George King stumbled upon Jeter's mother in a Tokyo convenience store searching for medicine for Charles's killer of a head cold.

"Why don't you just have the Yankees get you something?" King asked.

"We've never asked the Yankees for anything," Dot said, "and we never will."

Derek maintained the same approach. Clubhouse guys who were kept busy washing players' cars or filling their gas tanks or fetching their forgotten keys never received such requests from Jeter. "Derek's responsible enough to know when the needle's near empty, he's going to pull into a gas station," said Lou Cucuzza Jr., a visiting clubhouse manager who could not keep up with the requests from the David Ortizes and Zack Greinkes for autographed Jeter jerseys, requests the captain always granted.

"Alex is a great guy; he invites us to his house sometimes for family barbecues. . . . But he's different. He wants you to be more hands-on with him. He needs people to care for him a lot more than Derek."

Jeter was a giver, not a taker, and for much of his career A-Rod lived on the other end of the spectrum, lusting after perks, requesting his own cabana boy in the clubhouse.

Only this was the new Rodriguez, playing for the new Girardi, attending family parties with the new recruits, and winning games in the new Stadium. The Yankees were 13-15 when A-Rod sent that first pitch over the Camden Yards wall; they were 91-50 and up nine games in the division before everything new about the franchise cycled back to everything that was old.

Not an old Jeter, but the Jeter of old.

The NFL season was under way, and a pencil-necked shortstop was proving he was still the toughest athlete in New York. Jeter was in the midst of a stunning renaissance, looking as young and supple in his first year in the new Stadium as he had looked in the old place in '96.

Jeter was still Jeter, still the impeccably dressed Yankee who quietly sat in the back of the team plane wearing his headphones, watching his movies, largely ignoring the card games played by others. Still the responsible captain who was never seen in a hotel lobby looking disheveled, unshaven, or even remotely drunk or buzzed. Still the earnest ambassador who served as Captain America for Team USA in the World Baseball Classic.

But Jeter was playing the game with a new body, a new plan of attack. Jason Riley's training program had worked. Jeter had turned his glaring weakness — grounders to his left — into an actual strength, and he was enjoying one of the finest seasons of his career.

He was also giving Yankee Stadium crowds a fresh reason to celebrate him. Jeter was running down Lou Gehrig's franchise hits record of 2,721, the chase inspiring a love fest bigger than the feat itself. In fact, many sports fans were shocked to learn the Yankees of Ruth, Gehrig, DiMaggio, and Mantle never had a player who collected 3,000 career hits.

But this was the world's most famous ball team, Gehrig was bigger in death than he was in life, and Jeter was a dignified figure at a time when they came in short supply. The captain was perceived as so relentlessly team-oriented, so compatible with a franchise that did not put player names on the backs of their jerseys, Yankee fans were eager to seize upon any chance to salute him as an individual.

So they did just that on September 9, when Jeter ended an 0-for-12 stretch by dropping down a first-inning bunt for a base hit against Tampa Bay, by hitting a ground rule double in the fifth, and by ripping a hard grounder past a diving Chris Richards at first to tie Gehrig's record.

The home crowd exploded, and with the Rays holding a 2–0 lead, Jeter did not know whether to acknowledge the applause. He did not want to disrespect the visitors and defending American League champs, but the Rays took him off the hook, walking up to the dugout rail to clap along with the fans.

"[Jeter] carries himself in a manner that's worthy of passing Gehrig," Tampa Bay manager Joe Maddon said.

Twice Jeter doffed his helmet to the adoring masses. Truth was, he felt a greater connection with Gehrig than with the other Yankee titans of the past. Quiet and dignified, the Iron Horse was the anti-Ruth, just as he would have been the anti–A-Rod.

"One of the classiest people to ever play the game," Jeter called Gehrig.

Two nights later, a rainy September Friday, the Yankees staged a pregame ceremony to mark the eighth anniversary of the terrorist attacks that changed the world. The crowd of 46,771 honored the fallen, waited through an eighty-seven-minute rain delay, and then listened as Jeter walked to the plate with the elegant sound of Bob Sheppard booming over the public address system in his voice-of-God way.

At ninety-nine, Sheppard was no longer strong enough to work the Yankee games he had been working since 1951, but Jeter was not about to take a cut in the Bronx without that voice introducing him to the crowd. He asked Sheppard to record his voice so it could be played for the balance of the captain's career, and the P.A. announcer called that request one of the greatest compliments he had ever received.

So Sheppard shepherded him to the plate one more time. *Now batting for the Yankees, Numbah 2, Derek Jeter, Numbah 2.* The fans were standing and the camera lights were flashing until the mighty Casey struck out.

The captain went down on a curve ball from Baltimore's Chris Tillman before he ended the newspaper countdowns in the third inning, with puddles forming on the warning track and fans huddled under their wet ponchos. Jeter cut loose his classic inside-out swing on Tillman's 2-0 fastball and laced it past first base, past a diving Luke Scott, and into a deep corner of Yankee lore. The hit was nearly a carbon copy of the one that had tied Gehrig's record two nights earlier, nearly a carbon copy of a thousand other singles (or so it seemed) in Jeter's career.

The shortstop rounded first base, extended his arms wide, and clapped his hands together. It was 9:23 p.m., and Derek Sanderson Jeter stood as the most prolific Yankee hitter of them all.

Jeter approached the first-base coach, Mick Kelleher, and rested an arm on top of his head. The Yanks came pouring out of the dugout, led by Alex Rodriguez, and one by one they hugged their captain as the crowd roared its approval. Jeter raised his helmet high, waved it to all corners of the Stadium, and pointed and pumped his left fist toward his family's suite above the on-deck circle, where his parents, sister, and his serious girlfriend, actress Minka Kelly, had lifted their arms to the sky.

Wearing a military cap with the interlocking "NY," Kelly grabbed the pendant around her neck and looked up adoringly at the woman some close to Jeter expected to be her mother-in-law. Nick Swisher, up next, dug into the batter's box, but the fans kept chanting Jeter's name, forcing him to wave that helmet one more time.

Once again, Charles and Dot had ordered their son to enjoy this moment. "It's still hard to believe," Derek would say. "Being a Yankee fan, this is something I never imagined. Your dream is always to play for the team, and once you get there, you just want to stay and try to be consistent. This wasn't a part of it. This whole experience has been overwhelming."

Jeter was surprised by the sight of his teammates coming over the dugout railing, and he was touched by the number of fans who had waited out the rain. "They're just as much a part of this as I am," the captain said.

George Steinbrenner would call his shortstop during a second rain delay, and the failing Boss would release a statement through his publicist that began like this: "For those who say today's game can't produce legendary players, I have two words: Derek Jeter."

In a joint news conference called as the game was about to resume with a horde of second-stringers, A-Rod, Andy Pettitte, and Jorge Posada delivered an appreciation of Jeter past and present. Pettitte and Posada talked about the frail and terrified teenager they saw in Greensboro, North Carolina, and how that wisp of a kid grew into a man.

Rodriguez recalled his first meeting with the shortstop at that Michigan-Miami baseball game in '92 and thinking Jeter "just had this special feeling, that special look in his eye."

All these years later, A-Rod said, that special feeling and look could not be explained by any box score. "Fifty years from now," he said, "people are going to look at the back of [Jeter's] baseball card and see some crazy number of hits, maybe in the mid-3,000s or maybe even 4,000. But it's not going to capture half the story.

"For me, playing next to him I've learned so much. He's motivated me and inspired me. . . . Derek is the ultimate grinder. He's the ulti-

mate winner. . . . I don't think he's ever played any better than he's playing right now. . . . He's like a machine. He's like a robot."

Only Jeter was human enough to understand that his historic baseball achievement, at least on this night in this town, cried out for proper
perspective. He spoke of his team's role as goodwill ambassadors and
as entertainers providing a necessary sanctuary for a devastated city
after the 9/11 attacks.

On the eighth anniversary, he spoke of giving New Yorkers another
temporary reprieve. "This is a day everyone will continue to remember
forever in our country," Jeter said, "and I'm sure people's thoughts were
elsewhere. But at least for a little while, they had a chance to cheer
today."

Jeter gave them that gift, a gift that promised to keep on giving. At
thirty-five, the captain was ahead of the pace set by Pete Rose, who
retired at forty-five as the all-time career hits leader with 4,256. Jeter
scoffed at the notion that he could break that record ("Come on, man,
you're talking about another 1,500 hits") or that he ever sat around
thinking about it.

But one Jeter friend said the shortstop had brought up Rose in conversation and had asked about where the Hit King stood at Jeter's age.
The captain did acknowledge he wanted to play into his forties, and as
he was piecing together his fourth 200-hit season in his last five years,
and as he was on track to play in at least 148 games for the thirteenth
time in fourteen seasons, it appeared he could go on forever dumping
singles into right field.

It also appeared he could make that jump throw from the hole and
reach hard grounders up the middle for who knew how long. Jason Riley's regimen was largely responsible for Jeter's defensive rebirth, and
Kelleher's film work did not hurt, either.

The former big league infielder spent his off-season studying every
2008 grounder that went Jeter's way and found the captain was playing too shallow and setting his feet too late. Jeter realized he could
reach more balls by playing deeper, and by moving into a ready position earlier in a pitcher's delivery.

But this adjustment was not only about positioning. "Derek needed
somebody in his corner," Kelleher said. "He needed somebody to say,
'Hey, you can be better.'"

As a result, Jeter's sabermetric scores finally lined up with his standing among Yankee fans. For the first time, Jeter scored a positive number in John Dewan's Plus/Minus system, checking in at a plus 5 two years after his ghastly minus 34. The shortstop also nailed a positive Ultimate Zone Rating; according to FanGraphs.com, he scored a plus 6.4 two years after a minus 17.9.

"Jeter is Benjamin Button," said Oakland A's general manager Billy Beane, a sabermetric scholar whose charts had been most unkind to the shortstop in previous years. But late in the 2009 season, Beane looked down at those same charts and saw Jeter ranked as the third-best defensive shortstop in all of baseball.

"My God, it's amazing," Beane said. "My whole front-office career I've been waiting for Jeter to slow down, and this year he's as good as ever. His grace and elegance in everything he does, and his ability to be the same exact guy today that he was the day he stepped into the big leagues, is just incredible.

"It's hard to have a negative thought about the guy even as you are competing against him. . . . If you're in Fenway and [David] Ortiz hits a home run, as a GM you're going, 'Fuckin' Ortiz,' even though Ortiz isn't a guy you dislike. You would never say that word in front of Jeter's name. You can't deface it. You have the term 'Damn Yankees,' but there's never a 'Damn Jeter.'"

Beane was married to his metrics, if only because they helped him build a consistent contender on an absurdly small budget and helped him become the breakout star of *Moneyball*.

Only no matter how much he worshiped at the metric altar, Beane said, "One guy I'll never criticize if the metrics don't match up with the player is Derek Jeter. It's like someone saying they don't like the mole on Cindy Crawford's face. . . . As someone who believes in metrics, I'm here to give you the good news: I still think Jeter is an incredible player."

Beane was hardly alone. All over baseball, big-time talents — Troy Tulowitzki, Hanley Ramirez, and B. J. Upton among them — were wearing number 2 because Jeter wore number 2. The Yankee captain had established a living legacy — the kids who grew up admiring him now had their own legions of admirers.

And just as Jeter spoke of one day running a charitable foundation like Dave Winfield's, young players spoke hopefully of one day making the kind of difference Jeter had made with his Turn 2 Foundation.

Much the way the Yankees represented the Steinbrenner family business, Turn 2 was the Jeter family business. The shortstop was the founder, his father the vice chairman, his sister the president, and his mother the treasurer. Born over that pizza in a Detroit hotel room during Jeter's rookie year, Turn 2 had given more than $11 million to the cause of keeping kids away from alcohol and drugs, focusing its efforts in the Kalamazoo area, Tampa, and New York.

Jeter was touched by the letters he had received from parents thanking him for the support his foundation had given their children through troubled times. He established a program designed to compel high school students to set an example of community service, academic achievement, and social activism. The shortstop called it Jeter's Leaders, and according to his website, DerekJeter.com, he built it around what he called "10 pillars of leadership," which included morality, communication, being trustworthy, and leading by example.

Of course, Jeter was the ultimate lead-by-example captain, his mere presence inspiring his teammates to play at a higher level. The young pitcher Phil Hughes called Jeter "the pillar we all lean on" and spoke of visits the captain would make to the mound to calm his hyperactive mind.

"He'll call time and give you a couple of words of encouragement," Hughes said, "just to let you catch your breath. You don't see that from a lot of guys. Guys on defense are worried about their next at-bat, or they're waiting for the third out, but [Jeter's] going to do everything he can to help you win.

"When you're a young pitcher you're out there and it's like being a kid afraid of the dark. To have Derek Jeter there, it's like when you're that scared kid and your mom is there and it's, 'OK, things are better now.'"

Hughes described Jeter as "a larger-than-life figure" who was nonetheless "very approachable, a down-to-earth guy." As he grew older, Jeter took on more of a mentoring role with the younger Yankees.

On the night he tied Gehrig's hits record, Jeter marched to the mound in the first inning to order Joba Chamberlain to straighten up. Chamberlain had already surrendered two runs and had two men on and only one man out when the shortstop had seen enough.

"He doesn't really give too many like, 'I'm-getting-in-your-face' talks," Chamberlain said. This was one of them. Jeter sternly told the reliever to calm down and start making the pitches that had made him successful.

Joba struck out the next two batters and, while confined to an innings limit, retired the last eight Rays he faced.

Jeter did not only show tough love to the young Yanks. He remained willing to confront a veteran if the situation warranted it, even if that situation involved his closest friend on the team.

In 2008, an injured Jorge Posada had failed to show up for a rehab session one day after he traveled to Tampa with the Yanks' blessing. Posada was supposed to return the following day for a pregame session with trainer Gene Monahan, only he did not make it back in time.

Given that he had recently signed Posada to a four-year, $52.4 million deal, Brian Cashman was furious. When Jeter saw the GM in an agitated state and asked what was wrong, Cashman told him about Posada's absence. The next day, a Yankee employee who had witnessed Cashman's outburst and who later saw Jeter in the clubhouse told the GM, "Hey, I just want you to know that Derek jumped Posada's ass after you left."

In 2009, Jeter told a friend that he had spoken with Nick Swisher about taming his wild faux-hawk hairstyle; the captain apparently did not believe the hair was very Yankee-like. Asked about approaching Swisher, Jeter responded to a reporter, "Who told you that?" before declining comment. Far more often than not, with Yankees new and old, Jeter was a leader who believed in positive — if quiet — reinforcement.

On arrival in the Bronx, A. J. Burnett texted Jeter that he would be honored to have the captain playing behind him. "No," Jeter texted back, "it will be an honor to play behind you."

As it turned out, the honor belonged to every Yankee who watched Jeter's remarkable 2009 unfold. The captain elevated his traditional stats along with his sabermetric scores, finishing with a .334 batting average, a .406 on-base percentage, and more steals (30) than he had in 2007 and 2008 combined as his 103-59 Yanks won the AL East by eight games.

Jeter nailed down his eleventh division title and thirteenth postseason appearance in fourteen years as a full-time shortstop, and he did it by absorbing Cashman's criticism over dinner after the 2007 season and by using it to create a more athletic version of his aging self.

Some longtime Jeter teammates, friends, and observers were stunned he admitted to changing his fitness regimen in an attempt to improve his defense — conceding weaknesses, of course, never came easily to the captain.

One such teammate recalled being shocked years earlier when Jeter started doing quickness and lateral movement drills before pregame stretching, sometimes with fellow Yankees and fans watching. "I always thought he'd do that in the weight room or someplace nobody would see it," the teammate said. "He'd get out that ladder and step between the ropes, or he'd have on resistance bands around his ankles going side to side, and knowing his personality a few of us couldn't believe the first time he did that in full view."

In the end, if Jeter was strong enough to overcome his flaws, physical and otherwise, he still had failed for eight consecutive seasons to accomplish his one and only goal. He was tired of hearing about the parity in baseball created by revenue sharing. He was tired of hearing about smarter opponents, tired of hearing about the Red Sox and their two championships — on Jeter's watch — after an eighty-six-year drought.

The captain was running low on patience and time. He needed to win a World Series title, and who woulda thunkit:

He finally had the partnership with Alex Rodriguez to make it happen.

They sat at the same table inside a Minneapolis hotel ballroom, two happy couples celebrating a return to the American League Championship Series: Derek Jeter and actress Minka Kelly, Alex Rodriguez and actress Kate Hudson. The Yankees had swept Minnesota in their best-of-five Division Series, and the left side of their infield was the principal reason why.

Jeter batted .400 with an on-base percentage of .538; A-Rod batted .455 with an on-base percentage of .500. The shortstop hit a big home run in Game 1; the third baseman hit a bigger home run in Game 2, a two-run shot off closer Joe Nathan in the ninth that ultimately allowed Mark Teixeira to win it with his own homer in the eleventh.

In the seventh inning of Game 3, with the Twins leading 1–0 and with excommunicated ex-Yankee Carl Pavano back from the dead, Rodriguez homered off his former teammate before Jorge Posada did the same, sending the Yanks back to their hotel for a merry little feast.

Though the *Post*'s Page Six had reported Kelly and Hudson were picking up where Jeter and A-Rod left off — "Kate Hudson Feels Minka Kelly Brushback," read the headline — witnesses saw the two couples exchanging easy banter and generally enjoying each other's company.

It was just the four of them at a table for about an hour. "There were tables everywhere, a lot of different groups to sit with," said one witness. "So they literally chose to sit with each other."

One friend of Rodriguez's was glad he had moved on from Madonna and settled in with Hudson, whom the friend described as grounded enough to make for an ideal A-Rod partner for the long term. On the Minka front, a friend of Jeter's said the shortstop appeared more serious about the *Friday Night Lights* star than he'd been about past actresses, singers, and starlets.

But the relationship Yankee officials, players, coaches, and fans cared about most was the rapidly improving one between Jeter and Rodriguez, who did their Jordan and Pippen thing in the Twins series — Jeter scored four runs, and A-Rod drove him home for three of those four.

Rodriguez was a dynamic force against the Twins, good for six RBI, finally distancing himself from the horrific postseason numbers that had dogged him since the back half of the 2004 ALCS. With his own eyes, Jeter could see the value of a liberated Rodriguez.

"I've had conversations with Derek about this," said Buck Showalter, who managed Jeter briefly in 1995 before managing Rodriguez in Texas in 2003. "Derek understands Alex's positives and negatives. He loves the statistical return he gets from Alex, and he's come to understand the way Alex is."

This is what the rest of baseball feared, the coming together of the most talented player, Rodriguez, and the most resourceful player, Jeter.

A-Rod and Jeter were so different as people and athletes, common ground was harder to find than a Bucky Dent fan in Boston. Their contrasting experiences at the four-hour-and-fifty-minute 2008 All-Star Game at the old Yankee Stadium had said it all. Long after he was removed from the game, Jeter hung on the dugout railing through all fifteen innings, all the way until the American League won at 1:38 a.m.

Rodriguez? A day after he spoke of his love for the Stadium and all things pinstriped, A-Rod played four innings, showered, dressed, and bolted the premises to start his night on the town, leaving Jeter to see everyone to the door hours later.

Jeter and Rodriguez were the odd couple in every way. Even their pregame approaches to hitting were different; Jeter was not as maniacal or lathered up as Rodriguez in his preparation. The captain took about thirty to thirty-five swings before batting practice, another thirty to thirty-five during BP, and then another fifteen before the game. The shortstop was more of a feel hitter, someone who wanted to see his stride on video before making an adjustment.

"Derek's not one of those guys who does multiple tee drills or a net drill like Alex," said Yankees hitting coach Kevin Long. "Alex does a lot of very precise, detailed drills to help his swing, and Derek's not nearly as — I don't want to say anal, but he doesn't get as sophisticated with it."

Nothing Jeter did mirrored what Rodriguez did, and the rest of baseball only hoped their differences in style, skill, and personality would widen the divide between them, until the Yanks finally threw up their hands, swallowed a huge portion of A-Rod's contract, and traded him to another owner with stars in his eyes.

But when the Yankees clinched the AL East title, the papers ran photos no enemy of the Yankee state ever wanted to see.

These were not pictures of Rodriguez grabbing a reluctant Jeter the way the Babe grabbed a reluctant Gehrig. The photos captured a beaming Jeter lifting A-Rod's cap off his head with his left hand and pouring a bottle of bubbly over A-Rod's bowed scalp with his right.

At last, the captain had baptized Rodriguez a Yankee, and even those old October haunts, the Angels, were sweating the potential fallout. As it turned out, their fears were well founded.

The first run of the ALCS was scored by Jeter, who had singled before Rodriguez drove him home with a sacrifice fly. The captain added another RBI single, CC Sabathia outpitched John Lackey, and in Bronx temperatures unfit for a polar bear the Yankees took Game 1 from the warm-blooded Californians, 4–1.

The following night, again in Lambeau-like weather, Jeter hit a big homer; Rodriguez again hit a bigger one on an 0-2 pitch from Brian Fuentes to lead off the eleventh inning, Angels up a run; and the Yanks would win it in the thirteenth when Maicer Izturis made a wild throw to second base.

If the ending of this brutal, five-hour-and-ten-minute marathon was stunning, it was fitting at the same time. The Angels were supposed to be the most fundamentally sound team in the sport, with the smartest manager, Mike Scioscia, and yet they spent the first two games of the ALCS making the kinds of forced and unforced errors the top-heavy Yanks had always made against them.

Maybe their thinking caps were frozen under their ski masks and hoods. In the first inning of Game 1, Chone Figgins and Erick Aybar set the alarming tone by staring at each other as a pop-up fell untouched to the earth, allowing the Yankees another run and a 2–0 lead. In the thirteenth inning of Game 2, Figgins would fumble the remains of Izturis's errant throw as Jerry Hairston Jr. raced home and into a mob of Yankee teammates who knocked him down.

The Angels swore the weather did not affect them, but they did not look any more comfortable in the Bronx than Tom Landry's Cowboys looked in the Ice Bowl.

Scioscia's team never seemed right in this series and even extended its bungling ways to the base paths. The Angels did survive Jeter's lead-off homer and A-Rod's fourth-inning blast to win Game 3 in eleven innings, and they did barely overcome A-Rod's Game 4 pounding to win a topsy-turvy Game 5 and send the series back to New York.

But these were not the 2002 or 2005 Angels. Of greater consequence, these were not the 2002 or 2005 Yankees.

Game 6 was an efficient Pettitte-to-Joba-to-Mariano execution, and when the clock struck midnight, the great Rivera secured the last of his six outs, a strikeout of Gary Matthews Jr. that sent Jeter and Mark Teixeira running into Rodriguez's arms to celebrate A-Rod's first trip to the World Series.

"I couldn't be more excited," the slugger would say amid another champagne bath he was sharing with Jeter. "I feel like a ten-year-old kid."

Four years after he said he had played like a dog against the Angels, Rodriguez batted .429 with a .567 on-base percentage and 3 homers and 6 RBI. Jeter did not quite keep up with A-Rod, but he could smile over the first of his two homers in the series, the one that gave him 19 in his postseason career, or one more than Mickey Mantle or Reggie Jackson hit in theirs.

Of course, Mantle collected his 18 in 65 postseason games and Jackson collected his 18 in 77. Jeter would enter his first World Series since 2003 with 20 homers in 132 postseason games, trailing only Manny Ramirez (29) and Bernie Williams (22).

One by one, the singles hitter with the inside-out swing was taking down the mightiest of October sluggers. Working with the benefit of extra playoff rounds, Jeter would face the defending champion Philadelphia Phillies with more postseason hits (164), runs (94), and games played than any other man dead or alive.

Not that he cared about writing another edition of his record book; Jeter just wanted to end his World Series drought. And when someone asked Jeter what he would have said in 2000 if warned he would still have four trophies in 2009, the captain didn't blink.

"DAMN!" he said. "That's exactly what I would've said."

On the night of November 4, 2009, the Yankees stood twenty-seven outs away from their twenty-seventh championship, and their first in the new Stadium. The Steinbrenners had spent more than $1.6 billion in wages on this pursuit since losing their dynasty in the Arizona desert eight years earlier. A one-for-the-thumb victory for the core four Yankees — dynasty holdovers Derek Jeter, Mariano Rivera, Andy Pettitte, and Jorge Posada — would make the investment worth it.

The Yankees held a 3–2 lead over Philadelphia entering Game 6, and Cliff Lee's pitching and Chase Utley's power (the second baseman had tied Reggie Jackson's World Series record with five home runs) were the chief reasons the Phillies remained alive.

Lee dominated the Yanks in Game 1, allowing one run and six

hits — three of them to Jeter — in going the distance. But New York took the next three games, leaning on the lumber of Hideki Matsui and Alex Rodriguez, who struck out six times in eight hitless at-bats over the first two games in the Bronx before rediscovering his stroke in Philly.

Rodriguez slammed a Cole Hamels pitch off a TV camera in right field in Game 3, inspiring the first use of instant replay in postseason history (the double was upgraded to a two-run homer) and turning the World Series in the Yankees' favor.

A-Rod was hit by a pitch for the third time in the Series before he won Game 4 with an RBI double off Phillies closer Brad Lidge, and before he found that his two doubles and three RBI in Game 5 were not enough to eliminate the home team.

Philly was a proud reigning champ, but there was a grim sense of inevitability entering Game 6 at Yankee Stadium. Slugger Ryan Howard had twelve strikeouts and no homers in the first five games, and manager Charlie Manuel did not have a starter other than Lee capable of holding down Joe Girardi's lineup.

The Phillies were starting thirty-eight-year-old Pedro Martinez, who had done a serviceable job in the Game 2 loss but who wasn't even half the pitcher he had been when the Yanks ran him down in that epic Game 7 six years earlier.

And sure enough, before the 50,315 fans packed into the new Stadium, Martinez served up a two-run homer to Matsui in the second inning and a two-run single to Matsui in the third, after Jeter started the rally with a single of his own. Manuel was managing this game as if it were the middle of summer. At least when Grady Little stayed with Martinez much too long in the 2003 ALCS, Pedro was still Pedro, or damn close to it.

Manuel was working with the Jurassic Pedro, and yet he kept Martinez out there long enough for Matsui to pummel him in Round 2. By the time the Philly manager replaced Martinez with Chad Durbin after the fourth inning, it was too late.

Jeter smacked Durbin's fourth pitch for a double, then scored on Mark Teixeira's single to make it 5–1. Matsui would then belt a two-run double off J. A. Happ to make it six RBI on the night, to clinch the World Series MVP award, and to make the terms of the Phillies' demise a matter of how, not if.

It was only fitting that Jeter played a significant role in this clincher, contributing three hits and two runs and watching as the new A-Rod, the selfless A-Rod, agreed to accept two walks to help his team. Rodriguez refused to flail away in the hope of extending his hot streak and beating Matsui and everyone else to the MVP.

Jeter was the unofficial host of this World Series, just as he had been the unofficial host of the All-Star Game in the old Stadium. On the field before Game 1, Jeter kissed the First Lady, Michelle Obama, and the vice president's wife, Jill Biden, and he playfully mugged with Yogi Berra before posing for photos with all three. Jeter also caught the ceremonial first pitch thrown by Tony Odierno, the son of the U.S. commander in Iraq, Raymond Odierno, and a veteran of the Iraq war who had lost an arm.

The following day, Jeter ended up in a news conference before Game 2 to accept the Roberto Clemente Award for his community service. "You're a wonderful role model not only for the youth of America," Bud Selig said at the podium, "but also for our players. You have been the face of baseball for many years, and you're truly deserving of this award."

Selig would say he was proud to be the leader of a sport with Derek Jeter in it, and in full uniform the shortstop stepped to the podium and joked that he had the commissioner fooled, too.

Jeter did everything for the franchise and meant everything to the franchise. Appropriately enough, in a season that would see Jeter win a Gold Glove award, a Silver Slugger award, and a Hank Aaron Award, he secured the very last major league hit of 2009, a single off Ryan Madson in the eighth.

With two outs and the Yanks holding a 7–3 lead in the top of the ninth, Rivera finished what Pettitte had started. The greatest closer of them all got Shane Victorino to ground to second base, and as Robinson Cano was making his throw to first, his double-play partner was running forward in great anticipation, ready to throw his arms toward the black Bronx night.

Jeter and A-Rod ended up in a delirious scrum behind the mound, the weight of the world and the World Series lifted from their shoulders. Jeter had his first ring as a captain, a teary-eyed Rodriguez had his first ring, period, and the brand-new Stadium nearly crumbled around them.

After they ended up on a podium behind second base, there for the official coronation, Jeter held the trophy above his head and said, "It's good to be back. This is right where it belongs."

Soon enough the captain was outside the winning clubhouse, hugging his parents and sister while holding a bottle of Moët & Chandon. Jeter gathered his girlfriend, Minka Kelly, who was tucked tightly under a Yankee cap, and walked her into the clubhouse and toward his locker in the back, away from the madness unfolding in the heart of the room.

Jeter checked on Kelly, made sure she was all set in this dry corner of victory, and then went off to join the fun. "It feels better than I remember it," the captain said. "It's been a long time."

Jeter would grab Rodriguez around the neck, put him in a WWE chokehold, and pour champagne over the third baseman's head as he nearly dragged him to the ground, the two of them giggling the way they had on their sleepovers in a different life, bonus babies talking about someday playing on the same team. Yes, A-Rod had discovered it was a lot more fun to impact a World Series with his bat than with an opt-out clause in his contract.

Jeter and Rodriguez ended up with their famous girlfriends and their famous teammates at 1Oak, a trendy Chelsea club, where the Yankees took over the place the way the international soccer stars with the Cosmos used to take over Studio 54. Two mornings later, the Yanks all climbed aboard floats and rode in a ticker-tape parade.

"You feel like you're the president, waving," Jeter said. He had met President Obama at the All-Star Game, in the locker room, the two of them congratulating each other and speaking one biracial golden child to another.

"I've been a big fan for a long time," the president said before turning toward Jeter's American League teammates. "This guy's like the old guy around here now, huh?"

"I'm not the oldest," Jeter responded through a smile.

Just the most revered.

The ticker-tape parade was attended by a couple of million people, and for the fifth time Jeter was the recipient of the loudest cheers and the most marriage proposals.

"You could do this every day and you wouldn't get tired of it," he said.

It seemed as if Jeter had been doing it every day for the first five years of his career. He would play baseball, he would win in October, he would be honored for winning in October the right way.

New York watched him grow up, applauding his every baby step into manhood. *The Truman Show*, that was Jeter's story — the short-stop said so himself — and a loyal audience approved of the plot line.

As it turned out, the main character had a steady moral compass. Derek Sanderson Jeter did not just embody the pride of the Yankees as much as any mythic figure before him.

He proved a prince can become a king without lusting after the throne.

14

War

THE DEREK JETER who finished the 2010 season needing a new contract from the Yankees was not the Derek Jeter who finished the 2009 season as a five-time champ at the very top of his game.

The captain had endured his worst season as a pro, flailing his way to a career-low batting average of .270, a full 64 points below his average from the year before. Jeter established new personal lows in on-base percentage (.340) and slugging percentage (.370), and his saber-metric numbers in the field took a cruel turn south.

More than anything, Jeter transitioned from a young thirty-five to an old thirty-six. Overnight, the ageless wonder at short had devolved into the picture of Dorian Gray.

In the six-game American League Championship Series loss to the Texas Rangers, Jeter appeared positively glacial when measured against the Rangers' whiz kid, Elvis Andrus. The difference in range, bounce, and athleticism could not be ignored.

So Yankees fans understood why Jeter's contract negotiations wouldn't mirror the last round of talks between player and team a decade earlier, when Jeter had all the leverage and used it to make his $189 million score.

On the eve of the last great financial face-off between Jeter and the Yankees, the fans understood why Hal Steinbrenner told 1050 ESPN

Radio's Michael Kay that "things could get messy." They understood a couple of weeks later — with negotiations already under way — why team president Randy Levine told writers assembled at the general managers' meetings in Orlando the following:

"Now's a different negotiation than ten years ago. . . . This isn't a licensing deal or a commercial rights deal. He's a baseball player."

But the fans could not understand how the purest marriage in sports could descend into a food fight between a dignified icon and the only team he ever wanted to play for, the bitter contract talks stamping 2010 as a year Jeter only wished he could forget.

The captain's rocky 2010 actually started near the end of 2009, when his friend Tiger Woods was exposed as a serial adulterer in a scandal that would cost Woods his marriage and good name. Reports said that Jeter had introduced Tiger to one of his mistresses at the center of the storm, Rachel Uchitel, and that Jeter had also dated her at one time.

With so many superstar sports figures engulfed in scandal, Tiger and Jeter had represented the last men standing. That all changed when Woods crashed his Cadillac SUV into a fire hydrant and tree outside his home in the hours after the first Thanksgiving dinner of the rest of his life, unleashing a bimbo eruption to end all bimbo eruptions.

For Jeter, seeing his name connected to the Woods story in any way was an unfortunate development much too close for comfort.

"Man, they're trying to bring me into this thing with Tiger, and I've got nothing to do with it," Jeter told a friend. "You see why I didn't get married?"

In fact, reports had Jeter engaged and scheduled to be married to longtime girlfriend Minka Kelly in November of 2010 at Long Island's lavish Oheka Castle, reports that proved to be false. As it turned out, the captain spent that month fretting over an entirely different event in his life.

Jeter wanted badly to re-sign with the Yankees, and the Yankees wanted to grant that wish. But they wanted to grant it on their terms. They believed their shortstop was in a state of decline, and they planned on using their negotiating leverage the way Jeter had used his after the 2000 season.

If the captain's contract had expired after 2009, he would have been in line for another staggering nine-figure deal. But he spent 2010 hitting more ground balls than any other player in baseball. As the Yankees' leadoff man, Jeter hit a career-high 3.6 grounders for every ball he put in the air, according to FanGraphs.com, which also reported that Jeter swung at a career-worst 28.2 percent of pitches outside the strike zone.

The numbers painted a portrait of a ballplayer who had lost bat speed and confidence, a hitter desperate enough to cheat on the fastball. Pitchers kept attacking him low and inside, and Jeter kept slapping those balls harmlessly into the ground.

On September 15, the captain only hardened the belief that his skills were eroding when he faked getting hit by a pitch from Tampa Bay's Chad Qualls, a pitch that actually struck the knob of his bat. Jeter allowed an umpire to mistakenly award him first base, and most fans understood why.

But Jeter's absurd acting job was beneath him. As soon as the ball hit the knob, Jeter spun around, flung the bat, hopped about, and grabbed his left forearm in apparent agony, bending over and releasing an anguished cry. He gingerly extended his left arm for trainer Gene Monahan's inspection.

The home-plate umpire, Lance Barksdale, bought the act, if only because baseball's Honest Abe was performing it. Barksdale would eject the irate Rays manager, Joe Maddon, only to discover later that Jeter admitted he had pulled a fast one.

Players, coaches, and columnists were divided over the redeeming value — or lack thereof — of Jeter's little prank. Dodgers manager Joe Torre made the predictable case for his favorite player, saying, "Hell, yeah, he did the right thing. It's not like running a red light. Stuff you can do out on the field, whether you can get away with it, it's not being immoral. . . . Anything you can get away with is fine."

This from the same Torre who had rebuked A-Rod for yelling "Ha!" on a pop-up to successfully distract a Blue Jays fielder while running the bases.

In the end, this scene of a struggling Jeter cheating his way to first reminded some of the 1973 World Series scene of a forty-two-year-old Willie Mays on his knees at the plate, begging in vain for the ump to give his Mets a call.

Jeter was off-key all season. In July, ninety-nine-year-old public address announcer Bob Sheppard died two days before the eighty-year-old Boss, George Steinbrenner, died after suffering a massive heart attack.

Steinbrenner's death was the bigger story, of course, as he was a global figure who had become the most famous owner in the history of American team sports. Jeter was fond of Steinbrenner, the man who made him captain, and the feared employer who forever granted Jeter the exclusive privilege of dousing him with champagne in a winning October clubhouse.

Remarkably enough, the star owner and star shortstop had only one public run-in (when Steinbrenner suggested after the 2002 season that Jeter was partying too much), and even that tiff ended in a most amicable way — with the two of them dancing in a Visa ad.

So Jeter was the right Yankee to speak to the crowd before the first home game since Steinbrenner's death, the first game the Yanks played after the All-Star Game in Anaheim. Without reading from notes, the captain delivered an eloquent tribute to Steinbrenner and Sheppard and called them "two shining stars in the Yankee universe." It was another clutch performance by a shortstop who made a cottage industry out of them.

Only that morning, Jeter was angered by a column in the *Daily News* written by its longtime baseball voice, Bill Madden, who wondered how it was possible that not a single Yankee player, past or present, had bothered to show up for Sheppard's funeral the day before.

As the captain and the player who insisted that Sheppard's taped voice introduce him at the plate after the public address man retired, Jeter instantly became the face of the no-shows. Asked why he didn't attend the funeral, Jeter maintained that there are different ways of honoring a man's memory, a fair point for sure.

But when Jeter said, "To be honest with you, I didn't know his funeral was yesterday," many veteran Jeter watchers were stunned. For once, the shortstop had come to work unprepared. This marked the first time in Jeter's distinguished career that he had given a dog-ate-my-homework explanation for anything.

The captain survived the slip-up. A few days later, a *SportsBusiness Daily* survey of sports business executives and media personalities showed that Jeter was far and away the most marketable player in baseball. Jeter received thirty-nine first-place votes in the survey, and the runner-up, Albert Pujols, received all of two.

The shortstop remained a Madison Avenue heavyweight because of his looks, his relative humility, his ability to dodge controversy, and his talent for treating the biggest October games as if they were pickup games in the park.

"The greatest thing about Jeter," Alex Rodriguez said, "is he treats Game 7 of the World Series the same way as the first game of spring training, literally. I've never seen a player quite like that.

"He's Mr. Simplicity. He keeps it as simple as possible. All players can learn something from Jeter, because he's a master at it."

In August, after going homerless in forty-six at-bats, Rodriguez had blasted the 600th home run of his career the night after Jeter advised him to relax and try for a single. The captain shared his experiences in running down Lou Gehrig for the club's all-time hits record, and A-Rod seemed to take it to heart.

When Rodriguez crossed the plate, he was greeted by a beaming Jeter, who had scored ahead of him. The captain gave A-Rod a double high-five, and after the third baseman took his curtain call and retreated down the steps of the dugout, a smiling Jeter was waiting there for another hug.

Yes, their first championship together had improved an already improving relationship. "It's been huge," said general manager Brian Cashman. "The fact that they have a good relationship now, and it's seamless, it's just another distraction — like Alex supposedly can't hit in the postseason — that we don't have to hear about anymore. It's just another pressure valve relieved."

Only at season's end, the A-Rod–Jeter discussion didn't revolve around the return of their feel-good karma; it revolved around their age and loss of range, and whether the Yankees could win another title with them making like bronze statues on the left side of the infield.

Rodriguez was signed through the 2017 season and still had enough power at the plate to make for a credible designated hitter if needed. Jeter had no such power and for the first time was a Yankee without a contract.

But despite the questions raised by his 2010 performance, Jeter did arrive at the negotiating table with some friendly facts on his side.

He committed the fewest errors of his career (6), managed a league-best .989 fielding percentage, and won his fifth Gold Glove award (an honor mocked in many baseball corners), making him only the sixth shortstop to win at least five and the oldest American Leaguer to win one since a thirty-six-year-old Luis Aparicio claimed his ninth in 1970.

Jeter stood 106 games short of Mickey Mantle's franchise record of games played (2,401) and, of course, needed 74 hits to become the first Yankee to reach 3,000. No, the executives on the other side of the table — Cashman, Levine, and Hal Steinbrenner — couldn't ignore the history Jeter represented.

The captain was chiseling himself into the franchise's own Mount Rushmore, a truth captured a year earlier by one of the best young pitchers in the game, Florida's Josh Johnson, who pumped his fist after blowing a 96-mile-per-hour fastball by the Yankees' leadoff man. "Striking out Derek Jeter," Johnson said. "I'll remember that for the rest of my life."

Yes, Jeter's legend was a powerful force. Chris Webber, the former NBA All-Star, didn't remember the teenage Jeter from the time his AAU basketball team defeated the Kalamazoo Blues. But as a grownup, Webber said, "I've told that story in every bar I've ever walked into, that I once played basketball against Derek Jeter. And then in the parking lot afterward, I usually add that I struck him out once playing baseball."

For good reason: Jeter was the biggest star in the biggest city. He made New York an American League town, seizing it from the Mets, and he took the town from the Knicks, too.

Madison Square Garden was the place to be in the early to mid-nineties, and then two things happened that made a seat behind the Yankee Stadium plate more desirable than a courtside seat at the Garden.

Pat Riley left.

Derek Jeter arrived.

This is what Jeter and his agent, Casey Close, wanted to sell to the Yankees in their contract talks. The captain had been an invaluable asset to the brand, to the new Stadium, and to the YES Network, and he had never embarrassed the franchise the way Alex Rodriguez had.

Jeter was everything the Yankees wanted their mythology to be. He was the right man to make the final speech at the old Stadium across the street, the right man to pack up that DiMaggio sign he for-ever reached up and touched in the tunnel and carry it home with the memories.

Clyde King, the Steinbrenner aide who wanted Jeter demoted be-fore the start of his rookie season in 1996, would come to see Jeter as perhaps the greatest all-around shortstop of all time. "I played with Pee Wee Reese, and Jeter is better," King would say. "I had a ton of re-spect for Ernie Banks, but Jeter is better than him, too, because he can do it all."

Jerry Manuel, who had managed the White Sox and Mets, said he would take Jeter over Rodriguez, Nomar Garciaparra, Miguel Tejada, Omar Vizquel, and every other modern-day shortstop in his prime. "No question I would start my club with Jeter over all of those guys," Manuel said. "He gives so much to the game, and not to individual stats, that when the game's on the line it gives back to him."

So legions of Yankees fans were proud that their sons and daugh-ters chose to wear number 2, the most identifiable marker of an un-tarnished star. "If you wanted a son and didn't have one," said Leonard Biro, the father of Jeter's lifelong friend Doug, "Derek would be the person to be your son. His character is very high. . . . He's definitely a great example, unlike most of the others getting all that money."

Money. Derek Jeter was regarded as the ultimate money player, and yet one who never played for money.

Only in the winter of his discontent, the winter after his 2010 sea-son, Jeter was suddenly being defined in strictly financial terms.

As in, How much should the Yankees pay an aging singles hitter who had a slugger's impact on the franchise's legacy and bottom line?

Cashman, Levine, and Steinbrenner first met with Jeter and his longtime representative from Creative Artists Agency, Casey Close, on November 8 in Tampa. The meeting lasted several hours, and it opened with the Yankees assuring Jeter they wanted him to return, and with Jeter assuring the Yankees he wanted to play only for them. A good start.

Steinbrenner did a lot of the early talking, telling Jeter how much he meant to his father, to his family, and to the franchise as a whole. Hal promised Jeter he planned on keeping him a Yankee for life.

The captain responded by telling Steinbrenner he wanted the same thing. A better start.

But then it was time to do business, a time that would end up fracturing the bond between iconic player and iconic team.

"I just want what's fair," Jeter told the Yankees executives.

Steinbrenner handed over the meeting to Cashman and Levine, a hardened money man who had been the chief labor negotiator for Major League Baseball and who had served as New York City's labor commissioner and its Deputy Mayor for Economic Development, Planning and Administration under Rudy Giuliani.

Levine had clashed with Joe Torre before Torre bolted for Los Angeles. He did not want to send Derek Jeter through the same door.

Nor did Cashman, the former intern who rose through the organizational ranks by winning Boss Steinbrenner's perilous game of *Survivor*. Cashman wanted Jeter back, too, but the general manager was a fierce competitor whose modest physical stature belied his appetite for the fight. Cashman was Willie Pep in a golf shirt and slacks.

When the GM took over the meeting with a presentation on the state of Jeter's game, he pulled no punches. In his gofer days, Cashman used to help Yankee Stadium security people pull unruly drunks out of the stands. As an executive he had gotten tough with the likes of Bernie Williams and Johnny Damon, and in his 2007 dinner with Jeter the GM proved he wasn't afraid to get tough with the captain.

So with Jeter sitting right there in this first round of contract talks, Cashman raised the concerns the organization had about the captain's bat speed and range in the field, and his declining slugging and on-base percentages in two of the previous three seasons. It was a detailed and pointed critique, and Jeter did a slow burn while listening to it.

The agent, Close, had his say in response, emphasizing his client's tremendous impact on the franchise on the field and off, and the two sides parted without exchanging any hard numbers. If they didn't agree on a contract in this first sit-down, they did agree to keep the negotiations private. The captain would have it no other way.

Soon enough Jeter and the Yankees made their first informal offers. Close said his client was entitled to six years at $25 million a pop, and Cashman said he thought Close's client was worth three years at

$13 million a pop. These were parameters more than they were hard estimates, but still, the Yankees and their shortstop opened up the preliminary bidding three years and $111 million apart.

Yes, Hal Steinbrenner had it right. Things could get messy.

The Yankees increased their offer to three years and a $15 million wage, and Close countered with four or five years and a $23 million wage, which Cashman and Levine took to mean four years and a $23 million wage. The $111 million gap had been reduced to a $47 million gap.

It was progress, painful progress, but the Yankees made it clear that Jeter would have to do almost all of the compromising from that point forward. Meanwhile, Jeter and Close were stewing over what they believed to be the team's breach of their agreement to keep details of their talks out of the press.

Following Steinbrenner's radio remarks that the negotiations could get "messy" and that he needed to be mindful he was running a business, and Cashman's remarks that he didn't believe in paying players for milestones, Close told AOL FanHouse's Ed Price that Jeter agreed "with Hal's and Brian's recent comments that this contract is about business and winning championships. Clearly, baseball is a business, and Derek's impact on the sport's most valuable franchise cannot be overstated. Moreover, no athlete embodies the spirit of a champion more than Derek Jeter."

The agent thought that would be the end of it, but his client was bothered by what he perceived to be additional organizational leaks in the news media designed to make him appear greedy, even delusional. Jeter wasn't thrilled with Levine's comments at the GM meetings, either, the ones making it clear that the Yankees were prepared to pay the shortstop only for his on-field skills.

Jeter's father, Charles, was as unhappy as his son over the team's offer of a pay cut (the shortstop made $21 million in the final year of his $189 million deal), and over the way the captain was being portrayed in many corners of the media. That left Close in a difficult spot.

The Yankees were willing to keep Jeter the game's highest-paid middle infielder, they knew no competing team would offer Jeter a $15 million salary, and they knew Jeter wasn't leaving for a competing team anyway. The agent had no market for his client's services, no leverage, and no way to cloak the fact that Jeter was coming off his worst season.

Close kept coming back to everything the captain meant to the brand, the ballpark, and the network. The agent did raise Alex Rodriguez's monstrous $305 million contract (including up to $30 million in bonus money if he ultimately breaks the career home-run record) early in the negotiations, but A-Rod's deal wasn't something Close kept harping on.

The agent did remind the Yankees that they had given a ton of money to players who hadn't done a fraction of what Jeter had done for the franchise. None of it moved Cashman and Levine off their numbers.

They argued that Close used A-Rod's $252 million deal with Texas to land Jeter's $189 million, when both were shortstops, and that the Yankees had every right to use comparable players in negotiations this time around.

Levine and Cashman cited twenty-six-year-old Florida shortstop Hanley Ramirez, who had superior numbers to Jeter's and was making $11 million, or $4 million less than the Yankees were offering. They cited the Dodgers' Rafael Furcal ($12 million) and the Phillies' Jimmy Rollins ($8.5 million), among others.

Through grapevine intelligence, Levine was aware that Colorado was about to give twenty-six-year-old shortstop Troy Tulowitzki a seven-year extension that would leave him with $157.75 million over ten seasons, or an average of $15.775 million per. Despite the fact that Tulowitzki's stats blew away his idol's, the Yankees were quietly prepared to improve their offer to Jeter so that his average annual take would exceed the Colorado star's.

But the captain pushed for a salary of more than $20 million, and Close was being asked to pull a rabbit out of a hat that didn't exist. If the agent had always beaten the Yankees at the negotiating table, this time he was destined to lose.

With frustrations mounting inside the Jeter family and camp, with his client smoldering over a perceived campaign to make him look bad in the news media, Close decided to alter the game plan. He decided to go public despite warnings from Yankee officials that such a move could escalate hostilities and prove damaging to Jeter's image.

So when Close told *Daily News* columnist Mike Lupica that the

Yankees' negotiating stance was "baffling," that they "continue to argue their points in the press and refuse to acknowledge Derek's total contribution to their franchise," and that there was a reason "the Yankees themselves have stated Derek Jeter is their modern-day Babe Ruth," Cashman, Levine, and Steinbrenner lost it.

Steinbrenner was the one who would decide the appropriate Yankee response. After concluding that Close had hurt the family business with his words, the Boss's son ordered the Code Red and asked Cashman to carry it out.

With his phone as his only weapon, the general manager launched a media offensive with something of shock-and-awe tone. Cashman's money quote on Jeter was landed by ESPNNewYork.com's Wallace Matthews, and it went like this:

"We've encouraged him to test the market and see if there's something he would prefer other than this. If he can, fine. That's the way it works."

Meanwhile, Hal Steinbrenner's brother, Hank, weighed in by telling the Associated Press, "As much as we want to keep everybody, we've already made these guys very, very rich, and I don't feel we owe anybody anything monetarily. Some of these players are wealthier than their bosses."

Jeter was hotter than he'd ever been, hotter than he was over A-Rod's remarks ten years back. The captain was particularly upset at Cashman's dare to go test the market.

Suddenly Jeter was caught up in a tabloid feeding frenzy, the very thing he'd worked so hard to avoid his entire career. And from a safe distance, while he was sunning himself on a yacht by Cameron Diaz's side, A-Rod was loving every minute of it. Rodriguez was signed through his forty-second birthday, and he'd make a whole lot more than $15 million a year. The A-Rod–Jeter relationship was in a much better place, but the third baseman didn't mind finally seeing the shortstop caught up in an A-Rodian drama of his own.

In almost all of his interviews, Cashman pointed out that he still wanted to sign Jeter, and that he still believed Jeter represented the team's best option at shortstop. But the GM would also point out, "There are things we have concerns with — his performance over the last few years, and his age. And that has to be factored into the negotiation."

Jeter accepted Cashman's criticism in 2007. He wasn't accepting this.

The two sides had grown into enemy forces. Jeter and Close were looking at the Yankees the way the Red Sox were looking at them, and for a day or two the unthinkable was thinkable: maybe Jeter wouldn't finish his career in the Bronx after all.

With Cashman assuming the role of bad cop, especially in Jeter's eyes, Levine came up with a proposal that the GM and Hal Steinbrenner liked. Over the long Thanksgiving weekend, Levine pieced together an elaborate incentives plan that would allow Jeter to make additional millions in a fourth year of the contract if he played at a high level.

Levine was reviewing the details of his plan when Close reached out to Steinbrenner to arrange a second face-to-face meeting in Tampa. Understanding that the Yankees weren't going to be giving his client another megadeal, a truth he had to explain to the Jeters, Close was hoping to bridge the turbulent waters separating the two sides and get the best deal he could.

On November 30, Jeter, Close, and Creative Artists Agency attorney Terry Prince met with Cashman, Levine, and Steinbrenner. This summit lasted more than four hours, but Jeter was there for only the first forty-five minutes.

The captain's world had been turned upside down. His girlfriend, Kelly, had been named *Esquire*'s Sexiest Woman Alive (yes, *Esquire* owed Jeter one), and he had built himself a 31,000-square-foot waterfront mansion on Davis Islands in Tampa, where Jeter would have to make do with seven bedrooms and nine bathrooms.

Only his life didn't feel like an Everyman's fantasy at the start of this second meeting. Jeter opened by telling the Yankee delegation how upset he was that they made the negotiations public, and by telling Cashman how upset he was that the GM dared him to shop for a better offer.

When Jeter was done spewing, he tried to get up and leave before Cashman asked him to sit back down. The GM reminded Jeter that the

Yankees' offer was the highest offer. "You said all you wanted was what was fair," Cashman told him. "How much higher do we have to be than the highest offer for it to be fair?"

Cashman also blamed Close for making the contract talks public, a position Jeter and his agent rejected. They went back and forth for a bit before Jeter decided that his presence might hinder the process. As the captain excused himself, he made it clear Close was now authorized to make a deal.

The sides made significant progress over the balance of the summit, and the agent and Levine then spent a couple of days on the phone tweaking the proposal. Knowing it would be a wise idea to keep his client and Cashman apart, Close asked Levine to go see Jeter in his Manhattan apartment on the afternoon of December 3.

They met in the skyscraping Trump World Tower home Jeter had put on the market for $20 million, this while Cashman met with his other future Hall of Famer, Mariano Rivera, to work on the closer's free agent deal in Rivera's suburban Westchester home.

The Rivera talks were as quiet as Rivera himself, even as the Red Sox were making an attempt to extricate him from the Bronx. Jeter was the one who had to scratch and claw for his money while millions of fascinated fans looked on.

Inside his Trump home, Jeter told Levine he wanted more money added to the incentives clauses in the proposal. At the time the offer included bonuses for winning awards such as league MVP, World Series or League Championship Series MVP, Silver Slugger, and Gold Glove.

Jeter spent a couple of hours arguing that those awards are very difficult to win, and that the contract numbers didn't reflect the degree of difficulty. He made persuasive arguments. Levine absorbed the captain's points, called Cashman and Steinbrenner while Jeter called Close, and the two sides ended up a yard or two away from pay dirt.

As it turned out, Jeter made himself about $4 to $5 million in extra money in that meeting with Levine. The Yankees agreed to raise the ceiling on the incentives plan to $9 million, and that night the parties set up a meeting for late the following afternoon to close the deal at the Regency in the city.

The same men who attended the second meeting in Tampa ended up in a Regency suite on Saturday, December 4: Jeter, Close, and

Prince on one side; Cashman, Levine, and Steinbrenner on the other. They reached an agreement around 4:00 p.m. Everyone shook hands, hugged, and shared a laugh.

Derek Sanderson Jeter was still a Yankee.

Levine got fellow executives Lonn Trost and Jean Afterman on the phone to help dot the i's and cross the t's with Prince. The contract guaranteed Jeter $56 million over four years, with a player option after year three.

The captain would make $48 million in salary in the first three years and would receive another $3 million if he decided to buy his way out of the deal and into free agency, leaving him with $51 million and an average annual take of $17 million, better than Tulowitzki's $15.775.

Jeter would have the option to stay for the fourth and final season for an $8 million salary plus potential bonus money earned over the life of the contract that topped out at $9 million, making it possible for him to earn as much as $65 million in the deal.

Jeter would earn $4 million for winning a league MVP award and $2 million for finishing second through sixth in the voting. He could score an additional $1.5 million for a Silver Slugger, $500,000 for a Gold Glove, and $500,000 each for a League Championship Series MVP and a World Series MVP. Jeter would be eligible for any unearned bonuses during the fourth and final year of the contract.

In order to save the Yankees on luxury tax payments applied to their massive payroll, Levine persuaded Jeter to defer $7 million of his salary over the first three years, without interest, something the captain didn't want to do.

"I'm rooting for Derek Jeter; we all are," Levine would say. "I hope he hits all of his incentives so we end up paying him $17 million in that fourth year. It will be the happiest $17 million we've ever spent."

Before leaving the Regency, Jeter met separately with Cashman and Steinbrenner to begin repairing the relationship. They had a long and winding road ahead of them.

Some in baseball believed the Yankees were guilty of unnecessary roughness in their talks with Jeter. But just as many others, including some teammates of Jeter's, thought the team had offered the captain more than it needed to.

The deal was set to be announced on Tuesday, December 7, at George

M. Steinbrenner Field in Tampa. At last, Jeter would get that big press conference denied him in 2001. At last, he would get his day inside the tent.

The captain arrived in a blue pinstriped suit, and before he spoke, Cashman offered him a piece of advice.

"Tell the truth," the GM told Jeter. "Let's not have a fake press conference. Let them see how pissed off you are at me, let them know that. I'm a big boy. I can handle it."

Shockingly, Jeter took Cashman's advice. He stepped to the microphone, joked that he'd never had one of these press conferences before, and, with the YES Network cameras rolling, admitted he was pissed off by the way the negotiations went down.

"I'd be lying to you if I said I wasn't angry at how some of this went," Jeter said.

Angry. Nobody could recall Jeter using that word to describe his emotions about anything. Ever.

Jeter revealed his rage over Cashman's statement that he should go searching for a better offer from another team.

"I was pretty angry about it," Jeter said, "and I let that be known. I was angry about it because I was the one who said I wasn't going to [talk to other teams]. To hear the organization say, 'Go shop it,' and I just told you I wasn't going to, yeah, to be honest with you, I was angry about it."

Angry, angry, angry. It had taken fifteen years for the New York Yankees to make Derek Jeter angry.

"I never wanted to be a free agent," he said.

And now everyone understood why. Jeter had been scarred in the process. He'd been bloodied just as clearly as he was bloodied on that dive into the stands against Boston in 2004, and it would take some time to heal the wounds.

That night, outside Jeter's Davis Islands mansion, the captain's father reportedly pushed and grabbed a freelance photographer trying to take photos of his son. A long day and a longer year had taken their toll, and the captain wanted everything to return to the way it used to be. He wanted to trade the pursuit of a contract for the pursuit of another parade, never mind the pursuit of his 3,000th hit.

Derek Jeter, pride of the Yankees, couldn't wait for Opening Day.

Epilogue

◆

3,000

On the morning of Saturday, July 9, 2011, Derek Jeter showed up at Yankee Stadium a tense and burdened man. Jeter had built himself a Hall of Fame career by playing fearless baseball, but this was a rare day when he was consumed by the potential consequences of failure.

The captain was two hits shy of becoming the first Yankee to reach the magic number 3,000, and he desperately wanted to make history before the home crowd. A rainout the night before left Jeter with only two games in the Bronx before the All-Star break and then an eight-game road trip, and the shortstop had a feeling if he didn't finish his death march of a pursuit on Saturday, he wouldn't finish it on Sunday, either.

At thirty-seven, Jeter no longer radiated the can-do aura of his prime. He was batting .257, with an on-base percentage of .321 and a slugging percentage of .329, the worst numbers of his career, numbers that represented a plunge even from his dreadful 2010. Jeter had recently returned from a calf injury that cost him 18 games (the Yankees won 14 of them), and with more than half the season gone the shortstop had homered in only one game (he hit two at Texas on May 8).

The captain was a diminished player and presence in every way. Coming off his contract negotiations from hell the previous fall, when

Yankees management introduced him to a new brand of hardball, Jeter was scarred again in May after his good friend Jorge Posada pulled himself from the lineup before a nationally televised game against the Boston Red Sox, of all teams, because he felt disrespected by Joe Girardi's decision to bat him ninth.

After Posada gave Jeter a sanitized version of his insubordination — Posada had actually gone as far as telling general manager Brian Cashman he wanted out of the organization — the captain went public the following day with the opinion that his friend didn't need to apologize to his teammates. "My understanding is he told the manager he needed a day," Jeter said. "If that's the case, I don't see anything wrong with it."

Yankees officials were nearly as incensed by Jeter's comments as they were by Posada's actions. They summoned the captain to the principal's office, and Cashman, team president Randy Levine, and owner Hal Steinbrenner took turns on a conference call rebuking Jeter, a one-sided exchange that included a Steinbrenner lecture on a captain's responsibilities.

News of the conference call leaked, and Jeter predictably refused to reveal any meaningful details. Nine times over a brief meeting with reporters Jeter repeated what the team had said: "We're all on the same page."

But many inside the organization viewed the whole affair as a dry run for a much bigger demotion to come. Posada had been unceremoniously dumped as a catcher and reduced to a designated hitter — Cashman had informed him in a hospital room after Posada underwent a scheduled off-season exam — and felt unappreciated long before he was told to bat last against the Red Sox.

If a Jeter move from shortstop to, say, left field still seemed to be a concern for a distant season, people were already talking and writing about Jeter's inevitable move out of the leadoff role and toward the bottom of the order.

"And when it happens," one team official said, "that will definitely be a Defcon 1 day."

Was that day drawing near? The Yankees' hitting coach, Kevin Long, spent the off-season attacking a goal he first established late in

2010 — the elimination of Jeter's stride to the pitched ball. The short-stop tried his damnedest to keep his left foot planted in the box, to give himself more time to see the ball, but he ditched Long's program early in 2011 when he decided he was doing too much thinking at the plate for his own good.

But the old approach wasn't a major upgrade over the abandoned new approach, and so on June 13, when Jeter hobbled toward first after lifting a fly ball against Cleveland and then immediately headed down the dugout steps and into the clubhouse, he finally caught a break.

The grade 1 strain of his right calf sent him to the disabled list — a move he resisted, of course — and afforded him a sanctuary from the 24/7 scrutiny of his every futile swing. Even if he'd never admit it, Jeter needed the kind of getaway his Tampa-area mansion (known to the lo-cals as St. Jetersburg) would provide. Just like the pressure of chasing another big contract in 2010, the pressure of chasing 3,000 hits had gotten to him.

Jeter would go to Tampa to heal, and before he and his 2,994 hits boarded a plane, the captain made one request: he asked if he could work with Gary Denbo, his first minor league manager in 1993 and the one man in the organization who knew his swing best.

At the big league level, Long had enjoyed success with the likes of Robinson Cano, Curtis Granderson, and Nick Swisher; he also had a strong working relationship with Alex Rodriguez. But much as he tried, Long couldn't free Jeter from the jaws of a slump that had cov-ered a season and a half.

Cashman was the one to say yes or no to Jeter's request. It wasn't a no-brainer, not with Denbo on assignment with the Yankees' Florida State League club, and not with Long's ego staring at its own trip to the DL.

"I didn't really want to do it," Cashman said. "Gary had a job to do as a pro scout, and I didn't want to step on any toes. It kind of went back to the George [Steinbrenner] days of, 'Oh, Mel Stottlemyre, you can't help my pitcher? I'll just send him to Billy Connors.' But this was Derek Jeter making the request, so I looked past all of that. He felt it would really help him. Derek didn't demand it, he just asked, and to be honest, I don't remember anything Derek's ever really asked us to do for him."

Cashman got Denbo on the phone with Long, who had told the GM, "If Derek feels this will help him get better, I'm all for it." Long and Denbo compared notes, and the rehabilitation of Jeter's swing and mind was on.

Denbo focused on the fundamentals in the cage, on the hitting tee, almost as if he were teaching an eighteen-year-old Jeter all over again. The coach noticed the captain had been moving his head toward the ball, costing him precious time to study it. Denbo asked his pupil to concentrate on steadying his head and staying back.

While Jeter was away, his young and athletic replacement, Eduardo Nunez, was showing the kind of life in his bat and legs that had vanished from Jeter's game. The Yankees were winning, and their captain was feeling a growing sense of urgency to return as quickly as he could. He celebrated his thirty-seventh birthday during his rehab, a reminder of why the calf wasn't healing at his preferred pace.

By the time Jeter was ready to play a rehab game for the Double-A Trenton Thunder, he'd gone nearly three weeks since injuring himself. He was in the Thunder's lineup on Saturday night, July 2, the first of two minor league games he was scheduled to play before rejoining the Yankees in Cleveland, George Steinbrenner's hometown, on the Fourth of July, George Steinbrenner's birthdate.

Jeter was asked if he knew the story of Wally Pipp, the Yankee first baseman who famously lost his job to Lou Gehrig. "I do," the captain said. "That's why I'll be back Monday."

He'd arrived at Trenton's Waterfront Park nervous and a bit sleep-deprived; Jeter had done a lot of tossing and turning the night before. But to the delight of an overflow crowd of 9,000, the shortstop got a hit, ran without a hitch from first to third, and showed some range to his left by making a difficult play near the second-base bag. His right calf fully cooperated during this five-inning comeback.

"I felt better than I thought I would," Jeter said.

With Nunez tearing up the Mets in the Subway Series, and with the Yankees' replacement leadoff man, Brett Gardner, busy posting a .362 on-base percentage in the first-stringer's absence, Jeter played a quick six innings with Trenton the following night while wearing the Thunder's special holiday tribute jersey, a Captain America special. Jeter didn't look like any superhero at the plate or in the field, striking out with two men in scoring position, committing a throwing error, and botching a double-play ball before leaving the game after the sixth and scrambling to catch his plane.

"I got through it," Jeter said. At least his calf didn't hurt.

On arrival in Cleveland, back in the major leagues again, the shortstop voted in as an All-Star Game starter admitted, "I'm not happy with my first half." Despite Gardner's decisive edge in on-base percentage points, Girardi reinstalled Jeter as the Yankees' leadoff hitter, Gardner was dropped to ninth, and what had become a joyless march on 3,000 resumed at Progressive Field.

Jeter went 0 for 4 in his first game back, and didn't look much better than he did before he got hurt. Reporters and columnists closed in on him, and adding to the squeeze was the camera crew the captain had allowed into his life for an HBO documentary on the chase. Jeter never invites public examinations of his private thoughts, but he agreed to this intrusion — he even agreed to wear a wire for HBO and MLB Productions as he played — so his children-to-be could see their father do something no Yankee had ever done.

He managed two hits — a slow infield roller and a two-run double — in six at-bats the next night, and despite the fact that Jeter had played in four straight games (including the two in Trenton) on a potentially vulnerable calf, Girardi ran him out there again for the series finale in Cleveland.

The manager had slept on it and decided he had no choice. Jeter was hell-bent on getting number 3,000 during the upcoming four-game series in the Bronx with Tampa Bay, and he still needed four hits. Four hits in four games used to be a four-foot putt for Jeter, but not anymore.

The intense scrutiny made something so close seem so far away. "It's kind of hard to enjoy it," Jeter said, "when there's a lot of negativity that's out there."

The captain rewarded Girardi's faith by doubling in the last game in Cleveland, leaving him a more reachable three hits away when the

Yanks opened their series with Tampa Bay on July 7. Only the manager wasn't enjoying this any more than Jeter was. Girardi talked about trying to "wrap it up this weekend" and allowing his shortstop to "get back to just being Derek Jeter."

If that were possible. A celebration of Jeter's career had devolved into a running dissertation on his fading skills, and at times during this never-ending pursuit, Jeter looked like a dehydrated marathon runner in the twenty-sixth mile, ready to collapse and crawl his way home. He couldn't catch up to the high fastball, and when he did make contact, too often he couldn't get the ball out of the infield.

But when Jeter came to bat in the Stadium for the first time since June 13, the fans stood and cheered and suddenly brought him back to life. Jeter lashed at the first pitch he saw from the Rays' Jeff Niemann (the same pitcher who surrendered the Jeter hit that tied Gehrig's franchise record), and the ball landed safely in left center for a double and number 2,998. The captain felt so rejuvenated and relieved as he stood at second base, he started believing this would be the big night.

"That's what I thought," he said. "It didn't happen."

The crowd of 47,787 kept standing for him, chanting his name, and lighting up the Bronx night with their flashing cameras. The fans badly wanted their ticket stubs to become historical documents, and it wasn't to be.

Sean Rodriguez, Tampa Bay's third baseman, made a Graig Nettles–like diving stop on a Jeter shot down the line. With two outs in the ninth and the Rays up 5–1, the gods granted Jeter an extra at-bat when Kyle Farnsworth's strike three to Brett Gardner got past the catcher. About half the crowd was still in the ballpark, though it sounded like a full house. Jeter couldn't seize the moment. He hit a tapper to Rodriguez, and he was a half step too slow to beat it out.

The same gods that gave Jeter that extra at-bat took away four the following night, after the captain walked to his locker in the afternoon, surveyed the angry green blob covering New York on the weather map that was his computer screen, and realized Mother Nature was now messing with him as much as Father Time.

The heavy rain washed out the second game of the series and left the Yankees in an impossible spot. They could have imposed a regulation doubleheader on the Rays the following day, Saturday, or they could have done what they did — push for a day-night doubleheader on Saturday so they wouldn't lose the money they would've lost if they kissed away a gate.

"We're not interested in going from 81 home games to 80," said Cashman, who conceded that the decision was based on "business reasons."

Only the Rays were allowed to veto the day-night plan (they would've had no such power over a regulation doubleheader), and veto it they did. The Yankees were miffed, but the Rays were only protecting their best baseball interests. Evan Longoria, Tampa Bay's player rep and star third baseman, said his team needed to get healthy and that playing a split doubleheader wouldn't serve the cause.

The Friday night fans were devastated, and not only because some had flown in from faraway places and paid exorbitant prices for the hottest ticket in town. They were denied a chance to witness history, and handed a parting gift of a much less meaningful seat at a much less meaningful time. The Yankees and Rays agreed to make up the game on September 22, and the rain kept falling on Jeter's parade.

"Damn," the shortstop told himself. "Now we only have two games."

Two games at home before the All-Star break and the eight-game road trip through Toronto and Tampa Bay. Jeter had just announced he wouldn't be playing in the All-Star Game because he wanted to rest his calf. Of course, he also wanted to avoid a two-day interrogation in case he failed to reach 3,000 in the Bronx.

If his bailout upset baseball officials and All-Star ticket holders who hoped to pay tribute to Jeter's career, their feelings of disappointment would multiply tenfold Saturday afternoon, July 9, when Jeter conquered his demons and doubts in a staggering way.

Across a big league career that started in May of 1995, Jeter swore he was never afraid to fail. And yet he was afraid to fail against David Price, the Rays' big, hard-throwing lefty who had held Jeter to a .240 batting average in their head-to-head matchups. It didn't matter that in September 2008 Jeter had claimed the first hit Price had ever given up, belting a homer and tying Gehrig's record for most career hits at the Stadium.

It didn't matter that Jeter had batted .315 against Sunday's scheduled starter, James Shields. The captain could've been facing a couple of beer league pitchers over the weekend and he still would've felt overwhelmed by the stakes. He found it a lot easier being a clutch player in a team context than being one while chasing a new contract or a new milestone.

At least Jeter didn't have to worry about another rainout on July 9; it was a great day for baseball in the Bronx. Blue skies, white clouds, a game-time temperature of 84 degrees. The Stadium was packed, though Jeter couldn't view it as a full house: his mother Dot and sister Sharlee were booked for a previous engagement, the christening of Sharlee's child.

The captain's father, Charles, was representing the family in its suite above the first-base side. "I have every at-bat with you," Charles always told his son, and the old man was about to share five at-bats he would never forget.

Jeter was introduced in the bottom of the first by the voice of Bob Sheppard, and he arrived at the plate wearing a guard on his left shin, a pad on his left elbow, and an invisible piano on his back. He took a strike and a ball from Price before swinging through a 93-mph fastball on a big, almost amateurish cut that didn't inspire much optimism in the crowd.

Jeter took a close pitch to get to 2–2 and then lifted his arms and threw back his rump on an even closer pitch that Price wanted for strike three. Granted a generous full count from home plate umpire Jim Wolf, Jeter ordered himself to swing no matter what.

"He could've thrown [it] in the dugout," Jeter said, "and I would've swung. I'm telling you, I was not trying to walk."

Price did his opponent a favor and kept throwing the ball within his reach. Jeter fouled off back-to-back pitches to the right side before finally hitting one fair, a hard bouncer between short and third that dramatically altered the captain's approach to the day.

That piano had been lifted from his back. Jeter was at 2,999 hits with three or four more at-bats to go on Saturday, and then another four behind it on Sunday. Even he liked those odds.

"Huge," Jeter called that not-so-routine single through the hole.

He felt liberated, certain this home crowd of 48,103 would see him become the twenty-eighth man to amass 3,000 hits and the eleventh man to do it with one team.

In the third inning, after a diving Gardner was called out on a close play at first, the booing quickly gave way to deafening cheers as Sheppard's voice reintroduced the Yankee captain. Jeter tossed away his bat weight, and the home plate ump, Wolf, put in play specially marked balls in the highly unlikely event that the man of the hour sent number 3,000 over the Yankee Stadium wall.

Jeter had gone 286 at-bats since his last homer at home, an inside-the-parker on July 22, 2010, and he'd gone 358 at-bats at the Stadium since last putting one in the seats (he hit two against Houston on June 12, 2010). The safe bets had Jeter beating out a tapper to third, or fisting a blooper over the second baseman's head. Nobody was putting the mortgage on Jeter joining Wade Boggs — another improbable slugger — as the only men to make their 3,000th hit a home run.

With the fans on their feet, with the Yanks and Rays leaning hard on their dugout rails, Jeter exchanged small talk with the Tampa Bay catcher, John Jaso, stepped into the box, extended his right hand toward Wolf, and took a low, 94-mph fastball from Price for ball one.

This duel would also last eight pitches, with Jeter stepping out seven times to bang the barrel of his bat against his spikes, adjust his helmet, adjust his elbow pad, and then step back in. Price would throw him heat and off-speed stuff, everything he had. Jeter would take one vicious cut on a 2–1 count pitch he fouled straight back before his momentum sent him spinning across the plate and into the other box, leaving the fans to release a pained *ohhhhhhh*.

Jeter worked Price to a full count, again, before hitting a foul ball to the right side, and then another past third base. In his second at-bat, with the clock about to strike 2 p.m., number 2 dug back in and told himself he couldn't afford to look for a changeup or curve. "David Price throws 98 when he wants to," Jeter said. "David Price throws fastballs. He always throws a lot of fastballs."

Jeter also told himself to honor the work he did with Denbo and stay back and try to drive the ball up the middle. The captain didn't care if he hit a single, double, triple, or home run — "For me all of them count," he said — but he wanted no part of another one of those slow rollers to third base "and have that be replayed forever."

Jeter had one thought in his head: *Just hit it hard.* As Price prepared to deliver the final pitch of this encounter, he looked up at the scoreboard and saw a reminder that he'd surrendered that Gehrig-tying homer to Jeter two seasons earlier.

The fans were chanting the captain's name when Price let it go, the kind of 78-mph curveball the batter wasn't expecting. Jeter lifted his left foot in the air and planted it back in the dirt, leaned forward, then threw his hands toward the sinking ball as it cut across the plate. Jeter felt it explode off his black Louisville Slugger, and the hitter, catcher, ump, and pitcher suddenly shot their eyes skyward as the ball headed for the white clouds above left center.

Price dropped to one knee as if he'd just absorbed a hook to the ribs. Having ditched his bat with both hands, Jeter knew nobody was catching this one. Matt Joyce, the left fielder, drifted back to the wall as the Yankees' first-base coach, Mick Kelleher, started yelling, "That ball's outta here."

The ball landed above a State Farm sign in the left-center seats, and as Jeter rounded first he extended his arms wide and clapped his hands. The Stadium felt and sounded as if it were about to come down. As the Yankee captain passed him, Casey Kotchman, the Rays' first baseman, removed his cap and flipped it upside down in tribute.

Jeter didn't slow down his run around the bases to bask in the moment; of course he didn't. And yet the captain thought about so much on this historic trot — his family, his friends, his wish that his mother and sister could've been there to see him in this charmed state.

Waiting at the plate for Jeter was a receiving line of teammates, with Posada at the front. The designated hitter jumped into a beaming Jeter's arms, and then Mariano Rivera and a scrum of Yanks that included Alex Rodriguez, injured and out of the lineup, pounced on the captain and patted him hard on the head and back.

Jeter emerged from the pile without his helmet and fell into a series of embraces with teammates and coaches. A-Rod gave him a bear hug, laughed, and said, "That's unbelievable." On the third-base side, Jeter's former teammate Johnny Damon led some Rays onto the field to applaud their opponent.

Price had returned to his dugout during the celebration, and on the way in, his fellow pitcher Shields said to him, "That was a bomb," drawing a laugh from the shaken lefty.

Jeter pointed toward his father, friends, and girlfriend Minka Kelly in the family suite, and then reemerged from the dugout for a curtain call. He pointed to all corners of the Stadium and to the Rays gathered around the mound.

"They were looking my way and sort of clapping a little bit," Jeter said, "and so I was just acknowledging them, and actually felt bad that the game had to stop because you understand that [Price] is trying to win, they're trying to win a game. So it was almost like, 'I'm sorry. Hopefully we can get this thing moving again.'"

Yeah, they got it moving again. The fourth-youngest player to reach 3,000 hits immediately went to work on 4,000, ripping a double to left in the fifth, unleashing his classic inside-out swing on a liner past the second baseman in the sixth (if only to prove he could still do that too), and, finally and fittingly, with Gardner at third and the score tied and the infield playing in, winning the game with a weak, lunging bouncer up the middle.

"It would've been really, really awkward being out there doing interviews and waving to the crowd if we would've lost," Jeter said.

The first member of Club 3,000 to go 5 for 5 on his big day (Craig Biggio went 5 for 6 on his), Jeter met with the twenty-three-year-old cell-phone salesman who ended up with his home-run ball. As it turned out, Christian Lopez, a burly, six-foot-five former small college lineman, was another fan out of Central Casting, a Jeffrey Maier all grown up.

Rather than sell the ball for hundreds of thousands of dollars, and pay off a student loan debt of more than $100,000, Lopez decided to hand it over to Jeter free of charge. Just because he felt it was the right thing to do.

The Yankees gave Lopez some premium tickets and a bagful of bats, balls, and jerseys signed by Jeter, who thanked the fan for his generosity before walking into a news conference and making the kind of confession to the media he rarely made.

"I've been lying to you guys for a long time," Jeter said, "saying I wasn't nervous and that there was no pressure. There was a lot of pressure to do it here."

He did it on a career day, a day that defied reason. If this day came out of a Hollywood script, Jeter said, "I wouldn't even have bought it."

Wearing a DJ3K T-shirt carrying his own fist-in-the-air image, Jeter spoke of the tremendous relief he felt that it was over, that he could, in his manager's words, "get back to just being Derek Jeter."

For the balance of 2011, getting back to just being Derek Jeter meant going on enough of a post-3,000 tear to raise his batting average 40 points, to .297. It meant suspending the talk — at least temporarily — that he was washed up and headed for a plunge to the bottom of the order. It meant watching Mariano Rivera record his 602nd career save to break Trevor Hoffman's record. It meant helping the Yankees win their twelfth division title in his sixteen years as the starting shortstop.

It meant losing a five-game series to Detroit in the first round of the playoffs, a truth that usually rendered a season — by Jeter's own unforgiving judgment — a complete failure.

It meant having the ball field he grew up on at Kalamazoo Central High School named in his honor. It meant being named one of Barbara Walters's ten most fascinating people of the year. It meant shocking friends by breaking up with Minka Kelly and then, in the wake of a *New York Post* story that had Jeter sending female conquests home with thanks-for-the-memories autographed memorabilia, making up with Kelly and vacationing with her in Paris.

Jeter was heavily favored to remain of great gossip-page interest in 2012, much to his dismay. On the sports page, where the tributes had already faded to black, his every at-bat was likely to be scrutinized all over again.

Time wasn't on Jeter's side. Would he continue his resurgence as the Yankees' leadoff man, or would he return to his struggles at the plate and reignite the daily conversation about his declining skills and his advancing age?

Only this much was certain: nobody could take away that Saturday afternoon in July when Derek Jeter reminded millions of fans of what he used to be. On that day, in search of his historic hit, the captain was deathly afraid of hitting a slow roller to third.

He touched them all instead.

Acknowledgments

◆

The people who regularly cover Derek Jeter's Yankees do so with a professionalism matched only by the greatest of Jeter's teams. Their ranks include many friends and colleagues whose outsized talent and generosity helped shape this book.

Mike Vaccaro and Joel Sherman were invaluable resources and trusted wingmen, as were Jack Curry, Bob Klapisch, and Buster Olney. George King, Michael Kay, Ken Davidoff, Tyler Kepner, Dom Amore, John Harper, Sweeny Murti, and Suzyn Waldman were among those willing to share their experiences and wisdom, as were Wallace Matthews, Andrew Marchand, Tara Sullivan, Steve Politi, Brian Costello, Anthony McCarron, Dan Graziano, Roger Rubin, John Rowe, Jeremy Schaap, Ryan Ruocco, Dave Kaplan, Murray Bauer, and Michael Rosenberg. Friends and fellow authors Adrian Wojnarowski, Joe Posnanski, David Fischer, and Dan Wetzel were good enough to fill the roles of much-needed sounding boards, and the works of Harvey Araton, Ronald Blum, Erik Boland, Filip Bondy, Sam Borden, Pete Caldera, Marc Carig, Mark Feinsand, Jon Heyman, Bryan Hoch, Chad Jennings, Bill Madden, Ben Shpigel, Tom Verducci, and Gene Wojciechowski were among those that served as important guides.

The late, great Vic Ziegel showed me how to tell a story, and the late, great Bill Shannon showed me how to act on game day.

I owe a debt of gratitude to all the past and present Yankee players, coaches, and executives who gave their time and perspective to this project, and to R. D. Long, Nick Delvecchio, and other minor league teammates of Jeter's for their kindness and candor. The same goes for the high school, summer league, and basketball teammates and coaches out of Jeter's Kalamazoo youth, and the many big league executives and scouts who filled in too many blanks to count.

I would also like to thank Derek Jeter himself for agreeing to field questions for this book at his locker, as he was under no obligation to do so.

Sean Forman's baseball-reference.com, a required destination for all fans, proved to be a lifesaver in so many ways. FanGraphs.com, retrosheet.org, fieldingbible.com, thebaseballcube.com, baseballamerica.com's executive database, baseball-almanac.com, and LexisNexis were also terrific research tools.

Anthony Owens of Fisk University was a great help in tracking down Charles Jeter's former college coach and teammates. Paul Morgan of the *Kalamazoo Gazette* helped paint the portrait of Derek Jeter, high school star. Cathy Serra and the staff of the Kalamazoo Public Library provided published accounts of Jeter's scholastic career, and Jeff Idelson and Bill Francis of the National Baseball Hall of Fame provided dozens of clips on Jeter's professional career.

I want to thank many outstanding journalists and executives under the ESPNNewYork.com, ESPN, and 1050 ESPN Radio umbrellas for their trust, including Leon Carter, Rob King, Tim McCarthy, Dave Roberts, Jim Pastor, Norby Williamson, Justin Craig, Jon Scher, Matt Marrone, Kevin Jackson, and Pete Silverman. I would also like to note the overwhelming support I received from Stephen and Mac Borg, Frank Scandale, and John Balkun at the *Record* of New Jersey.

My literary agent, David Black, is the Jeter and Jordan of his trade, and a hell of a nice guy to boot. For some reason he believed in me long before I wrote three books on his watch.

At Houghton Mifflin Harcourt, Megan Wilson and Larry Cooper cared about this project as much as I did, and that meant a ton. On cue, Barbara Wood did a wonderful job copyediting the manuscript and filling in the potholes. For the second time my editor, Susan Canavan, challenged me to be better on every page of every chapter and showed again why she's among the very best at what she does.

Finally, this book wouldn't have been possible without my dearest friends, Tracey and Kyle O'Connor, whose unconditional love and understanding forever inspire me to make it all the way home.

A Note on the Author's Interviews and Sources

◆

Derek Jeter agreed to do a number of clubhouse interviews for this book during the 2009 season but did not agree to do a lengthy sit-down. In piecing together the narrative, I leaned on scores of interviews with Jeter that I either conducted or participated in over the course of his fifteen-year career.

Of the dozens upon dozens of players, coaches, managers, and executives approached to discuss Jeter specifically for this book, only a handful declined. Alex Rodriguez and Joe Torre were among that handful. Their quotes on these pages were pulled from previous interviews and news conferences, including some in which I participated.

Following is a list of people who granted interviews for this book, including those who consented to multiple interviews. Some people in and around Jeter's baseball life, including teammates and club officials, requested and received anonymity so they could speak candidly about the shortstop without impacting their relationship with him.

AUTHOR'S INTERVIEWS

Ace Adams, Bob Alejo, Bob Altman, Brian Altman, Fern Altman, Jeff Antolick, Bronson Arroyo, Charlie Atkinson, Brad Ausmus, Billy Beane, Gene Bennett, Yogi Berra, Elridge Blake, John Blundell, Aaron Boone, Mike Borzello, Larry Bowa, Jim Bowden, Mike Buddie, A. J. Burnett, Homer Bush, Brian Butterfield.

Robinson Cano, Steve Caruso, Brian Cashman, Chad Casserly, Rick Cerrone, Earl Clary, David Cone, Norm Copeland, Alex Cora, Pat Courtney, Lou Cucuzza Jr., Rob Cucuzza, Chad Curtis, Johnny Damon, Ken Davidoff, Nick Delvecchio, Gary Denbo, Bucky Dent, Mark DeRosa, Rick Down, Mariano Duncan, Jim Duquette.

Dave Eiland, Kevin Elfering, Theo Epstein, Bill Evers, John Flaherty, Whitey Ford, Andy Fox, Pat Freehan, John Frey, Nomar Garciaparra, Clarence Gardner, Shirley Garzelloni, Joe Girardi, Monter Glasper, Nick Green, Dick Groch.

Walter Hall, David Hart, Charlie Hayes, Trey Hillman, Mike Hinga, John Horshok, Orlando Hudson, Phil Hughes, Marie Jackson, Reggie Jackson, Bill James, Courtney Jasiak, Derek Jeter, Tommy John, Eric Johnson, Roger Kahlon, Howie Karpin, Michael Kay, Mick Kelleher, Pat Kelly, Clyde King, George King, Bob Klapisch.

David Larson, Al Leiter, Randy Levine, Jim Leyland, Jim Leyritz, Bill Livesey, Kevin Long, R. D. Long, Matt Luke, Mitch Lukevics, Monsignor Thomas Madden, Dick Maier, Jane Maier, Jeffrey Maier, Kevin Malone, Charlie Manuel, Jerry Manuel, Tino Martinez, Kate Mascali, Lori Mascali, Tony Massarotti, Hideki Matsui, Stump Merrill, Gene Michael, Doug Mientkiewicz, Omar Minaya, Julian Mock, Gene Monahan, Wayne Moore, Paul Morgan, Chad Mottola, Jamie Moyer, Kenyon Murray, Mike Mussina.

Ray Negron, Jeff Nelson, Beryl Newhouser, Mark Newman, Gary Nickels, Dan O'Brien, Buster Olney, Paul O'Neill, Chris Oosterbaan, Ogi Overman, Sally Padley, Dustin Pedroia, Tony Pena, Andy Pettitte, Steve Phillips, Jim Pittsley, Jorge Posada.

Scott Raab, Tim Raines, Cody Ransom, Sandy Rehberg, Jose Reyes, J. P. Ricciardi, Jason Riley, Mariano Rivera, Keith Roberts, Francisco Rodriguez, CC Sabathia, Eric Saland, Matthew Saland, Dan Shaughnessy, Gary Sheffield, Joel Sherman, Buck Showalter, Aaron Small, Ulric Smalls, Dr. James Smith, John Smoltz, Matt Stairs, Mike Stanton, Julia Ruth Stevens, Art Stewart, Darryl Strawberry, David Sussman.

Mark Teixeira, Rob Thomson, George Tiedemann, Michael Tiedemann, Ray Tiedemann, Ryan Topham, Gary Tuck, Sonny Vaccaro, Bobby Valentine, Ron Villone, Jose Vizcaino, Romel Wallace, Ron Washington, Bob Watson, David Weathers, Jeff Weaver, Chris Webber, John Wetteland, Mickey White, Greg Williams, Dave Winfield, Charlie Wonsowicz, David Wright, Jason Zillo, Don Zimmer, Barry Zito, Don Zomer.

NOTES

The following is a chapter-by-chapter summary of additional sources that contributed to this book.

1. The Kalamazoo Kid

"Castles of the United States," Tiedemann Castle, http://www.dupontcastle.com.

CenterStage with Michael Kay, featuring Derek Jeter, YES Network, 2004.

ESPN SportsCentury profile of Derek Jeter, ESPN, 2003.

Fisk University, history, http://www.fisk.edu.

Joe Gergen, "Everyone's Hero: It's Time for Young Star to Cash In," *Newsday*, November 5, 1996.

Derek Jeter with Jack Curry, *The Life You Imagine: Life Lessons for Achieving Your Dreams* (New York: Crown, 2000).

LeRoy E. McWilliams with Jim Bishop, *Parish Priest* (New York: McGraw-Hill, 1953).

Ian O'Connor, "For Yanks' Jeter, Life Is Beautiful: 'If This Is a Dream, Don't Wake Me,'" *USA Today*, October 26, 1999.

John Tiedemann, Inc., history, http://www.johntiedemann.com.

Kelly Whiteside, "Born to Be a Bomber," *Sports Illustrated*, November 13, 1996.

2. The Draft

ESPN SportsCentury profile of Derek Jeter, ESPN, 2003.

Andy Latora, "Jeter, Topham Draw Large Group of Scouts," *Kalamazoo Gazette*, April 12, 1992.

Major League Scouting Bureau Free Agent Scouting Reports, Jim Terrell, Dick Colpaert, and Carroll Sembera on Derek Jeter, April–May 1992.

Paul Morgan, "Jeter Inks Deal for $800,000," *Kalamazoo Gazette*, June 29, 1992.

New York Yankees Free Agent Scouting Report, Dick Groch on Derek Jeter, April 1992.

Buster Olney, *The Last Night of the Yankee Dynasty: The Game, the Team, and the Cost of Greatness* (New York: HarperCollins, 2004).

Joel Sherman, *Birth of a Dynasty: Behind the Pinstripes with the 1996 Yankees* (Emmaus, PA: Rodale, 2006).

3. E-6

Jeter and Curry, *The Life You Imagine.*

Tom McEwen, "Jeter's Path Wasn't Always the Smoothest," *Tampa Tribune*, June 24, 1999.

Paul Morgan, "Jeter Holding His Own in Rookie League," *Kalamazoo Gazette*, August 19, 1992.

Ian O'Connor, "Close to Perfect," (White Plains, NY) *Journal News*, October 26, 1999.

4. Rookie of the Year

Dave Anderson, "Sports of the Times: Jeter Made Difference for Yankees," *New York Times*, September 26, 1996.

Jack Curry, "Psst . . . Showalter Had 2d Chance," *New York Times*, December 3, 1995.

John Giannone, "Short Stories: Jeter: Errors Can't Shake Him," *New York Daily News*, March 31, 1996.

Charles Jeter, *Sports Illustrated* Sportsman of the Year award ceremony, December 1, 2009.

Ian O'Connor, "Desert Bomber Buck Can't Lose His Yankee Bond," *New York Daily News*, February 25, 1996.

Sherman, *Birth of a Dynasty.*

5. Champion

Mark Bradley, "'27 Yankees Might Lose to These Guys," *Atlanta Journal-Constitution*, October 22, 1996.

MLB.com, *Baseball's Best*, 1996 World Series video.

Ian O'Connor, "Kid's Fame Is in Reach," *New York Daily News*, October 10, 1996.

6. Perfection

Bob Finnigan, "Rodriguez, Jeter Share Shortcuts to Success," *Seattle Times*, August 19, 1996.

Paul Hoynes, "Home with No Ring: Indians Again Fall Short of Main Goal," *(Cleveland) Plain Dealer*, October 15, 1998.

George King, *Unbelievable! The Historic Season of the 1998 World Champion New York Yankees* (New York: HarperCollins, 1998).

Ian O'Connor, "Derek & Partner Can Seal It with Ring," *New York Daily News*, February 10, 1998.

O'Connor, "For Yanks' Jeter, Life Is Beautiful."

O'Connor, "Torre Saddled with the Boss," *New York Daily News*, March 25, 1998.

Dotson Rader, "Mariah Carey: 'I Didn't Feel Worthy of Happiness,'" *Parade*, June 5, 2005.

Alan Schwarz, "Long at Short," *Inside Sports*, August 1997.

7. Dynasty

Ken Davidoff, "Livin' La Vida Loca; For Jeter, a Balancing Act," *The Record*, July 13, 1999.

Josh Dubow, "Torre's Cancer Dampens Strawberry's Return," Associated Press, March 10, 1999.

Fred Goodall, "Yankees, Trying to Improve on Perfection, Trade for Clemens," Associated Press, February 18, 1999.

Derek Jeter, *GameDay: My Life On and Off the Field* (New York: Three Rivers Press, 2001).

George King and Jonathan Mayo, "Jeter $5M, Yankees 0: Yank SS Keeps Winning," *New York Post*, February 17, 1999.

Jack O'Connell, "Trade Hits 'Boomer' Like Bombshell," *Hartford Courant*, February 19, 1999.

Ian O'Connor, "Clemens Finally Lives Up to His Reputation, and to Others' Expectations," *(White Plains, NY) Journal News*, October 10, 1999.

O'Connor, "If the Yankees Were Smart, They Would Invest in Jeter Now," *(White Plains, NY) Journal News*, February 24, 1999.

Buster Olney, "Jeter Seeks Improvement, Right Down to Core," *New York Times*, February 20, 2000.

Adrian Wojnarowski, "Jeter Learned from a Master; Yankee's Grandfather Set Early Example," *The Record*, February 24, 1999.

8. The Flip

Mark Feinsand, "Yanks Learned Their Importance on 9/11," MLB.com, September 8, 2006.

MLB.com, *Baseball's Best*, 1996 World Series video.

MLB.com, *Baseball's Best*, 2001 World Series video.

Ian O'Connor, "Championships Matter First for Jeter," *(White Plains, NY) Journal News*, January 23, 2001.

O'Connor, "Jeter's Sister Gives Mother a Present to Remember," *(White Plains, NY) Journal News*, May 14, 2001.

O'Connor, "Yankees Charm Wizard Wooden," *USA Today*, November 2, 2001.

Olney, *The Last Night of the Yankee Dynasty*.

Scott Ostler, "Jeter Makes All the Difference for N.Y.; Jeter Heart and Soul of This Yankee Club," *San Francisco Chronicle*, October 18, 2001.

Scott Raab, "Jackpot!" *Esquire*, April, 2001.

Lawrence Rocca and Jon Heyman, "$189M but Still Short-Changed," *Newsday*, February 10, 2001.

Henry Schulman, "Jeter's Athletic Play Saves Yankees; Backup Relay Flip to Home Plate Catches Giambi," *San Francisco Chronicle*, October 14, 2001.

Joel Sherman, "It's Pin-Strife at Camp Chaos — Jeter Drops the Ball as Captain," *New York Post*, February 21, 2007.

Joe Torre and Tom Verducci, *The Yankee Years* (New York: Doubleday, 2009).

Tom Verducci, "2009 Sportsman of the Year: Derek Jeter," *Sports Illustrated*, December 7, 2009.

9. New Guys

Dom Amore, "Testing Part of Labor Talks," *Hartford Courant*, May 30, 2002.

Harvey Araton, "Forget About Blame. It's a No-Fault Collision," *New York Times*, April 2, 2003.

Bill Campbell, "Thankful for a Steal of a Chance; Rivera Trying to Make Things Right in Minors with Rangers," *Dallas Morning News*, April 16, 2002.

Marc Carig, "A-Rod Delivers Again as NY Yankees Celebrate at BBWAA Awards," NJ.com, January 24, 2010.

CenterStage with Michael Kay, featuring Derek Jeter, YES Network, 2004.

Murray Chass, "Contract Omission Says It All for Yanks," *New York Times*, February 11, 2005.

Chass, "What's $32 Million More? Yanks Sign Contreras," *New York Times*, December 25, 2002.

Wayne Coffey, "Boss Looks Back, Warns Jeter & Joe in Exclusive Sitdown with News," *Daily News*, December 29, 2002.

Josh Dubow, "Rivera Released by Yankees, Accused of Stealing from Jeter's Locker," Associated Press, March 12, 2002.

ESPN SportsCentury profile of Derek Jeter, ESPN, 2003.

Bob Gillies and Greg Gittrich with Kristoffer Garin, "Jeter Sweeter: A-Rod Says OK as Ex-Date Is Seen with Yankee Star," *Daily News*, August 19, 2001.

Bob Klapisch, "Who's in Charge? Boss Tweaks Torre with Jeter Move," *The Record*, June 4, 2003.

Scott Miller, "Infamous Huckaby Still Chasing Elusive Big-League Dream," CBS SportsLine.com, March 23, 2004.

Ian O'Connor, "Jeter's Value Is Slipping," *(White Plains, NY) Journal News*, February 25, 2003.

O'Connor, "Yankees' Matsui Shows All-American Traits," *USA Today*, October 21, 2003.

Roger Rubin, "Party On: Jeter Fires Back at Boss by George, Won't Change Lifestyle," *Daily News*, February 4, 2003.

Michael Silver, "Prince of the City," *Sports Illustrated*, June 21, 1999.

Bernie Williams, BBWAA awards dinner, January 23, 2010.

Steve Wilstein, "Jeter Answers the Boss," Associated Press, February 13, 2003.

10. Alex

Ronald Blum, "A-Rod Officially Dons Yankees Pinstripes," Associated Press, February 17, 2004.

Howard Bryant, "Boo Birds Brutal; Fans Merciless on Yanks Stars," *Boston Herald*, April 26, 2004.

CenterStage with Michael Kay, featuring Derek Jeter, YES Network, 2004.

Forbes magazine, MLB franchise values, April, 2004.

Matt Lauer, Alex Rodriguez interview, *Today* show, NBC, February 27, 2004.

Tony Massarotti and John Harper, *A Tale of Two Cities: The 2004 Yankees-Red Sox Rivalry and the War for the Pennant* (Guilford, CT: The Lyons Press, 2005).

Ian O'Connor, "Jeter Should Look to Yankees History and Another Captain for Guidance," *USA Today*, February 24, 2004.

11. The Great Divide

Dom Amore, "This One Makes Blood Boil; Angry Torre Blames Lack of Effort," *Hartford Courant*, June 11, 2005.

Gordon Edes, "Ortiz Raps HR, MVP Voting," *Boston Globe*, September 11, 2006.

Elias Sports Bureau.

Bob Klapisch, "A Heavy Burden; Rodriguez Says It's Up to Him to Capture October for Yanks," *The Record*, January 30, 2005.

Joe Torre with Tom Verducci, *Chasing the Dream: My Lifelong Journey to the World Series* (New York: Bantam, 1997).

Howard Ulman, "Nixon Criticizes A-Rod," Associated Press, February 15, 2005.

Mike Vaccaro, "Tip of the Captain," *New York Post*, March 6, 2005.

12. Moment of Truth

Baseball Info Solutions, http://www.baseballinfosolutions.com.

John Dewan, "Plus/Minus System," *The Fielding Bible*, http://www.fieldingbible.com.

FanGraphs.com, Ultimate Zone Rating, http://www.fangraphs.com.

Michael Hoban, *Fielder's Choice: Baseball's Best Shortstops*, Booklocker.com, 2003.

Bill James, "Jeter vs. Everett," *The Fielding Bible*, http://www.fieldingbible.com.

Tyler Kepner, "Baseball; Sunshine Amid Clouds," *New York Times*, May 13, 2007.

Ian O'Connor, "The Boss to Torre: Win, or Else; 'His Job Is on the Line,' Yankee Owner Warns," *The Record*, October 7, 2007.

13. Rebirth

John Dewan, "Plus/Minus System," *The Fielding Bible*, http://www.fieldingbible.com.

FanGraphs.com, Ultimate Zone Rating, http://www.fangraphs.com.

Derek Jeter, Q&A, *Sports Illustrated* Sportsman of the Year award ceremony, December 1, 2009.

Jeter, "10 Pillars of Leadership," http://www.DerekJeter.com.

R. D. Long, "A-Rod Represents the Collapse of an Empire," Uncommon Knowledge Blog, September 19, 2008.

Ian O'Connor, "Lessons from a Gentle Giant; A Mellower Girardi Rips a Page from Coughlin's Playbook," *The Record*, March 3, 2009.

Epilogue: 3,000

"Derek Jeter 3K," MLB Productions in collaboration with HBO Sports, July 28, 2011.

Yankees vs. Tampa Bay Rays Broadcast, YES Network, July 9, 2011.

Bibliography

Books

Giles, Patrick. *Derek Jeter: Pride of the Yankees*. New York: St. Martin's Paperbacks, 1999; Sports Publishing Inc., 1999.

Jeter, Derek. *GameDay: My Life On and Off the Field*. New York: Three Rivers Press, 2001.

——. *The Life You Imagine: Life Lessons for Achieving Your Dreams*. With Jack Curry. New York: Crown, 2000.

King, George. *Unbelievable! The Historic Season of the 1998 World Champion New York Yankees*. New York: HarperCollins, 1998.

Massarotti, Tony, and John Harper. *A Tale of Two Cities: The 2004 Yankees-Red Sox Rivalry and the War for the Pennant*. Guilford, CT: The Lyons Press, 2005.

McWilliams, LeRoy E. *Parish Priest*. With Jim Bishop. New York: McGraw-Hill, 1953.

O'Connell, Jack. *Derek Jeter: The Yankee Kid*. Sports Publishing Inc., 1999.

Olney, Buster. *The Last Night of the Yankee Dynasty: The Game, the Team, and the Cost of Greatness*. New York: HarperCollins, 2004.

Sherman, Joel. *Birth of a Dynasty: Behind the Pinstripes with the 1996 Yankees*. Emmaus, PA: Rodale, 2006.

Torre, Joe. *Chasing the Dream: My Lifelong Journey to the World Series*. With Tom Verducci. New York: Bantam, 1997.

——. *The Yankee Years*. With Tom Verducci. New York: Doubleday, 2009.

Vaccaro, Mike. *Emperors and Idiots: The Hundred-Year Rivalry Between the Yankees and Red Sox, from the Very Beginning to the End of the Curse*. New York: Doubleday, 2005.

Magazines

Baseball America   *Forbes*
Esquire   *GQ*

Inside Sports   *Sport*
New York   *The Sporting News*
Parade   *Sports Illustrated*

Newspapers/Wire Services

Associated Press   *New York Daily News*
Atlanta Journal-Constitution   *New York Post*
Boston Globe   *New York Times*
Boston Herald   *San Francisco Chronicle*
(Cleveland) Plain Dealer   *Seattle Times*
Dallas Morning News   *St. Petersburg Times*
Greensboro (NC) News & Record   *Tampa Tribune*
Hartford Courant   *USA Today*
Kalamazoo Gazette   *(White Plains, NY) Journal News*
Newark (NJ) Star-Ledger   *Woodland Park (NJ) Record*
Newsday

Websites

http://espn.go.com   http://www.dupontcastle.com
http://newyork.yankees.mlb.com   http://www.fangraphs.com
http://sportsillustrated.cnn.com   http://www.fieldingbible.com
http://www.baseballamerica.com   http://www.fisk.edu
http://www.baseball-almanac.com   http://www.johntiedemann.com
http://www.baseballinfosolutions.com   http://www.mlb.com
http://www.baseball-reference.com   http://www.nexis.com
http://www.cbssports.com   http://www.retrosheet.org
http://www.derekjeter.com   http://www.thebaseballcube.com

Videos/Broadcasts

CenterStage with Michael Kay, featuring Derek Jeter, YES Network, 2004.
ESPN SportsCentury profile of Derek Jeter, ESPN, 2003.
Game Broadcast Clips: Fox, MSG Network, YES Network.
Matt Lauer, Alex Rodriguez interview, *Today* show, NBC, February 27, 2004.
MLB.com, *Baseball's Best*, 1996 World Series, 2001 World Series videos.

Index